Wigwam and War-Path

Yours Truly
A B Meacham

Wigwam and War-Path

The Modoc Indian War 1872-3,
by an Active Eyewitness

Hon. A. B. Meacham

LEONAUR

Wigwam and War-Path
The Modoc Indian War 1872-3, by an Active Eyewitness
by Hon. A. B. Meacham

First published under the title
Wigwam and War-Path; or the Royal Chief in Chains

Leonaur is an imprint of Oakpast Ltd

Copyright in this form © 2013 Oakpast Ltd

ISBN: 978-1-78282-098-7 (hardcover)
ISBN: 978-1-78282-099-4 (softcover)

http://www.leonaur.com

Publisher's Notes

Contents

Preface   7

Introduction   9

Early Reminiscences, Pow-E-Shiek's Band   13

Overland: Blood for Blood   27

Indians and Miners   32

Diamond-Cut-Diamond   41

Policies on Trial—"Oneatta."   49

Senatorial Brains Beaten by Savage Muscle   60

Phil Sheridan's Old Home   77

Stopping the Survey—Why   89

The Aged Pair—Birthplace of Legends   101

Dangerous Place for Sinners   109

The Parson Brownlow of the Indian Service   115

No Place Like Home—Squaws in Hoops and Chignon   129

"How-Lish-Wampo," King of the Turf   132

Snake War—Fighting the Devil With Fire   146

The Council With the Snake Indians—O-Che-O   157

Over the Falls—First Election   171

Klamath Court—Elopement Extraordinary   182

Omelets and Arrows—Big Steam-Boilers   193

Modoc Blood Under a Flag of Truce   200

Blue Eyes and Black Ones, Which Win?—Tobey Riddle   214

Burying The Hatchet—A Turning-Point   234

U. S. Senators Cost Blood—Fair Fight—Open Field   247

Mourning Emblems and Military Pomp   258

Peace or War—One Hundred Lives Voted Away by Modoc Indians   265

Gray-Eyed Man on the Warpath   273

Olive Branch and Cannon Balls—Which Will Win?   281

Captain Jack a Diplomat—Shoot Me If You Dare   300

Who Had Been There—Who Had Not   309

Under a Woman's Hat—The Last Appeal   313

Assassination—"Kau-Tux-E"   324

Harnessed Lightning Carrying Awful Tidings   345

Killed in Petticoats   355

Fighting the Devil With Fire a Failure   368

Betrayed   381

Modoc Butchers Outdone   395

Weakness Under Chains   414

The Execution   441

The Two Gibbets   458

Appendix to Chapter Six   475

Appendix to Chapter Eight   481

Preface

The Hon. A. B. Meacham has committed to me the difficult and delicate, yet delightful task of revising the manuscript and arranging the table of contents of the present work.

I have endeavoured to review every page as an impartial critic, and have, as far as possible, retained, in all its simplicity and beauty, the singularly eloquent and fascinating style of the gifted author. The changes which I have made have been, for the most part, quite immaterial—no more nor greater than would be required in the manuscript of writers commonly called "learned." In no case have I attempted (for the attempt would have been vain) to give shape and tone to the writer's thoughts. His mind was so full, both of the comedy and the tragedy of his thrilling narrative, that it has flowed on like a mighty torrent, bidding defiance to any attempt either to direct or control.

None, it seems to me, can peruse the work without being charmed with the love of justice and the fidelity to truth which pervade its every page, as well as the manly courage with which the writer arraigns *Power* for the crime of crushing *Weakness*—holding our government to an awful accountability for the delays, the ignorance, the fickleness and treachery of its subordinates in dealing with a people whose very religion prompts them to wreak vengeance for wrongs done them, even on the innocent.

For the lover of romance and of thrilling adventure, the work possesses a charm scarcely equalled by the enchanting pages of a Fennimore Cooper; and, to the reader who appreciates truth, justice, and humanity, and delights to trace the outlines of such a career as Providence seems to have marked out for the author, as well as for the unfortunate tribes whose history he has given us, it will be a reliable, entertaining, and instructive companion.

Mr. Meacham's thirty years' experience among the Indian tribes of the North-west, and his official career as Superintendent of Indian affairs in Oregon, together with his participation in the tragic events of the Lava Bed, invest his words with an authority which must outweigh that of every flippant politician in the land, who, to secure the huzzas of the mob, will applaud the oppressor and the tyrant one day, and the very next day clamour mercilessly for their blood.

D. L. Emerson.

Boston, Oct. 1, 1874.

Introduction

The chapter in our National history which tells our dealings with the Indian tribes, from Plymouth to San Francisco, will be one of the darkest and most disgraceful in our annals. Fraud and oppression, hypocrisy and violence, open, high-handed robbery and sly cheating, the swindling agent and the brutal soldier turned into a brigand, buying promotion by pandering to the hate and fears of the settlers, avarice and indifference to human life, and lust for territory, all play their parts in the drama. Except the negro, no race will lift up, at the judgment-seat, such accusing hands against this nation as the Indian. We have put him in charge of agents who have systematically cheated him. We have made causeless war on him merely as a pretext to steal his lands.

Trampling underfoot the rules of modern warfare, we have made war on his women and children. We have cheated him out of one hunting-ground by compelling him to accept another, and have robbed him of the last by driving him to frenzy, and then punishing resistance with confiscation. Meanwhile, neither pulpit nor press, nor political party, would listen to his complaints. Congress has handed him over, gagged and helpless, to the bands of ignorant, drunken and brutal soldiers. Neither on its floor, nor in any city of the Union, could his advocate obtain a hearing. Money has been poured out like water to feed and educate the Indian, of which one dollar in ten may have found its way to supply his needs, or pay the debts we owed him.

To show the folly of our method, examine the south side of the great lakes, and you will find in every thirty miles between Plymouth and Omaha the scene of an Indian massacre. And since 1789 we have spent about one thousand million of dollars in dealing with the Indians. Meanwhile, under British rule, on the north of those same lakes, there has been no Indian outbreak, worth naming, for a hundred years, and hardly one hundred thousand dollars have been spent directly on the Indians of Canada. What is the solution of this astounding riddle? This, and none other. England gathers her Indian tribes, like ordinary citizens, within the girth of her usual laws. If injured, they complain, like other men, to a justice of the peace, not to a camp captain.

If offenders, they are arraigned before such a justice, or some superior court. Complaint, indictment, evidence, trial, sentence, are all after the old Saxon pattern. With us martial law, or no law at all, is their portion; no civil rights, no right to property that a white man is bound to respect. Of course quarrel, war, expense, oppression, robbery, resistance, like begetting like, and degradation of the Indian even to the level of the frontiersman who would plunder him, have been the result of such a method. If such a result were singular, if our case stood alone, we should receive the pitiless curses of mankind. But the same result has almost always followed the contact of the civilized and the savage man.

General Grant's recommendation of a policy which would acknowledge the Indian as a citizen, is the first step in our Indian history which gives us any claim to be considered a Christian people. The hostility it has met shows the fearful demoralization of our press and political parties. Statesmanship, good sense and justice, even from a chief magistrate can hardly obtain a hearing when they relate to such long-time victims of popular hate and pillage as our Indian tribes. Some few men in times past have tried to stem this hideous current of national indifference and injustice. Some men do now try. Prominent among these is the author of this volume. Thirty years of practical experience in dealing with Indians while he represented the government in different offices; long and familiar acquaintance with their genius, moods, habits and capabilities, enable and entitle him to testify in this case. That, having suffered, at the hands of Indians, all that man can suffer and still live, he should yet lift up a voice, snatched almost miraculously from the grave, to claim for them, nevertheless, the treatment of men, of citizens, is a marvellous instance of fidelity to conviction against every temptation and injury.

Bearing all over his person the scars of nearly fatal wounds received from Indians, he still advocates Grant's policy. Familiar with the Indian tribes, and personally acquainted with their chiefs, with the old and young, men and women, their sports and faith, their history and aspirations, their education and capacity, their songs, amusements, legends, business, loves and hates, his descriptions lack no element of a faithful portrait; while his lightest illustrations have always beneath the surface

10

a meaning which cannot fail to arrest the attention of the American people, and enable them to understand this national problem. Never before have we had just such a witness on the stand. Brilliant and graphic in description, and exceedingly happy in his choice of topics, he gives us pages startling and interesting as a novel. While his appeals stir the heart like a clarion, he still keeps cautiously to sober fact; and every statement, the most seemingly incredible, is based on more than sufficient evidence.

I *commend this book to the public*—study it not only as accurate and striking in its pictures of Indian life, but as profoundly interesting to every student of human nature,—the picture of a race fast fading away and melting into white men's ways. His contribution to the solution of one of the most puzzling problems of American statesmanship is invaluable. Destined no doubt to provoke bitter criticism, I feel sure his views and statements will bear the amplest investigation. His volume will contribute largely to vindicate the President's policy, and to enable, while it disposes, the American people to understand and do justice to our native tribes.

(Signed,)   Wendell Phillips.

CHAPTER 1

Early Reminiscences, Pow-E-Shiek's Band

"Oh, that mine enemy would write a book!" With that ominous warning ringing in my ears, I sit down to write out my own observations and experiences, not without full appreciation of the meaning and possible reiteration of the above portentous saying. In so doing I shall endeavour to state plain facts, in such a way, perhaps, that mine enemies will avail themselves of the privilege.

Hoping, however, that I may disarm all malice, and meet with a fair and impartial criticism, based on the principles of justice both to myself and to the peoples of whom I write, I begin this book with the conviction that the truths which I shall state, though told in homely phrase, will nevertheless be well received by the reading public, and will accomplish the purposes for which it is written; the first of which is to furnish reliable information on the subject under consideration, with the hope that when my readers shall have turned the last leaf of this volume they may have a better understanding of the wrongs suffered and crimes committed by the numerous tribes of Indians of the north-west.

Born on the free side of the Ohio River, of parents whose immediate ancestors, though slave-holders, had left the South at the command of conscientious convictions of the great wrong of human bondage, my earliest recollections are of political discussions relating to the crime against God and humanity; of *power* compelling *weakness* while groaning under the oppression of wrongs to surrender its rights.

Coupled with the "great wrong" of which I have spoken, occasionally that other wrong, twin to the first, was mentioned in my

13

father's family; impressed upon my mind by stories I had heard of the treatment of Indians who had in early days been neighbours to my parents, driven mile by mile toward the setting sun, leaving a country billowed by the graves of their victims mingled with bones of their own ancestors. What wonder, then, that, while rambling through the beech woods of my native State, I should speculate on the remnants of ruined homes which these people had left behind them, and walk in awe over the battle-fields where they had resisted the aggressive march of civilization?

While yet in childhood my parents migrated to what was then the "Far West." Our new home in Iowa was on the outskirts of civilization, our nearest neighbours being a band of Sacs and Foxes,—"Saukees." This was the beginning of my personal acquaintance with Indians.

The stories that had kindled in my heart feelings of sympathy and commiseration for them were forgotten for a time in the present living history before my eyes.

I was one of a party who in 1844 assisted the government in removing Pow-e-shiek's band from the Iowa river to their new home in the West. The scenes around the Indian village on the morning of their departure were photographed on my mind so plainly that now, after a lapse of thirty years, they are still fresh in my memory, and the impressions made on me, and resolves then made by me, have never been forgotten, notwithstanding the terrible dangers through which I have since passed.

The *impression* was, that *power* and *might* were compelling these people to leave their homes against their wishes, and in violation of justice and right. The resolution was, that, whenever and wherever I could, I would do them justice, and contribute whatever of talent and influence I might have to better their condition.

These impressions and resolutions have been my constant companions through a stormy life of many years on the frontier of Iowa, California, and Oregon.

The bloody tragedy in the Lava Beds, April, 1873, through which the lamented Christian soldier, Gen. Canby, and the no less lamented eminent preacher, Dr. Thomas, lost their lives, and by which I had passed so close to the portals of eternity, has not changed my conviction of right, or my determination to do justice to even those who so earnestly sought my life. Narrow-minded, short-sighted men have said to me, more than once, "I reckon you have suffered enough to cure all your fanatical notions of humanity for these people!"

I pity the heart and intelligence of any man who measures principles of justice and right by the gauge of personal suffering or personal interest. It is unworthy of enlightened Christian manhood.

"By their works ye shall know them." So may these people of whom I write be adjudged in the lights of 1874; so shall this nation be adjudged; so judge ye the author of this book.

The spring of 1845, Pow-e-shiek's band of Sacs and Foxes were removed from their home on Iowa River, twenty-five miles above Iowa City, Iowa, to Skunk River, one hundred miles west. Eighteen or twenty teams were hired by the government to convey the household goods and supplies.

Among the number who furnished teams, my father was one, and I went as captain of the ox-team. The Indians were assembled at the "Trading Post" preparatory to starting. While the wagons were being loaded, some of them were gathering up their horses and packing their goods, ready for shipment; others were making the air vocal with wails of grief over the graves of their friends, or from sadness, consequent on leaving the scenes of a life-time.

I wonder not that they should reluctantly yield to inexorable fate, which compelled them to leave their beautiful valley of the Iowa. "*The white man wanted it,*" and they must retreat before the onward march of empire, notwithstanding their nationality and their ownership of the country had been acknowledged by the government, when it went into treaty-council with them for the lands they held. This was not on the plea of "eminent domain," but on account of the clamour for more room for the expanding energies of a growing population.

"The white man wanted it," tells the story, as it has been repeated, time after time, since the founding of the Colonies in America.

I do not know that, in this instance, any advantage was taken of these Indians, except that advantage which the powerful always have over the weak. But I do know that if they had been allowed a choice, they never would have consented to leave the graves of their fathers. 'Twas easy to say, "It was a fair transaction of selling and buying."

So is it a business transaction when a man buys the lots adjoining your own, and builds high walls on three sides, erects powder magazines and glycerine manufactories, corrupts city councils, and, by means of extra privileges and excessive taxation, compels you to sell your valuable property for a mere song, by saying, "Take my price for your property, or run the risk of being blown up."

Is it a fair "business transaction," after he has thus forced the

15

trade?

What though he does faithfully pay the contract-price? Does it atone for the first moral wrong, in legally forcing the sale? And how much more aggravated the injury becomes, when, through his agents, or his sons, he "legitimately," under various pretences, permits the unfortunate seller to be robbed, by paying him off in "chips and whetstones," that he does not desire nor need, so that in the end he is practically defrauded out of his property, and finds himself at the last payment, homeless and penniless.

All done, however, under the sanction of law, and in the shade of church-steeples, and with sanctimonious semblance of honesty and justice.

The picture is not overdrawn. The illustration is fair, or, if deficient at all, it has bean in excess of advantage to the principal, not the victim. The latter has accepted the situation and suffered the consequences.

To return to Pow-e-shiek's band leaving their home. Who shall ever recount the sorrows and anguish of those people, while they formed in line of march, and turned their eyes for the last time upon the scenes that had been all the world to them? What mattered it though they realized all the pangs their natures were capable of, in those parting hours, with the uncomfortable promises that the ploughshare of civilization would level down the graves of their fathers, before their retreating footprints had been obliterated from the trail which led them sadly away? They were "Injins;" and they ought to have been in better luck than *being* "Injins."

Such was the speech of a white man in whose hearing I had said some word of sympathy on the occasion. I did not like the unfeeling wretch then, and have not much respect for him, or for the class he represents. Now I may have charity and pity, too, for all such. Charity for the poverty of a soul so devoid of the finer sensibilities of "common humanity that make mankind akin;" pity for a heart overflowing with selfishness, made manifest in thoughtless or spiteful speech.

The trying hour in the lives of these Indian people had come, and the long cavalcade moved out along the line of westward march, wagons loaded with corn and other supplies. The old men of the tribe, with darkened brows and silent tongue, sat on their horses; the younger ones, with *seeming* indifference, in red blankets, feathers, and gaudy paints, moving off on prancing ponies, in little squads, to join the funeral pageant; for so it was. They were leaving the cherished scenes of childhood to hunt for sepulchres in the farther West.

16

The women, young and old, the drudges of the Indian household, as well as homes, where the sunlight of civilization *should* warm the hearts of men, and move them to truer justice, were gathered up, and preparing their goods for transportation, while bitter tears were flowing and loud lamentations gave evidence of the grief that would not be repressed, and each in turn, as preparations were complete, would lift the *papoose*-basket with its young soul to altitudes of mother's back or horse's saddle, and then, with trembling limbs, climb to their seats and join the sad procession, adding what of woeful wailing seemed necessary to make the whole complete with sights and sound that would bid defiance to painter's skill or poet's words, though, in the memory of those who beheld it, it may live as long as the throbs of sympathy which it kindled shall repeat themselves in hearts that feel for human sorrow.

The first day's journey measured but four miles; the next, six; and at most never exceeded ten or twelve. I did not understand, then, why we went so slow. It may have been necessary to "kill time," in order to use up the appropriation for the removal. When "camp" was reached, each day the wagons were "corralled;" that is to say, were drawn together in a circle, one behind another, and so close that when the teams were detached, the "pole" laid upon the hind wheel of the next forward wagon would close up the gap, and thus complete the "corral," which was to answer the double purpose of "penning the oxen when being yoked up," and also as an extempore fort in case of attack by the Sioux Indians.

The *wick-e-ups*—Indian tents—were scattered promiscuously around, as each family might elect. After dinner was over the remainder of Uncle Sam's time was spent in various ways: horse-racing, foot-racing, card-playing, shooting-matches by the men, white and red, while the women were doing camp-work, cooking, getting wood, building lodges, etc.; for be it understood, an old-style Indian never does such work any more than his white brother would rock the cradle, or operate a laundry for his wife. The old men would take turns standing guard, or rather sitting guard. At all events they generally went out to the higher hills, and, taking a commanding position, would sit down all solitary and alone, and with blanket drawn around their shoulders and over their heads, leaving only enough room for vision and the escape of smoke from their pipes.

In solemn silence, scanning the surroundings, hour after hour thus wore away. There was something in this scene suggesting serious con-

The Lone Indian sentinel

templation to a looker-on, and I doubt not the reveries of the lone watchman savoured strongly of sadness and sorrow, *may be* revenge.

Approaching one old fellow I sought to penetrate his mind, and was rewarded by a pantomimic exhibition, more tangible than "Black Crook" ever witnessed from behind the curtains, while recuperating his wasted energies that he might the more seemingly "play the devil."

Rising to his feet and releasing one naked arm from his blanket, he pointed toward the east, and with extended fingers and uprising, coming gesture quickly brought his hand to his heart, dropping his head, as if some messenger of despair had made a sudden call. He paused a moment, and then from his heart his hand went out in circling, gathering motion, until he had made the silent speech so vivid that I could see the coming throng of white settlers and the assembling of his tribe; and then, turning his face away with a majestic wave of his hand, I saw his sorrow-stricken people driven out to an unknown home; while he, sitting down again and drawing his blanket around him, refused me further audience. Perhaps he realized that he had told the whole story, and therefore need say no more.

Often at evening we would gather around some grassy knoll, or, it may be, some wagon-tongue, and white and red men mingled together. We would sit down and smoke, and tell stories and recount traditions of the past. Oftenest from Indian lips came the history of wars and dances, of scalps taken and prisoners tortured.

At the time of which I write the "Saukies" were at variance with the "hated Sioux," and, indeed, the latter had been successful in a raid among the herds of the former, and had likewise carried away captives. Hence the sentinels on the outpost at evening.

Just at dusk one night, when the theme had been the "Sioux," and our thoughts were in that channel, suddenly the whole camp was in a blaze of flashing muskets. We beat a hasty retreat to our wagons— which were our only fortifications—with mingled feelings of fear and hope; fear of the much-dreaded Sioux, and hope that we might witness a fight.

My recollection now is that *fear* had more to do with our gymnastic exercises round about the wagon-wheels than *hope* had to do with getting a position for observation. But both were short-lived, for soon our red-skinned friends were laughing loud at our fright, and we, the victims, joined in to make believe we were not scared by the unceremonious flight of a flock of belated wild geese, inviting fire from the warriors of our camp; for so it was and nothing more. Still it was enough to make peace-loving, weak nerves shake, and heated brain to dream for weeks after of Sioux and of Indians generally. I speak for myself, but tell the truth of all our camp, I think.

The destination of our chief, Pow-e-shiek, and his band was temporarily with "Kisk-ke-kosh," of the same tribe, whose bands were on Desmoines River. There is among all Indians, of whom I have any knowledge, a custom in vogue of going out to meet friends, or important personages, to assure welcome, and, perhaps, gratify curiosity.

When we were within a day or two of the end of our journey, a delegation from Kisk-ke-kosh's camp came out to meet our party, and, while the greeting we received was not demonstrative in words, the younger people of both bands had adorned themselves with paint, beads, and feathers, and were each of them doing their utmost to fascinate the other. The scene presented was not only fantastic, but as civilized, people would exclaim, "most gay and gorgeous," and exhilarating even to a looker-on.

At night they gathered in groups, and made Cupid glad with the battles lost and won by his disciples. Then they danced, or, to ears polite, "hopped," or tripped the light fantastic *moccasin* trimmed with beads, to music, primitive, 'tis true, but music made with Indian drums and rattling gourds. They went not in waltz, but circling round and round, and always round, as genteel people do, but round and round in single row, the circling ends of which would meet at any particular point, or all points, whenever the ring was complete, without reference to sets or partners, and joining in the *hi-yi-yi-eia-ye-o-hi-ye-yi;* and when tired sit down on the ground until rested, and then, without coaxing or renewed invitation, joining in, wherever fancy or convenience suited; for these round dances never break up at the unwelcome sound of the violin,—not, indeed, until the dancers are all satisfied.

The toilets were somewhat expensive, at least the "outfit" of each maiden cost her tribe several acres of land,—sometimes, if of fine figure, several *hundred* acres,—and not because of the long trails or expensive laces, for they do not need extensive skirts in which to dance, or laces, either, to enhance their charms; for the young gentlemen for whom they dressed were not envious of dry goods or fine enamel, but rather of the quality of paint on the cheeks of laughing girls; for girls will paint, you know, and those of whom I write put it on so thick that their *beaux* never have cause to say, "That's too thin."

The boys themselves paint in real genuine paint, not moustaches alone, but eye-brows, checks, and hair. They wore feathers, too, because they thought that feathers were good things to have at a round dance; and they followed nature, and relieved the dusky maidens of seeming violation of nature's plain intention.

As I shall treat under the head of amusement the dances of Indians more at length, I only remark, in this connection, that the dance on this occasion, while it was a real "round dance," differed somewhat from round dances of more high-toned people in several ways, and I am not sure it was not without advantage in point of accommodation to the finer feelings of discreet mammas, or envious "wall-flowers." At all events, as I have said on former pages, the whole set formed in one circle, with close rank, facing always to the front, and enlarged as the number of the dancers grew, or contracted as they retired; but each one going forward and keeping time with feet and hands to the music, which was low and slow at first, with short step, increasing the music and the motion as they became excited, until the air grew tremulous with the sounds, rising higher and wilder, more and more exciting, until the lookers-on would catch the inspiration and join the festive ring; even old men, who at first had felt they could not spare dignity or muscle either, would lay aside their blankets until they had lived over again the fiery scenes of younger days, by rushing into the magnetic cordon, and, with recalled youth, forget all else, save the soul-storming fury of the hour, sweetened with the charm of exultant joy, over age and passing years.

And thus the dance went on, until at last by degrees the dancers had reached an altitude of happiness which burst forth in simultaneous shout of music's eloquence, complete by higher notes of human voice drawn out to fullest length.

The dance was over, and the people went away in groups of twos and threes. The maidens, skipping home to the paternal lodge without lingering over swinging gates, or waiting for answering maids to ringing bells, crept softly in, not waking their mammas up to take off for them their lengthened trails, but perhaps with wildly beating hearts from the dance to dream-land.

The young braves gathered their scarlet blankets around them, and in couples or threes, laughing as boys will do at silly jest of awkward maid or swain, went where "tired Nature's sweet restorer" would keep promise and let them live over again the enchanting scenes of the evening, and thus with *negative* and photograph would *feel* the picture of youth their own.

21

The older men, whose folly had led them to display contempt for age, went boldly home to lodge where the tired squaws had long since yielded to exhausted nature, and were oblivious to the frolics of their *liege lords.*

Mrs. Squaw had no rights that a brave was bound to respect. It was *her* business to carry wood, build lodges, saddle his horse, and lash the *papoose* in the basket, and do all other drudgery. It was *his* to wear the gayest blanket, the vermilion paint, and eagle-feathers, and ride the best horses, have a good time generally, and whip his squaws when drunk or angry; and it was nobody's business to question *him.* He was a *man.*

Now, if my reader has failed to see the picture I have drawn of Indian dances, I promise you that, before our journey is ended, I will try again a similar scene, where the music of tall pine-trees and tumbling torrents from hoary mountains will give my pencil brighter hues and my hand a steadier, finer touch.

The arrival of our train at the camp of Kisk-ke-kosh called out whatever of finery had not been on exhibition with the welcoming party who had come out to meet us. And when the sun had gone down behind the Iowa prairies the dances were repeated on a larger scale.

The following day we were paid off and signed the vouchers. Don't know that it was intended; don't know that it was not; but I do remember that we were allowed the same number of days in which to return that we had occupied in going out, although on our homeward journey we passed each day two or three camps made on the outward journey. I ventured to make some remark on the subject, suggesting the injustice of taking pay for more time than was required for us to reach home, and a nice kind of a churchman, one who could drive oxen without swearing, said in reply, "Boys should be seen and not heard, you little fool!"

He snubbed me then, but I never forgot the deep, earnest resolve I made to thrash him for this insult when "*I got to be a man.*" But, poor fellow, he went years ago where boys *may* be heard as well as seen, and I forgive him.

We met the rushing crowds who were going to the "New Purchase;" so eager, indeed, that, like greedy vultures which circle round a dying charger and then alight upon some eminence near, or poise themselves in mid air, impatient for his death, sometimes swoop down upon him before his heart has ceased to beat.

So had these emigrants encamped along the frontier-line, impatient for the hour when the red man should pull down his *wigwam*, put out his council-fires, collect his squaws, his *papooses*, and his ponies, and turn his back upon the civilization they were bringing to take the place of these untamed and savage ceremonies. While the council-fire was dying out, another was being kindled whose ruddy light was to illuminate the faces, and warm the hands of those who, following the westward star of empire, had come to inherit the land, and build altars wherefrom should go up thanks to Him who smiled when he created the "beautiful valley" of the Iowa.

How changed the scene! Then the gray smoke from Indian lodge rose slowly up and floated leisurely away. Now from furnace-blast it bursts out in volume black, and settles down over foundry and farm, city and town, unless, indeed, the Great Spirit sends fierce tempests, as an omen of his wrath, at the sacrilege done to the red man's home.

Then the forest stood entire, like harp-strings whereon the Great Spirit might utter tones to soothe their stormy souls, or rouse them to deeds in vindication of rights he had bequeathed.

Now they live only in part, the other part decaying, while groaning under the pressure of the iron heel of power.

Bearing no part in sweet sounds, unless indeed it be sweet to hear the iron horse, with curling breath, proclaiming the advance of legions that worship daily at Mammon's shrine, or bearing forward still further westward the enterprising men and women who are to work for other lands a transformation great as they have wrought for this.

Then on the bosom of the river the red man's children might play in light canoe, or sportive dive, to catch the mimic stars that seemed to live beneath its flow, to light the homes of finny tribes who peopled then its crystal chambers.

Now, it is turgid and slow, and pent with obstructions to make it flow in channels where its power is wanted to complete the wreck of forests that once had made it cool, fit beverage for nature's children, or is muddied with the noisy wheels of commerce, struggling to rob the once happy home of Pow-e-shiek, of the charms and richness of soil that nature's God had given.

The prairies, too, at that time, were like a shoreless sea when, half in anger, the winds resist the ebb or flow of its tides; or they may be likened to the clouds, which seem to be mirrored on their waving surface, sporting in the summer air, or, at the command of the Great Spirit, hurry to join some gathering tempest, where He speaks in tones of thunder, as if to rebuke the people for their crimes.

Where once the wild deer roamed at will is enlivened now by the welcome call of lowing herds of tamer kind.

The waving grass, and fragrant flowers, too, gave way to blooming maize of finer mould.

The old trails have been buried like the feet that made them, beneath the upturned sod.

And now, while I am writing, this lovely valley rings out a chant of praise to God, for his beneficence, instead of the weird wild song of Pow-e-shiek and his people at their return from crusades against their enemies.

Who shall say the change that time and civilization have wrought, have not brought nearer the hour, "When man, no more an abject thing, shall from the sleep of ages spring," and be what God designed him, "pure and free?"

No one, however deeply he may have drank from the fount of justice and right, can fail to see, in the transformation wrought on this fair land, the hand of Him whose finger points out the destiny of his peculiar people, and yearly gives token of his approbation, by the return of seasons, bringing rich reward to the hands of those whom he has called to perform the wonders of which I write, in compensation for the hardships they endured, while the transit was being made from the perfection of untamed life to the higher state of civilization.

While we praise Him who overrules all, we cannot fail to honour His instrumentalities.

The brave pioneers, leaving old homes in other lands to find new ones in this, have made sacrifices of kindred, family ties, and early associations, at the behest of some stern necessity (it may be growing out of bankruptcy of business, though not of pride and honour, or manly character), or ambition to be peers among their fellows.

Or, mayhap, the change was made by promptings of parental love for children whose prospects in life might be made better thereby, and the family unity still preserved by locating lands in close proximity, where from his home the father might by some well-known signal call his children all around him. Where the faithful watch-dog's warning was echoed in every yard, and thus gave information of passing events worthy of his attention enacting in the neighbourhood. Where the smoke from cabin chimneys high arose, mingled in mid air, and died away in peaceful brotherhood. Where the blended prayer of parent and child might go up in joint procession from the school-house-churches through the shining trees that answered well for steeples then, or passing through clouds to Him who had made so many little groves, where homes might be made and prepared the most beautiful spots on earth for final resting-place, where each, as the journey of life should be over, might be laid away by kindred hands, far from the hurrying, noisy crowds, who rush madly along, or stop only to envy the dead the ground they occupy, and speculate how much filthy *lucre* each sepulchre is worth.

Others went to the new country with downy cheeks of youth, and others still with full-grown beards, who were fired with high ambition to make name, fame, home, and fortune, carrying underneath their sombre hats bright ideas and wonderful possibilities, with hearts full of manly purposes, beating quickly at the mention of mother's name or father's pride, sister's prayer or brother's love.

And with all these to buoy them up, would build homes on gentle slope, or in shady grove, and thus become by slow degrees "one among us."

I was with the first who went to this new country, and I know whereof I write. I know more than I have told, or will tell, lest by accident I betray the petty jealousies that cropped out; when Yankee-boys, forgetting the girls they left behind them, would pay more attention to our western girls than was agreeable to "us boys."

Others there were who had followed the retreating footsteps of the Indians. These were connecting links between two kinds of life, savage and civilized. Good enough people in their way, but they could not bear the hum of machinery, or the glitter of church-spires, because the first drove back the wild game, and the devotees who worshipped beneath the second, forbade the exercise of careless and wicked noises mingling with songs of praise.

A few, perhaps, had fled from other States to avoid the consequences of technical legal constructions which would sadly interfere with their unpuritanical ways. But these were not numerous. The early settlers, taken all in all, possessed many virtues and qualifications that entitled them to the honour which worthy actions and noble deeds guarantee to those who do them. They had come from widely different birthlands, and brought with them habits that had made up their lives; and though each may have felt sure their own was the better way, they soon learned that honest people may differ and still be honest. And to govern themselves accordingly, each yielded, without sacrifice of principle, their hereditary whims and peculiar ways, and left the weightier matters of orthodoxy or heterodoxy to be argued by those who had nothing better with which to occupy their time than to muddle their own and other people's brains with abstruse themes.

The "early settlers" were eminently practical, and withal successful in moulding out of the heterogeneous mass of whims and prejudices a common public sentiment, acceptable to all, or nearly so. And thus, they grew, not only in numbers but in wealth, power, intelligence, and patriotism, until today there may be found on the once happy home of Pow-e-shiek a people rivalling those of any other State, surpassing many of them in that greatest and noblest of all virtues, "love for your neighbour."

No people in all this grand republic furnished truer or braver men for the holocaust of blood required to reconsecrate the soil of America to freedom and justice, than those whose homes are built on the ruins of Pow-e-shiek's early hunting-grounds. Proud as the record may be, it shall yet glow with names written by an almost supernal fire, that warms into life the immortal thought of poets, and the burning eloquence of orators.

We are proud of the record of the past, and cherish bright hopes of the future. But with all our patriotic exultations, memory of Pow-e-shiek's sacrifices comes up to mingle sadness with our joy. Sadness, not the offspring of reproach of conscience for unfair treatment to him or his people by those who came after he had gone at the invitation of the government, but sadness because he and his people could not enjoy what other races always have, the privilege of a higher civilization; sadness, because, while our gates are thrown wide open and over them is written in almost every tongue known among nations, "Come share our country and our government with us," it was closed behind him and his race, and over those words painted, in characters which he understood, "Begone!"

CHAPTER 2

Overland: Blood for Blood

In 1846 Pow-e-shiek came with his band to visit his old home. We were "early settlers" then, and had built our cabins on the sloping sides of a bluff overlooking the valley below. From this outpost we descried the bands of piebald ponies and then the curling smoke, and next the poles of his *wick-e-ups* (houses); and soon we saw Pow-e-shiek coming to make known his wish that he might be permitted to pasture his stock on the fields which we had already robbed of corn. The recognition in me of one who had assisted in removing his people seemed to surprise and please him, and for a moment his eye lit up as if some fond reality of the past had revived the friendship that had grown out of my sympathy for him in his dark hour of departure from his home.

And when I said, "This is my father, and my mother, these my sisters and my brothers, and this place is our home," he gave to the welcoming hands a friendly grasp in evidence of his good intentions, and then assured us that no trouble on his part should grow out of his coming, and that, if his young men should do any dishonest acts, he would punish them; that he had come back to spend the winter once again near his haunts of olden times, perhaps to kill the deer that he thought white men did not care about since they had so many cattle and swine. We accepted his assurance, and believed him to be just what he pretended,—a quiet, honest old chief, who would do as he agreed, nor seek excuse for not doing so.

The dinner hour had passed, but such as we had my mother set before him, and he did not fail to do full justice to everything upon the table. He made sure that his *papooses* should complete what he began by making a clean sweep into one corner of his blanket to bear it to his lodge. After dinner he drew out his pipe, and filling it with *kin-*

ni-ki-nick (tobacco), and lighting it with a coal of fire, he first sought to propitiate the Great Spirit by offering up to him the first puff of smoke; next the devil, by blowing the smoke downward, and saved the third for himself; and after that he offered to the fourth person in his calendar, my father, the privilege of expressing his approval. But, as he was not a smoker himself, he passed the pipe to his oldest son, intimating his desire that he should be represented by proxy. I, willing to do his bidding, in friendship for our guest, *it may be*, or perhaps from other personal motives, soon reduced the *kin-ni-ki-nick* to ashes and handed back the empty pipe to Pow-e-shiek. I knew not that I had transgressed the rules of politeness until afterwards, when I offered a pipe to our strange-mannered guest, he, with dignity, drew a puff or two and then passed it back, with an expression of countenance which declared unmistakably that it was meant for reproof.

If I felt resentment for a moment that a savage should presume to teach me manners, I do not feel that I was the only one who might be greatly benefited by taking lessons of unsophisticated men and women of other than white blood; not alone in simple politeness, but also in regard to right and justice, whose flags of truce are never raised *ostensibly* to insure protection, but *really* to intimidate the weak and defenceless, who dared to stand up for the God-given rights to home and country.

Pow-e-shiek made preparations to return to his lodge, and we, boy-like, followed him out of the cabin door, and while he was saying goodbye he espied a fine large dog that we had, named Van, though the name did not indicate our politics. Pow-e-shiek proposed to trade a pony for "old Van," and we were pleased at first, because we thought the pony would do to ride after the "breaking team" of dewy mornings in the spring. But when we learned that "Van" was wanted by the chief to furnish the most substantial part of a feast for his people, we demurred. "Old Van," too, seemed to understand the base use to which he was to be put, and reproached us with sullen side-looks; and the trade was abandoned, and would have been forgotten only that Van was ever afterward maddened at the sight of Pow-e-shiek or any of his race.

The winter passed, and our red neighbours had kept their promise, for although neither the granary nor any other building was ever locked, nothing had been missed, and our mutual regard seemed stronger than when the acquaintance was renewed. When spring had fully come, Pow-e-shiek, punctual to his promise, broke up his camp

BULL-DOG TRADE.

and went away.

Occasionally, for years afterwards, his people came back to visit; but *he no more.*

Years have passed, and he has joined the great throng in the happy hunting-grounds.

When the gold fever was at its height, in 1850, in company with others I journeyed overland to the new Eldorado. While *en route*, we heard much of Indians, of their butcheries and cruelties; I think there was good foundation for the stories. Indeed, we saw so many evidences of their handiwork, in new-made graves and abandoned wagons demolished, that there could be no reasonable doubt of their savage treatment of those who came within their power.

While *I do not now, never have, and never will attempt to justify their butcheries, yet it is but fair that both sides of the story be told.*

When our party was at "Independence Rock," in 1850, and no Indians had disturbed the passing travellers, near where we were then, we "laid over" a day, and within the time a man came into camp and boasted that he had "knocked over a *buck* at a distance of a hundred yards," and when the query was made as to the whereabouts of his game he produced a *bloody scalp*. He gave as an excuse that the Indians had frightened an antelope he was trying to kill, and that he shot the Indian while the latter was endeavouring to get away. Is it unreasonable to suppose that the friends of the murdered Indian, when he came not to the lodge at nightfall, would hunt him up, and that, when his brother or friend saw his scalpless head, he should avow to avenge his death?

Doubtless he did avenge both himself and his tribe, and he may have slain many innocent persons in retaliation for this foul deed.

As to the cause of the Indian troubles on the Humbolt River, during the summer of 1850, I know nothing. Probably they originated in some lawless act similar to the one above described. In September following I loaned a rifle to a miner who was going out on a prospecting tour. On his return he proposed to buy it, saying that "it was a good one, he knew, because he tried it on an Indian, shooting from one bluff to another; and," said this civilized white man, "I dropped him into the river, and he went where all good Injuns go."

Later in the season two friendly Indians came into the town of "Bidwell's Bar," and, although no evidence was produced against them, they were arrested on "general principles," it was said; and while threats were made of hanging them on "general principles" too, *better*

30

counsels prevailed, and they were placed in charge of a guard, who were to convey them to "Long's Bar," and turn them over to the sheriff to be held for trial.

The guard returned in a short time, and reported that the prisoners had "slipped down a bank and were drowned." It was, however, understood that they were killed by the guard "to save expense." Following this accident several white men were murdered by Indians, it was said, although the murdered men, it was evident, had met death through *other instrumentality than bows and arrows.*

A company was raised to go out and punish the offenders. On their return they reported grand success in finding Indian *rancheros,* and in the wholesale butchery they had committed. Do you wonder that twenty or thirty white men were *riddled with arrows within a short time, after such manly conduct, by the brave butchers of Indian women and children?*

I have not at hand the data from which to mention in detail the various Indian wars that harassed the miners of California. Suffice it that they were of frequent occurrence, and, indeed, continued until the mountain bands of Indians were broken up. If the truth could be heard from the lips of both the living and the dead, we should hear many things *unpleasant to the ears of white men* as well as Indians, and, perhaps, discreditable to both. I doubt not such revelation would support the declaration I here make,—that *bad white men* have always been the instigators of the bloody deeds through which so many innocent persons have passed on to the other life.

The proofs are not wanting in almost every instance in support of this statement. That the Indian is vindictive, is true; that he is brave, cunning, and inhuman to his enemies is also true; but that he is faithful to his compacts, whenever fairly dealt with, is *not less true.*

CHAPTER 3

Indians and Miners

Walla-walla, Washington Territory,
February 4th, 1863.

Dear Brother (Suisun City, Cal.):—

I have found a good country and more business than I can manage alone; come and help me. Better leave your family until you can see for yourself. You may not like it, though I do. Money is plenty, everything new, and prices keyed up to old "forty-nine" times.

Your brother,

H. J. Meacham.

Lee's Encampment, fifty miles south of Walla-Walla,
on top of Blue Mountain, March 6, 1863.

My Dear Wife (Suisun, Cal.):—

"*Eureka.*" Come; I am camping in four feet of snow, and cooking meals in a frying-pan, and charging a dollar; selling "slap jacks" two bits each; oats and barley at twelve cents, and hay at ten cents per pound, and other things at same kind of prices; can't supply the demand. Go to William Booth, San Francisco, and tell him to ship you and the children with the goods, to Walla-Walla, Washington Territory, *via* Portland, Oregon, care Wells, Fargo & Co.'s Express.

A. B. Meacham.

These two letters are copied here, to carry the reader and the writer over a period of twelve years, leaving behind whatever may have transpired of interest to the work now in hand, to be taken up on some other page, in proper connection with kindred subjects of later date.

Lee's Encampment is located near the summit of the Blue Mountains in Oregon, on the great highway leading from the Columbia River to the rich gold fields of Idaho and Eastern Oregon. It is fifty miles south of Walla-Walla, and is also one of the out-boundaries of the Umatilla Indian Reservation, occupied by the Walla-Walla, Cayuse and Umatilla Indians.

The roads leading out from the several starting-points on the Columbia River, to the mines above-mentioned, converge on the Reservation, and, climbing the mountain's brow, on the old "Emigrant trail," cross over to Grand Round valley.

During the spring of 1863, the great tide of miners that flowed inland, to reach the new gold fields, necessarily passed through the Reservation, and thence *via* Lee's Encampment. This circumstance of location gave abundant opportunity for observation by the writer. Of those who sought fortunes in the mines, I might write many chapters descriptive of the motley crowds of every shade of colour and of character, forming episodes and thrilling adventures. But my purpose in this work would not be subserved by doing so, except such as have bearing on the subject-matter under consideration.

Of the thousands who landed at Umatilla City and Walla-Walla, *en route* to the "upper country," few brought means of transportation overland. There were no stages, no railroads; and what though Haley & Ish, Stephen Taylor, and many others, advertised "saddle trains to leave for the mines every day of the week, at reasonable rates," which were, say, sixty dollars, on ponies that cost perhaps forty dollars; yet there were hundreds that could not get tickets even at those rates. The few who engaged *reserved seats* were started off on saddle-horses of various grades, under the charge of a "conductor," whose principal duty was, not to collect fares, but to herd the kitchen mules,—every train had with it one or more animals on whose back the supplies and blankets were carried,—and indicate the camping places by pulling the ropes that loosed the aforesaid kitchens and blankets, when, like other trains, at the pull of the rope, the whole would stop, and not be startled into unnecessary haste by "twenty minutes for dinner" sounded in their ears. One or more nights the camp would be on the Reservation, thus bringing travellers and Indians in contact.

I have said that many could not get places, even on the backs of mules, or Cayuse ponies. Such were compelled to take "Walkers' line," go on foot and carry blankets and "grub" on their backs. The second night out would find them also on the Reservation, and those who had the wherewith, purchased horses of the Indians; some, perhaps, without consulting the owners. Not stealing them! No. A white man would not do so mean a thing; but ropes are suspicious things when found in the pack of one of "Walker's" passengers, and if a pony was fool enough to run his head into a noose, the handiest way to get clear of him was to exchange with some other man of similar misfortune, and then it was not stealing in the eyes of honest white men.

If the Indian missed his property, and, hunting along the line, found him under a white man, you might suppose he could recover his horse. Not so, my lord! Not so. The white man had proof that he had bought him of some other man, may be an Indian. Such was sometimes the case, for I do not believe that all men are honest, white or red; and these red men were not behind the white in sharp practice; and it is safe to say, that those of whom I am writing now were peers of those who sought to outwit, them.

The horses of saddle trains would sometimes "stray away,"—often those of freighters,—and, since time was money, and strangers might not understand the "range," the Indians were employed to hunt for the straying animals, and paid liberally if they succeeded; and thus it *made the stock of other trains restless, and often they* would run away—and so the business increased, and the Indians grew wealthier, notwithstanding their own sometimes followed off a rope in the hands of white men.

The road, along which this stream of miners poured, left the valley of Umatilla on the Reservation, leading up the mountains. Near the foot of the hill, but with a deep ravine or gulch intervening, and on another hill,—part really of the valley, though sloping toward the former,—was The "Trading Post,"—Indian's sutler store. 'Twas here that saddle trains and "Walker's line," halted for the night, or "to noon" and rest, after travelling a fourteen-mile "stretch."

The "Walker" passengers were already worn out, with heavy packs of picks and pans, bottles and blankets. The situation of the post, with reference to the mountain, was to an observer like standing on the sloping roof of one house and measuring the "pitch" of the one adjoining, making it seem much steeper than it really is. So with this mountain. True, it required a broad upward sweep of vision to take in the height. On the first bench, one mile above, the trains and men seemed to be transformed into dogs and boys. On the second bench, two miles up, they looked still smaller. On the third, three miles up, they very closely resembled Punch and Judy driving a team of poodles. The Indians found here a market for their horses, and sometimes did a livery business, in Indian style.

A stalwart son of Erin, standing against the wall of the store to "rest his pack," after looking at the trail leading up the mountain, said to the merchant doing business there, "I say, misther, is it up that hill we go?" Hearing an affirmative answer, he looked again at each bench, his brow growing darker the higher his eye went; at length he gave vent to his estimate of the undertaking by saying, "By the howly St. Patrick, if me own mother was here in the shape of a mule, I'd ride her up that hill, sure! I say, Misther Injun, wouldn't you sell us a bit of a pony for to carry our blankets an' things over the mountain with?"

The Indian had been in business long enough to understand that, and replied, "*Now-wit-ka mi-ka pot-luetch. Chic-a, mon, ni-ka is-cum, cu-i-tan!*"

"Och! Mister Injun, don't be makin' fun of a fellow, now, will ye? It's very sore me feet is, a-carrying me pick and pan and cooking-traps. Why don't you talk like a dacent American gentleman?"

"*Wake-ic-ta-cum-tux,*" said Tip-tip-a-noor, the Indian.

"Don't be playin' your dirty tongue on me now, or I'll spoil your beautiful face so I will."

Drawing his arms out of the straps that had kept the pack in position on his shoulders, and lowering it "aisy," to save the bottle, he began to make demonstrations of hostile character, when Mr. Flippin, the post-trader, explained that Tip-tip-a-noos had replied to his first request, "Yes, you show the money, and I will furnish the horse;" and he had replied to the second, "I don't understand you."

"And is that all he says? Shure, he is a nice man, so he is. Shan't I swaten his mouth wid a dhrop from me bottle?"

"No," says Flip., "that won't do."

"Away wid yees; shure, this is a free counthry, and can't a man do as he plases with his own?"

"Not much," replied Flip.

"I say now, Mike, will you join me in the byin' of a bit of a pony for to carry our blankets and things?"

The man addressed as Mike assented to the proposal, and soon Tip-tip-a-noos brought a small pinto calico-coloured horse; and after some dickering the trade was completed by Pat, through pantomimic signs, giving Tip to understand, that if he would follow down into the gulch, out of sight of Flip., he would give him a bottle of whiskey, in addition to the twenty dollars.

The pony was turned over to Pat and Mike. The next move was to adjust the packs on the Cayuse. This was not easily done. First, because the pony did not understand Pat's jargon; second, they had not reckoned on the absence of a pack-saddle. Flip., always ready to accommodate the travelling public, for a consideration, brought an old cross-tree pack-saddle, and then the lash-ropes,—ropes to bind the load to the saddle. Pat approached the pony with outstretched hands, saying pretty things in Irish brogue; while Mike, to make sure that the horse should not escape, had made it fast to his waist with a rope holding back, while Pat went forward, so that at the precise moment the latter had reached the pony's nose, he reared up, and, striking forward, gave Pat a blow with his fore-foot, knocking him down. Seeming to anticipate the Irishman's coming wrath, he whirled so quick that Mike lost his balance and went down, shouting, "Sthop us, sthop us; we are running away!" Pat recovered his feet in time to jump on the prostrate form of Mike, going along horizontally, at a furious gait, close to the pony's heels. The Cayuse slackened his speed and finally stopped, but not until Mike had lost more or less of clothing, and the "pelt" from his rosy face.

When the two Irishmen were once more on foot, and both holding to the rope, now detached from Mike's waist at one end, and buried into the wheezing neck of the Cayuse at the other, a scene occurred that Bierstadt should have had for a subject. I don't believe I can do it justice, and yet I desire my readers to see it, since the renowned painter above-mentioned, was not present to represent it on canvas.

Think of two bloody-nosed Irish lads holding the pony, while he was pulling back until his haunches almost touched the ground, wheezing for breath, occasionally jumping forward to slacken the rope around his neck, and each time letting Pat and Mike fall suddenly to the ground, swearing in good Irish style at the "spalpeen of a brute" that had no better manners, while Mr. Indian was laughing as he would have done his crying,—away down in his heart. Flip., and *others* looking on, were doing as near justice to the occasion as possible, by laughing old-fashioned horse-laughs, increasing with each speech from Pat or Mike.

Occasionally, when the Cayuse would suddenly turn his heels, and fight in pony style, Pat would roar out Irish, while the horse would compel them to follow him, each with body and limbs at an angle of forty-five degrees, until his horseship would turn again, and then they were on a horizontal awhile. Securing him to a post, Pat said, "Now, be jabers, we've got him." After slipping a shirt partly over his head, to "blind" him, they proceed to *sinche*—fasten—the pack-saddle on him, and then the two packs. When all was lashed fast, and a *hak-i-more*—rope halter—was on his nose, they untied him from the post, and proposed to travel, but Cayuse did not budge. Mike pulled and tugged at the halter, while Pat called him pretty names, and, with outspread hands, as though he was herding geese, stamping his foot, coaxed pony to start. No use. Flip. suggested a sharp stick. Pat went for his cane, like a man who had been suddenly endowed with a bright idea. After whittling the end to a point, he applied it to the pony.

The next speech that Irishman made was while in half-bent position. With one hand on the side of his head, he anxiously addressed Tip. "Meester Injun, is me ear gone—Meester Injun, what time of night is it now? I say, Meester Injun, where now is the spalpeen of a pony?"

Mike had let go of the rope soon after Pat applied the sharp stick, and was following the retreating blankets and bottles, ejaculating, "The beautiful whiskey! The beautiful whiskey!"

When Pat's eyes were clear enough, Meester Injun, without a smile, pointed to the valley below, where frying pans and miners tools were performing a small circus, much to the amusement of a band of Cayuse horses, who were following Pat's pony with considerable interest.

I don't think the goods, or the whiskey either, were ever recovered by Pat and Mike, but I have an idea that "Tip-tip-a-noor" had a big dance, and slept warm under the blankets, and possibly a big drunk.

Of course, reader, you do not blame Irishmen for their opposition to "The Humane Policy of the Government."

The Indian, however, if detected in unlawful acts, was sure of punishment under the law, no matter though he may have been incited to the deed by whiskey he had bought of white men, who vended it in violation of law. This commerce in whiskey was carried on extensively, notwithstanding the efforts of a very efficient agent to prevent it.

Men have started out on "Walker's line," carrying their blankets, and in a day or two they would be well mounted, without resorting to a "rope" or money to purchase with, and obtain the horses honestly too; that is to say, when they practised self-denial, and did not empty the bottles they had concealed in their packs. One bottle of whiskey would persuade an Indian to dismount, and allow the sore-footed, honest miner, who carried the bottle, to ride, no matter though the horse may have belonged to other parties. I have heard men boast that they were "riding a bottle," meaning the horse that bore them along had cost that sum.

Such things were common, and could not be prevented. Young "Black Hawk" learned how to speak English, and make brick, and various other arts, through the kindness of the superintendent of the State's Prison. These things he might never have known, but for the foresight of some fellow who disliked the fare on "Walker's" line.

The question is asked, "What was the agent doing?" He was doing his duty as well as he could, with the limited powers he possessed. But when he sought to arrest the white men who were violators of the laws of the United States, he was always met with the common prejudices against Indian testimony, and found himself defeated. But, when he was appealed to for protection against Indian depredations, he found sympathy and support, and few instances occurred where guilty Indians escaped just punishment.

I knew the agent well, and doubted not his sense of justice in his efforts to maintain peace.—If he did not mete out even-handed justice in all matters of dispute between white men and Indians, the fault was not his, but rather that of public sentiment. When coloured men were "niggers," the Indian "had no rights that white men were bound to respect."

He who proclaimed against the unjust administration of law so unfavourable to the Indians, in courts where white men and Indians were parties, was denounced as a fanatical sentimentalist, and placed in the same category with "Wendell Phillips" and "Old John Brown," whose names, in former times, were used to deride and frighten honest-thinking people from the expression of sentiments of justice and right.

I wish here to record that, although we did a large amount of business with white men and Indians, we never had occasion to complain of the latter for stealing, running off stock, or failing to perform, according to agreement, to the letter, even in matters left to their own sense of honour.

On one occasion, "Cascas," a Reservation Indian, who was under contract to deliver, once in ten days, at Lee's Encampment, ten head of yearlings, of specified size and quality, as per sample, at the time of making the bargain, brought nine of the kind agreed upon and one inferior animal. Before driving them into the corral, he rode up to the house, and calling me, pointed to the small yearling, saying that was "no good;" that he could not find "good ones" enough that morning to fill the contract, but if I would let the *"Ten-as-moose-moose"*—small steer—go in, next time, he would drive up a *"Hi-as-moose-moose"*—big steer—in place of an ordinary yearling. If I was unwilling to take the small one, he would drive him back, and bring one that would be up to the standard.

I assented to the first proposition. Faithful to the promise, he made up the deficiency with a larger animal next time, and even then made it good.

Another circumstance occurred which asserted the honesty of these Indians. After we had corralled a small lot of cows purchased from them, one escaped and returned to the Indian band of cattle, from which she had been driven. Three or four years after, we were notified by the owner of the band that we had four head of cattle with his herd. True, it was but simple honesty, and no more than any honest man would have done; but there are so many who would have marked and branded the calves of that little herd, in their own interest, that I felt it worthy of mention here to the credit of a people who have few friends to speak in their behalf. Notwithstanding their lives furnish many evidences of high and honourable character, yet they, very much like white men, exhibit many varieties.

In pressing need for a supply of beef for hotel use, I called on "Tin-tin-mit-si," once chief of the Walla-Wallas (a man of extraordinary shrewdness, and possessed of great wealth, probably thirty thousand dollars in stock and money), to make a purchase. He, silently, half in pantomime, ordered his horse, that he might accompany me to the herds. Taking with us his son-in-law, John McBerne, as interpreter, we soon found one animal that would answer our purpose. The keen-eyed old chief, with his blanket drawn over his head, faced about, and said, "How much that cow weigh?"

"About four hundred and fifty pounds," I answered.

"How much you charge for a dinner?"

"One dollar," I responded.

"How much a white man eat?" said "Tin-tin-mit-si."

I read his mind, and knew that he was thinking how to take advantage of my necessity, and, also, that he was not accustomed to the white man's dinner. I replied, "Sometimes one pound."

"All right," quoth Indian; "you pay me four hundred dollars, then what is over will pay you for cooking."

"But who will pay me for the coffee, sugar, butter, potatoes, eggs, cheese, and other things?" I replied.

While Johnny was repeating this speech the old chief moved up closer, and let his blanket slip off his ears, and demanded a repetition of the varieties composing a Christian dinner; and, while this was being done, he looked first at the interpreter, then at me, and said, in a surly, dry tone, "No wonder a white man is a fool, if he eat all those things at once; an Indian would be satisfied with beef alone."

After some mathematical calculations had been explained, he agreed to accept forty-five dollars, a good, round price for the cow. And I drove away the beast, while "Tin-tin-mit-si" returned to his lodge to bury the money I had paid him along with several thousand dollars he had saved for his sons-in-law to quarrel over; for the old chief soon after sent for his favourite horse to be tied near the door of his lodge, ready to accompany him to the happy hunting-grounds, where, according to Indian theology, he has been telling his father of the strange people he had seen.

CHAPTER 4

Diamond-Cut-Diamond

It was understood, in the treaty stipulation with the government and these people, that they were to have the privilege of hunting and grazing stock in common with citizens on the public domain. In the exercise of this right, they made annual journeys to Grand Round and other valleys, east of the Blue mountains, driving before them, on these journeys, their horses. They were often thus brought in contact with white settlers, and sometimes difficulties occurred, growing, generally, out of the sale of intoxicating liquors to them by unprincipled white men.

Indians are not better than white men, and, when drunk, they exhibit the meaner and baser qualities of their nature as completely as a white man. Deliver us from either, but of the two, an intoxicated white man has the advantage; he is not held responsible to law. The Indian has one privilege the civilized white brother is not supposed to enjoy. He can abuse his family, and as long as he is sober enough can whip his squaw; but woe be to him when he gets past fighting, for then the squaw embraces the opportunity of beating him in turn, and calls on other squaws to assist in punishing her lord for past as well as present offences.

The chiefs generally watch over their men, to prevent the purchase of liquor by them. "Homli," chief of the Walla-Wallas, sometimes punished his braves in a summary manner for getting drunk, using a horsewhip in the public streets. However worthy the example, I believe that it was not often followed by others of either race.

The annual visits of which I have spoken occurred in the latter part of June, when the mountain sides of Grand Round valley were offering tempting inducements in fields of huckleberries. The valley, too,—where not enclosed and turned to better use,—was blooming

41

with Indian "*muck-a-muck*," a sweet, nutritious root called *ca-mas*, with which the Indian women filled baskets and sacks, in which to carry it to their homes for winter use.

The beautiful river of Grand Round was inviting the red men to war against the shining trout and salmon, that made yearly pilgrimage to greater altitudes and cooler shades, there to woo and mate, and thus to people the upper waters with finny children, who would, in time of autumn leaves, go to the great river below, and come again when mountain snows, now changed to foaming torrents, hastened to the river's mouth, and tempting salmon flies had come from their hiding places, and swarmed on bush and bank, to lure the fish onward and upward, or beguile them to the fisher's net, or hidden spear, if, perchance, they were warned away from angler's line, or escaped the lightning arrow of Indian boys.

Then, too, this beautiful garden of the mountains wore its brightest hues on plain and sloping hills and cultured field. The farmers were idle then, and often went to join the red men in racing horses, and chasing each other in mimic wars. Sometimes the two would engage in trades of wild Cayuses (Indian horses), teaching each other how to tame these fiery steeds. Great circus shows were these, in which the red man might for once laugh at the white man's clumsy imitations of red men's daily recreations.

Again, the red man had sweet revenge for sharper practice which he had felt at the hands of his white brother. Selecting some ill-natured beast, whose tricks he well knew, he would offer him at a price so low, that some white man who was tired of going to his neighbours for a ride, or had a hopeful son anxious to imitate little Indian boys in feats of horsemanship, would purchase him. Then fun began, to witness which the town sometimes turned out. The colt, unused to civilized bit or spur, would, like his former owner, show contempt for burdens he was not made to bear without "bucking." When, with bridle and saddle, and rider, all new, surrounded by scenes unlike his colt-ship's haunts, he was called upon to forward move, he would stand as if turned to marble, until by persuasion of whip and spur he'd change his mind.

Then, with a snort, a bound, or upward motion of his back, his nostrils buried in the dust, he'd whirl and whirl until the rider dizzy grew, of which circumstance he seemed aware, when, with all his power brought into quick use, he sent the rider in mid-air or overhead, and straightway bent each bound toward his former home, followed by loud shouts of laughter, made up of voices joined of every kind and age, except perhaps that of the disgusted father—who had sundry dollars invested in furniture on the runaway's back—and the crying boy in the dust.

The chances against the new owner's boy ever "putting on much style" on that pony were not very numerous. Fearing as much, the next proposition was to sell the pony back to "Mr. Injun" at a heavy discount; which was done much against the wishes of the dethroned boy, whose aspirations for western honour were thereby "nipped in the bud."

A lawyer of "La Grande," celebrated for his shrewdness in business generally, and who was the father of several enterprising sons, made an investment in Cayuse stock, for the benefit of the aforesaid boys, and fearing that he, too, might go in mourning over the money thus spent, in fatherly tenderness determined that he himself would ride the pony first.

The horse was saddled, and led by a long rope to the office door. The lawyer said, "Now, Charley, I'll fool that pony, sure. I'm little, you know, and he'll think I'm a boy." The rope was made fast to an awning-post, and then, in presence of a hopeful audience, he mounted slowly, though in full lawyer's dress, a bell-crowned "plug" (hat) included. When softly springing in the stirrups, to assure himself all was right, and confident that his "nag" was there, subject to his will, he essayed to display his horsemanship. But pony was not ready then. The lawyer called for whip and spurs, and without dismounting they were furnished, and while holding out his foot to have the spur put on, remarked that "he did not half like the white of the pony's eye. But, boys, I'll stick while the saddle does."

With sober face and eye fixed on the ears in front, he coaxed again, and with soft speech sought to change the pony's mind. But he was not ready now, until he felt the rowel stick into his sides, and then away went horse and rider together, to the end of the rope, where the pony stopped, though the lawyer did not, until his head had struck the crown of his hat; and not then even, but, going at a furious rate, the lawyer, hat, and torn trowsers had landed all in a heap on the other side of the street; the awning-post gave way, and the lawyer's Cayuse went off, with a small part of the town following him.

The language used by him on this occasion consisted not of quotations from Blackstone, or the Bible either, unless in detached words put strangely in shape to answer immediate use. It is not safe to say anything about fooling ponies, in court or elsewhere, in the town of La Grande, unless the speaker wants war. That lawyer, although a stanch Republican, and liable to be a candidate for Congress, is strongly opposed to President Grant's peace policy with Indians,—the Umatilla Indians in particular.

To say that Chief Homli and his tribe enjoyed little episodes, growing out of horse-trading with the citizens of La Grande, is too gentle and soft a way of telling the truth, and have it well understood, unless we add the westernism "hugely."

These visits had other beneficial results than those growing out of trade, since they extended over the Fourth of July, when all the people of the valley came together to celebrate the "nation's birthday," when, with fife and drum, the country-folks would join with those in town, who "marched up a street and then marched down again," to the willow-covered stand, where readers and orators would rehearse, one, the history of the "Declaration," the other, repeat some great man's speech.

The tables groaned beneath the loads of viands, spread by gentle women's hands. The reader and the orator of the day would take positions at either end, and the meek chaplain in between, while the bashful country boys would lead up their girls, until the table had been filled. Homli and his people, dressed in Fourth-of-July regalias, would look on from respectful distance, and wonder what the reader meant, when he said, "All men are born free and equal," and wondered more to hear a wicked orator protest that the "flag above was no longer a flaunting lie." The Indians were then serving in the house of a foolish old man, named Esau. When fair lips refused longer to taste, and manly breast was filled too full for utterance, Homli and his people were invited to partake. Some of his people accepted the gift of the remnants; but he, Homli, never.

In the absence of better pastime, the crowd would come again to the grand stand, to give opportunity for disappointed spouters to ventilate pent-up patriotism. Homli, too, made a speech, and with keen rebuke referred to days gone by, when white men had come to his lodge, and craved his hospitality; how his women had culled their berry-baskets to find something worthy of the white man's taste, and how the finest trout had been offered in proof of friendship for the stranger guest, and boasted that he had given the finest horses of his band to help the stranger on, and sent an escort of trusty braves to direct him over all doubtful trails. He boasted, too, that no white man's

44

blood had ever stained his hand, even when he was strong, and they were weak; then, with well-made gesture, pointed to the valley, once all his own, and covered with antelope and feathery tribes.

No houses, fields, or barns marred then the beautiful valley of the mountain. Turning half around, he gazed at people and town, and sadly motioned to the mountain-sides, robbed of fir and pine, and seemed to drink in, what, to him, was desolation made complete. With eye half closed, he mused a moment, and then broke forth like some brave soul that had mastered self, and was reconciled to the inexorable destiny that his mind had seen in store, declared that he would be a man himself, with white man's heart, and that his people would yet join with pride in the coming celebrations.

The triumph of civil hopes over savage mind was complete, and when the change was realized by the lookers-on, they gathered round the chieftain, and gave him welcome to a brotherhood born of a nation's struggles to redeem mankind, when the white men were few and Homli's people numerous as the stars that looked down on the rivers of this beautiful land. Who shall remember the mild reproof of Homli, when he, under the humane and enlightened policy of the government, shall have made good this declaration to be a white man in heart and practice?

Little things sometimes move in harmony until they unite, and make up an aggregate of causes, whose combined power becomes irresistible for good or ill to peoples, tribes, and nations.

The chieftain of whom I write had, at various times, felt the thongs that bound him to his savage habits loosening, little by little, until at last, under the influence of the patriotic joy of freemen, he himself had stepped from under a shadow that was once a benison, but had now, because of his enlightenment, become a barrier to his happiness.

The change was real, and the heart that had come laden with reproach to his neighbour, and felt the sting of slighted manhood, now exulted in the recognition he had found in the sunshine of American Independence, and the warm hands of freedom's sons, who bade him welcome to a better life.

No human brain can correctly measure the influence of such events. Homli, as I have said, was a chief of the Walla-Wallas, who, in conjunction with the Umatillas and Cayuses, occupied the reservation spoken of as "Umatilla" (horse-heaven), it being the original home of the tribe bearing that name. In 1856, the three tribes above named united in treaty council with the government, represented by the la-

45

mented J. I. Stevens and General Joel Palmer.

This treaty was conducted with firmness and on principles of justice, the Indians having, in this instance at least, half "the say." By the terms agreed upon, a portion of country was reserved by the three tribes for a permanent home, to be held jointly by them. It is located on one of the tributaries of the Columbia, known as the Umatilla River. The out-boundaries measured one hundred and three miles, covering a country possessing many natural advantages, conducive to Indian life, and of great value in the transfer of these people from a barbarous to a civilized condition.

Its surface is diversified with rich prairie lands, producing an excellent quality of bunch grass,—so called because of its growing in tussocks,—covering not more than half the surface of the round, the remainder being entirely devoid of vegetation, very nutritious and well adapted to grazing.

The mountains are partly covered with forests of pine and fir, valuable for commercial and building purposes. The streams are rapid, with bold shores, abounding in latent power, waiting for the time when labour and capital shall harness its cataracts to machinery, whose music will denote the transformation process going on in the forest of the mountain; the fleeces from the plain, and in the cereals they contain, in embryo, for better use than shading herds of cattle and Indian horses, or its fleeces made traffic for traders and shippers, who enrich themselves by taking them in bulk and returning in manufactured exchanges; or for its fields to lie dormant and idle, while commerce invites and starving people clamour for bread they might be made to yield.

True, its almost unbroken wilderness, echoing the call of cougar or cayote (*ki-o-te*); its tall grass plains, tangled and trembling with the tread of twenty thousand horses; its valleys decked with carpets of gorgeous flowers,—fit patterns for the costumes of those who dance thereon,—or speckled with baby farms, belonging to red-skinned ploughmen, or shaded by the smoke of council *wigwams*; its waters sometimes shouting, as if in pain, while hurrying headlong against the rock, or, laughing beneath the balm-wood trees at the gambols of its own people, or, divided into an hundred streams, go rushing on, still playing mirror for the smiling faces of the youths, whose hearts and actions take pattern after its own freedom; true, indeed, that this lovely spot of earth seems to have been the special handiwork of the Almighty, who had withheld from other labours the choicest gems of beauty, that he might make a paradise, where youth could keep pace with passing years, until the change of happy hunting-grounds should be noted only by the wail of weeping widows, or sighs of sorrowing orphans.

'Twas to this Indian paradise that Homli returned from his summer visit, his heart laden with new feelings of pride; for he had been recognized as a man. If he did not then begin to enjoy the realization of his hopes, there were reasons why he did not that few have understood.

Born to a wild, free life, possessed of a country such as few over enjoy, with a channel of commerce traversing his home; brought in constant contact with white men, some of whom, at least, he found to be soulless adventurers, ever ready to take advantage of his ignorance of trade; confused and bewildered by the diversity of opinions on political and religious subjects; witnessing the living falsehood of much of civilized life; but half understanding the ambitions of his "new heart," or the privilege he was entitled to; with the romance of his native education in matters of religion, its practical utility to satisfy his longings that reached into the future, or to meet the demands of conscience, where duty led him, or anger at insult drove him; the performance of its ceremonies, connecting social with religious rites.

Added to these the power that his red brethren who were yet untouched by the finger of destiny, and were luxuriating in idle, careless life, enhanced by the sight of the hardened hands and sweating brows of those who sought to find admission to circles where labour insures reward; confused when witnessing the enforcement of laws "that are supposed to be uniform in operation," by the outrageous partiality shown; treated with coldness and distrust, because of his colour; envied of his possessions, to which he had an inalienable right, by deed from God, and confirmed by the Government of the United States; compelled to hear the constant coveting of others for it, and to hear government denounced because it did not rob him of his home; to see distrust in every action toward him; his manhood ignored, or crushed by cruel power; his faith shaken; treated as an alien, even in his birthplace; taunted with the threat that when he planted his feet on higher plains, he should be crowded off, or forced to stand tottering on the brink; his fears aroused by the threats he overheard of being finally driven away; of speculations on the future towns that should spring up over the graves of his fathers, when he was not there to defend them.

Added to all these discouragements the oppressions of his would-be teachers, in moral ethics and religion; demanding his attendance

47

on ceremonies that were intangible, incomprehensible, to his mind, made more unbearable by the tyranny of his red brethren, growing out of their recognition of church-membership, and the consequent arrogance, even contempt, with which they spoke of his religious habits and ceremonies; unable to reconcile the practices of these people with the precepts of their priest; ostracised from those, who, while untouched by the hand of Christianity, had mingled voice and prayer with him in wilder worship; finding friends among white men, whose hearts were true, but who, instead of soothing his troubled feelings by patiently teaching him charity and liberal-minded views touching matters of religious practice of his Catholic friends and their ministers, would pile the fagots on the burning altar 'twixt him and them, increasing distrust, making the breach wider, thus becoming alienated from the other chiefs, How-lish-wam-po, of Cayuse, and We-nap-snoot, of the Umatillas, and those of their tribes who had been led, by ministrations of priest and chief, to the solemn masses of the church: if then Homli failed to be a "white man" in heart, on whom does the responsibility rest?

I have not dealt in fiction, but have stated the circumstance plainly, the truth of which will not be questioned by those whose personal knowledge qualifies them for passing judgment, unless, indeed, it be those whose minds have been trained to run in narrow, bigoted grooves, whose hearts have never felt the warming influences of the high and pure love for truth that characterizes a noble Christian manhood, and whose measure of right is made by the petty and selfish interest of himself, who, with the judgment of a truckling demagogue, barks for pay in popular applause or political reward.

For the present, I leave my readers to chide Homli for his failure, if, indeed, they can, with the facts before them. As to the responsibility, I shall discuss the subject fully and fearlessly on some future page of this work, where the argument for and against the several "policies" may be made and applied in a general way in the consideration of the subject of "Indian civilization."

CHAPTER 5

Policies on Trial—"Oneatta."

In the fall of 1866, the "Oregon Delegation," in Washington, proposed the name of the author of this book for appointment as Superintendent of Indian Affairs in Oregon.

President Johnson, on inquiry, learned that he was not a "Johnson man," and, of course, refused to make the nomination.

The recommendation of the author's name was made without his solicitation or knowledge. On the accession of President Grant, the recommendation was renewed, the nomination was made and confirmed by the Senate of the United States; bonds filed, oaths of office administered, and notice given to my predecessor; and on the 1st of May, 1869, I assumed the duties of the office indicated.

The new administration had the Indian question in transit, between three policies: The old way, "*Civil Service*," "*The War Department Policy*," and General Grant's "*Quaker Policy*."

With good intention, doubtless, the several policies were put on trial.

Oregon superintendency and all its agencies were assigned to the tender care of the War Department policy, and I was ordered to turn over my office to an officer of the army, even before I had performed an important official duty. Remonstrance was made by the people of Oregon against the change.

A compromise was effected. I was retained as superintendent, and Hon. Ben. Simpson, agent at Siletz, and Capt. Charles Lafollette, agent at Grand Round also of the civil service policy. The remainder of the agencies were assigned to officers of the army. This mixing up of elements was somewhat embarrassing for a time.

I began again my official duties. From the records in the superintendent's office, Salem, Oregon, I learned the location and something

49

of the condition of the several agencies under my charge.

"*The Coast Reservation,*" covering three hundred miles of the Pacific coast, embraced several stations, or agencies, comprising not more than one-third the territory within its boundaries. It had never been ceded to the government, neither acquired by conquest, but was set apart by an act of Congress for the benefit of the several tribes of the Willamette valley. It is partly timbered and generally mountainous. It abounds in resources suitable to Indian savage life.

Once this wild region had been peopled with deer and elk, whose plaintive call had led the cougar to his feast, or quickened the steps of the huntsman, whose steady nerves enabled him to glide through the tanglewood, bearing with him images of his children (who, dependent upon his archery, awaited his return); and of faithful *clutch-men* (squaws), whose eyes would kindle at sight of hunter, laden with fruits of the chase, that were to be food and clothing for her little ones. These forest trees had stood sentinels, guarding its people, from the gaze of tamer huntsmen, and from the rough ocean winds that sweep the coast; or, uttering hoarser sounds, or sighing songs, warning of coming storms, that sometimes beat the white-winged ship, laden with merchandise, from foreign lands, against the rocky shore (whose caverns were the refuge of sea-lions), or, echoing back Pacific's roar, were waiting for the debris from wrecks of stately crafts, or coming of sea-washed mariners.

Then, at such perilous times, the peoples of this wild western verge of continent would, in pure charity, build warning-fires on higher bluffs, at nightfall, and thus give signals of danger; or, mayhap, they sometimes built them to decoy, in order to avenge insult (or wrong, real, or imaginary) of some former seaman, who had repaid them for good will by treacherous act of larceny of some dusky maiden, or black-eyed boy, or stalwart warrior, carried away to other lands.

Tradition's living tongue has furnished foundation for the pictures I have made. And many times to listening ears the story has been told, changed only in the name of maiden, or boy, or braves, as date or location gave truth to the sorrowing tale.

Living still, on a home set apart by the State, are two chieftains of a western tribe, whose people tell, in story and in song, how, at a certain sign of danger to a ship, they went out over the breakers in a hollow-tree canoe, to meet the white "*tyee*" of the "great canoe," and in pity for the poverty of his knowledge of sea line had proffered him shelter in a quiet nook of land-locked ocean, until such time as the Great Spirit might give evidence of anger past, by smiling on the boisterous waves that had made sport of man's puny efforts to control his own going.

These chieftains, in dainty craft, had won the captain's confidence, and, by consent of favouring winds and rolling seas, with trust he follows past lone rocks that stand above the sunken reef, and through the foamy passage, guarded by "headlands" on either side; past bars, unseen, that break huge rollers into waves of shorter measure; past, still past, the homes of fishermen on shore, until at last his sails flapped approval on the mast, the keel complains of unaccustomed touch, and anchors dropped in fathoms short to the bed of a bay that gives evidence of welcome, by sending its sands to surface, speckled with mica or sparkling with grains of gold.

Thus the white man's big canoe found rest, and sailors crowded the rail to give signs of gratitude to the strange, strong-armed pilots.

The captain let down his stairs, that they might come on deck and exchange mutual feelings of each heart. On the one hand, that of thankfulness, that misfortunes make mankind akin, and used such occasions to teach the lion that the mouse may be his master when circumstances bring his ability into demand.

The white man felt gratitude, and made proof of it by loading the red man's "hollow tree" with rich stores of choice sugars from the islands, blankets made in colder zones; with clothing that illy fitted the red man's limbs; with lines, and nets, and hooks, and spears of foreign make, and with weapons of fiery breath and noisy mouth, that poorly mated the bow and arrow, though mating good by force of execution the loss in warning talk.

The chieftains, too, gave back, with answering hand and smiling face, the gladness of their hearts that they had found opportunity to serve the white man.

When they departed, the "*tyee*" bade them come *again*. This was a great day for the chieftain's *household*, when they landed beneath the willow trees near their *e-li-he* (home). The women, with great, wondering eyes at the sight of so many *ic-tas* (goods), began to unload the "hollow-tree canoe," and, as each article new to them came in sight, they would wonder and chatter and try them on, until at last they stood clothed in sailor's garb, of jacket, pants and shoes. To their camps they came, loaded with the precious freights, and, coming to their own, the little ones would cry and run, shouting, "*Hal-lu-me, til-li-cum*" (strangers); nor would they trust to their mothers' voices until they

51

had put aside their costumes.

These chiefs still laugh at the surprise they felt at sight of what they supposed to be the new-found friends, until the merry *cluchmen* (women) shouted, "*Cla-hoy-em-six, tyee?*" (How do you do, chief?) They quickly rose from their cougar skin and panther's pelt, caught the bogus sailors, and quickly robbed them of their borrowed clothes.

That night, while the sun was going to rest in his bed of flaming billows, on the ship's deck and on the sand of the red man's floor, happy hearts bade each "Goodnight." The white man was happy now that his home was gently rocked by flowing tides. The red men, happy with their *til-li-cums*, retailing in guttural notes their great adventures, and dancing the *pot-lach* dance (giving dance), would stop, and with their hands divide the prizes won, without thought of shells, or Indian coin, or white man's *chick-a-mon* (money). When "tomorrow's sun" had climbed over the craggy ledges of the coast mountain, and sent out his fiery messengers to announce his coming, they came to the vessel's deck, and found no watchman there. They peeped into the forecastle and cabin, and waked the slumberers up to welcome the new morn begun on the bosom of Ya-quina Bay.

At the Indian lodge, the soft voice of *cluchman*, mingling with the murmur of rippling rills, that from snow-banks high on the mountain side came hurrying down to quench the thirst of sailor or of savage; maybe, the briny lips of the sea-monster or salmon fish, that come in to rest from surging waters and bask awhile in the smooth currents of the bay.

The chiefs arose and made breakfast on foreign teas and island sugars, and when in new attire, with *cluchman* in beads and fine *tattoo* (an adornment of savage tribes), with noses pierced by long polished shells, that made an uncouth imitation of a dandy's moustache, with *papoose* in basket hung with bells, or lashed to boards with wild-deer thongs, and slung on mother's back, secured with sealskin belts worn on the brow. To make the whole a complete picture of Indian life, the dogs were taken in, and then sitting in the prow to give command, the "hollow-tree canoe" was pointed toward the ship. The loud hurrah of sailors, that was intended to give welcome, was at first construed to be a warning, and quick the "hollow-tree canoe" was turned about, each paddle playing in concert to carry the frightened visitors away, while *cluchmen* and maidens, with woman's privilege, screamed in terror of expected harm.

The chief soothing them, and looking back descried the *tyee* captain, with beckoning hand and signs recalling him to fulfil his purpose, and make the visit. He bade the oarsman cease, and, while his canoe moved on from acquired motion, though slower going, while he backward gazed, he, with noiseless paddle, again brought the prow towards the sides of the "big canoe."

Slowly and cautiously he, with his precious cargo, floated nearer and nearer still, with eyes wide open, to detect any sign of treachery, sometimes half stopping at suggestions of frightened mothers or timid maidens, and then anon would forward move; still, however, with great caution, until at last the two canoes were rocking on the gentle tide in closest friendship.

The seamen who made this welcome port came on deck, with a sailor's pride of dress, wide-legged trowsers, and wider collars to their shirts over their shoulders falling, and with wide-topped, brimless caps. When the newcomers had passed their fright, and the old chief had climbed on deck to be sure that all was safe, he called his family, and, though the jolly tars went down to assist them, they remained waiting for some further proof of friendship.

While their eyes were upward turned, and Jack's were downward bent, two pairs (at least) met midway, and told the old, old tale over again.

On deck, and leaning over the rail, stood a youthful sailor, with deep, earnest eyes. These had met the gaze of another, the daughter of the pilot chief. Silently the arrows flew; and, without honeyed word, or war-whoop, the battle went on, until, by special invitation of looks, Oneatta came aboard, and stood beside the smiling pale-face; and soon the older women followed with the baby baskets until all were there except the dogs, who cried at the partiality shown to the master and his family.

The scene on deck was novel. The *tyee* captain and the chief were teaching each other the words with which to give token of hospitality and gratitude; half-sign, half-word language 'twas, though, in which exchanges of friendly sentiments were told.

The sailors, with the women and maidens, had organized a school, on a small scale. Merry laughter often broke at the clumsy efforts of white man's tongue to imitate Indian *wa-wa* (talk). The little ones received the touch of rough fingers on dimpled chin, and turned like frightened fawns away to listen to the tinkling of the little bells above their heads.

The chief had brought with him richest offerings of venison and fish; the women, specimens of handiwork in beads and necklaces, which they offered in exchange for such articles of bright-hued colours as the sailors might have bought in other lands.

The bargains were quickly made, each side proud of success in securing something to remind them of the visit.

The chief signified his intention to return to his home on the beach, when the good captain, not to be outdone in matters of courtesy, brought fresh supplies of various kinds, and had them stowed away in the "hollow-tree canoe."

When the parting came, to prove his good will, the *tyee* captain promised to return the visit. Oneatta had said to Theodore, the sailor, "Come;" and he, with eyes doing service for his lips, had made promise. The red chief and his family withdrew, and soon they were riding the laughing waves in the "hollow-tree canoe."

Thus the day had passed and joined the happy ones gone before it; and bells had called the sailors to the deck, and the Indian chief reposed his limbs on the uncut swath of willow grass, and waited for the approach of night, that he might, by signal fires, call his kinsmen to the *pil-pil* dance; a dance in honour of each Indian maiden when she "comes out."

Oneatta had demanded of her parents this honour, and, since custom allowed this privilege, she on that day reached an era in her life, when she chose to be no longer a child.

Her father, the chief, wondered at this sudden change of manner wrought, but, yielding to his doting child, gave his assent. The picture I am making now is true to the life of many a maiden, who may follow Oneatta's history, whose faces take their hue of colours that give token of their race.

Some of them may recall their "coming out" 'neath dazzling chandeliers, on carpets of finest grain, in dresses trailing long, in which they stepped with timid gait to softest music, of silver lyre, or flute, or many-voiced piano.

But Oneatta's parlour was lighted up with glittering stars, that had done service long, and brighter grew to eyes of each new *belle*, who had, from time to time, lent first a listening ear to soft-voiced swain.

The carpets were brightest green, and sanded by waves stranded on the beach at the flowing of the tide.

The music was grandly wild, a combination of the hoarse drum, or angry roar of sea-lions, mingling with the deep bass voice of waves, breaking on the rocks, while, soft and low, the human notes came in to make the harmony complete to ears long trained to nature's tunes.

The maiden, whose heart was now tumultuous as the scenes around her, had dressed with greatest care in skirts of scarlet cloth, embroidered with beads and trimmed with furs of seal and down of swan. Her arms, half bared, were circled with bands of metals; her neck, with hoofs of fawns, or talons of the mountain eagle; pendent from her ears, rattles of the spotted snake; the partition of her nose held fast a beautiful shell of slender mould; her cheeks, rosy with vermilion paints; while in her raven hair she wore a gift from her pale-faced lover, brought from some far-off shore, intended for some other than she who wore it now. It was but a tinsel, yet it fitted well to crown her whose eyes were dancing long before her beaded slippers had touched time upon the sanded floor.

The circular altar, built of pebbles of varied colours, was lighted up with choicest knots of pine from fallen trees.

The watch on board the "big canoe" was set, and down its swinging stairway the *tyee* captain, mate, and sailors descended to the waiting boat; then softly touched the oars to smiling waves, and steady arms kept time to seamen's song in stern and bow, guided, meanwhile, by the altar fire. Over the glassy bridge they flew, and touched the bank beside the "hollow-tree canoe."

With hearty hand the chieftains bade them welcome, and gave silent signal for the dance to begin, while the *tyee* captain and his men took station at respectful space. The dancers came, and, forming round the maiden's altar fires, awaited still for her to come from lodge.

The pale-faces, lighted up with blaze from knotty wood, with folded arms and curious wonder stood gazing on the scene.

One among the number had scanned the merry circle of bashful Indian boys and timid girls; his face bespoke vexation at his disappointment, for he had failed to catch the eye of Oneatta.

She came, at length, tripping toward the festive throng, and spoke to him ere the dance began, not by smile, or deed, or word, but in Cupid's own appointed way, that never lies. He, as every other swain can do, read it in her eyes, and made answer in ways that do not make mistake.

When the circle had closed round the altar, the song of gladness broke forth from the lips of the tattooed and painted red chins, and from the drum of hoarser sound, and then the happy dancers, without waiting for partners, went with lithesome step in gay procession round. Louder rang the music, quicker grew the steps, each time round; the little invisible arrows flew from sailor-boy to Indian maiden, and from maiden to sailor-boy; glancing each against the other, would rustle and then go straight to target sent, until at last the maiden tired grew, her bosom overladened with the arrows Cupid's quiver had supplied. She bade the dancers stop, and with native grace, and stately step, she stood beside her lover without a thought of wrong; for she was Nature's child, and had not felt the thongs of fashion's code, which forbid her to be honest.

Her tiny hand was pressed between the hard palms of the captive sailor, for he had been fighting a battle where each is conquered only to be a conqueror.

Oneatta led the sailor-boy to join those who, with wondering eyes, had waited for her return. He took his place beside his tutor now, to learn how a step unused by tamer people might make speech for joy and gladness.

The dance was ended. Pale faces, and red ones, too, had lost sight of the stars, and were lulled to sleep by the rocking tides or muffled song of rippling waters, or by the breakers beating the rocky shores of Ya-quina.

Day followed day, and each had a history connecting it with its yesterday and prophesying for the morrow. The sailor-boy went not on duty now, for his "chummies" stood his watch. He spent much time at the *e-li-he* of the tree chief, or with Oneatta went out in a small canoe to watch the fishermen spear the fattened salmon.

Sometimes they rambled on the mountain side beneath the *mansinetta* trees, and exchanged lessons in worded language. He told her of his home, where cities and towns were like the forest of her native home; of people who outnumbered the stars above, and of bright-coloured goods, of beautiful beads and shells; and by degrees he won her consent to go from her native land, to leave country and kindred, all for the sake of the promised happiness he could give.

The sailor made confident of his captain, and glowing pictures painted of his princess, and what he would do with her when to his mother's home he came.

The honest captain found objection to the plan of carrying her away, and sent for "Tyee John" (for so they called the chieftain then), and made him understand how the young people had become betrothed.

The face of Tyee John grew dark at first, and he was impatient to be gone; but kindly words and presents hinted at brought him to consider. He proposed that the sailor-boy should become one of his tribe, and make his home with them, and then he could be his son.

The conference was transferred to the *e-li-he* of Tyee John. The sailor would not consent to remain on this wild shore, and made vows to come again and bring Oneatta.

At length by rich presents given, and promises of more when he should come, the compact was made, to the joy of the Indian maiden and her sailor lover.

The sea gave a favouring breeze. The sails repaired, the *tyee* captain made known his will to ride again the bounding waves. Oneatta bade farewell to sorrowing mothers, sisters, brothers, giving each a token to keep until her coming. O foolish Oneatta! you know not what you do! You act now from example of your fairer sisters, who listen to the wooing notes of foreign lips. We pity you as we do them. You have not thought how strange will be the customs, manners and life of those with whom you are to mingle. A time may come when you will long for the caresses of your rude mother, to hear the merry shouts of brothers, to gaze into the face of your dark-eyed father; perhaps long to hear love in native accents spoken by the young brave who has given you choicest gems of ocean's strand and mountain cliffs.

We see you yet when your kinsmen tell of you in song, or story, your dark eyes brimming with tears of hope and sorrow mingled.

You reach the side of the "big canoe." We see the brave and manly sailor-boy, who hastened to catch your trembling hand, and help you up the swinging steps, and when on deck you stand, we see the sailor's chums, from the ship-yards above, gaze down on you and him, with glances half of envy, and half of pleased surprise.

And now we see you startle at the fierce command of the mate, to heave the anchor up, then their response drawn out in lengthened "Aye-aye, sir," and singing, while they work, the seamen's song; and how wide your dark eyes open at sight of whitened sails, outspreading like some monster swan, and the troubled, anxious look you give to the humble *e-li-he* of childhood, as it passed away, as if moving in itself, and the headlands that seem floating towards you, and the great water that came rushing to meet you.

We see, too, your father, Tyee John, in his "hollow-tree canoe," leading the way, and pointing to some sunken rock, or shallow bar, or hidden reef, until he rounds to in proof of danger past to the "big canoe."

How its huge white wings fold up at a signal from the *tyee* captain!

57

FAREWELL TO ONEATTA

And then your father comes board, and stands in mute attention to the ceremonies of seamen's marriage law. And you, in innocence, give heed to word or sign until you are bound in law to the fortunes and freaks of a roving sailor-boy.

When Tyee John turns away, hiding his tears in his heart, while yours run down your cheeks, we see him reach his canoe, and you hanging over the sides of the ship to catch a last glance of his eye.

And then the white wings are spread again, and soon he grows so small that his paddle seems but a dark feather in his hand, and your old home recedes, and you have caught the last glimpse you ever will, of the mountain sinking in the sea, and you, *alone*,—no, not alone, for your sailor-boy is with you, now drying the tears from your dusky cheeks.

Oneatta, we leave you, with a prayer that your life may not be as rough as the seas that drove the "big canoe" into Quina bay. Whether your hopes have blossomed into fruition, or have been blasted, we know not, nor if you still live to be loved or loathed. We only know that your silver-haired sire sits on the stony cliff, overlooking the mouth of the harbour, and watches passing sails, or hastens to meet those that anchor, and repeat the old question over and over, *Me-si-ka, is-cum, ni-ka-hi-ak-close, ten-as-cluchman, Oneatta?* (Have you brought back my beautiful daughter, Oneatta?)

When Cupid comes with pale-faced warrior to the dusky maiden now, they repeat the warning tale, with *Ni-ka-cum-tux Oneatta*. (I remember Oneatta.)

CHAPTER 6

Senatorial Brains Beaten by Savage Muscle

The story I have related is but one of the many that belong to this region, and for the truth of which, witnesses still live, both whites and Indians; another reason I introduce it here is to show my readers who may think otherwise, that Indians—savage as they are at times, often made savage by their religion—have *hearts*. Again and again shall I refer in this work to the red man's emotional nature, and to his religion. I cannot do so too often, as the reader will admit before he turns the last leaf.

This agency is located west of the coast range of mountains, and bordering on the Pacific Ocean. The valleys are small, irregular in shape, fertile and productive, with prairies interspersed with forests of fir; picturesque almost beyond description. At some points the mountains reach out into the ocean, forming high headlands whereon are built light-houses, to guard mariners against the dangers of the coast. Long white sandy beaches stretch away for miles, and are then cut off by craggy bluffs.

At the southern boundary of Siletz—two miles from the line— may be found a beautiful bay, navigable inland for thirty miles. The banks are varied in altitude; undulating hills, with rich alluvial bottom lands intervening. The greatest width of bay is perhaps four miles, and occasionally cut into channels by beautiful islands narrowing inland to receive the small river Ya-quina. Midway between the mouth of the river and the ocean entrance to the bay, extensive oyster-beds exist.

This "Chesapeake" of the Pacific was once a part of Siletz reservation. The discovery of the oyster-beds, and also of the numerous forests of timber accessible to navigation, attracted the attention of the white men; and the old, old story was again rehearsed,—"*The white men wanted them.*"

That it was wanted by the white men was *sufficient*, and no ambitious candidate for Legislature or Congressional honours *dare* oppose the violation of a solemn compact between the United States Government and the Indians, who had accepted this country in compensation for their homes in Umpyua and Rogue River valley. It was *cut off*, and given to commerce and agriculture in 1866.

That an equivalent was ever made to the Indian does not appear from any records to which I have had access. It is, however, asserted, that a small sum was invested in stock cattle, for the benefit of Siletz Indians. There are two approaches to Siletz from the valley of Willamette; the principal, *via* Ya-quina River and bay; the other, over the mountain by trail. My first visit was by the former. In September, 1869, in company with Hon. Geo. H. Williams, then U. S. Senator, now Attorney General of the United States, Judge Odeneal, since my successor in office, and other citizens, we reached the head of navigation late on the evening of the 12th. We remained over night at "Elk Horn Hotel. The following morning, in the absence of steamer, we took passage in small row-boats, propelled by Indians.

The adventures of the day were few, only one of which I shall refer to now. Our U. S. Senator, who had done much for reconstruction in the Senate, challenged one of our Indians for a trial of muscle at the oars. The challenge was accepted, and senatorial broadcloth was laid aside, and brain and muscle put to the test. After a short race the prow of our boat ran into the bank on the side where brains was at work. For once at least, muscle proved more than a match for brains, and, besides, an Indian had won a victory over a great *tyee*. Now although our senator had proven himself a match for other great senators in dignified debate, he was compelled to listen to the cheers of our party in honour of a red man's triumph over him. I doubt if those who of late defeated him, when a candidate for the highest seat in our halls of justice, felt half the gratification that "To-toot-na-Jack" did that morning when the *tyee* dropped the oar, exhausted and disgusted with his failure to hold even hand with a red brother, who was *not a senator*.

After a row of twenty miles, we landed within a half hour's ride of Siletz. The agent, Mr. Simpson, met our party with saddle-horses.

While *en route* a horse-race was proposed; the dignified gentleman turning jockey for the nonce. In fact, the entire party engaged in a run. The road passed over low hills, covered with timber and tall ferns.

61

While the Congressional and Indian Departments were going at a fearful speed, a representative of the latter went over his horse's head, and soon felt the weight of the United States Senate crushing the Indian Department almost to death.

The parties referred to will recognize the picture.

This was not the first time, or the last either, that the Senate of the United States has "been down on the Indian Department."

Without serious damage, both were again mounted, and soon were fording Siletz River,—a deep, narrow stream, whose bed was full of holes, slight—"irregularities," as defaulters would say.

We crossed in safety, except that one horse carried his rider into water too deep for wading. It matters not who the rider was, or whether he belonged to Congress or the Indian Department.

On reaching the prairie a sight presented itself, that gives emphatic denial to the oft-repeated declaration, that Indians cannot be civilized.

Spread out before us was a scene that words cannot portray. The agency building occupied a plateau, twenty feet above the level of the valley. They were half hidden by the remnants of a high stockade that had been erected when the Indians were first brought on to the agency fresh from the Rogue River war. At that time a small garrison was thought necessary to prevent rebellion among the Indians, and to secure the safety of the officers of the Indian Department.

It was, doubtless, good judgment, under the circumstances. Here were the remnants of fourteen different tribes and bands, who had been at war with white men and each other, and who, though subjugated, had not been thoroughly "*reconstructed.*"

They were located in the valley, within sight of the agency, and were living in little huts and shanties that had been built by the government.

Each tribe had been allotted houses separated from the others but a few hundred yards at farthest. They drew their supplies from the same storehouse, used the same teams and tools, and were in constant contact. They had come here at the command of the United States Government, in chains, bearing with them the trophies of war; some of them being fair-haired scalp-locks, and others were off red men's heads. Think for a moment of enemies meeting and wearing these evidences of former enmity; shaking hands while each was in possession of the scalp-locks of father or brother of the others!

But, at the time of the visit referred to, no sentinel walked his rounds. No bayonet flashed in the sunshine on the watch-tower of the stockade at Siletz. The granaries and barns were unbarred; even Agent Simpson's own quarters were unlocked day and night. Fire-arms and tools were unguarded; Indians came and went at will, except that Agent Simpson had so taught them that they never entered without a preliminary knock. The Indian men came not with heads covered, but in respectful observance of ceremony.

The kitchen work and house-keeping were done by Indian women, under the direction of a white matron. The agent's table afforded the best of viands. Tell the world that Indians cannot be civilized! Here were the survivors of many battles, who, but a few short years since, had been brought under guard, some of them loaded with chains, and with blood on their hands, who were living as I have described.

Sometimes, it is true, the remembrance of former feuds would arouse the sleeping fires of hatred and desire for revenge amongst themselves, and fights would ensue. But no white man has ever been injured by these people while on the Reservation, since their location at Siletz.

This statement is made in justice to the Indians themselves, and in honour of those who had control of them, both of whom merit the compliment. Amongst these people were Indian *desperadoes*, who had exulted in the bloody deeds they had committed. One especially, braver than the rest, named Euchre Bill, boasted that he had *eaten the heart of one white man*.

This he did in presence of Agent Simpson, during an effort of the latter to quell a broil. The agent, always equal to emergencies, replied, by knocking the fellow down, handcuffing him, and shutting him up in the guard-house, and feeding him on bread and water for several days, after which time he was released, with the warning that, the next time he repeated the hellish boast, he would "not need handcuffs, nor bread and water." Bill understood the hint. The agent remarked to us that "Bill was one of his main dependants in preserving order."

During our visit we went with the agent to see Euchre Bill. He was hewing logs. On our approach he dropped the axe, and saluted the agent with "Good-morning, Mr. Simpson," at the same time extending his hand. When informed of the personality of our party, Bill waved his hat, and made a slight bow, repeating the name of each in turn.

We looked in on the school then in progress; we found twenty-five children in attendance. They gave proof of their ability to use

63

the English language, and understand its power to express ideas; the lessons were all in primary books. Their recitations were remarkable. Outside of books they had been instructed in practical knowledge, and answered readily in concert to the questions, Who is President of the United States? What city is the capital? Who is Governor of Oregon? Where is the capital located? Who is Superintendent of Indian Affairs? What year is this? How many months in a year? When did the count of years begin? Who was Jesus Christ? And many other questions were asked and readily answered. The boys were named George Washington, Dan Webster, Abe Lincoln, James Nesmith, Grant, Sherman, Sheridan,—each answering to a big name. "Dan Webster" delivered in passable style an extract from his great prototype's reply to Hayne. The school also joined the teacher in singing several Sunday-school hymns, and popular songs. Short speeches were made by visitors and teachers.

We were much encouraged by what we saw, and left *that* schoolhouse with the belief that Indian children can learn as readily as others when an opportunity is given them. I have not changed my conviction since; much of its prosperity was due to the teacher, William Shipley, who was fitted for the work and gave his time to it. We also called at some of the little settlements. The agency farm was tilled in common; notwithstanding we saw many small gardens around the Indian houses, growing vegetables, and in one or more "*tame flowers.*" At one place several men were at work on a new house, some of them shingling, others clinking cracks. One man was hewing out, with a common axe, a soft kind of stone for a fire-place.

We entered the house of "Too-toot-na Jack," the champion oarsman. He welcomed his vanquished rival in the boat-race above referred to, and his friend, and offered one an armchair, and stools to the remainder. His wife came in, and Jack said, "This is my woman, Too-toot-na Jinney. She is no fool either. She has a cooking-stove in the kitchen." Jinney was much older than her husband; but that was not unusual. She was a thrifty housewife, and was a financier,— had saved nearly one thousand silver half-dollars; and what she lacked in personal charms, on account of tattooed chin and gray hairs, she made up, like many a fairer woman, in the size of the buckskin purse wherein she kept her coin. Jack seemed fully to appreciate the good qualities of his "woman;" not because he had access to her fortune, but because *she* was old and *he* was young, and the chances were that *he* would be at *her* funeral.

That hope has made many a better fellow than Too-toot-na behave with becoming reverence for his wife. But "*many a slip 'twixt cup and lip*" applies to all kinds of people. Jack never realized on *his investment. He* went *first*, and Jinney is now a rich widow, and has no doubt marriage offers in abundance.

We were present on "court day," the agent holding it for the adjustment of all kinds of difficulties among his people. In such cases he appoints juries from among the bystanders, always taking care to select such as had no tribal affinities with the parties to the suit. He had a sheriff in every tribe, and on occasions where their own friends were interested he summoned others to act. He *himself* was the *court and high sheriff*, and always *sat* with a large hickory cane, called "Old Moderator."

My readers may smile at this kind of a gavel; but it was a practical and useful thing to have in such courts,—much more potential than Blackstone or any other kind of commentaries, unless, indeed, it be the last revised edition of Samuel Colt.

The records of that court were sometimes made on untanned parchment; by which I mean, my poor, unsophisticated reader, that these Indian citizens would sometimes forget very willingly to observe the decorum due before that august tribunal, and fall to making a record for themselves and on one another with fists, clubs, whips, knives, pistols, and other lively weapons, until the good Judge Simpson completed that record by a vigorous application of the aforesaid hickory club, and some of the citizens had editions for personal adornment.

The walls of the court-room had transcript fragments done in carmine,—or, to be better understood, in "claret." Court day had been announced to the visitors while at breakfast. The senator had been a successful lawyer before entering the political arena; the judge was then in the enjoyment of a lucrative practice; the superintendent had done something in the law line in county courts before justices of the peace.

The court-room was crowded, the doorways and windows were occupied, and black shining eyes were glistening through every crack, all anxious to see and hear. These people, of Siletz especially, were apt imitators, and more readily fell in with the vices and frivolities of civilization than with its virtues and proprieties.

The assembly was composed of the greatest variety of character, colour, costume, and countenance ever found in any court-room.

Women were there, learning law. Perhaps, they had, woman-like, intuitively snuffed the purer air of freedom that is soon to sweep over our beautiful country and blast the hopes of demagogues who now *rule*, without *representing*, the better portion of the people.

Old chiefs were there to learn wisdom, to take with them to the hunting-grounds above. Don't chide them, reader. They never had an even chance in this life; let them have it in the next, if possible.

The boys were there, and why not? They were looking forward to a time when an Indian will be as good as a negro, if they behave as well. They had an eye to political and pecuniary affairs. In fact, the people were all there except camp-watchers and sick ones.

When our party were seated, the "Moderator" touched the floor, and soon all was silent.

These Indians are fond of "law," and since the old law and new—that is to say, Indian and white men's—were somewhat mixed up, it was a difficult matter to execute justice uniformly. Agent Simpson, being a practical man, had not sought to enforce the white men's law any further than the Indian comprehended it.

The Indian lawyers were on hand ready for business. The first case called was for assault and battery. The court and the visitors had been partial witness of the little fight, which occurred the day previous to the trial, on the "*plaza*," in front of the agent's headquarters. The contestants were clutchmen (women); *the cause of war*, the only thing that women ever fight about,—*a man*.

The statement in court was to the effect that one woman had stolen another woman's husband. The parties were arraigned, the statement made concerning the case, and the matter compromised by sending both parties to the "*Sku Kum*" House (Guard House).

The next case called was that of a man charged with unlawfully using a horse belonging to someone else. The accused was ordered to pay for the offence about what the real service of the animal was worth; no damages were allowed. The third case was somewhat similar to the first.

One of Joshua's people—name of a tribe—claimed damage for insulted honour, and destruction of his domestic happiness.

A Rogue River Indian had, very much after the fashions of civilized life, by presents and petty talk, persuaded the wife of the aforesaid warrior to elope with him. The old history of poor human nature had been repeated. The villain deserted his victim, and she returned to her home. Her husband, with observing eyes discovered more *ic-*

tas (goods) in the woman's possession than could be accounted for on honourable grounds, and demanded an explanation. She made "a clean breast," and agreed to go into court with her husband and claim *damages*, not divorce; for I have before remarked that Indians were eminently practical. The husband demanded *satisfaction*. The accused, whose name was "Chetco Dandy," would have accorded him the privilege of a fight; but that was not the satisfaction demanded. The husband had made his ultimatum. *Two horses* would settle the unpleasantness. Chetco, however, owned but one. The court decided that he should make ten hundred rails, and deliver the horse to the injured husband, with the understanding that the latter was to *board* him while doing the work.

I can't resist a query: how long a white man, under such arrangements, would require to make ten hundred rails. The husband was satisfied, his honour was vindicated, and he owned another horse. After the docket was cleared, a council talk was had.

These people had been placed here by the government, in 1856, numbering then, according to Superintendent Nesmith's report for 1857, 2,049 souls, representing fourteen bands; and although, in 1869, they numbered little more than half as many, they kept up tribal relations, at least so far as chieftainship was concerned. In the council that day one or two of the chiefs represented tribes in bands of ten or twenty persons; and one poor follow, the last of his people, stood alone without constituency. He was a chief, nevertheless.

I cannot report here the reflection that such a circumstance suggests,—only that he, with the usual solemn face of an Indian in council, seemed the personification of loneliness.

The speeches made by these people evinced more sense than their appearance indicated. They were dependent on the government, and felt their helplessness. When the usual speeches had been made preliminary to business talk, I said to them that I was gratified at the advancement they had made, considering the circumstances, and that I was willing for them to express their wishes in regard to the expenditure of money in their interest.

They were loath to speak on this matter, because they had never been consulted, and a recognition of their manhood was more than they had expected. After some deliberation, during which they, like bashful boys, asked one another, each nudging his neighbour to speak first, old Joshua at last arose, half hesitatingly, and said, "Maby, I don't understand you. Do you mean that we may say what we want bought for us? Nobody ever said that before, and it seems strange to me."

I had consulted the agent before making this experiment, and he had doubted the propriety; not because he was unwilling to recognize their manhood in the premises, but he feared they would betray weakness for useless articles, and thereby bring derision on his efforts to civilize them. Perhaps it might establish a precedent that would be troublesome sometimes.

He exhibited great anxiety when Old Joshua rose, lest he would disgrace his people by asking for beads, paint, and powder, and lead, and scarlet cloth. I can see that agent yet, with his deep-set eyes fixed on the speaker, while he rested his chin on his cane. Old Joshua spoke again, and, though he was considered a "terrible brave on the war-path," and had passed the better portion of his life in that way, now when, for the first time in his life, he was called upon to give opinions on a serious matter, concerning the investment of money for his people, he appeared to be transformed into a *man*. He *was* a man. Hear him talk:—

> I am old; I can't live long. I want my people to put away the old law (meaning the old order of things). I want them to learn how to work like white men. They cannot be Indians any longer. We have had some things bought for us that did us no good,—some blankets that I could poke my finger through; some hoes that broke like a stick. We don't want these things. We want *ploughs*, *harness*, chick-chick (*wagons*), *axes*, good hoes, a few blankets for the old people. These we want. We have been promised these things. They have not come.

The agent's face relaxed; his eyes changed to pleased surprise. Other chiefs spoke also, but after the pattern that Joshua had made, except that some of them complained more, and named a former agent, who came poor and went away rich. No Indian suggested an unwise investment. We assured them that they should have the tools and other goods asked for; and *that promise was kept*, much to the gratification of the Indians and agent.

I have not the abstract at hand, but I think I purchased for them soon after $1,200 worth of tools and twenty sets of harness, and that a few blankets were issued.

But, to resume the council proceedings. These people were clamorous for allotments of land in severalty. Their arguments were logical, they referring to the promises of the government to give each man a home. The land has been surveyed, and, if not allotted to them, I do not know why it has not been done.

The subject of religion was discussed at some length. The agent, willing to advance "his people," had given them lessons in the first principles of Christianity. He had taught them the observance of Sunday, had forbidden drinking, gambling, and profanity. He invited ministers to preach to them, and, when necessary, had been their interpreter. There were several languages represented in the council; the major portion of the Indians understood the jargon, or "*Chi-nook*," a language composed of less than one hundred words; partly Indian, Spanish, French, and "Boston." The latter word is in common use among the tribes of Oregon and Washington Territory to represent white men or American.

The Christian churches have enjoyed the privilege of ministry to these people since they were first located on the Reservation.

The Catholic priests, who had baptized some of these people, were very zealous. Occasionally, the Methodist itinerant called and preached to them. The labours of neither were productive of much good, because they did not preach with simplicity, and could not, therefore, preach with power. It would be about as sensible for a Chinaman to preach to Christians, as for the latter to preach to Indians in high-flown words, abstruse doctrines, or abstract dogmas. One case will illustrate.

A very devout man of God visited the agency, with, I doubt not, good intentions. He preached to these people just as he would have done to white men. He talked of Jesus Christ, the Saviour of the world; besought them to flee from the wrath to come; that Jesus Christ was the Saviour of the red men as well as white men; that he had died for the sins of the world; that he rose again the third day and ascended into heaven.

The discourse was interpreted to the Indians by an *employé* on the Reservation. A few days after, a *Si-wash*, the usual word for Indian, who answered to the name of Push-wash, entered into conversation with the above-named *employé*, by saying, "What you think about that Sunday-man's talk,—you think him fool?"

"No; he is a good man; he has plenty of sense."

"What for he swear all time?"

"He did not swear; he talked straight."

"What for he say Jesus Christ so many times? All the time he talk the same."

"That was all right; he told the truth; he did not talk wrong."

"You think me fool? What for a good man die for me? I am not a bad man. I did not tell him to die."

"The Jews killed him, they did not like him."

"You say Jews kill good man?"

"Yes, they kill him, and he come to life again on the third day."

"You think he came to life? I don't believe they kill him. He not live anymore."

"Yes; everybody will live again some time."

"You suppose a bad Indian get up, walk 'bout again, all the same a good man?"

"They will all rise, but they won't all be good."

"What for the Sunday man tell that? He say Jesus Christ die for bad Indian too? Say he go to heaven all the same as a good Indian, good white man; that aint fair thing. I don't no like such religion."

A few days afterwards the man who reported this dialogue passed near the grave of an Indian, and found it covered with stones and logs. He learned afterwards, that Push-wash had explained to other Indians the meaning of the "Sunday-man's talk," and they had piled stones and logs on the graves of their enemies, to prevent them rising from the dead.

The reader will thus appreciate the necessity for sending ministers who are qualified to preach to these people; otherwise they may do the savage more harm than good. Farther on in the work I shall discuss more fully this most important of all questions, with special reference to the difficulties in the way of treating with the Indians, in consequence of their numerous and peculiar religious beliefs, which few white men know anything about.

I left Siletz with a favourable opinion of the people, and the prospects before them. Notwithstanding the many impediments in the way of their civilization, the transformation from a wild savage to a semi-civilized life had been wrought in fourteen years.

In this connection I submit the last annual report of Hon. Ben. Simpson,[1] late United States Indian agent at Siletz. I do so, because whatever of progress these people may have made was under his administration as Indian agent, and believing the short history presented by him will be of interest to my readers.

He is a gentleman of unimpeachable integrity, though blessed with enemies whose assaults have polished his character like a diamond.

1. See Appendix.

Whatever vices these Indians may have exhibited to his successor,— Gen. Palmer,—they were not the results of Mr. Simpson's management, or example; but rather the natural consequences of association with profligate soldiers and other white men, during the first years of their residence on the Reservation.

Gen. Joel Palmer was recommended as Mr. Simpson's successor by the Methodist Church. He went to his duty with long experience, and in many respects well fitted for the work.

Scarcely had he assumed the duties of his office, with a new set of employés, before he was made to realize that poor human nature will in most cases control human action. Ingratitude is said, by Indian haters, to be characteristic of those people. Better be honest and say it of mankind.

I have said that he selected a new set of officers. Among them was one chosen on account of his religious habits,—habits, I say, not character,—who had lent a listening ear to the call, "Go preach my Gospel to all nations." This man answered this urgent call, and Agent Palmer employed him. No sooner had he unfurled the banner of Christianity among these people, than he began in a clandestine way to undermine Agent Palmer. Unfortunately for the agent, this preacher had been recommended by the same church for position. This gave him influence. He made use of it. He proposed to other officers of the agency that if they would assist in ousting Palmer he would retain them in their respective positions.

To consummate this act of religious villainy, he circulated reports against the man, whose kindness fed him and his family, that he (Palmer) had men in his employ who were "not, strictly speaking, Christians; that he was not competent to discharge the duties of his office." The agent found, what nearly every officer has learned sooner or later, that his position was of doubtful tenure, and felt the sting of this man's treachery so severely that he proposed to resign.

Brother —— is determined to oust me, and I reckon I will let him have the position. He wants it, and I don't care to worry my life out fighting for an Indian agency.

This is the substance of the speech Agent Palmer made to me as superintendent. I said to him, "Do no such thing. Go back to your agency and tell that man to roll his blankets and be off, or you will put him in irons. Then discharge every accomplice he has, and select good, true men instead."

71

Brother Palmer replied that "the church recommended Brother ——, and I don't like to do such a thing." I prevailed on him to withdraw his resignation; and on his return to Siletz, he discharged Brother ——. But the war was continued against him until Agent Palmer demanded a successor to relieve him; and after a short administration he retired without having Christianized the Siletz Indians.

I have mentioned this episode for the reason that I desire full justice done a man who meant well, with a sincere hope that those having the appointing power may be made to reflect a moment before making nominations for office in deference to the demands of any church, and without regard to the fitness of the appointee.

I have due respect for church members, and recognize the necessity of having men of moral character among the wards of this government.

Gen. Palmer, with his long experience, was, in many respects, qualified for his position; but he was a poor judge of character. I may be censured for making these comments, but they are just, nevertheless; as was the opinion I gave of the aforesaid Brother ——, when his name was proposed as a missionary to the Siletz Indians, by the presiding elder of the district.

I answered him, "That man's face says he would undermine his father, to forward his own interests."

The elder said in reply, "Brother Meacham, you must be mistaken; he is a good, Christian man, and will be a great help to Brother Palmer." In courtesy to the presiding elder, I consented, with the remark, "Try him; but he will make a thorny bed for Brother Palmer."

Here is the history. It is not written to bring ridicule on the church nominating him.

Siletz agency has been established fourteen years, during which time five agents have represented the government. Some of them have been good men for the position.

Although these Indians are not up to the standard of moral character, or church requirements, a great change has been wrought, and credit should be given to whom it is due.

Uncouth these Indians on Siletz may be, but let truth speak for them, and you will hear of how they came to this new home captives, and in chains, under guard of bayonets, borne on shoulders of men wearing the uniform of the U. S. A.

You will hear how these men were stationed among them to guard them, and compel obedience to the mandates of a government that permitted the grossest outrages on their rights, and made no effort to redress their wrongs.

You would hear, too, of a people living in careless indolence on Umpyua and Rogue Rivers, in southern Oregon, when disturbed by the advent of white men, who came with prejudices against them, who disregarded their rights, denied them the privilege of living on the land God had given them, who failed to protect them from the outrages committed by vicious white men; of the indiscriminate war-fare that was carried on against them for resenting such insults; of their native land left in ruins, where the wail of weeping pale-faces over slain friends mingled with their own lamentations on taking leave of the homes of their earliest life.

Truth would tell of the many crimes committed by and against them, since their residence at Siletz; of how they have been punished for their own misdeeds, and have seen those who sinned against them go unpunished.

Be patient, you half-savage people! Death is rapidly healing your wounds and curing your griefs. Those who survive may, in time, be given homes. The lands have been surveyed for these people, but have not yet been allotted. Nothing could do more to revive them than the consummation of this promise.

Some of them have lived with white men as labourers, and have learned many things qualifying them for this great boon. Surely a magnanimous government will complete this great act of justice to a helpless people. May God speed the day!

ALSEA AGENCY.

It is located on the coast Reservation south of Yaquina bay. The people are "salt chuck," or saltwater Indians, and the majority of them were born on the lands they now occupy; hence they are the most quiet and well-behaved Indians in Oregon.

They are easily controlled, and are making progress in civilization. But few in number, and of the character I have named, they have never taken part in any of the many wars that have made Oregon "the battle-ground of the Pacific coast."

A sub-agency was established over them in 1866. The pay of sub-agent is $1,000 *per annum*, without subsistence or other allowance. The Alsea people being non-treaty Indians,—that is to say, they have no existing treaty with the government; no funds being appropriated especially for them,—they are sustained entirely from the "Incidental

73

Funds" for Oregon Superintendency.

The fact that the Alsea Indians have always been easily managed has been to their disadvantage in securing government aid. Had they been more refractory, they would have been better treated. This sounds strangely, and yet I declare it to be true. Why should government reward them for being peaceable? They have asked for buildings; the government gave them huts. They asked for schools and churches; but no school-house stands out in the bleak ocean winds of their home; no church-bell calls them to hear the wonderful story of a Saviour's love. Notwithstanding the wealth of their successors peals forth in loud strains which echo on foreign shores, no hammer rings out its cheering notes on anvil of theirs.

This little agency demonstrates the fact, that the only *sure* way for Indians to secure attention is *through blood*. Our government follows the example of the father of the Prodigal Son, with this remarkable difference, that it abuses its dutiful children, while it fawns upon and encourages the red-faced reprobates, by *rewarding* them for their rebellious deeds.

The department farm at Alsea was made by government, on Indian land, ostensibly for the Indians' benefit. It is located on a bleak plain, that stretches away from the ocean surf to the foot of the coast range mountains. It produces potatoes and oats. The mountains are high and rugged, and covered with dense forests of fir and cedar timber; much of the former has been "burnt." A heavy undergrowth has become almost impenetrable except for wild animals or Indian hunters.

The cedar groves cover streams of water that will in time be of great value, when turned on to machinery with which to convert the cedars into merchandise for foreign markets. The streams are plentifully supplied with fish. No long list of *employés* answer to the command of an agent at Alsea. In some respects it is the better way, inasmuch as it is to the interest of the agent to teach his wards the more common arts of handiwork. In this way, the improvements have been made by Indian labour, under the direction of an agent; and now, while I write, these people are coming slowly up towards the gate that *should* open to them a way to the brotherhood of man.

Efforts are being made to reduce the area of the Reservation, and, should they succeed, these people who have cost the government so little of blood or treasure, will be compelled to yield; only repeating, "Might versus Right." I am not opposed to reduction of the limits of the coast Reservation, if these people, who have already given up

74

so much beautiful country, shall be provided with schools, churches, shops, and other means whereby they may be compensated, and, in the mean time, prepared by civilization for the new life that awaits the survivors, that, a few years hence, may be left to represent their people.

The government owes to these humble Indians all I have suggested, and, in addition, a home marked out and allotted in severalty, made inalienable for one or two generations.

But, however deserving they may be, it is doubtful if they ever enjoy the boon they crave. Few in number, peaceable in disposition, unknown to the world by bloody deeds, the probabilities are that the white man will encroach on their lands, a few miles at a time, until at last, hemmed in by a civilization they cannot enjoy, they will gradually mix and mingle, becoming more licentious and corrupt by association with vicious white men, and in a generation or two will be known only by a few vagabonds, who will wander, gipsy-like, through the country, a poor, miserable fag-end of a race.

Perhaps a few may take humble positions as labourers, and attain to a half-way station between savage and civilized life. Another few will become slaves to King Alcohol, and their chief men, lying around whiskey mills, drunken, debauched, despised, will drop back again to mother earth, mingling with the soil their fathers once owned.

Thus the people of Alsea will pass away. I pity you, humble, red-skinned children of the Pacific surf! You were happy once, and carelessly rode in your canoes over the shining sands of your native beach, or chased the game on the mountain side, little dreaming of the coming of a human tide which would swallow you and your sea-washed home, or carry both away out on the boundless expanse of a civilization whose other shores you could not see had sepulchres ready for your bones. You have spent your lives with your feet beating the paths your fathers made centuries ago; but your children shall follow newer trails, that lead to more dangerous jungles than those trod by your ancestors. Strange demons they will meet, before whom they will fall to rise no more.

Your fathers watched the shadows of Alsea mountain moving slowly up its western front, making huge pictures on its sides, and gazed without fear on the sun dropping under the sea, wondering how it found its way under the great ocean and high mountains, to come again with so much regularity; or perhaps they believed, as others do, that the Great Spirit sent a new "fire-ball" each day, and nightly quenched it in the sea. You now see the shadows climb the mountain, fitting emblem of the white man's presence in your land, and read in the setting sun the history of your race. Better that you had never heard the sweet sounds of civilized life than that you, with feet untrained, should follow its allurements to your destruction.

You, that once gave to the beautiful mountain streams smile for smile, are now haggard and worn, giving only grim presages of your doom.

Others of your race have avenged their ill-fortunes with the tomahawk, and, in compliance with their religion, have rejected offers of a better life than they knew. But you—you have yielded without war, and, like helpless orphans thrown on the cold world, have accepted the mites given grudgingly by your masters, who treat with contempt and ridicule your cherished faith, who misconstrue your peaceful lives into cowardice. They have fixed their eyes on your home. They will make Alsea river transform the forest on its banks into houses, towns, and cities. They will make the valley where you now follow the government plough, to yield rich harvests of grain, and they will convert the ocean beach into a fountain of golden treasure. A few years more, and the noise of machinery will wake you early from your slumbers. The roar of ocean's breakers will mingle with the hum of busy life in which you may have no part. The white man's eyes will dance with gladness at the sight of your mountains dismantled of their forests, and the glimmer of coming sails to bear away the lofty pines.

Yours will weep at the sacrilege done to your hunting grounds; theirs will gaze on the wide Pacific, and see there the channels that will bring compensation to them for the spoils of your home. Yours will recognize it only as the resting-place for the bones of your people. The white man says, "Your fate is fixed,—your doom is sealed." Few hearts beat with sympathy for you; you are unknown and unnoticed. You must pass away, unless, indeed, the white race shall, from the full surfeit of vengeance upon you and yours, at last return to you a measure of justice.

He who dares appeal in your behalf is derided by his fellows. A proud, boastful people, who claim that human actions should be directed by high motives and pure principles, treat with contempt every effort made to save you from destruction. Strong may be the heart of the Indian chief to resist the encroachments on his people's rights, but stronger still the arm of a government that boasts rebellion against oppression as its foundation stone.

CHAPTER 7

Phil Sheridan's Old Home

GRAND ROUND INDIAN AGENCY

I made my first official visit to this agency in the latter part of September, 1869. Captain Charles La Follette was then acting agent.

The road from Salem was over a beautiful country, settled by white men, who had transformed this once wild region into a paradise. The first view of the agency proper was from a high ridge several miles distant. On the right and left were clustered the houses of the several tribes, each one having been assigned a location. Their houses were built of logs or boards, and rudely put together. Every board had cost these poor people an acre of land; every log counted for so much money given in compensation for their birthrights to the soil of the matchless valley of the Willamette.

As we stood on the dividing ridge separating this agency from the great valley I have mentioned, looking toward the west, we beheld, nearest on the left, old Fort Yamhill, with its snowy cottages, built for the accommodation of the officers of the army in the days when the gallant Sheridan was a lieutenant, and walked its parade-grounds with a simple sword dangling by his side and bars on his shoulder, holding beneath his military cap a brain power waiting for the sound of clanking chains and thundering cannon to call him hence to deeds of valour that should compel the laurel wreath of fame to seek his brow, little thinking then, while guarding savages, that, away off in the future, his charger would impatiently call him from repose, and bear him into the face of a victorious enemy with so much gallantry that he would turn an apparent defeat into a glorious victory.

Immediately on our right were the huts of the people for whose especial intimidation the costly palaces and beautiful cottages had been built. The huts or houses were built on the hillside sloping toward the valley. They presented the appearance of a small, dilapidated inland town that had been "cut off" by a railroad; but they were peopled with Indians who were trying to imitate their masters.

Farther away on the left was another little group of houses, occupied by the chief of the Santiams and his people. The sight of this man's home recalled a part of his own history, suggestive of romance, wild, it is true, but real, nevertheless.

Many years ago, this chief was a young warrior, and his people were at peace with the white race, and were not then "wards of the government," but were living on their native hills, in the vicinity of Mount Jefferson, standing sentinel over the snowy peaks of the Cascade mountains, on whose sides were sitting, like great urns, clear, cold lakes, sending forth little streamlets, murmuring and whispering, and sometimes leaping, like boys going home from play, joining other merry, laughing streamlets, rushing madly along through forests of firs and sugar-pines, whose dropping cones startled the wild game from their repose.

'Twas here this young warrior's home was nestled, beneath the outstretched arms of giant cedars, or sheltered by some quiet nook or cove. Here he had learned the arts of his own people, and passed the winters by, until alone he could chase the fawns or climb the mountain-peak, and gather trophies with which to ornament his neck or fill his quiver.

A pale-face man from distant Missouri had come to this far country to escape the familiar sounds of civilization, where he might imitate the Indian in his freedom and his pleasures. He brought with him his family, and built his cabin near a fountain, to which medicine men would sometimes come or send their patients for recovery.

This white man had a son, with down just cropping on his chin, who, "chip of the old block," as he was, seemed half Indian already, and, fond of wild sports, soon made the acquaintance of young Santiam. The friendship grew, and the rivalry of *archer* and *gunner* often drew them into dispute. Still they were friends.

The archer claimed that he could creep, and noiselessly shoot from cover, without giving alarm, until his quiver should be empty, and thus bring down the chary buck or spotted fawn. The gunner would aver that he could do better execution at greater distance. These trials of skill were often made, and each time the difference 'twixt white and red skin seemed to diminish. The young pale-face would sling his gun and straightway bend his steps toward the camp of Santiam. By signs that he had learned, he took the young chief's trail, and followed through wooded plains, or up the mountain side, until they would hail each other, and then, by agreement, would separate to meet again at some appointed place, laying a wager who would be most successful in the chase of black-tailed deer or mountain sheep.

The hill-sides had put on autumn hues, and the loftier hills were dressed in winter's garb, and gave warning to the denizens who spent their summers near their peaks, that cold weather would soon drive them to the hills beneath for refuge from the blasts that howl above the roar of mountain lion or jumping torrents.

The keeper of the fleecy clouds had given sign of readiness, and, in fact, had begun to spread the winter's carpet down, to preserve the tender grasses for the antlered herd, which would return in open spring to train their limbs for daring feats, in defiance of the feathered arrow, or his neighbour, the loud-talking gun.

Santiam, to anticipate their coming, had started in the early morn, while yet the sun was climbing the eastern slope of Jefferson, and, leaving a sign imprinted in the snow, for his friend to read, hurried on, hoping that from ambush he might send his arrow home to the panting heart of the bounding deer. His friend, anticipating the coming of his rival, had already gone by another route to the trysting place; while waiting there for valley-going game, he spied a grizzly bear, and, without knowing the habits of the monster, he took deliberate aim and fired, but failed to bring his bearship to the ground.

These fellows, when undisturbed, are sure to run; but when the leaden ball had pierced this one's pelt, he exhibited the usual bear-ish indications of resentment for insult offered. The pale-face hunter stood his ground, and sent another ball, merely to persuade his enemy to desist. To those accustomed to this kind of fight, I need not say that every shot made the matter worse. These kings of the Cascades yield not to showers of leaden hail or flocks of flying arrows until the life of their enemy or their own gives victory. With lumbering gait and open mouth, he closed upon the hapless hunter, and had borne him to the ground, when Santiam reached the scene. He hesitated not on which side he would volunteer. Snatching from his belt a hatchet, and a well-tried knife, he, too, closed on the grizzly, and drew his attention from his friend, who, in turn, would attack the wounded monster, and thus alternating between two enemies, he grew more furious and regardless of consequences.

Rallying again to renew the desperate struggle, though his life was ebbing fast, he threw his great body on the pale-faced hunter, when Santiam, with well-aimed steel at his heart, closed the battle. His friend had been severely wounded, and lay prostrate on the ground; his torn garments dripping in blood, his own, and that of his dread enemy, mingled. The young chief soon had a blazing fire, and then tying up the wounds of his friend, to stop the flow of blood, he hastened to his home for aid.

Returning with a *cluchman* of his tribe, he found his friend sinking fast. Making a hasty litter of pine limbs, they bore the wounded hunter to his home. The mother, at the sight of her son so mangled, like a true heroine, overcame her fear, and made preparation for his comfort. The sister, in her quiet way, brought refreshment for her brother, and while the father and his comrade, the "medicine man," were joining their skill to provide remedies for the wounded one, young Santiam, acting from the precepts of his people, had hurried back to the battle-ground, and, with his *cluchman's* help, soon stripped the pelt from the dead beast, and brought it to the home of his white rival, and then the "medicine man," with faith based on tradition's usage, bound up the wounds therewith.

The days went slowly by, until the danger was passed. Santiam went not to the chase, unless for choicest food for his friend, but waited beside the couch of his comrade for his recovery; sometimes joining with the sick man's sister in watching his slumbers, or, may be, touching hands in ministering to his wants.

She, with missionary spirit, sought to teach Santiam words, and the history, too, of her people, their ways, and higher life than he had known. He was apt at learning, as my reader may discover by his speech, recited in this book, made in council years after. His dark eye kindled as some new knowledge found way to his understanding, and his heart grew warmer at the sound of voice from pale-faced *cluchman*. If history be true, her eye kindled too, at the coming of the quiet step of the young comrade of her brother, and her heart felt a new, strange fire, that sent its flame to her cheeks in tell-tale roses.

Novice though he was in civilized ways, he was a man, and with quick perception made the discovery that he now cared more for his comrade's sister than for him; and that even the sister thought of her brother in the third person.

This Missouri man had not yet recognized the growing love be-tween his daughter and young Santiam; and the mother, too, without recalling the youthful days of her own wooing,—perhaps she had none, but years before, in obedience to a custom of her own people, had listened to a proposal, and accepted, because she might "do no better,"—did not recognize the signs of coming trouble to her household, in the rustic courtship going on. Why do parents so soon forget their wooing days, and hide the history from their children, when so nearly all that human nature endures of woes, or enjoys of bliss, comes through the agency of the emotions and affections of the heart?

This guileless girl, cut off from association with her own people by action of her father, and in gratitude for the young chief's kindness to her brother, had, under the prompting of the richest emotions that God had given, opened her heart in friendship first and invited the visitor to share so much; little dreaming that, when once the guest was there, he would become a constant tenant, against whose expulsion she would herself rebel.

The young chief himself did not realize that the finest, warmest feelings of the human heart are supposed by greater men to be confined to the same race or colour. Perhaps he thought the Great Spirit had made all alike, not fixed the difference in the hue of the skin. He was a free man; did not know that civilization had raised a barrier between the races. He had, without knowing what he did, found the barrier down, and passed beyond in natural freedom, and, without thought of wrong, had given full freedom to his heart.

The winter passed, and spring had sprinkled the hillside with flowers. The wilder herds had fled from the huntsman's horn, and climbed again to pleasure-grounds, where the tender grasses cropped out from retreating snow-fields. The rival hunters had again resumed the chase, and spent whole days in telling stories of the past, or living over the battle of the preceding autumn. Each rehearsal made them better friends, and confidence grew mutual. Santiam, with freedom, spoke to his white brother of the "fire in his heart,"—so these people speak of love,—of the sister whom he loved. Who ever told a fellow that he loved his sister without making friendship tremble for the result?

The pale-face boy of whom I am writing still lives, (1875), though grown into gray manhood, to verify this story. When Santiam had told his story, her brother was quiet and thought in silence, while the warrior talked on, of how he would be a "white man" and put away his wild habits, and be his brother. The other promised that he would consult his family, and thus they parted for the night.

The morning found Santiam at the cabin of the "settler," little dreaming that the friendship they had shown him was so soon to be withdrawn. He saw the ominous word refusal in the cold reception that he met. One pair of eyes alone talked in sympathetic glances. He waited to hear no more.

I would like to accommodate my readers with what would make this romantic story run on until some happy denouement had been found, and then resume my work; but I dare not be false to history. The white man moved away. The Indian remained until, through misunderstanding between his people and the white race, war ensued; the frontier rang out the fearful challenge of battle, and victims of both races were offered up to appease insult and thirst for vengeance. The white hunter and his father united with others in a war of extermination against the Indians, while they left a home defenceless.

Young Santiam refused to war against the white man. He gave protection to the cabin that sheltered his love of other days. The maiden is maiden yet; and, though gray hair crowns her head, she is still faithful to the vows made to her Indian lover in her girlhood. Whether she condemns the usage of society that forbade her marriage, or blesses it because it saved her from a savage life, we know not. She may blame her parents for their short-sighted action in isolating her from those congenial to her heart, by locating on the frontier where she met Santiam; surely, not for prohibiting her marriage to him.

Santiam, at the close of the war, removed with his people to Grand Round Agency, where he lived since. Hear him talk in the Salem council of 1871, and judge him by his speeches. Faithful to his compacts, he remains on his home. Few of those who meet him when he visits Salem know of this romance of his life, but hundreds give him the hand of friendship.

To resume, Grand Round valley, the name of which suggests its size and shape, lay stretched out before us, a beautiful picture from Nature's gallery, embellished by the touches that Uncle Sam's greenbacks had given to this agency in building churches, halls, and Indian houses, together with a large farm for general use, and small ones for individuals.

At every change of government officers, Reservation Indians show the liveliest interest, and have great curiosity to see the new man. My arrival was known to all the people very soon. The Indians of this agency were more advanced in civilization than those of any other in Oregon. They had been located by the government, fifteen years previously. Many of them were prisoners of war, in chains and un-

82

GRAND ROUND AGENCY.

der guard, and had been subjugated, through sheer exhaustion; others were under treaty. Their very poverty and the scanty subsistence the government gave, was to them a blessing. Permitted to labour for persons who lived "outside," passes were given each for a specified time. Thus their employers became each a civilizer.

At the time of my first official visit, they had abandoned Indian costume, and were dressed in the usual garb of white men; many of them had learned to talk our language. At my request, messengers were sent out, and the people were invited to come in at an early hour the following day. Before the time appointed they began to arrive. A few were on foot, the remainder in wagons, or on horseback; the younger men and women coming in pairs, after the fashion of white people around them, all arrayed in best attire, for it was a gala day to them. I noticed that in some instances the women were riding side-saddles, instead of the old Indian way, astride.

The children were not left at home, neither were they bound in thongs to boards, or swinging in *papoose* baskets; but some, at least, were carried on the pummel of the father's saddle. They were clothed like other children. Strange and encouraging spectacle, to witness Indian men, who were born savages, conforming to usages of civil life. When once an Indian abandons the habits and customs of his fathers, and has tasted the air which his more enlightened brother breathes, he never goes back so long as he associates with good men.

These people, in less than twenty years, under the management of the several agents, had been transformed, from "Darwin's" wild beasts, almost to civilized manhood, notwithstanding the croaking of soul-less men who constantly accuse United States agents of all kinds of misdemeanours and crimes.

When they were first located, they numbered about twenty-one hundred souls. At the time of which I write, they had dwindled away to about half that number.

When the hour for the talk arrived the people filled the council house, and crowded the doors and windows, so that we found it necessary to adjourn to the open air for room and comfort. The agent, La Follette, went through the form of introducing me to his people, calling each one by name.

This ceremony is always conducted with solemnity; each Indian, as he extends the hand, gazing steadfastly into the eye of the person introduced. They seem to read character rapidly, and with correctness equal to, and sometimes excelling, more enlightened people.

First, a short speech by Agent La Follette, followed by the "Salem *tyee*,"—superintendent. I said that "I was pleased to find them so far advanced in civilization; that I was now the 'Salem *tyee*.' You are my children. I came to show you my heart, to see your hearts, to talk with you about your affairs."

Jo Hutchins—chief of Santiams—was first to speak. He said: "You see our people are not rich; they are poor. We are glad to shake hands with you and show our hearts. You look like a good man, but I will not give you my heart until I know you better." Louis Neposa said: "I have been here fifteen years. I have seen all the country from here to the Rocky Mountains. I had a home on Rogue River; I had a house and barn; I gave them up to come here. That house on that hill is mine;" pointing towards the house in question.

Indian speeches are remarkable for pertinency and for forcible expression, many of them abounding in flights of imagination and bursts of oratory. Much of the original beauty is lost in the translation, as few of them speak in the English language when delivering a speech. Interpreters are often illiterate men, and cannot render the subject-matter with the full force and beauty of the original, much less imitate the gesture and voice.

During my residence in the far West, and especially while in government employ, I have taken notes, and in many instances, kept verbatim reports, the work being done by clerks of the several agencies. I have selected, from several hundred pages, a few speeches, made by these people, for use in making up my book. It will be observed that the sentences are short, and repetitions sometimes occur. In fact, these orators of nature follow nature, and repeat themselves, as our greatest orators do, and their skill in the art of repetition is something marvellous. This is peculiar to all Indian councils, though not always recorded. The following are word for word, especially Wapto Dave and Jo Hutchins' speeches:—

Black Tom said: "I am a wild Injun. I don't know much. I have not much sense. I cannot talk well. I feel like a man going through the bushes, when he is going to fight; like he was thinking some man was behind a bush, going to shoot him. I have been fooled many times. I don't know much. Some *tyees* talk well when they first come. I have seen their children wearing shirts like those they gave me; maybe it was all right. I don't know much."

Solomon Riggs—chief of the Umpyuas—said: "I am not a wild man. I have sense. I know some things. I have learned to work. I was born wild, but I am not wild now. I live in a house. I have a wagon and horses that I worked for. They are mine. The government did not give them to me. That woman is my wife, and that is my baby. He will have some sense. I show you my heart. I want you to give me your heart. I don't want to be a wild Injun." See speech of Solomon Riggs in Salem Council.

All the "head men" made short speeches, after which we came to business talk. Superintendent Meacham said: "I see before me the remnants of a great people. Your fathers are buried in a far country. I will show you my heart now. You are not wild men. You are not savages. You are men and women. You have sense and hearts to feel. I did not come here to dig up anything that is buried. I have nothing to say about the men who have gone before me. That is past. We drop that. We cannot dig it up now. We have enough to think about. I do not promise what I will do, except I will do right as I see what is right. I may make some mistakes. I want to talk with you about your agent. I think he will do right. He is a good man. I will help him. He will help me. You will help us. You are not fools. You are men. You have a right to be heard. You shall be heard. We are paid to take care of you. Our time belongs to the Indians in Oregon. The government has bought our sense; that belongs to you. The money in our hands is not ours, it is yours. We cannot pay you the money. The law says we must not; still it is yours. You have been here long enough to have sense. You know what you want. You can tell us. We will hear you.

"If you want what is right we will get it for you. You need not be afraid to speak out. The time has come when a man is judged by his sense, not his skin. In a few years more the treaty will be dead. Then you must be ready to take care of yourselves. You need not fear to speak. Nobody will stop your mouth. We are ready now to hear you talk. We have shown our heart. Now talk like men. I have spoken."

A silence of some moments followed. The chiefs and head men seemed taken by surprise. They could not comprehend or believe that the declarations made were real; that they were to be allowed to give an opinion in matters pertaining to their own interests. I would not convey the idea that my predecessors had been bad men. They were not; but they had, some of them, and perhaps all of them, looked on these Indians as wards, or orphan children. They had not recognized the fact that these people had come up, from a low, degraded condition of captive savages, to a status of intelligence that entitled them to consideration. The people themselves had not dared to demand a hearing. They were subjugated, and felt it too; but I know in their hearts they often longed for the boon that was offered to them.

It is due to the citizens who occupy the country adjoining this agency, in whose employ the Indians had spent much time in labour on farm, wood-yards, and various other kinds of business, that they had, by easy lessons, and, with commendable patience, taught these downtrodden people that they had a right to look up. "Honour to whom honour is due."

Wapto Dave, a chief of a small band of Waptos, was the first to speak. He delivered his speech in my own language:

> The boys all wait for me to speak first; because me understand some things. We hear you talk. We don't know whether you mean it. Maybe you are smart. We have been fooled a heap. We don't want no lies. We don't talk lies. S'pose you talk straight. All right. Me tell you some things. All our people very poor; they got no good houses; no good mills. No wagons; got no harness; no ploughs. They get some, they work heap. They buy them. Government no give em. We want these things. Maybe you don't like my talk. I am done.

Jo Hutchins—Chief of Santiams—said:

> I am watching your eye. I am watching your tongue. I am thinking all the time. Perhaps you are making fools of us. We don't want to be made fools. I have heard *tyees* talk like you do now. They go back home and send us something a white man don't want. We are not dogs. We have hearts. We may be blind. We do not see the things the treaty promised. Maybe they got lost on the way. The President is a long way off. He can't hear us. Our words get lost in the wind before they get there. Maybe his ear is small. Maybe your ears are small. They look big. Our ears are large. We hear everything. Some things we don't like. We have been a long time in the mud. Sometimes we sink down. Some white men help us up. Some white men stand on our heads.
> We want a school-house built on the ground of the Santiam people. Then our children can have some sense. We want an Indian to work in the blacksmith shop. We don't like half-breeds. They are not Injuns. They are not white men. Their hearts are divided. We want some harness. We want some ploughs. We want a saw-mill. What is a mill good for that has no dam? That old mill is not good; it won't saw boards. We want a church.

87

Some of these people are Catholics. Some of them are like Mr. Parish, a Methodist. Some got no religion. Maybe they don't need religion.

Some people think Indians got no sense. We don't want any blankets. We have had a heap of blankets. Some of them have been like sail-cloth muslin. The old people have got no sense; they want blankets. The treaty said we, every man, have his land. He have a paper for his land. We don't see the paper. We see the land. We want it divided. When we have land all in one place, some Injun put his horses in the field; another Injun turn them out. Then they go to law. One man says another man got the best ground. They go to law about that. We want the and marked out. Every man builds his own house. We want some apples. Mark out the land, then we plant some trees, by-and-by we have some apples.

Maybe you don't like my talk. I talk straight. I am not a coward. I am chief of the Santiams. You hear me now. We see your eyes; look straight. Maybe you are a good man. We will find out. *Sochala-tyee,*—God sees you. He sees us. All these people hear me talk. Some of them are scared. I am not afraid. *Alta-kup-et,*—I am done.

Here was a man talking to the point. He dodged nothing. He spoke the hearts of the people. They supported him with frequent applause. Other speeches were made, all touching practical points. The abstract of issues following that council exhibit the distribution of hardware, axes, saws, hatchets, mauls, iron wedges; also, harness, ploughs, hoes, scythes, and various farming implements. The reasonable and numerous points involved many questions of importance, which were submitted to the Hon. Commissioner of Indian Affairs, Washington city.[1]

1. See Appendix.

CHAPTER 8

Stopping the Survey—Why

Without waiting for red tape, we proceeded to erect a new saw-mill. The Indians performed much of the necessary labour. With one white man to direct them, they prepared all the timber, built a dam, and cut a race, several hundred yards in length, and within ninety days from "breaking ground" the new saw-mill was making lumber.

The Indians formed into working parties and delivered logs as fast as the mill could saw them. Mr. Manrow, a practical sawyer, was placed in charge of the mill, and, with Indian help only, he manufactured four to eight thousand feet of lumber per day. He subsequently remarked that "they were as good help as he wanted."

The understanding before commencing work on the mill was to the effect that it was to belong to the Indians on Grand Round Agency, when completed. Those who furnished logs were to own the lumber after sale of sufficient quantity to pay the "sawyer," the whole to be under control of the acting agent.

Misunderstandings seem to have arisen between the agent and Indians, growing out of the sale of lumber manufactured by the mill. The only misunderstanding that could have arisen, was that wherein the Indians claim that "the government would pay the expense of running it,"—the saw-mill,—and they—the Indians—should have the lumber to dispose of as they thought best, claiming the right to sell it to the whites outside of the Reservation.

It was so agreed and understood as above stated, that the government agent was to manage the business, pay the sawyer, and meet such other expenses as might *accrue, out of the sale of lumber, and the remainder to belong to parties furnishing logs*, with the privilege of selling to persons wherever a market could be found. If any other plan has been adopted, it is in violation of the agreement made with the Indians at the council that considered the question of building the mills. A full report of that council was forwarded to the commissioner at Washington, was filed in the office of Superintendent of Indian Affairs, Salem, Oregon, and was, or should have been, recorded on the books at Grand Round Agency.

The *Indians* of Grand Round *own* the *mills*. The funds invested in their erection did not belong to agent or government. It was the Indians' money, and was so expended by their knowledge and request. The sweat of these people was dropped in the long race, cut for the mills. Every stick of timber in them was prepared, partly at least, by Indian labour. They had accepted this little valley at the bidding of a powerful government, who had promised them mills (see treaty of 1866), and had constructed inferior machinery, at enormous expense, that had never been worth one-half the greenbacks they had cost.

These people have advanced more rapidly in civilization than any other Indian people on "the coast." They had learned a great amount of useful knowledge while working for the white men, to make a living for their families, when the government had failed to furnish subsistence for them. They were now ready to take care of their interests, when men paid to instruct them had performed their duty.

If these Indians are ever to manage for themselves, why not begin with easy lessons, while they have, or are supposed to have, an agent, whose duty it was to stand between them and the stronger race with whom they are to mingle and associate?

I repeat that these Indian men own the mills, and are entitled to the proceeds, and that it is, and was, an agent's duty to transact such parts of the business as the Indians could not themselves. What if it did require labour and care to prevent confusion? The agent was paid for his time, his business talent, and, if he was unwilling or incompetent, he was not in a proper position.

The agent says, "I have allowed them one-half the lumber made, when they wished to use it for building purposes, retaining the other half for the department, until such time as it can be used in improvement, or otherwise disposed of for their common benefit." If the department required lumber, let the Indians be the *merchants*, and receive the pay. To dispose of it for their benefit was to compel those who were willing to labour to support those who were not. Working parties were organized among them by agent La Follette, and they were to enjoy the privilege, of furnishing saw-logs in turn; thus encouraging enterprise among them. Klamath Indian mill furnished several thousand dollars' worth of lumber for the Military Department at Fort Klamath, and for outside people too, and the proceeds were paid to the Indians who did the work, or it was invested in stock cattle for them. In the name of justice I protest, as a friend of the Indians, against the confiscation, by our government, of labour and lumber belonging to the Indians of Grand Round Agency.

Reference has been made to the allotment of land to these people. The letter following will give the reader some idea of the manner in which it was done, and the various questions that were to be considered in connection with this important episode in the lives of these people.[1]

The enrolment referred to was completed. The surveying was done by Col. D. P. Thompson, United States Deputy Surveyor.

While he was engaged in doing this work, the Indians assisted materially, and followed him in crowds, each anxious to see where the lines would run, whether they would conform to their preconceived hopes or not.

The thoughts of these men—for they were men—must have been very comforting at the prospect of promises being at last fulfilled. Many years had passed, *waiting, waiting,* waiting for the time to come when they should have homes "like white men." They well understood the arrangement in regard to the amount of land that was to be given to each. I have not the "Willamette Treaty" before me, but, from memory, state, that each *grown person* was to have twenty acres, with ten acres additional for each minor child.

Col. Thompson, the surveyor, relates, that while engaged in surveying near the house of a "Wapto" Indian, said Indian came to him with a very serious face, and requested the suspension of the work. The colonel, being a humorous man, and patient withal, entertained the petition, but demanded to know the reason why the survey should stop.

"Wapto" said, in jargon, "Indian *Neeseka-nan-itch-mi-ka, is-cum,* twenty acres; *Nika cluchman is-cum,* twenty acres; *Ni-ka ten-us-cluchman is-cum,* ten acres; *Nika ten-us-man is-cum,* ten acres; *Ma-mook,* sixty acres; *Al-ka.* You see I get twenty acres, my squaw get twenty acres, my daughter get ten acres, my son get ten acres, making sixty acres in all. *Spose Mesika Capit mamook icta elihe, Kau-yua nika is cum,* seventy acres. Suppose you stop surveying, and wait awhile, I can get seventy acres, may be eighty acres. *Cum-tux,*—understand?"

1. See Appendix.

The colonel took the hint, when the Indian pointed to the small lodge, fitted up expressly, as the custom among these people is, for important occasions of the kind intimated above.

Whether he changed his course in surveying, he did not say, but went on to relate, that a few days after the above conversation, the same Indian came to him and said, *"Nika-is-cum, Ten-is-man"*—"I have another boy."—*"Klat-a-wa-ma-mook-elihe"*—"Go on with the survey."—*"Nika is-cum,* seventy acres"—"I get seventy acres." He seemed much elated with the new boy, and the additional ten acres of land.

The surveying was completed, but "red tape" was in the way of allotment, much to the satisfaction of some of the people, who were hoping for as good fortune as "Wapto," in the same way; others, who were hopeless of such luck, were anxious for the lands to be set apart at once, because each newcomer made the chances less in securing good homes, by being crowded of to make room for the additions that such events demanded.

The allotment has finally been made. The people are overjoyed, and they start off on this new order of life with commendable zeal. I have no doubt of their ability to maintain themselves, when they shall have been admitted to the new relationships in life. While they have been long in bondage, treated as dependents, and begrudged the valley wherein they have been placed by the government, they have, nevertheless, attained to a status of manhood that entitles them to consideration. They fully appreciate such evidences of recognition, and should be consulted in regard to the expenditure of their funds, the appointment of agents and *employés*, the selection of church ministries and school teachers.

During one of my official visits they assembled to the number of nearly one hundred, and paraded on horseback, for a grand demonstration. They were well dressed, and well mounted on good horses. After performing various evolutions, they drew up in front of the agency office in a half circle. The leader then made a speech, a portion of which I copy here, from the memoranda made at that time. It was in American language, and began:

Mr. Meacham: You our chief. We look on you as our father. We show you how we get along. We think we white men now. We no Injuns now. We all Republicans. We know 'bout the big war. We no Democrats. One man he live with me—he Democrat—us boys all laugh. He get shamed; he good 'publican now. These all our horses, we work for 'em. S'pose you want us work road, all right; s'pose you tell us pay the tax, all right. Sometime we vote just like a white man. All right. S'pose the President want soldier, we are white men; we know all about everything; we can fight. We are not boys; we know about law. That's all right. "We want to hear you talk. You talk all the same; you talk to white men. Some of these people don't understand, we tell them; you go ahead, talk all the time.

Meaning I should make a speech without waiting to have it interpreted.

I felt then that I was their servant. The government was paying me for my time, and whatever of ability I might have. I was not there to make a hurried call, and go away without doing them good.

My remarks were, substantially, that I was glad to see them appear so much like white men; that the government would give them lands, and would do right by them. A few years ago, a great many black people were slaves; now everybody is free. Every man is counted by his sense and conduct, *not* by his colour. You men are almost white in your habits. You are doing well; you have made a good start. After the land is allotted, you will each have a home, and in four years the treaty will be dead; then you can come up with the white man. You will pay taxes and vote.

Dave said: "There is something else we want you to talk about. Some of us Injuns are Catholic; some of us are not. The Catholics don't want to go to the other meetings. They don't talk all the same. We want to understand about this religion."

The agency was, at that time, under the supervision of the Methodist Church. A Catholic priest had been labouring with these people for many years, and had baptized a large number of them.

The assignment of agencies was made without proper knowledge of the religious antecedents of the people. Many of them had been, from time to time, under the teaching of other churches, especially the Methodist Episcopal Church. They had also formed their ideas from association with the farmers, for whom they had worked at various times. I realized then, as I have often done, the very embarrassing circumstances that surrounded the subject.

If I have ever doubted the feasibility of the church policy, it was because no well-defined regulations were ever made. Regarding these matters it is a doubtful question which of the churches named had priority of right to minister to the people of Grand Round Agency. Though the Catholics had been many years among them, the Methodists had, at an earlier date, taught them in matters pertaining to religion.

I fully realized the importance of Dave's request, and so deferred action until the Catholic father could be summoned. Father Waller, one of the early founders of Methodist missions in Oregon, was present. When the former arrived, the subject was again brought up. In the mean time, however, a new question arose, and an incident occurred worthy of a place in this connection.

The habits of these people are their lives really, and when an old custom is abolished, the substitute may be clumsily introduced, and not well understood. I refer to the marriage law. The old way was to buy the girl, or make presents to the parents until they gave consent for the marriage. The new order of things forbade this way of performing this sacred rite.

The hero of this episode—Leander—was a fine, handsome young fellow, who belonged to Siletz Agency, and from his agent had learned something of the working of the law. Siletz and Grand Round Agencies are within one day's ride.

The heroine—Lucy—lived on the latter, with her parents, who were "Umpyuas."

Leander had obtained a pass—permission—from his agent, stating the object of the visit, and had been well drilled in regard to his rights under the "new law." He had proposed, and, so far as the girl's consent was concerned, been accepted. But the parents of Lucy could not be so easily conciliated.

It is true they had assented to the new law, but were reluctant to see Lucy marry a man, and go away to another agency to live. I think, however, the absence of presents had something to do with their reluctance. Leander had promised his agent that he would stand by the new law,—make no presents to the parents.

The "old folks" founded their objection on other grounds when submitting the case for settlement. Leander requested a private interview with me. He then stated that he was willing to pacify the old folks by making a present or two, if he thought Mr. Simpson would not find out about it. He declared he never would return to Siletz without Lucy; said he thought she was a good young *cluchman*; he loved her better than any on Siletz. "She is stout; she can work; she can keep house like a white woman. She is no squaw. I want her

94

mighty bad. You s'pose you can fix it all right? I don't want them old folks mad at me. They say if she goes away now she get no land. Can't she get land at Siletz? They don't care for her. They want some *ictas* (presents); they want me to wait until you give the land; that's what they want."

I promised to arrange the matter for him somehow, although I could see the difficulties that embarrassed the marriage, as indicated by Leander's talk.

Had the allotment of lands been made, no objections would have been had on that score. The father and mother called upon me, wishing advice. Grand Round was, at this time, without a general agent, and was running in charge of a special agent,—Mr. S. D. Rhinehart; hence the duties of an agent were devolved upon the superintendents, and one of the important duties is to hear the complaints, and adjust all matters of difference.

The "old folks" were much excited over this affair of their daughter Lucy, who had, as her white sisters sometimes do, given evidence of her interest in the question, by declaring she would marry Leander, and possibly said something equivalent to the "there now" of a spoiled girl.

They were much affected. The father's chief objection, I think, was to prospective loss of ten acres of land; the mother's, the companionship and services of her daughter, added to a mother's anxiety for the welfare of her child. She shed some real tears, woman-like.

The father said, when he would wake up in the morning and call "Lucy," she could not hear him, and that he would be compelled to go for his horse when he wanted to ride. Lucy had always done that kind of work for him.

The conference was protracted, for I recognized in this affair a precedent that might be of great importance to the Indians of Grand Round Agency hereafter. I foresee, in the future, some stony-hearted Indian hater, scowling while he reads this mention of sentiment and feeling on the part of Indians. Scowl on, you cold-blooded, one-sided, pale-face, protected in your life, your rights, and even your affections, by a great, strong government!

Finally, all the parties interested were taken into the council. The mother put some pertinent questions to Leander.

"Do you ever drink whiskey? Do you gamble? Will you whip Lucy when you are mad? Will you let her come to see me when she wants to?"

95

Leander's answers were satisfactory, and, I think, sincere. He promised, as many a white boy has to his sweetheart's mother, what he would not have done to a mother-in-law. That relationship changes the courage, and loosens the tongue of many a man.

Lucy was not slow to speak her mind on the subject. "*Leander, Clat-a-wa-o-koke-Sun-Siletz. E-li-he, hi-ka-tum-tum, ni-ak-clut-a-wa.* (Leander goes to Siletz, my heart will go with him, today.) *Ni-ka-wake-clut-or-wa-niker, min-a-lous.*" ("If I don't go, I will die.") This settled the question.

Being the first marriage under the new law, it was decided to make it a precedent that would have proper influence on subsequent weddings. The ladies resident at the agency, were informed of the affair, and requested to assist the bride in making preparations for the ceremony.

Leander was well dressed, but he required some drilling. Dr. Hall, the resident-physician, assumed the task, and calling two or three boys and girls to the office, the ceremony was rehearsed until Leander said, "That's good. I understand how to get married."

The people came together to witness the marriage. The men remounted their horses, and formed in a half circle in front of the office, women and children within the arc, all standing. The porch in front of the office was the altar. Father Waller, with his long white hair floating in the wind, stood with Bible in hand. A few moments of stillness, and then the office door opened, and Leander stepped out with Lucy's hand in his.

The doctor had arranged for bridesmaids and groomsmen. As they filed out into the sunlight, every eye was fixed on the happy couple. The attendants were placed in proper position, and then the voice of Father Waller broke the silence in an extempore marriage service. Leander and Lucy were pronounced man and wife, and, the white people leading off, the whole company passed before the married pair and offered congratulations.

Great was the joy, and comical the scene. One of the customs of civilized life was omitted, that of kissing the bride. Father Waller could not, consistently, set the example, the doctor would not, and, since no white man led the way, the Indian boys remained in ignorance of their privilege.

The horsemen dismounted and paid the honour due, each following the exact model, and if one white man had kissed the bride, every Indian man on the agency would have done likewise.

One young man asked the bridegroom in Indian, "*Con-chu-me-si-ka-ka-tum-tum?*" ("How is your heart now?")"*Now-wit-ka-close-tum-tum-tum-ni-ka.*" ("My heart is happy now.") I have witnessed such affairs among white people, and I think that I have not seen any happier couple than Leander and Lucy.

The dance, in confirmation of the event, was well attended. It being out of Father Waller's walk in life, and my own also, we did not participate in the amusement. But we looked on a few moments, and were surprised to see the women and girls dressed in style, somewhat grotesque, 'tis true, but all in fashion; indeed, in several fashions.

Some of them wore enormous hoops, others long trails, all of them bright-hued ribbons in their hair. Some with chignons, frizzles, rats, and all the other paraphernalia of ladies' head-gear. The men were clad in ordinary white man's garb, except that antiquated coats and vests were more the rule than the exception. Black shining boots and white collars were there. A few had gloves,—some buckskin, some woollen; others wore huge rings; but, taken all in all, the ball would have compared favourably with others more pretentious in point of style, and even elegance.

These people were apt scholars in this feature of civilization. The music on the occasion was furnished by Indian men, with violins. Few people are more mirthful, or enter with more zest into sports, when circumstances are favourable, than do Indians.

The day following the wedding, a general council, or meeting, was held. Father Waller of the Methodist, and Father Croystel of the Catholic Church, being present, the subject of religion was taken up and discussed. The facts elicited were, that many of the Indians, perhaps a majority, were in favour of the Catholic Church. The remainder were in favour of the Methodist, a few only appearing indifferent.

Neither of the fathers took part in the "talks." My own opinion, expressed then and since, on other occasions, was, that the greatest liberty of conscience should be allowed in religious practice. That the people should honour all religions that were Christian. No bitter feelings were exhibited. I attended, at other times, the Catholic Church exercises, conducted by Rev. Father Croystel. The Indians came in large numbers, some of them on horses, but the majority in wagons; whole families, cleanly clad and well behaved.

Those who belonged to the Catholic Church were devout, and assisted the father in the ceremonies and responses. The invitation was extended to any and all denominations to preach; on one occasion a minister came by invitation, and preached in the office. The attendance was not large, but the *employés* of the agency monopolized all the available benches. They seemed to think that the Indians had no rights. The preacher began his discourse, and, after dilating on the word of God, with a prosy effort to explain some abstruse proposition in theology, for half an hour, my patience became exhausted, and I arose and made the suggestion that, since the meeting was for the benefit of the Indians, something should be said which they might understand. More seats were provided, and the preacher started anew, and when a sentence was uttered that was within the comprehension of those for whom the preaching was intended, it was translated. This meeting, however, did not do them very much good, because it was not conducted in a way that was understood by the Indians.

The man who was trying to do good had undoubtedly answered when someone else had been called of God to preach the gospel. He would, perhaps, have made a passable mechanic, but he had no qualifications for preaching to Indians. He was not human enough. He was too well educated. He knew too much. Had he been *less learned*, or possessed more *common sense*, he might have been competent to teach great grown-up children, as these Indian people are, in the Christian religion.

A short colloquy overheard between two of the red children he had been preaching to would have set him to thinking. The talk was in the Indian language, but, translated, would have run in about the following style:—

"Do you understand what all that talk was about?"

"No; do you? Well, he was talking wicked half the time, and good half the time. He was telling about a man getting lost a long time ago. Got lost and didn't find himself for forty years. That's a big story, but maybe it is so. I don't know. Never heard of it before."

I need not say to the reader, that this minister had been preaching about Moses. Perhaps he was not to be censured. He may have done the best he could. He did not know how to reach an Indian's heart.

The schools at this agency were not flourishing. The reason was that the mode was impracticable. Schools were taught with about as much sense and judgment as the preaching just referred to.

After several years of stupid experimenting, at an expense of many thousands of dollars, there was not among these Indians half a dozen of them who could read and understand a common newspaper notice. The fault was not with the pupils; it was the system.

The Indians of this agency are farther advanced than those of any others in Oregon, in everything that goes to make up a civilized people. They have, since the allotment of lands, made rapid progress, and bid fair to become rivals of other people in the pursuit of wealth, and other characteristics that make a people prosperous. Some of them are already the equals of their white neighbours in integrity of character and business tact. They have abandoned their old laws and customs, and have been working under civil laws. They elect officers and hold courts, somewhat after the manner of a mock legislature; in other words, they are practising and rehearsing, in anticipation of the time when they shall become citizens.

Like all other races, they learn the vices much quicker than the virtues of their superiors. It cannot be denied that they follow bad examples sometimes, especially intemperance; but when considered fairly, taking note of the influences that have been thrown around them; the many different agents, and kinds of policies under which they have lived; the fact that they were wild Indians sixteen years ago; that they have been kept in constant fear of being removed; hope deferred so often and so long; that they were remnants of many small tribes; that their numbers have decreased so rapidly,—then they stand out in a new light, and challenge commendation.

Lift your heads, Indians of Grand Round! you are no longer slaves; you are free.

This agency, with the people who are there now, and who have been there as government officers and *employés*, would furnish material for volumes of real live romance; racy stories, sad tales, great privations, disease, death and suffering make up the history of such places. No character required to make a thrilling drama, a bloody tragedy, or comic personality, would be wanting. Better live only in tradition, or fireside story, than in printed page. The latter would embarrass men who have passed through some of the chairs of office, and poor fellows, too, who have sponged a living off of "Uncle Sam," and cheated the people of thousands of dollars, and months of labour, that they were paid for doing. Let the history die untold, since it could not restore justice to either government or people. Some of those who have administered on Grand Round Agency have left the Indians in much better condition than they found them, and will live forever in the memory of those they served so faithfully.

Before leaving this agency I would state one feature of Indian life that exists everywhere, but it is less prominent on this than other agencies.

I refer to the *poor* and the *old*. Perhaps the last Christian virtue that finds lodgement in Indian hearts is regard or reverence for age, especially old women. They are drudges everywhere, and when too old to labour are sometimes neglected.

Poor, miserable-looking old women, blind, lame, and halt, charity would shed more tears at your death than your children would. While this deplorable indifference for them exists to a fearful extent, there are notable exceptions, particularly among the Grand Round Indians. In every council they were found standing up and pleading for something to be done for the old and poor. These old creatures nearly always hobble to the meetings, and although they seem fair specimens of the Darwinian theory, they, nevertheless, have feelings and gratitude even for small favours. A grasp of the hand seems to impart a ray of sunshine to their benighted faces.

A few years more, and all the old ones will be gone, and their successors will take the vacant places with prospects of more humane treatment than they have hitherto received.

Heaven pity the *poor* and old, for man has little for them that casts even a glimmer of hope, save on their waiting tombs!

CHAPTER 9

The Aged Pair—Birthplace of Legends

The scene changes, and we stand on the deck of a river steamer with its prow pointed eastward.

For hours we have steamed along in the shadows of the Cascade mountains, through deep, dark *cañons*, with walls so high that the smoke-stack of our little boat seemed like a pipe-stem. "Puny thing" it is. Yet it bears us over boiling eddies and up rapids that shoot between high rocks like immense streams of silver from the great furnace of creation.

We are startled at the sound of the whistle on our deck, and grow anxious when the nearest *cañon* answers back, and still another takes up the sound, and the echo turns to its original starting-point, and finds its own offspring talking back in fainter voice, until it dies away like the rumbling of some fast-retreating train rushing through the open field or wooded glens.

Soon we are on board the thundering train, whirling away toward the upper cascades, swinging around curves and beneath ledges, and overhanging the rushing floods hundreds of feet below. As we fly swiftly along, the conductor, or someone familiar with this cascade country, points out the battle-grounds where the red men fought white men for their homes. The battle was a fierce one, and lasted several days, when the Indians withdrew.

There are traditions yet among Indians and white settlers; and it is related that in former times the Indians who lived along the banks of the Columbia were employed to assist the white men in transporting goods over the portages (or carrying places), and they were ill-treated by their employers, and their rights disregarded.

The invasion of the country was not the most grievous complaint. They were furnished whiskey, were debauched, and corrupted as a people, until virtue was unknown among their women; the men themselves selling their wives and daughters for the basest purposes. Degraded, polluted, and in despair, they sought to wreak vengeance on their seducers.

If those who debased them were the only victims, no just condemnation could be pronounced against them.

There is a feeling of respect for the man, though a savage he may be, who defends his home, and resents imposition even at the risk of life. But humanity revolts against the butchery of innocent persons, no matter what the colour may be, or the cause of provocation of race against race.

A few survivors of the Cascade tribes may be found now, (as at time of first publication), on Warm Springs and Yak-a-ma agencies.

The traveller on the Columbia meets, occasionally, a man and his family, still lingering around their old homes, living in bark-covered huts, sometimes employed in labouring for the Steam Navigation Company, who transport the commerce that passes through the mountain at this point. These stragglers are poor, miserably degraded savages, and are not fair specimens of their race.

An old Indian legend connected with the Cascades has been repeated to tourists over and over again. It has been written in verse, in elegant style and forceful expression, by S. A. Clark, Esq., of Salem, Oregon, published in February number of *Harper's Magazine* for 1874. The poem is worthy of perusal, and ought to make the author's fame as a poet.

The substance of the legend is to the effect, that many, many years ago, before the eyes of the pale-faces had gazed on the wonders of the Cascades, the river was bridged by a span of mountains, beneath which it passed to the ocean; that to this bridge the children of Mount Hood on the south, and those of Mount Adams on the north, made yearly pilgrimage, to worship the Great Spirit, and exchange savage courtesies, and to lay in stores of fish for winter use. The Great Spirit blessed them, and they came and went for generations untold.

They tell how the exchange of friendship continued, until at length a beautiful maiden, who had been chosen for a priestess, was wooed and won by a haughty Indian brave of another tribe. On her withdrawal from the office her people became indignant, and demanded her return. This was refused, and when, on their annual visit, they came from the north and from the south, bitter quarrels ensued, until, at last, fierce wars raged, and the rock spanning the river became a battle-ground. *Soch-a-la tyee*—God—was vexed at the children, and caused the bridge to fall. Thus he separated them, and bade each abide where he had placed them.

The legend still lives fresh in the memory of these Indians, and they respect the command. Few have changed their residences. The ragged mountains on either side support well the historic tale. High, bald summits stand confronting each other, and it requires no effort of the imagination to see the Great Bridge as it is said once to have stood, and to hear rising on the winds, the weird, wild songs of the people at the time of sacrifice.

At the place where this legend had its origin the "Columbia" is crowded by its banks into so narrow a channel that an Indian might, with his sling, make a stone to trace the curves of the ancient arch. The waters rush so swiftly that the keenest sight can scarcely keep the course of timber drift in view. The river's bosom is smooth above this rapid flow, and, widening, takes the semblance of a lake, in whose depth may be seen the trees that once were growing green, but now to stone have turned; they never move before the breeze; they sway not, nor yet can yield to the gentle currents, still standing witnesses of the legend's truth.

Midway between the shores an island stands, fashioned and fitted for a burial-ground of the tribes that had oft, in ages past, made use of it at nature's invitation, and had borne to this resting-place the warriors whose spirits passed up to the happier lands; while the body resting here might wait for the coming of some Great Prophet, who should bid the bones to rise and become part and parcel of human forms, and mingle with those who remain to build the nightly fires and feed the mouldering bodies of their dead, until the great past should be re-born and live again attended by all the circumstances of savage life.

Sitting in the pilot-house of the steamer *Tenino*, beside "McNulty," her captain, hear him tell how these people come, at certain times, to pay honour to their dead; how, in years gone by, from the *Tenino* he could see the old *sachems* sitting bolt upright in their wooden graves and calmly waiting, watching, with sightless eyes, for the coming hour foretold before they died; how, with fleshless hands, they clutched the rotting handle of the battle-axe of flint or fishing-spears.

Then see his eye kindle while he tells you of relic-hunters from the

103

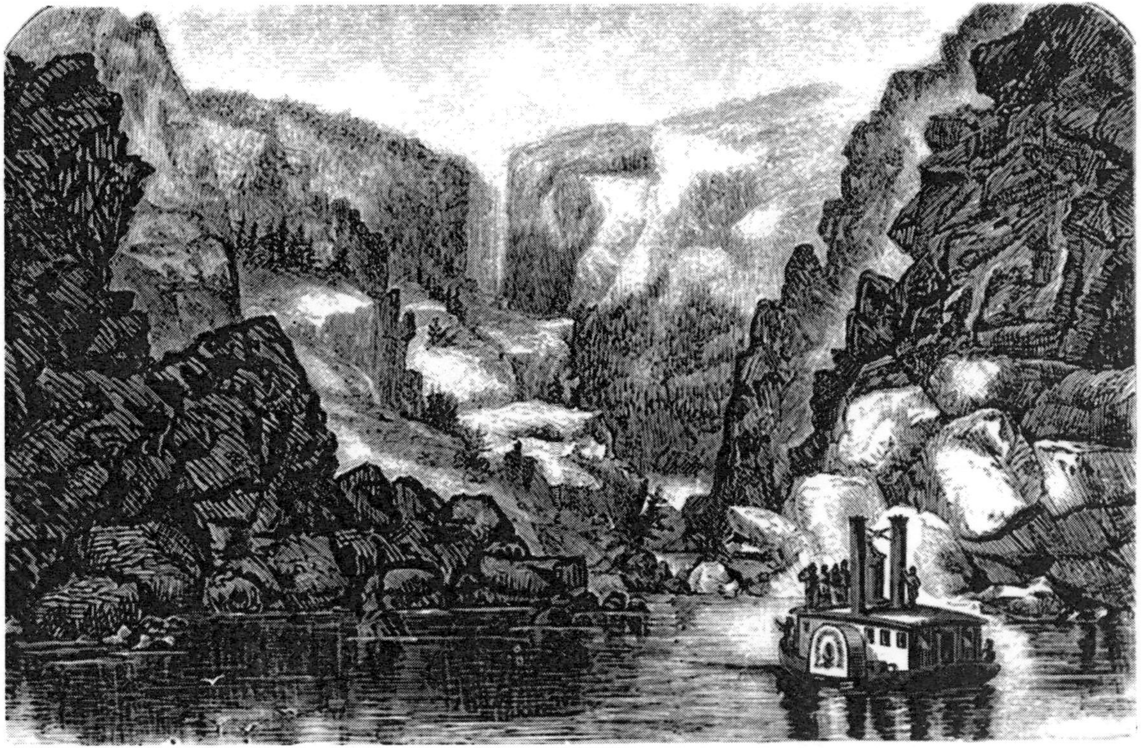

The birthplace of Indian legends

East, who came on board the *Tenino* with boxes and lines and other devices for relic-hunting, and requested that he would land them on the shores of this lone island. You will feel the fire of that eye warming your heart towards the dead, and living too, when it declares in full sympathy, with the rich Irish voice, "That while he commands the *Tenino no grave-robbers* shall ever disturb the old heroes who sit patiently waiting for their resurrection. No sacrilegious foot shall leave his vessel's deck to perpetrate so foul a deed!"

You will honour him still better when you learn that, in his whole-hearted generosity, he declares that "No man shall ever disturb the repose of the congregated dead, on that little island, while he lives, and escape unpunished."

Brave, fearless captain, many years have you passed daily in sight, and scanned their sepulchres; self-appointed guardian, you have been true to the impulse of a noble heart; you have exalted our opinion of the race you represent; and for your fidelity to the cause of a common humanity, and especially to the race whose dark faces seldom light up from recognition by those whose power has been but the destruction of their own, do we thank you.

May many winters come and go before their snows shall bring to you old age; and when, at last, the *Tenino* shall be laid aside, may you still be guardian of this spot, so sacred to many a sad and hopeless heart.

Leaving behind, on our upward journey, the burial-ground of the mountain tribes, in charge of the faithful McNulty, we pass beneath high rock cliffs, sometimes near beautiful valleys, with farm cottages and lowing cattle on hillside pastures. Through the deep *cañons* that cut the table mountains in twain, as if made on purpose for tourists' delight, Mount Hood, the father mountain, comes suddenly in view; the beauty much enhanced when seen through nature's telescope, made by rifts in solid rocks, with sky-lights reaching to the stars above. Words may not give even a faint outline of the scene. McNulty, though for years he has gazed on this sublime painting,—at morning, when the shadows cover the telescope, but light the mountain up; and at evening, too, when both were shaded,—sees new beauties at every sight; and, not content to worship all alone, he rings his call to the engineer, and the vessel slackens her speed, and "rounds to" in proper place, while the captain calls his guests to the grandest banquet that earth affords, and points out the beauties as each one paints the panorama on his soul.

105

See, there the old Father Hood stands, with his wreath of snow, which he has worn since the time when man was unknown. Sometimes he hides his hoary head in clouds, unwilling to witness the injustice done the puny children who have played around his feet for generations past. We see his own sons, still in primeval manhood, with heads crowned with fir or laurel, standing at his side and looking up, are ever ready to bear the winter's burdens that from his shoulders fall.

Again we glide on the smooth surface of the shining river until we hear repeated the captain's call to witness now how impartial God has been, and to prevent any jealousy that might arise, has made on the other shore, looking northward, twin telescope to the first, and twin mountain, too, for now we see another hoary head, rich in clustered snow-banks that ornament her brow. Mother Adams stands calmly overlooking her daughters, who modestly wear garlands of wild wood-vines, and heavy-topped fragrant cedars. She feels her solitude, and when "Hood" draws his mantle over his majestic shoulders, she, too, puts on a silvery veil of misty wreath, or, in seeming anger, drapes in mourning and weeps; the deluge of her tears giving signs of willingness to make friends again. And then these two old mountains smile and nod, and looking above the clouds that covered the heads of younger ones, they, giants in solitude, become reconciled. The lesser ones then peep through the rising mist, and smile to catch their estranged parents making up.

Leaving these grand scenes, the mountains, smaller, waste away into gentle hills, and we feel that we have passed the portals of a paradise, shut out from ocean storms by great barriers of rocks. The river grows narrow, the banks are perpendicular walls of solid rocks of moderate height. Rounding a turn in the river, suddenly comes to view "The Dalles," a small city near the river brink, nestling in an amphitheatre, formed by curved walls of rocky bluffs. In times past The Dalles was a starting-point for the mines of Eastern Oregon and Idaho, and was, also, the seat of a United States fort. Its streets have felt the tread of merchant princes, and miners of every grade and colour; of the tramping of bands of Indian ponies brought here to be sold or to parade some red man's wealth; of heavily ladened wheels bearing merchandise.

Busy throngs peopled then its streets, but now they are less merry; business has taken long strides toward surer success and larger life. Long years ago it was a great resort for Indians, who came to feast and gamble, and exchange captive slaves. Many old legends date from this post, and some of them are rich in historic truths; others in romance of human lives, and, others still, of fairy tales and ghostly stories.

A few miles above the city the river passes between almost perpendicular walls of stone, while through the narrow gorge the water leaps from ledge to ledge in quick succession, making huge billows of the rushing current, so rapid that no steamer or canoe has ever upward passed, though both have downward been in perfect safety. At this point the great schools of salmon, on their journey to the lakes and smaller streams, halt to rest, and thus prepare themselves for more severe struggles and more daring feats. Here the red men have, year after year, come to lay in supplies of salmon.

These fisheries are of great value, and, when the Portland, Dalles, and Salt Lake Railroad is completed, will become sources of untold wealth, furnishing Eastern markets with choicest salmon. Before leaving this fishery, I would state, for the information of by readers, that the Indians have some peculiar ideas about salmon. They "run" at regular seasons of the year, and the Indians gather on the banks and make preparations for catching and preserving them; but they do not take the *first* that come up, because they believe that, since the "Great Spirit" furnishes them, they should be permitted to pass, in his honour, and because the *first* that come are supposed to be bolder, and will succeed in getting to better spawning-grounds in higher streams.

The females always precede the males, who follow several weeks later. No Indian would make use of the first fish caught, because of the sacrilege. As soon, however, as the "run" fairly begins, the Indians, in their way, give thanks, by dancing and singing. The ceremonies of opening the fishing seasons are serious and solemn in character.

The manner of taking salmon varies. Sometimes they use dip nets, attached to long poles resting in a crotch or fork, or, maybe, pile of rocks, as a fulcrum. Others, with spears made of bone, pointed at each end, attached by a strong cord of sinew at the middle to a shaft made of hard wood, with three prongs in the end, of each of which a socket is made, wherein one end of the bone spear is thrust, the cord attachment being of sufficient length to permit the escape from the socket of the spear.

Thus equipped a fisherman thrusts the three-tined spear into the water at random, and when a salmon is struck, the spear leaves the shaft; but, still secure, turns athwart the fish, and his escape is impossible. When he is landed the fisherman's work is done. The fish is turned over to the women and boys, and carried to a convenient camp, where the work of drying them is performed by first beheading and then splitting them in two lengthwise. They are spread on long scaffolds built on poles, and with occasional turning are soon dried by the air and sun. The average weight of salmon at this fishing is about fifteen pounds, though sometimes much greater. Some have been taken weighing sixty-five pounds each, and many of them forty pounds.

Another noticeable fact is that the nearer the ocean they are taken the better. Those which succeed in stemming the many rapids *en route* to the headwaters are poor and thin, and of little value. They often ascend streams so small that they can be caught with the hand. It is doubtful whether they ever return to the ocean.

CHAPTER 10

Dangerous Place for Sinners

Leaving "The Dalles" early one morning in February, 1870, with Dr. W. C. McKay as guide, I set out on my first visit to Warm Springs Agency. Our route was over high grassy plains, undulating, and sometimes broken by deep *cañons*, occasionally wide enough to furnish extensive farm lands. Tyghe valley is traversed by two rivers that flow eastward from the foot of the Cascade mountains. It was, originally, a very paradise for Indians. It is a paradise still; but not for them. "White men wanted it;" hence our present visit to Warm Springs.

In 1855 the several Indian tribes occupying the country east of the Cascade mountains, as far up as John Day's, south of the Columbia River, and north of the Blue mountain, met in Treaty Council those who had been selected as the representatives of the government.

The Indians confederated, settling all their difficulties as between different tribes, and also with the government. They went into this council to avoid farther hostilities. From Dr. W. C. McKay I learned that a body of troops were present; that the Indians insisted on Tyghe valley as a home; that the government refused, and that the council continued for several days; that, finally, under threats and intimidations, the Indians agreed to accept a home on what is now "Warm Springs Reservation," the government agreeing to do certain things by way of furnishing mills, shops, schools, farms, etc.

At this time certain members of the Tenino band were in possession of, and had made improvements of value near, "The Dalles." Under special agreements in treaty council these improvements were to be paid for by the government.

Nineteen years have passed, and John Mission and Billy Chinook have not yet received one dollar for the aforesaid improvements. These men were converts to Christianity under the ministration of Father

Waller and others, who were sent out by the Methodist Church as missionaries. These Indians are still faithful to the vows then taken.

Here is a good subject for some humane, sentimental boaster of national justice to meditate upon.

Had these men broken their compact with the government, they would have been punished; and, had they been like other Indians who have figured in history, they would have been at last rewarded; not because the government is prompt to do them justice, but because they would have *compelled* justice to come to them, though filtered by blood through the bones of innocent settlers and sweetened by tears and groans of widows and orphans.

Strong language this, I admit; but history supports the declaration. For nineteen years have these two humble red-skinned men waited patiently for remuneration; for nineteen years have they waited in vain. Poor fellows, I pity you! Had you a vote to give, your claim might have been paid years ago. Then some ambitious politician, anxious to secure your suffrage, would have importuned the department at Washington to do you justice; and the department, anxious for influence in Congress, would have recommended payment, and some member would have found it to his interest to "log-roll" it through. But you are unfortunate; you cannot vote. You are no trouble; you are peaceable and faithful, and you *dare* not now make any noise about your claim. You are dependent on a government that has so much more important business to look out for, you are unknown.

Rebel once against your masters, and millions would be expended to punish you. A few thousands would make you rich, and would redeem the honour of the other "high contracting power." But you will not be made glad now in your old age, because you are but "Injuns," and the good ones of your people "are all underground." So say your white brethren, who now own what was once your country. Be patient still. The God, of whom you learned from the lips of the honoured dead, will yet compel a nation of conquerors to drink the bitter dregs of repentance, and though you may never handle one dollar of the money due you, your children may. And somewhere in the future your race may come upon the plane where manhood is honoured without the question of ancestry being raised.

Climbing a steep bluff, going south from Tygh valley, we look out on an extensive plain, bordered by mountain ranges, facing us from the further side. Forty miles brings us, by slow and ever-increasing easy grades, to the summit of the plain, where the road leads down a mountain so steep, that two common-sized horses cannot even manage a light carriage without rough-locking the wheels. From the starting-point into the chasm below, a small stream, looking like a bright ribbon that was crumpled and ruffled, may be seen. Down, down we go. Down, still down, until, standing on the bank of Warm Springs river, we behold the ribbon transformed into a rapid rushing current of snow-water, whose very clearness deceives us in respect to its depth. We drive into it at a rocky ford, and we are soon startled with the quick breathing of our team, while the water seems to rise over their backs, and we, standing on the seat, knee deep, encourage our horses to reach the other shore.

For nineteen years has the business of this agency been transacted through this current. We are on the other side, vowing that "Uncle Sam" *must* and *shall* have this stream bridged. So vowed our predecessors, and so our successors, too, would have vowed had they ever passed that way. A few miles from the crossing and near our road we see steam ascending, as if some subterranean monster was cooking his supper and had upset his kettle on the fires where it is supposed wicked people go. The nearer we came to the caldron the more we were convinced that our conjectures were correct, and stronger was our resolve to keep away from such places. Brimstone in moderate quantities scattered along the banks of this stream adds to our anxiety to reach a meeting-house, where we may feel safe.

This spring gives name to the Reservation, though twelve miles from the agency; to reach which, we climb up, up, up once more to another high sterile plain, devoid of everything like vegetation save sage bush. Mile after mile we travel, until suddenly the team halts on a brink, and we, to ascertain the cause, alight. Looking down, away down below glimmer a dozen lights. Tying all the wheels of our vehicle together and walking behind our team for safety, we go down into this fearful opening in the surface of the earth, and find "Warm Springs Agency" at the bottom of the chasm.

The country comprising this Indian Reservation is desolate in the extreme; the only available farming lands being found in the narrow *cañons* hemmed in by high bluffs. The soil is alkaline and subject to extreme drought.

The Indian farms are small patches, irregular in shape and size. They were originally enclosed by the government at great expense.

Remnants of the old fences may be seen, bearing witness of the way in which government fulfilled its promises: round blocks of wood, on some of which the decaying poles still lie, the blocks being from ten to twenty feet apart; above them other poles were staked, and thus the fences were made.

Calculation on the cost of this fencing would probably exhibit about five dollars per rod. In later years the Indians have rebuilt and improved fences and houses.

The department farm occupies the *best* portion of the valley, and is cultivated for the benefit of the *department*; seldom, if ever, furnishing supplies or seed for Indians. The government buildings are generally good, substantial and comfortable for the *employés*.

The schools are not well attended, and are of but little value to the Indians,—the fault, however, resting principally with the Indian parents, who seem to have but little control over their children, and do not compel attendance.

A large number of the Indians are professedly Christian, and are making progress in civilization. The remainder are followers of "*Smoheller*," the great dreamer,—a wild, superstitious bigot,—whose teachings harmonize with the old religions of these people. The Christian Indians are anxious for their young men to learn trades, and become like white men in practices of life.

The others are tenaciously clinging to the old habits of wild Indians,—isolating themselves from the Christian Indians and the agent.

Thus a wide difference is manifest among these people, apparently growing out of their religions. This is the real cause of difference; but why this difference exists is a question that is not difficult to answer.

The Indians who were located near the agency, where they could attend Christian service, were almost all of them Christianized; while those whose houses were remote from the agency, thus left to care for themselves, were followers of "*Smoheller*." Had these people been permitted to select Tygh valley, in 1855, *all* of them might have been civilized; because then all would have had productive farms and been under the immediate eye of the agent.

If, then, they were compelled to accept homes that did not furnish them the means of subsistence and employment, it is the natural conclusion and the legitimate result of the bad management of the government when making the treaty under which the Indians accepted this great fraud in lieu of their own beautiful homes.

The climate of Warm Springs differs materially from that of Grand Round, Siletz, or Alsea, being sheltered by the Cascade mountains from the heavy rains of the Willamette valley, but, being much higher, is dryer, and in winter much colder. The mountains act as a great refrigerator; hence snows are common, though seldom to an extent that prevent cattle and horses from living through without being fed.

The people are somewhat different in physique and habit. They are braver, and more warlike, and, in times past, have demonstrated their right to that character. Since they became parties to the treaty of 1855, they have, in the main, been faithful to the compact, the exceptions being those who were led away by the religion of "*Smoheller.*" Nothing serious has yet grown out of this "new departure." What may occur hereafter depends entirely on the management of the department.

In the treaty of 1855 the confederated bands of middle Oregon reserved the right to the fishery at "The Dalles," of which I have written at some length, on a former page. In 1866 a supplemental treaty was made with them by my predecessor,—the late Hon. J. W. P. Huntington,—by which the Indians released all claim to said fishery. The consideration was paltry, but was promptly paid by the government, and has long since been expended.

The Indians who were parties to the two treaties referred to declare, most emphatically, that they did not understand the terms of the latter one; that they only consented to relinquish, so far as the *exclusive right* to take salmon was considered; but that they supposed and understood that they were still to enjoy the privilege in common with other people. A careful examination of the said treaty discloses the fact that they had entirely alienated all their right and interest thereto.

When the lands covering these fisheries were surveyed and selected as State lands, they were taken up by white men and enclosed with fences, preventing the Indians and others from having access thereto except on payment of a royalty or rental. The Indians, not understanding the right of the parties in possession, opened the enclosure, and really, in violation of law, went to the grounds where they and their fathers had always enjoyed, what was to them almost as dear as life, the privilege of taking salmon.

A compromise was made, the Indian Department paying the claimant the damage done to the growing crops through which the Indians had passed to the fishery. I submitted the question of releasing this land to the department at Washington, and also to the State land officers. The government, and State land agent, Col. Thos. H. Cann, manifested a willingness to do justice to the wards of the government.

No further action was ever taken, to my knowledge, by the federal authorities. I suppose that it was overlooked and forgotten. The injustice stands yet a reproach to a forgetful government.

"A bargain is a bargain," so says the white man; and truly enough it may be held right in a legal view to compel the Indians to submit to whatever ey may agree to. But there was a wrong done them in this instance that ought to have been undone. The plea, that so long as they were permitted to make annual visits to the Columbia river to take fish, would interfere with their civilization, because of the bad influences of vicious white men with whom they came in contact, and urged in justification of the treaty whereby they yielded their rights in the premises, was a severe commentary on American Christian civilization, but may have been just.

It is a fact that cannot be questioned, that the virtue of the natives, until debauched by association with *low whites*, is far above that of the latter, and that the Indian suffers most by the contact. Had the commissioners who conducted the treaty of 1855 consented to select Tygh valley for a Reservation, no necessity would have existed for the Indians to obtain fish for subsistence.

Warm Springs Agency I have and ever will declare to be unfit for civilized Indians to occupy. Since they were compelled to take up their abode thereon, not one season in three, on an average, has been propitious for raising farm products. When a people hitherto accustomed to ramble unrestrained, are confined on a reservation that has not the necessary resources to sustain them, they should be permitted the privilege of going outside for subsistence.

Shame on a powerful people who would deny them this privilege; yet it is done. While these Indians on Warm Springs have had many hindering causes why they should not progress, they have nevertheless made decided advancement in the march from savage to civilized life. The fact of their living on unproductive soil has not been the only impediment in their way. To enable my readers to understand more fully this subject, I will introduce the subjoined letter from the present acting agent on Warm Springs Reservation,—Captain John Smith. Early in February, 1874, I addressed a letter to him, stating my purpose of writing this volume, and requested him to furnish me with such facts as he would be willing to have appear in my book over his own signature.

CHAPTER 11

The Parson Brownlow of the Indian Service

To my readers of the Pacific coast, I need say nothing in commendation of this writer. He is too well known to require an introduction. But that his communication may be appreciated by those who do not know "The Captain," it may be well to state that he is a member of the old-school Presbyterian church, has long resided West, is respected by all who know him, as a man of unimpeachable honour and integrity. His heart is in his work, and he talks and acts toward the Indians under his charge more as a father than as an officer. A zealous churchman and partisan, he is positive in character, and fearless as a speaker; while he may be lacking in some minor qualities, he has so many important and useful ones that qualify him for his position, that the deficiency, if any, is not felt. As a Christian civilizer of Indians he ranks with Father Wilber, of Yakama, and other noble-hearted men.

Warm Springs has been assigned to the Methodist Church; yet so much confidence has Captain Smith inspired by his success, that they have not recommended his removal. In this they have consulted the higher and purer motives that should, and often do, control men in important matters. *He* should be permitted to hold his office *during life.*

This communication, coming from such a man, is worthy of careful consideration; touching, as it does, the key-notes of the great question of the Christianization of the Indians.

Warm Springs Agency, Oregon.

Hon. A. B. Meacham:—

My dear Sir,—Believing that the work you contemplate publishing is designed to teach the minds of men the capability of the Indian race to be morally, religiously and socially advanced; and having had the experience of a residence of some seven years among the confederate tribes and bands of Middle Oregon, as agent; and further believing that I have in some degree mastered the great problem of their civilization, I willingly contribute anything that may serve to give your readers a correct idea of the progress they have really made; and they are still going forward.

It will be necessary to go back to the time I first came among them. A more degraded set of beings I am sure did not exist on the earth, nor was the condition of most of the Indians on this coast much better.

The mind of man would not conceive that human beings could get so low in the scale of humanity as they were; and I am sure, if they had been left to the instincts of their own wild and savage natures, they could never have been so low down as they were.

God's holy Sabbath was set apart as a day of licentiousness and debauchery. Drinking and gambling had become common. Their women were universally unchaste, and were taught to believe that lewdness was a commendable practice, or even a virtue.

Diseases and death were entailed on their posterity. The men had to submit at the point of the bayonet; the consequence was, the Indians had lost all confidence in the honesty and integrity of white men.

This state of affairs was principally owing to the military being brought into close proximity to them. Some of the officers had built houses, and were living with Indian women.

After I came here (the military having been removed previously) the Snake Indians commenced making raids on the Reservation.

I was asked "if I wished the military to protect us." I answered, "No." I preferred the raids of the Snake Indians to the presence of the soldiers; for I doubted if I would be able in twenty years to wipe out the evidences of the military having been amongst them; and I am sorry to say, that the agents and *employés* set over them to teach them had also contributed largely to their degradation.

One of the agents has been frequently heard to say, "that he thought the best way to civilize the Indians was to *wash out* the colour." They had accomplished what they were able to in that line. While it is certain that one agent came here a poor man, and went away wealthy, to say nothing of the lesser pickings which employers and contractors were allowed to take.

How to restore the lost confidence in the white man seemed on my arrival a herculean task. My first work was to get rid of all contaminating influences, by discharging bad men and filling their places with good, moral, and religious persons. The reformation at first seemed slow, but gradually increased from day to day. I was soon able to start a Sabbath school, and divine services were held every Sabbath.

The Indians, old and young, were placed in classes, and appropriate teachers set over them. Soon our large and commodious house of worship was filled to its utmost capacity by old and young, male and female, all seemingly eager to pick up the crumbs of comfort that fell from God's holy word; and from Sabbath to Sabbath this was continued.

Then came a change; officers from the army were ordered to relieve agents. The Sabbath was soon disregarded; Christian and moral men had their places made unpleasant, and were compelled to resign. Their places were filled by others who cared for nothing of the kind, and everything was relapsing into its former condition.

When I was again permitted to return I found things but little better than when I first came. However, I immediately set to work again, and, I think I can truly say, with full success. We have now three Bible-classes that read a verse around, and seem to comprehend very well what they read.

The old men are all in a class, and a person is appointed to read a chapter and explain it to them every Sabbath day. Many who cannot read can quote a large amount of Scripture. Quite a number, both men and women, lead in prayer, and many families maintain family worship, seemingly living Christian lives. We give out a psalm; many of the young people find it about as readily as we do, and can lead the music. The first week of the new year was observed as a national prayer-meeting, which was well attended; some for the first time acknowledging Christ as their Saviour. We have at this time nearly one hundred professing to live Christian lives, and we seem to be adding, from day to day, such as I hope will be saved. Our day-school has been a great success for the last two years; before that it was a failure, and I am now convinced that it was the fault of the teachers not understanding the management of Indian children. We have quite a number of children who read and speak fluently, commit to memory easily, using the slate to advantage, demonstrating their capability to learn as readily as white children, provided they can have the same advantages.

There are white children in the school who do not advance as rapidly as some of the Indian children, thus exploding the general opinion that, as a race, they are merely imitative beings, but cannot originate an idea. The true Indian character, I fear, is very little understood, and still it seems almost anybody can write lectures on it, and with about as much truth in them as Æsop's fables contain.

I have found them much more susceptible of moral and religious advancement than the white man, giving them the same opportunities; and I account for it in the fact that you never find an infidel among them unless made so by white men. They all acknowledge a Supreme Being that overrules all things. They may have a very crude notion of the worship due to such a Creator, but so soon as they are taught the true worship, they become very zealous, and they have no scoffers to discourage them.

One fatal error has been in admitting them into churches, without any change of heart, to enjoy all its privileges; consequently they were not restrained by any inward principle, and never became any better. To make a Christian religious, intelligence, as well as zeal, is necessary. If we are to be judged by God's law, we should be acquainted with it, and it is as needful for an Indian as for a white man to know *that* law in order to become a Christian.

The Catholics take them into the church, whether converted or not; and they are never made any better, but rather worse, for they are kept ignorant and superstitious. This was the case here, and these Indians are well aware of these facts. I have my doubts if a single Indian can be found on this coast that has been made any better by the Catholics.

I am credibly informed that they say mass in the morning, then run horses and play cards the remainder of the day; and all this

118

under the eye of the priest.

At the time of my coming here polygamy was indulged to the fullest extent. Their women were bought and sold, and used as beasts of burden, and when old, were kicked out at pleasure, to get their living as best they could, or die of want.

I immediately set myself to work to remedy this evil, by telling them it was in violation of God's holy word; then I was asked why we did not put a stop to it among the Mormons. I finally succeeded in securing a law prohibiting it in the future; allowing all who had more than one wife to get rid of her as best they could, but any one violating the law should be punished by fine or imprisonment.

I was soon after enabled to pass an amendment that where there was more than one wife, if one wished to leave, their husbands had no control over them. Under this rule nearly all had left.

On last Sabbath, a woman got up in church and said she was fully convinced that she had been living in violation of God's holy word. She had lived with her husband a long time; he had always treated her well, and she loved him,—but she loved her Saviour more, and for the sake of heaven and happiness she had to give him up. She was much affected. I was reminded of the words of our Saviour when he said, he had "found no such faith, no, not in Israel."

Her confession has led others to the same conclusion; and I think we can truly say, the days of polygamy are ended among these people, or soon will be. The merchandise of their women was a source of great annoyance to them. Their girls brought from three to ten head of horses, owing generally to the manner their parents were able to dress them for the market. This system was very hard to get rid of, but it has entirely ceased for the last three years. By law they are required to be married by the agent; for violation of this law they are punished. No divorces are granted, except in cases of adultery. Cards, or any other devices for gambling, found about their premises, make them liable to a fine of twenty-five dollars, or ten days' work on the highway; as does, also, gambling, or drinking ardent spirits, and refusing to tell where it was obtained. Adultery is severely punished; and now I am able to add another law entirely prohibiting polygamy.

Our court consists of the "Head Chief" and six selected men,—

the agent presiding, an Indian acting as sheriff, who arrests and brings into court all offenders, and subpœnas witnesses. The councils are always opened by prayer by some of the Indians. Their agricultural affairs and social relations have undergone a great change. When I came among them they were wrapped up in their filthy blankets, eating their meals—if meals they could be called—off the ground like the pigs.

They had but few houses. Their crops probably did not exceed three hundred bushels in any season; they were living on the roots they digged in the mountains and the fish they caught in the streams, and not one pound of anything on the Reservation. I purchased for them a limited amount of seed—they packing it forty miles. This enabled them to raise five thousand bushels of wheat, with a good supply of assorted vegetables.

This seemed to give them new life, and they have been steadily increasing ever since.

Their crop, the last season, has been estimated at from twelve to fifteen thousand bushels of wheat, with an abundance of vegetables of all kinds.

Now they have some forty houses, with logs hauled and lumber partly sawed for perhaps twenty more.

Many families sit around tables well furnished with the luxuries common with white people. As to their dress, they will compare very favourably with many country congregations.

The women and children come to church clean and nice, many of them dressed equal to white women.

I have built a house, 18 × 42 feet, for a female school. In this house, if I shall remain here a short time longer, I shall expect to accomplish much, as I propose to teach their women domestic economy,—a thing they are very little acquainted with, as are they also with the preparation of vegetable foods, to make them palatable; and for this reason they are less used than they should be, and they depend too much on the chase and fisheries.

This makes it necessary to leave their homes at times, and keeps up filthy habits, and their homes are not made comfortable as they would be if they looked to the ground for support; and they could be better induced to give up the chase and become settled and comfortable, much to the benefit of their health.

During the last year probably less than one half of the usual number left the Reservation in search of food, and I find the increase in numbers has been surprising. In roaming around, their children can never be educated, as they only come to school in the winter months, and forget what they learn by the next winter.

The sooner Indians can be brought to look to the earth for a support, the better; or, in other words, the Bible and the plough are the only civilizers of the human family.

That has been my experience with these Indians, notwithstanding the scoffs and jeers of *infidels*, who would like to bring all mankind down to a level with the wild and barbarous Indians; and these are generally the kind of men who wish them transferred from the civil to the military authorities.

This experiment has been tried, and we have seen the result. They may have been in some measure controlled, but never made any better,—always worse. Their object has been to control them,—not to civilize them.

President Grant's humane policy *has done more towards civilizing the Indians than all things heretofore done*; and it is yet in its infancy, while everything that could be has been brought to bear against it, to make it unpopular if possible.

Here let me say a word in regard to yourself. I have the fullest confidence that the earnest manner in which the work was seconded and pushed forward during your superintendency has greatly contributed to its success among the Indians of Oregon, who, I think, can compare favourably with any others in the United States.

Good results were apparent among these Indians, and I presume also others, immediately after the holding of that general council at Salem in the fall of 1871. What they saw and heard there gave them faith in the good intentions of the government towards them, and encouraged them to try and do something for themselves; and your general manner of treating and talking to them was well calculated to inspire them with confidence and a desire for improvement.

These Indians have been repeatedly advised to leave the Reservation by designing men, on the ground that under the fourteenth amendment to the Constitution they are citizens, entitled to both settle where they please, and to enjoy all other rights appertaining to citizenship.

They have succeeded in drawing away something over a hundred, who are roaming over the country; and some fears are entertained that should the military attempt to force them to return there may be trouble, and perhaps a repetition of Modoc scenes.

If this should be the case, the fault clearly would not be with the policy of the administration, but with its enemies, who by their mischievous interference have induced the Indians to leave.

I think the facts will bear me out in the statement that if the only contact of the Indians with the whites had been with true Christian men, there never would have been any, or, at least, very little trouble with them.

The cases are not wanting where men of high moral and Christian character have succeeded admirably in controlling Indians, by showing decision and firmness where it was needed, leniency and favour where it was appreciated, and dealing honestly and honourably in all things.

The results shown, where the contact was between them and such men, even though it did not continue for any great length of time, indicate clearly enough what might have been the present condition of these "wards of the nation" if none but good influences had been brought to bear upon them. We should have heard fewer details of revolting massacres, there would have been fewer costly wars and campaigns, that now go to fill up the pages of U. S. history; and it is no idle fancy, but a logical deduction, to presume that they might at present be self-supporting, instead of at the expense they now are, and must be for some time to come; if indeed they were not able to contribute something to the support of the government. Very much might be said on this subject, but as you probably prefer facts to theories, incidents to deductions, I will not intrude mine upon you.

Hoping that your work may be successful in assisting to lead people to form just and correct conclusions and ideas in regard to the Indian question,

I remain,

Yours respectfully,

John Smith,

U. S. Indian Agent at Warm Springs, Oregon.

Here is a man talking of a subject who knows whereof he writes;

so far at least as relates to his own experience and observation.

His success, as declared by his letter, is established by many living witnesses, and the anthems of praise that go up from this mountain home of the red men.

The reader who peruses the foregoing letter will not fail to discover that Captain Smith's heart is in the work, and that he is animated by a true Christian spirit in his labours with his people.

I do not, however, endorse all his strictures on the effects of the Catholic Church, in its labours in behalf of the Indian race. I know many worthy men, who are honestly labouring for them, who are members of the Catholic Church. There is a difference in the polity of that and Protestant Churches, and, however strong my own prejudices may be in favour of the latter, I am not insensible to the fact that the Catholic Church has manifested a great interest in these people. Let them be judged by their works.

Unfortunately for the world, Christianity has not, and does not, divest its followers of the common inheritance of poor weak human nature, and of the passions and prejudices that close our eyes to the virtues and honour due those who differ from us. More charity, more justice, preached and practised, would make man far happier.

In December, 1871, I visited Warm Springs Agency. I remained several days; during which time a series of meetings were held at the agency. From the record kept of that meeting I make a short synopsis. Agent Smith, when his people were assembled in the schoolhouse, called on an Indian to offer prayers. I confess that I was somewhat surprised to witness the response, by a man whose childhood had been passed in a wild Indian camp, and whose youth had witnessed scenes of warfare against the white man, and who had been compelled to accept this poor home, in lieu of the beautiful prairies of "John Day's" river country,—the name of a branch of the Columbia. A hymn was sung by the people. Nowhere have I ever seen exhibited a more confiding trust in God than was shown by them.

After the preliminaries were over, a discussion was opened on the several matters pertaining to the interests of the Indians,—their church, school, business matters, investment of funds, etc.

The social and civil customs were brought up. We insisted that polygamy was a great crime, and that they should abolish the law permitting it.

The meeting increased in interest and earnestness for several days. We finally proposed that those of them who were willing should come out squarely and renounce all their old ways, and take new names, or, at least, add to their old ones a plain American name. The people were warmed in their hearts. The occasion was one of intense interest. Here were those who had come up from a low, debased condition, through the labours of Christian white men, until they stood on the threshold of a higher life than they had as yet known. It was to them an important step.

The speeches made gave evidence of thought and forecast of mind. They did not rush blindly forward without counting the cost.

This scene reminds me of a Methodist camp meeting in olden time, when people were moved by some invisible power to flee from the wrath to come; when the preacher would call, and exhort, and pray, and a great overshadowing presence touched all hearts, and drove away careless thoughts and selfish purposes, and the multitude would seem to melt and mingle in common sympathy; when saints could throw their arms around sinners, and make them feel how much they loved them, and how earnestly they desired their salvation; when brave old sinners hesitated, faltered and trembled, and strong, brave Christians would then renew the contest in behalf of religion.

Men who had knocked elbows for life would meet at a common altar, or gather in knots and surround some stubborn, hard-hearted sinner, who, with thoughtful brow, would whittle sticks and spit, and whittle again, sometimes throwing the chips away from him, indicating "I won't;" and then, when some more pointed word of argument, or love, was sent home to the sinner's heart, he would turn the stick and whittle the chips toward him, thus saying, "I may;" until at last, when the preacher calls, "Who will be the next?" the repentant one drops his stick, shuts his knife, draws his bandanna to his eyes, starts forward, escorted by his pious exulting friends, who clear the way for the now penitent man.

The preacher comes down from the stand, clapping his hands, and with streaming eyes shouts, "Thank God, another sinner has turned to the Lord!" extends his hand, and utters a few kind words in the listening ear, and resumes, "Who will be the next?"

A cowardly sinner, who dares not come out from the world, and is not brave enough to stand before the battery of divine power, turns and flees, not from the wrath to come, but from the means that are intended to make him whole. He is followed by kind-hearted Christian friends and brought back, and he, too, surrenders; and the preacher says, "Thank the Lord!" and the brethren shout, "Amen! Amen."

And thus the work goes on until all are converted, or give evidence of penitence, save, perhaps, some strong-willed, hard-hearted, cool-headed one, and then especial efforts are made in his behalf. If he does, at last, yield his stubborn will, the joy is unbounded.

This picture I have made, is a true one of western camp-meetings, and equally true of the Indian meeting held at Warm Springs in December, 1871. I was to that what the presiding elder was to a camp-meeting. Capt. Smith was the "preacher in charge." After one or two days of speech-making, when all hearts were thoroughly aroused, the proposition above referred to was made. I shall never forget the scene that followed. "Who will be the first to throw away his Indian heart, laws, customs, and be from this day henceforth a white man in everything pertaining to civilization?" Silence reigned; all eyes turned toward "Mark," head chief. He realized the situation, saw how much of the welfare of his people depended on his example. He saw, besides, his three wives and their ten children.

He arose slowly, half hesitating, as though he had not fully made up his mind what to do. The presence of his women embarrassed him. He said, "My heart is warm like fire, but there are cold spots in it. I don't know how to talk. I want to be a white man. My father did not tell me it was wrong to have so many wives. I love all my women. My old wife is a mother to the others, I can't do without her; but she is old, she cannot work very much; I can't send her away to die. This woman," pointing to another, "cost me ten horses; she is a good woman; I can't do without her. That woman," pointing to still another, "cost me eight horses; she is young; she will take care of me when I am old. I don't know how to do; I want to do right. I am not a bad man. I know your new law is good; the old law is bad. We must be like the white man. I am a man; I will put away the old law."

Captain Smith, although a Presbyterian, behaved then like an old-fashioned Methodist, shouting, "Thank God! Thank God, the ice is broke!"

Mark remained standing, and resumed: "I want you to tell me how to do right. I love my women and children. I can't send any of them away; what must I do?" The old chief was moved, and his upheaving breast gave proof that he was *a man*. Silence followed, while he stood awaiting the answer,—a silence that was felt.

Here was a people, in the very throes of a new life, making effort to overcome the effects of savage birth and education. The heart of this question was bared. This old superstition was still lingering in their lives, part and parcel of the very existence of the people. It remained with them even after they had put away their religious faith and accepted that of their Christian teachers.

We had long before seen the struggle that it would cost,—the embarrassments that polygamy threw into the question. Our mind was made up, or we thought it was, and, motioning the chief to be seated, we arose and said:—

I know how much depends on my words. This is a great question. It has always been a hard thing to manage. My heart is not rock. I sympathize with you; Captain Smith feels for you. We will tell you what to do. No man after this day shall ever marry more than one woman. No woman shall ever be sold. The men that have more than one wife must arrange to be lawfully married to one of them. The others are to remain with him until they are married to other persons, or find homes elsewhere. If they do not marry again, the husband must take care of them and their children.

After a few moments, the chief arose, and said, "I understand; that is right. I will give all my wives a choice. I will be a white man from this day;" and then, advancing toward the desk, he was welcomed by friendly greeting from the white men present.

Holding him by the hand I said to him, "I welcome my red brother to our civilization. You are now a man; our people do not consider the colour of a man; it is his heart, his life. What name will you take?"

He hesitated, looking down for a moment; then raising his eyes to my own with earnest gaze, he inquired if he might take my name, saying that he liked it because it sounded well.

Acknowledging the compliment, I extended my hand, and addressed him as Mr. Mark Meacham, which was greeted with great applause. His second wife, Matola, arose and made a short speech, inquiring what was to become of her and her children. "Is your heart made of stone? Can I give Mark up? No I won't; he will want my children. I want them. I won't go away. I am his wife. I am satisfied with being his second wife; we did not know it was wrong. Nobody told us so. We get along well together. I won't leave him; I am his wife."

The plan was explained, and she was reconciled. John Mission was next to follow Mark, saying, "that when he was a small boy, he first heard about the new law. He had waited for the time when his people would come to it. They have come now. I am glad in my heart. I give you my hand."

Billy Chinook said, "I throw away the law my fathers made. I take this new law. I have two wives. They are both good. If anybody wants one of my wives, he can have her; if he don't, she can stay. Long time I have waited for the new law. It has come. I give you my hand."

Hand-shaking was renewed, and then one after another arose and made short speeches, and came forward and were enrolled; the captain growing warmer and more enthusiastic as each new name was entered on the roll. Nearly one hundred had come out squarely, and we adjourned the meeting to the following day.

On reassembling, next morning, the invitation was renewed, and nearly all of the men present surrendered. Sitting moody, gloomy, silent, was a tall, fine-looking fellow, with a blanket on his shoulders. His name was Pi-a-noose.

He had been called on several times, but had not responded until near the close of this civil revival. Unexpectedly he laid aside his blanket and arose. Every eye was turned on this man, because he had opposed every new law. While he was a peaceable, quiet man, he was a strong one, and had always exercised great influence, especially with the younger men.

He began to talk,—breaking a breathless silence, because it was supposed that he would take a stand against the new law,—the Indian way of speaking of all new rules. His speech was one of vast importance to his hearers, and was as follows:—

I was born a wild Indian. My father was a wild Indian. A long time I have fought you in my heart. I have not talked much; I wanted to think. I have thought about the new law a great deal. I thought I would not have the new law. My heart says No! I cannot fight against it any longer. I am now going to be a white man. I will give up the old law.

He advanced towards the desk, and the captain, unable to restrain his emotions of pleasure, gave vent to exclamations of gladness by slapping his hand on the desk, while tears came to his eyes in proof of his pleasure. The handshaking that followed was of that kind which expressed more than words. A throng gathered around Pi-a-noose, congratulating him.

Here was a scene that would have touched the heart of man possessed of any feeling,—a savage transformed into a man! The world scoffs at such sentiments, because it seldom witnesses a spectacle so

127

grand in human life. Indians who have passed into that new life are like white men newly converted to Christianity. Our meeting adjourned with great demonstrations of pleasure on the part of all interested.

The captain called his *employés* together for prayer-meeting. A few Indians were present, taking part in the exercises. Strange sounds,— those of prayer going up from an Indian agency, where, in years agone, shouts of revelry and bacchanalian songs arose from throats that were used to the language of the *debauchee*; even officers, if history be true, had taken part in the disgraceful orgies.

This agency has two classes of Indians—one that are anxious to advance; the other who, adopting the religion of white men, are loth to abandon their old habits. The former are fast coming up to the estate of civilized, Christianized manhood. A few years more and the treaty will expire, and then those who are qualified should be admitted to citizenship, and the remainder removed to some locality where they could find suitable lands for cultivation. This will not probably be done. The government owes these people a debt that it may be slow in paying.

The Dalles fishery should be returned to them, and a peaceful enjoyment of its privileges guaranteed. Captain Smith should be permitted to remain with those for whom he has done so much, and who regard him with reverence. This may not be either, because the success of party will require another change in the policy.

A new administration may change the whole plan of civilization, and remand these Indians back to the care of their first masters, or into the hands of the politicians. In either event, it will be a misfortune to those who have advanced so much under the humane policy of the present administration. Warm Springs has had but two agents in eight years. This agency has legends and romantic stories connected with its people, one of which I propose to give in other connections.

CHAPTER 12

No Place Like Home—Squaws in Hoops and Chignon

Umatilla Agency has been mentioned on former pages. I return to it now to say something more of its people. It is under the management of the Catholic Church. It has had but *four* agents in ten years, is on a great thoroughfare between the Columbia River and Idaho. It has a good climate, abundant resources, and is of great value. An effort was made during 1871, to induce the Indians to consent to a removal.

The council convened at Umatilla Agency, Oregon, August 7th, 1871, consisting on the part of the government, of Superintendent A. B. Meacham, Agent N. A. Coonoyer, of Umatilla Agency, and John S. White, a citizen of Umatilla County, Oregon.

Hon. Felix Brunot, chairman of Indian Commission, was present; also, many of the citizens of the surrounding country. The council was organized with A. B. Meacham, president, Mathew Davenport, secretary, Donald McKay and P. B. Pamburn, as interpreters. The council continued six days, during which time the questions at issue were fully discussed. A few of the speeches made will be sufficient to give a correct understanding of the argument for and against the sale of their lands.[1]

The Indians were entirely untrammelled, and spoke without intimidation. After the council had been in session four days, in reply to the remarks of a chief, that they were not ready to talk yet, it was said, "We want you to talk first all you have to say."

This council was conducted on fair terms. The Indians freely expressed their wishes and mind on the subject, and the white men ac-

1. See Appendix to Chapter 12 for the several speeches on the subject of removal.

129

cepted the result.

On all the western coast there is not a fairer land than Umatilla. I do not wonder that the Indians love their homes on this reservation. They are, however, somewhat divided in religious practice; one part being members of the Catholic Church, the remainder Dreamers,— followers of *Smoheller*. Some of them have made advancement in civil life.

Wealth has been to them a curse, and not a blessing. Many of them have large herds of horses and cattle, and have not felt the necessity for labour. The few who have farms are prosperous, the land being of excellent quality, climate favourable, and market convenient. At the Oregon State Fair, 1868, some of them were awarded first prizes for vegetables.

Surrounded, as they are, by white men, they have been worsted by the contact.

Unlike the Indians of Grand Round, who owe much of their prosperity to the citizens for whom they laboured, the Indians of Umatilla are a rich, thrifty, proud people. They are fond of sports and games, and yield slowly to the advice of agents to abandon their habits. A few noticeable instances, however, to the contrary, are How-lish-wam-po, We-nap-snoot, and Pierre, together with a few others, who live in houses like citizens. Another instance is that of the widow of Alex McKay, a half-breed. This woman, of Indian blood, has been educated by white persons, keeps house in a respectable manner, dresses after fashion's style, though about one year behind it. When white ladies adopt new fashions this "Susan" waits to see whether it is perpetuated, and then adopts it just about the time her fairer sisters abandon it.

During one of my official visits, I was invited to "a social" at Susan's house. In company with the agent and his family I attended. The refreshments served would have done credit to any house-wife in any frontier country, though the manner of serving them was rather comical. Each person went to the table, taking edibles in hand, while coffee for twenty persons was served in, perhaps, half-a-dozen cups, passing from one to another.

The Indian women who were present were dressed "*à la Boston:*" painted cheeks, high chignons, immense tilting hoops, and high-heeled bootees.

The men were in citizen costume, Susan refusing to admit either man or maiden in Indian dress.

The dance, or *hop*, was also Boston, with music on a violin by a native performer. The first was an old-fashioned "French four." When the set was formed, they occupied the floor, leaving little room for wall-flowers. Dancing is a part of Indian life in which they take great pleasure.

In this instance the music was slow, very slow at the commencement, but increased in time, growing faster, while faster went the flying hoops, and faster yet went the music; and then the dancers would chase each other in quick succession through the figure until the fiddles failed and the dancers, exhausted, sat down. No cold kind of amusement, that.

After refreshments were again served, another set was formed, and gone through in the same manner. I noticed in this affair that the maidens selected partners.

Susan, in reply to the remark on the change, said that "the boys liked all the girls for partners, but the girls don't always like all of the boys for partners. The boys have had their own way long enough." This is an enterprising woman, and believes in woman's rights. She is doing her people much good, in their amusements especially. Nature's children, as well as those of higher society, are blessed with joyful spirits, and a longing for recreation.

Susan has sense enough to know that she cannot, even if she would, prevent dancing, and wisely concludes to draw her people away from the old, uncouth, senseless dances of savages. Being herself a good Catholic, she is zealous for her church, and, since dancing is not prohibited, she succeeds in leading them into communion with religious people.

Whether the hearts of these converts are changed, I know not; their manners and customs are, and their ideas of right and justice much improved. For this reason, I commend this woman for her efforts to break up old, heathenish customs.

CHAPTER 13

"How-Lish-Wampo," King of the Turf

Umatilla is known to be a great country for horses. I doubt if anywhere on this continent there can be found horses of greater speed or powers of endurance.

The feats performed by those people on horseback are wonderful, and past belief by those who know western horses.

How-lish-wam-po, chief of the Cayuse (Kiuse), is owner of several thousand horses. He is a stout-built man, has a dark complexion, wears his hair just clear of his shoulders, and is now past middle age.

This man is a natural horseman, and a match for any man of any race in matters pertaining to horses. He is really king of the turf in the Umatilla country.

In conversation with him regarding horses, he remarked to me that he had horses that could carry a man one hundred miles in a day, and bring him home the next day. I shook my head, when he proposed to back his judgment by betting twenty horses. I am satisfied that he could have won the wager.

The racing habits of these people are well known, and many a white man has found more than his match.

I remember, one day in the spring of 1867, a man and boy passing my residence on the mountain bordering the Reservation. They were leading a fine-looking horse, with a fancy blanket over him. I suspected his purpose, and inquired his destination. In his answer I detected a rich Irish brogue and a tone that sounded somewhat familiar.

"It's meself that's going down to the Umatilla 'Risivation,' to have a bit of sport with the 'Injuns.' You see, I've been in Idaho this few years, and I've made me a nice bit of a stake; and I thought that, when I'd be going home, I might stop off at the Umatilla, and get even with them red-skinned boys that swindled me and Mike Connelly out of a few dollars when were going up,—so they did."

A few words of explanation, and I recognized him as the fellow who had, in partnership with another, bought an Indian pony, of which mention has been made in a previous chapter. I felt sympathy for him during his first adventure, and I did this time also, and said to him, "Be careful, Pat; you will lose all your money."

"Och! never fear; that fellow there has claned them all out in the Boi-se basin. Oh, but he is a swange cat, so he is; and he will show them how to take a poor man in when he's foot-sore and tired, so he will, too. Now, do you mind what I'm telling yous? That lad here can tell you how he flies. Och! but he's a swate one, so he is."

Pat went on his way with his heart full of hope. A few days after, the boy who had gone down with him returned homeward. To my inquiry about how Pat made out, racing horses, he shrugged his shoulders and replied, that "*the Injuns cleaned us out!*"

Another party, who had heard of the Umatilla race horses, passed down toward the Reservation. This man's name was French Louie. He had several fine racers with him. I learned his destination, and gave him a few words of caution. But he replied that he "knew what he was about." He had "a horse that had '*swept the track*,' all the way from the Missouri River, at Denver City, Salt Lake, Boi-se, and Baker City. Never fear. I'll teach those Indians something they never knew, before I get through with them."

Poor fellow, I felt sorry for him. On his arrival on the Reservation he found chances to invest his money. The men he came to teach were apt scholars in tricks that are shrewd.

He led out a horse, and made a small bet and *lost*, as he *intended* to. The next run the Indians played *him* the same game, until, thinking he had learned the speed of their horses, Louie proposed to wager all his money, horses, saddles, and, in fact, stake everything upon one race.

That man and his attendants went home on little ponies which the Indians gave them in charity.

How-lish-wam-po, chief of the Cayuses, is the owner of a horse with which he has challenged any and every sporting man in the country.

Several parties have visited Umatilla, bringing with them men and boys to drive home the herds of Indian horses they were "going to win."

One party imported a horse for the express purpose. He made known his desire, and he, too, soon found opportunity for an investment. The preliminaries were arranged, and the race was to be run over the Indian race-course, which was located on the bottom lands of Umatilla river, smooth, level turf, over two miles and a half in length.

At one end of this course a post was planted, round which the racers were to turn, and come back to the starting-point, making a distance of a little over five miles and a quarter.

Joe Crabb, the owner of the imported horse, had been present at a race months previous, when How-lish-wam-po had *permitted* his horse to be beaten; and as he had measured the distance, marked the time, and subsequently tested the speed of his horse with the winner, on that occasion, he, of course, had a "dead thing."

The white men came with groom and riders, making a camp near the Indian, standing guard over his own horse, to prevent accident.

The Indians were not so careful of their horse; at least Joe Crabb thought they were not, and, since everything is fair in gambling as in war, he concluded to *know* for himself how the speed of these two horses would compare.

He thought, as thousands of other white men have, that it was no harm to cheat an "Injun," no matter by what means.

There is a general belief that Indians sleep when their eyes are shut, and especially just *before daylight*.

Sending a careful, trusty man to get the Indian horse, leaving another in his place, he led his own out on the prairie, and made a few trials of speed with the two. The result was satisfactory. He found that his horse was able to distance the other.

Now How-lish-wam-po was the owner of two horses very nearly alike,—one the racer; the other half-brother to him, but not so fleet. They were "Pinto"—spotted horses; so the deception was complete.

The Indian horses are never stabled, groomed, shod, or grain-fed. Their system of training differs from a white man's very much. After a race is agreed upon, the animal is tied up to a stake or tree, and if he is fat, they starve him down, giving him only water. If, however, he is in good condition, they lead him out to grass, an hour or so, each day, and at nightfall they run him over the course.

In this instance the half-brother was tied up and put in training, and left *unguarded*, with the *hope* that Crabb would steal him out, and try his speed. Sure enough, he fell into the trap that How-lish-wam-po set for him. The real race-horse was miles away, under proper training.

The fame of this wonderful winner had spread far and wide, as did the news of the approaching contest.

When the morning agreed upon arrived, the roads leading to the valley of Umatilla gave full proof of the interest the people of the surrounding country had in this important affair.

They came from places several hundred miles distant, and from the settlements surrounding the Reservation.

The little towns furnished their quota, and the farmers excused themselves for going, hoping, as they told their wives at home, that they should meet someone with whom they had business. And through various devices nearly every man, and a part of the women, also, found excuse to be there.

I know how that was done; at least, I heard men tell how they managed.

People who never gambled with dollars, and would blush to own they were fast people, found their way to Umatilla.

The race-course which I have described was parallel with a low range of grassy hills, that rose by gentle slopes from the valley to an altitude of fifty to one hundred feet.

Long before the time for the race, carriages, buggies, wagons, and horses, might be seen standing on the hills, or driving over the green sward, while at the standing-point was assembled a great motley crowd, on foot and horseback.

The Indians were in their gala-day dress,—paints, feathers, long hair, red blankets; in fact, it was a dress-parade for white and red men too.

The manner of betting at an Indian race differs somewhat from affairs of the kind among white men. One man is selected as a stake-holder for all moneys. Horses that are wagered are tied together and put under care of Indian boys. Coats, blankets, saddles, pistols, knives, and all kind of personal effects, are thrown into a common heap and tied together.

As the starting-hour approaches, two judges are elected,—one white man and one Indian. But two are required, since the horses run out, turn the stake, and come back to the starting-point. The first horse to get home is winner. No account is made of the start, each party depending on his shrewdness to get the better in this part of the race.

Indians are enthusiastic gamblers, and have a certain kind of pride,

135

and to do them justice, honour, as well, in conducting their races. No disputes ever arise among themselves, and seldom with white men, growing out of misunderstandings, either about starting or the outcome. They take sides with their own people always, and bet, when the chances are against them, from pride.

The prevailing idea that they are always cool and stoical is not correct. They become very much excited at horse-races, but not generally until the race begins. While the preliminaries are being arranged, they are serious, even solemn-looking fellows, and with great dignity come up with the money to bet. "Capable of dissembling," I should think they were, from the cool face of How-lish-wam-po, when the money is being counted out by the hundreds, in twenty-dollar gold-pieces,—not a few, but handfuls of twenties. One could not have detected the slightest twinkle in his eye, or other sign that he knew that Joe Crabb had *stolen his horse*, and *run* him secretly. Cool, calm, earnest as if he were saying mass, this chieftain came up and handed over his money to the stake-holder, while numerous bets were being arranged between the other Indians and white men. Horses were wagered, and tied together, and led away. Many a fellow had brought extras with him, for the express purpose of gambling, expecting of course to take home twice the number in the evening.

Crabb had confided his secret about his stolen run to a few friends, and advised them to *go in*, and win all the horses they wanted. There was no danger; he knew what he was talking about. He had the Indian's horse's speed by time, and also by trial.

This thing leaked out, and was communicated from one to another. Some pretty good men, who were not accustomed to betting, became anxious to win a pony or two, and laid wagers with the Indians.

The trick that Crabb had played was finally made known to How-lish-wam-po. He and his people were cooled down, and seemed anxious to have the race come off before more betting was done.

This made the white men more anxious, and they urged, boasted, and ridiculed, until, in manifest desperation, the Indians began to bet again, and the *noble* white man generously took advantage of the Indian's hot blood, and forced him to make many bets that he appeared to shun.

The horses were brought out to start, and while the imported horse of Crabb's looked every inch a racer, the other stood with head down, a rough-haired, uncouth brute, that appeared then to be a cross between ox and horse.

The presence and appearance of the horses was the signal for another charge on the Indians, and a few white friends they had, who, having learned from the chief, the truth of Crabb's trick, came, in sympathy for the Indian, to his rescue.

Money, coats, hats, saddles, pistols, pocket-knives, cattle, horses, and all kinds of property, were staked on the race.

The Indians, in their apparent desperation, drove up another band of ponies, and in madness wagered them also.

Those of my readers who are accustomed to exhibitions around our "fair grounds," on days of "trials of speed," may have some idea of the scene I am trying to describe, except that few of them have ever seen so many horses tied together, and so large a pile of coats, blankets and saddles, as were staked upon this occasion.

When the final starting-time came, a pure-minded, innocent man would have felt great pity for the poor, dejected-looking Indians, at the sight of their faces, now so full of anxiety; and, certainly, the Pinto, who stood so unconcerned, on which they had staked so much, did not promise any hope; while his competitor was stripped of his blanket, disclosing a nice little jockey saddle, and silver-mounted bridle, his whole bearing indicating his superiority.

His thin nostrils, pointed ears, and arched neck, sleek coat, and polished limbs, that touched the ground with burnished steel, disdaining to stand still, while his gayly-dressed rider, with white pants tucked into boots embellished with silver-plated spurs; on his head, a blue cap, and with crimson jacket, was being mounted, requiring two or three experts to assist, so restless was this fine, thorough-bred to throw dirt into the eyes of the sleepy-looking Indian horse, which stood unmoved, uncovered, without saddle or bridle, or anything, save a small hair rope on his lower jaw, his mane and tail unkempt, his coat rough and ill-looking.

On his right side stood a little Indian boy, with head close-shaved, a blanket around him, and to all appearances unconscious that anything unusual was expected.

The other rider's horse was making furious plunges to get away.

How-lish-wam-po was in no hurry, really; indeed things were going very much to the satisfaction of that distinguished individual.

He was willing to see the other man's horse chafe and fret,—the more the better; and he cared nothing for the sponge that was used to moisten the mouth of the great racer.

Look away down the long line of white men and Indians; and on the low hills, above, see the crowd eager to witness the first jump!

The chief gives a quiet signal to the Indian boy. The blanket dropped from the boy's shoulders, and a yellow-skinned, gaunt-looking sprite bestrode the Indian horse, holding in his left hand the hair rope, that was to serve him for a bridle, and in his right a small bundle of dried willows.

Presto! The stupid-looking brute is instantly transformed into a beautiful animated racer. His eyes seemed almost human. His ears did not droop now, but by their quick alternate motion giving signs of readiness, together with the stamping of his feet, slowly at first, but faster and more impatiently the moment it was intimated he might go; and the other was making repeated efforts to escape, his masters manoeuvring for the advantage.

The little Indian boy managed his horse alone as the chief gave quiet signs. Three times had they come up to the scratch without a start. Crabb seemed now very solicitous about the race. I think, probably, he had by this time found the "hornet in his hat;" at all events, he was pale, and his rider exhibited signs of uneasiness.

At length, thinking to take what western sportsmen call a "bulge," he said, "Ready!"—"Go," said the little Indian boy, and away went twenty thousand dollars in the heels of the Indian horse, twenty feet ahead before the other crossed the mark, making the gap wider at every bound.

Away they sped, like flying birds. The crowd joined in shouts and hurras, hundreds of all colours falling in behind and following up.

Away go the flying horses, and several thousand eyes following the *yellow rider*, still ahead, as they grow smaller and smaller in the distance, until the Indian horse turns the stake at the farther end in advance. Now they come, increasing in size to the eye as they approach, the *yellow rider* still in advance. Crabb gasps for breath, and declares that his horse "will yet win."

The eagle eye of the old chief lights up as they come nearer, his rider still leading. Excitement is now beyond words to tell. Look again!—the Indian boy *comes alone*, rattling his dry willows over a horse that was making the fastest time on record, considering the nature of the turf.

The Indians along the line fell in, and ran beside the victorious racer, encouraging him with wild, unearthly shouts, while he comes to the starting-point, running the five miles and one-fourth and eighty-three yards in the unprecedented time of *nine minutes* and *fifty-one*

THE HORSE RACE.

seconds; winning the race and money, much to the joy of the Indians and their few friends, and to the grief of Crabb and his many friends. He, without waiting to hear from judges, ran down the track nearly a mile, and, rushing up to the gay jockey, with silver spurs, white pants, blue cap, and crimson jacket, who had dismounted, and was leading the now docile, fine-blooded English racer by his silver mountings, inquired, "What's the matter, Jimmy?"—"Matter? Why, this hoss can't run a bit. That's what's the matter."

Do my readers wonder now that so many white men, along the frontier line, declare that all good "Injins are three feet under the ground"?

Before leaving this subject, it is proper to state that How-lish-wam-po gave back to Crabb the saddle-horse he had won from him, and also money to travel on; and with a word of caution about stealing out his competitor's horse, and having a race all alone, remarking dryly, *"Me-si-ka wake cum-tux ic-ta mamook ni-ka tru-i-tan klat-a-wa* (You did not know how to make my horse run). *Cla-hoy-um, Crabb"* (Goodbye Crabb).

I will further state that many years ago these Indians had exchanged horses with emigrants going into Oregon, across the plains, and that this celebrated Indian race-horse is a half-breed.

The old chief refused to sell him, saying, "I don't need money. I have plenty. I am a chief. I have got the fastest horses in the world. I bet one thousand horses I can beat any man running horses."

He refused an offer of five thousand dollars for this renowned courser. Several efforts have been made to induce him to take his horse to the State fair.

He at one time consented, saying, "I will take my horse just to show the white men what a race-horse *is*." But he was unwell when the time came, and failed to go.

The question has been raised, whether this horse actually made the time reported. *I believe* he did. Competent white men have measured the course carefully, and several persons kept the time, none of whom marked over ten minutes, while others marked less than nine-fifty.

If any man is sceptical, he can find a chance to leave some money with How-lish-wam-po. The chief don't need it, because he has thousands of dollars *buried*, that once belonged to white men.

But he is human, and will take all that is offered, on the terms Joe Crabb made with him.

If there are real smart sports anywhere who desire a fine band of

140

Indian horses, they have here a chance to obtain them, without stealing. Take your race-horses to Umatilla, and you won't wait long. The probabilities are, that you may be disgusted with the *country very soon*.

For the benefit, it may be, of some of my readers, I would suggest that you have only to lead out the horse you propose running, and name the amount and distance. The Indians will find the horse to match the amount and distance, anywhere from fifty yards to one hundred miles. Don't be tender-hearted if you should win a few hundred ponies. They won't miss them. They only *loan* them to you to gamble on.

Having a long-standing acquaintance with How-lish-wam-po, as a neighbour, and subsequently as his "high *tyee* chief," I am authorized to say to Commodore Vanderbilt, Robert Bonner, "Uncle" Harper, Rev W H H Murray, or any other horse-fancier, clerical or unclerical, that a sufficient forfeit will be deposited by How-lish-wam-po, and his friends, in any bank in Oregon, to defray the expenses of any party who will measure speed with his horse, on his own turf, five and a quarter miles, turning a stake midway the race; said expense to be paid on the condition that the said parties win the race; in which event they can return with ponies enough to overload the Union Pacific Railroad, and make business for the "Erie" for a long time to come; with the proviso that How-lish-wam-po's race-horse is alive and in condition to make the run, as we believe that he is at this present writing, 1874.

Parties seeking investments of the kind will receive prompt attention by addressing How-lish-wam-po, chief of Cayuse, Umatilla Reservation, Oregon, *care Joe Crabb, Esq.*

This latter gentleman has been hunting this kind of a contract, in behalf of How-lish-wam-po, for several months, *unsuccessfully.*

The Umatilla Indians rear horses by the thousands, never feeding or stabling, but always herding them, when the owner has enough to justify the expense of hiring an Indian herder. The horses run in bands of fifty to one hundred, and seldom mix to any considerable extent. If however, there should be several bands corralled together, the master-horse of each band soon separates them. When turned out on the plains they are very exacting, and many a battle is fought by these long-maned captains, in defence, or to prevent the capture, by the others, of some one of their own.

Cayuse horses are small, from twelve to fifteen hands high; are of every shade of colour, and many of them white or spotted, bald-faced, white-legged and glass-eyed. They are spirited, though easily broken to the saddle or harness. As saddle-horses they are far superior to the common American horse, and for speed and power of endurance they have no equals.

The Indians are accurate judges of the value of their animals and have strong attachments for them; seldom disposing of a favourite except in case of real necessity.

The small scurvy ponies are sold in large numbers, for prices ranging from five to twenty dollars each. A medium-sized saddle-horse sells for about forty dollars; a first-rate horse, one hundred dollars; and if a well-tried animal that can make one hundred miles one day, and repeat it the next, one hundred and fifty dollars.

The small, low-priced ponies are capable of carrying a common man all day long, without spur or whip. They are bought by white men for children's use, and for ladies' palfreys. They are docile, tractable, and fond of being petted. I know a small white pony, with long mane, and not more than forty inches in height, that was taught many tricks,—going through the hotel dining-room, kitchen, and parlour; sometimes following his little mistress upstairs; lying down and playing dead horse, kneeling for prayers, asking for sugar, by signs; in fact,—a fine pet. And yet the little fellow would canter off mile after mile with his mistress.

Major Barnhart, of Umatilla, owned a small Cayuse, about thirteen hands high, that would gallop to the Columbia River, thirty-one miles, in two hours, with a man on his back, and come back again at the same gait.

I once made an investment of five dollars in an unbroken pony, paid an Indian one dollar to ride her a few minutes, took her home and gave her to a little daughter, who named her "Cinderella." After a few days' petting, she often mounted and rode her fearlessly.

This one was a bright bay, with a small star in the forehead, with long mane extending below the neck, a foretop reaching down to its nose.

The Indians teach their horses, by kindness, to be very gentle. Often on the visits which they make to old homes, a little *pic-i-ni-ne* (child) is securely fastened to the Indian saddle, and the horse is turned loose with the band.

On all their journeys they drive bands of ponies, presenting a grotesque scene: horses of all ages, sizes, and colours; some of them loaded with camp equipage, including cooking arrangements, tin pans, kettles, baskets; also bedding of blankets, skins of animals; always the rush matting to cover the poles of the lodge, and going pell-mell, trotting or galloping. The women are chief managers, packing and driving the horses.

An Indian woman's outfit for horseback riding is a saddle with two pommels, one in front, the other in the rear, and about eight inches high. The saddles are elaborately mounted with covers of dressed elk-skins, trimmed profusely with beads, while the lower portion is cut into a fringe, sometimes long enough to reach the ground.

These people seldom use a bridle, but, instead, a small rope, made of horsehair, in the making of which they display great taste. It is fastened with a double loop, around the horse's lower jaw. They carry, as an ornament, a whip, differing from ladies' riding-whips in this, that the Indian woman's whip is made of a stick twelve inches long, with a string attached to the small end, to secure it to the wrist. The other, or larger end, is bored to a depth of a few inches, and in the hole is inserted two thongs of dressed elk-skin, or leather, two inches wide and twenty in length.

The Indian woman is last to leave camp in the morning, and has, perhaps, other reasons, than her duties as drudge, to detain her; for she is a woman, and depends somewhat on her personal appearance especially if she is unmarried. If, however, she is married, she don't care much more about her appearance than other married women, unless, indeed, she may have hopes of being a widow some day. Then she don't do more than other folks we often see, who wish to become widows, said wish being expressed by feathers, and paint on the face and hair.

However, these Umatilla Indian maidens, who have not abandoned the savage habits of their people, are proud and dressy, and they carry with them, as do the young men, looking-glasses, and *pomatums*, the latter made of deer's tallow or bear's grease.

They also, I mean young people especially, carry red paints. Take, for illustration, a young Indian maiden of Chief Homli's band, when on the annual visit to Grand Round valley.

Before leaving camp she besmears her hair with tallow and red paint, and her cheeks with the latter. Her frock, made loose, without corset or stays, is richly embroidered with gay-coloured ribbons and beads, and rings of huge size, with bracelets on her wrists and arms.

Then suppose you see her mount a gayly caparisoned horse, from the right-hand side, climbing up with one foot over the high saddle, sitting astride, and, without requiring a young gent to hold the horse, place her beaded-*moccasined* feet in the stirrups, and, drawing up the parti-coloured hair rope, dash off at what some folks would call break-neck speed, to join the caravan.

No young man had ever caught up her horse from the prairie, much less saddled it. But, on the other hand, she has probably brought up and saddled for her father, brother, or friend, a horse and prepared it for the master's use.

The young men who are peers of this girl do not wait to see her mounted and then bear her company. Half an hour before, they had thrown themselves on prancing steeds, and with painted cheeks, hair flowing, embellished with feathers, and necklaces of bears' claws, and brass rings, and most prominent of all, a looking-glass, suspended by a string around the neck.

The women manage the train and unpack the horses, make the lodge in which to camp, while their masters ride along carelessly, and stop to talk with travellers whom they meet; or it may be dismount at some way-side house and wait until it is time to start for the camp, where the lodge is built for the night.

There are, however, Indian men who are servants, and these assist the women.

When the site of the camp is reached, our young squaw dismounts, and, throwing off her fine clothes, goes to work in earnest, preparing the evening meal, while the gay young men, and the old ones, too, lounge and smoke unconcerned.

Remember, I am speaking now of Homli's band of the Walla-Wallas. There are Christianized Indians on Umatilla Reservation, that have left behind them their primitive habits,—men of intelligence, whose credit is good for any reasonable amount in business transactions, and who occupy houses like civilized people. But the major portion are still wrapped in blankets, and thoroughly attached to the old customs and habits of their ancestors. They have a magnificent country, and are surrounded by enterprising white men, who would make this land of the Umatilla the most beautiful on the Pacific coast.

It may be many years before these people will consent to remove. In one sense it does seem to be a wrong, that so many prosperous homes as this should afford, must be unoccupied.

In another sense it is right, at least in that those who live upon it now are the lawful owners, and therefore have a right to raise horses on land that is worth five, ten, and twenty dollars per acre, if they choose. So long as they adhere to their old ways, no improvements may be expected. They will continue to raise horses and cattle, to drink whiskey and gamble, becoming more and more demoralized year by year; and in the meantime vicious white men will impose on them, often provoking quarrels, until some political change is made in the affairs of the government, and the present humane policy toward them will be abandoned, and then their land will become the spoils of the white man. It were better for these people that they had a home somewhere out of the line of travel and commerce; or, at least, those who continually reject civilization. It is not to the disadvantage of those whose hearts are changed that they should remain. While the government protects them they will enjoy the advantage of inter-course with business men. With those, however, who do not evince a willingness to become civilized, it is only a question of time, when they will waste away, and finally lose the grand patrimony they now possess.

I do not mean that it will ever be taken by force of arms, for the sentiments of justice and right are too deeply seated in the hearts and lives of the people of the frontier to permit any unjustifiable act of this kind to be committed; but designing men will, as they have ever done, involve good citizens in difficulties with Indians, who, so long as they cling to their superstitious religion, will retaliate, shouting "blood for blood;" and then the cry of extermination will be extorted from good men, who do not and cannot understand or recognize this un-just mode of redress.

Under the treaty with these Indians, they are to enjoy the privilege of hunting and grazing on the public domain in common with citizens; but this right is scarcely acknowledged by the settlers of places they visit, under the treaty.

CHAPTER 14
Snake War—Fighting the Devil With Fire

The south-western portion of Oregon is a vast plain, whose general altitude is nearly four thousand feet above the level of the sea. A greater part of it is an uninhabited wilderness of sage-brush desert. A few hundred Indians have held it for generations, except the narrow belts of arable lands along the streams. There, Indians are commonly called "Snakes," deriving the name from the principal river of the country.

The overland route to Oregon traverses this region for hundreds of miles. Many years ago the emigrants became engaged in a war with the few scattering bands of Indians along the route, and for many years hostilities continued. The origin of the first trouble is not known by white man's authority. The Indian story is to the effect that white men began it to recover stock, which they, the Indians, had purchased from other tribes. This may be correct, and may not; but that a relentless war was carried on for years there is no doubt, and, that in the aggregate, the Indians got the better of it.

The great overland route to the mining regions of Idaho in early days passed through this hostile country. Many valuable lives were lost, and a great many hundreds of horses, mules, and cattle were stolen. The Snakes were daring enemies, and brave fellows on the warpath, successful in making reprisals, and, having nothing but their lives to lose, were bold and audacious scouts. They kept a frontier line of several hundred miles in length in constant alarm. Life was unsafe even within the lines of settlement.

Owyhee-Idaho country was one of the bloody battle-grounds, the Indians waylaying travellers along the roads, and from cover of sage-

146

brush, or ledge of rocks, firing on them, and, in several instances, attacking stages loaded with passengers. At one time the stage was fired into on the road between Boise City and Silver City. The driver—Charley Winslow—and four passengers were killed and scalped. At another time, within ten miles of a mining town of two thousand inhabitants, Nathan Dixon, the driver of a stage-coach, was shot through the body and fell in the boot of the stage, a passenger by his side taking the lines and driving the stage-load of passengers out of danger. Poor "Nate!"—he paid the penalty of too brave a heart. He had been offered an escort at the station but one mile away, and declined it, saying, "He was not made to be killed by Indians."

H. C. Scott, a ranchman living on Burnt river, Oregon, with his family, consisting of a wife and two children, went in a two-horse wagon to visit a neighbour two miles away. On their return they were fired on by Snake Indians. Mr. Scott received his death-wound, his wife was also shot through the body, but with heroic coolness took the lines of the team, and drove home, with her murdered husband struggling in death on the floor of the wagon, his blood sprinkling her children and herself. She lived but a few hours and was buried with him. The children were unharmed, although several volleys were discharged after the flying team and its load.

On the road from "The Dalles" to Cañon City many skirmishes were had with these Indians. On one occasion they attacked the stage carrying passengers and the United States mail. The driver, Mr. Wheeler, was shot with a slug cut from an iron rod that had been used to secure the tail-board of a freight-wagon. The slug passed through his face, carrying with it several teeth from both sides of his upper jaw. Strange to relate, he drove his team out of further danger.

Not unfrequently freighters would lose the stock of entire trains, numbering scores of animals. Packers, too, lost their mule-trains. Lone horsemen were cut off, and murder, blood and theft reigned supreme in the several routes through the "Snake country."

A party of eighty-four Chinamen were killed while *en route* to the mines of Idaho. Helpless, unarmed Chinamen, they are game for the savage red men, and the noble-hearted white men also. One man, commenting on this occurrence, remarked that, "they had no business to be Chinamen. The more the Indians killed, the better." Instances of Indian butchery might be multiplied.

But, on the other hand, they in turn suffered in the same inhuman manner. Independent companies were organized to punish them, and punishment was inflicted with ruthless vengeance. Innocent, harmless Indians were murdered by these companies. Women were captured, or put to death. One circumstance will illustrate this feature of Indian warfare, as carried on by the white men. Jeff Standiford, of Idaho City, went in pursuit of savages with a company of white men and friendly Indians.

A camp was found and attacked. The men escaped, the women and children were captured. The old, homely women were shot, and killed; the children were awarded to the whites who distinguished themselves in their great battle against helpless women and children. The better-looking squaws were sold to the highest bidder for gold dust to pay the expenses of the expedition. But the fame of the company was established as "Indian fighters." When we hear of Indians doing such deeds, we cry "extermination," nor stop to learn the provocation.

This kind of Indian war continued several years, during the "great rebellion." One feature or sanitary cure on the part of the Snake Indians I do not remember to have seen in print. While they were poorly armed, and were cut off from supplies of ammunition, and especially of lead, they cut up iron rods from captured wagons, without any forges, into bullets. On the persons of Indian warriors who were killed and captured,—I say captured, because many were killed and carried off by their friends, to prevent mutilation, and because of their fidelity to each other,—were found iron slugs, stones that were cut into the shape of balls, and wooden plugs one or two inches in length, and one inch in diameter. These latter were used by them to stop haemorrhage. When a warrior was struck by a bullet, he immediately inserted a wooden stopper in the wound. Rude surgical treatment this, and yet they claim it to be of great value.

This "Snake war" afforded abundant opportunity for frontiersmen to learn the manly art of killing Indians; and they did learn it, and learned it well. Volunteer companies were enlisted to stand between the white settlers and the Snake Indians, while the regular army was withdrawn to assist in putting down the rebellion; and they *stood* there, some of them, and others *lay* there, and they *are* lying there to this day.

The famous Oregon poet, Joaquin Miller, earned his spurs as a war-man out on the plains fighting Snake Indians, and many others of less celebrity did likewise. But the handful of Snake Indians were harder to conquer than General Lee or Stonewall Jackson. General Lee touched his military hat with one hand, and passed over his sword with the other to General Grant, under the famous apple-tree, some months before.

E-he-gan, We-ah-we-wa and O-che-o had pulled down their war-feathers in presence of General Crook. When the drums of the Union army were beating the homeward march, General Crook was ordered to the frontier to whip the Snakes. Some of the regiments of the regular army were sent out to relieve the volunteers who garrisoned the military posts. Many a brave fellow who had returned from fighting rebels went out there to die by Snake bullets, and in some instances to be scalped.

They found a different enemy, not less brave, but more wily and cunning, who were careful of the waste of ammunition. These Snake Indians were not content to make war on white men, but continued to invade the territory of other Indians; particularly that of Warm Springs Reservation, and occasionally of the Umatilla; also, to capture horses and prisoners.

Among the exploits in this line, the carrying off a little girl, daughter of a chief of the Warm Springs, was the most daring, and perhaps the most disastrous, in its results to the Snakes; daring, because committed in broad daylight, and inside the lines of white settlements.

The affair created great excitement when it was known among the friends of the child's parents. No people are more intensely affected by such occurrences than Indians. This feeling is very much enhanced by the knowledge that captives are often sold as slaves into other tribes. Hence this capture was disastrous to the Snake Indians, because it aroused the fire of hate among the "Warm Springs," and sent many of their braves to the warpath.

General Crook being the *right man in the right place*, and finding that his regulars could not successfully cope with the Snakes, called for volunteers from Umatilla and Warm Springs Reservation. A company of Cayuse Indians, under the leadership of the now famous Donald McKay, went from the former, and another company, under command of Dr. Wm. C. McKay, an older brother of Donald's, from the latter agency. I know nothing of the theology of Gen. Crook, whether he is posted about the war-policy of his Satanic Majesty, but he struck it this time,—"fighting the devil with fire."

These Indians were enlisted with the understanding that they were to have, as compensation for their services, the booty won from the "Snake Indians;" but were armed and rationed by the Government.

The father of the captured girl promised to award the brave who should recapture her, with her hand; or, in other words, she was to be the wife of the man who brought her in.

In those days, no well-established Indian law recognized the necessity for a marriage ceremony, neither prevented a brave from taking as many wives as he was able to buy, or otherwise obtain.

Hence this captive girl became a prize within reach of any brave who went on the warpath, and could succeed.

This tempting bounty, together with a love of plunder and the thirst for revenge, added to the ambition of the Indians to do something that would entitle them to the recognition of their manhood by white men, made recruiting easy to accomplish, and the two companies were quickly made up. The enlisted Indian scouts, when supported by the government and furnished with arms and ammunition, clothed and mounted, were just the thing Crook had been wanting.

The Snakes had learned that soldiers in blue were poor marksmen, and that they could drive them by strategy. But as one of the chiefs related afterward, when they saw blue coats slip from their horses and take to the brush, giving back shot for shot, they were astonished. Then, too, the scouts under the McKays, Indians themselves, tracked them over plain and mountain, until they were forced to fortify, and, they became desperate.

Meanwhile this wily general, divested of his official toga, was out with his Indian scouts, one of whom said he looked like "*a-cul-tus-til-le-cum*"(a common man), but he "*mum-ook-sul-lux-ic-ta-hi-as-tyee-si-wash*,"("makes war like a big Indian chief.")

General Crook, giving his Indian scouts permission to take scalps and prisoners, under savage war custom, very soon compelled the Snake chiefs to sue for peace.

This result was brought about by the "Warm Springs" and "Umatillas," under the leadership of the McKay brothers, who advised a winter campaign. General Crook, with rare good sense, availing himself of their wisdom and experience, pursuing the Snakes, in midwinter, over the high sage brush plains, and through the mountains.

The Snakes were under the leadership of three several chiefs. E-E-gan's band, infesting the frontier on Burnt and Owyhee Rivers, Eastern Oregon, numbering never more than three hundred warriors, had been reduced to less than two hundred, by the casualties of war; We-ah-we-wa's band, of about the same number, swinging along between Burnt river and the Cañon City country.

Against these Donald McKay, with the Umatilla Indian scouts, was sent, supported by a company of the United States cavalry.

Donald was eminently successful in his scouting expedition, in recapturing horses, taking scalps, and, what has since been of more importance to him, in also retaking the captured daughter of the Warm Spring chief.

She was not found with her original captors, it being a common practice with Indians, and especially when at war, to pass captives out of the hands of the original captors, and, whenever practical, in exchange for other slaves.

Those who may meet this famous scout, Donald McKay, and his pretty little Indian wife, Zu-let-ta (Bright Eyes), would never suspect that she had served three years as a slave among the Snake Indians, and that the great stalwart fellow was her deliverer; yet such is the truth.

The third division of the Snake tribe was under the famous chief Pe-li-na, whose battle-grounds and warpaths were east of the Cascade mountains, and south of the Warm Spring Reservation.

During one of the engagements incident to this Snake war, he was killed in a fight with Dr. McKay's Warm Spring scouts. He was probably the most daring and successful leader the Snake Indians have ever had.

On his death, a chief named O-che-o assumed command, and conducted the last battle fought by this band. Harassed and driven by the combined power of United States soldiers and their Indian allies, they made at last a stand, and fought bravely, but were overpowered, and finally compelled to surrender.

When they came in with hands dyed with the blood of innocent victims, and offered to shake hands with General Crook, he refused; and placing his own behind him, coolly said, "When you prove yourselves worthy—not till then."

They were subjugated, and accepted the terms, "unconditional surrender"—without treaty or promise, except that of protection or subsistence on the part of the Government and an acknowledgment of its authority, and the promise of obedience on the part of the Indians.

At Warm Springs Agency an Indian, who had been with Crook, invited me to visit the department barn with him.

He led the way, climbing up gangways and ladders, until we reached the upper garret. He pointed to a dark-looking pile in one corner resembling a black bear-skin. On examination I found they were scalps. The scout remarked that he did not know how many

151

were there now, because white men carried them off, and Capt. Smith, the agent, forbade them from touching them; that when they came home from "Crook's war," at the great scalp-dance they had sixty-two. He appeared to regret that the men who had cut them off the hated Snakes' heads could not be permitted to ornament their shot-pouches with them. I selected one or two as reminders of the handiwork of the scouts, and also as specimens of the long black hair of the Snake Indians. I haven't them now. For a while they hung in my office; but the doors were sometimes left unlocked, and they were missing. Pretty sure, they are now playing switch for a couple of handsome ladies residing,—well, no odds where.

If my reader will accompany me awhile we will visit the "Snake country," and see it for ourselves. From the home office at Salem, Oregon, our route leads us down the beautiful Willamette valley, via Portland; thence once again up the Columbia by steamer and rail, through "the Cascades," seeing new beauties each time in things we had not noticed on former trips. On the right a mountain stream leaps off a rock six hundred feet, and turns to mist, forming a perpetual cloud, that hides its main course, but pours its constant rain into a great pool below, and, overflowing, leaps again two hundred feet, and lighting on stony bed, made deeper and softer each century, it comes out to a smiling, sparkling silver sheet beneath the evergreen forests, and joins the river in its flow to the briny deep.

On the left we see Castle Rock, on which Jay Cooke built a fine air-castle when the North Pacific Railroad was built *upon paper*, intending to match the ideal with the real in time, to sit on its summit, and, from the tower of his mansion, wave his welcome to the panting iron charger on his arrival from Duluth, *en route* to the great metropolis of the northwest.

Jay Cooke failed; the iron courser is stabled at Duluth; the metropolis is covered with heavy forests, and the hum of busy life is not heard very much at Puget Sound, and Castle Rock stands solitary and alone like some orphan boy.

So it will stand, for its mother mountains look on it with contempt, from its very insignificance. It is a pity Cooke can't build the castle,—pity for this lonely rock, who bathes his feet in the boiling waters of the river.

"Rooster Rock" is still worse off, for he is surrounded by water too deep for him to wade, though he may keep his head above the flood.

Onward, upward we go, passing old rock towers and Indian burial-grounds, catching a glimpse of Father Hood, who seems in ill-humor now, and frowns, with dark clouds on his brow. Maybe he is angry with Mother Adams, on the north, who smiles beneath her silvery cap, while he scolds and thunders. The tables may yet turn with these mountain monarchs, and Hood may laugh while Mother Adams weeps. We will keep an eye on them for a few days, as our journey leads us toward the "Snake country."

We are at "The Dalles." Our commissary, Dr. W. C. McKay has made preparation for the journey; we are no longer to be hurried by steam so fast we cannot have the full benefit of the scenes we pass.

The doctor is a native of the mountains, and boasts that he is "no emigrant or carpet-bagger either;"—that his father's blood was mixed with Puritan stock from Boston, and his mother knew how to lash him to the baby board and swing him to her back with strong cords, while she promenaded behind her husband, or gathered the wild huckleberries.

He is now, 1874, *en route* for the east with a troupe of Indians from Warm Springs and the Modoc Lava Beds.

Few who meet him will suspect he is the one of whom I write, unless I describe him more accurately. Educated in Wilbraham, Mass., at his father's expense, he graduated with honour, and returned to his native land a strong, well-built, handsome gentleman. He married a woman of his own blood, fully his equal in culture.

The doctor has taken part in nearly all the important Indian affairs of Oregon and Washington Territory for a quarter of a century; sometimes as interpreter or secretary for treaty councils, and sometimes as United States Resident Physician, and again as leader of friendly Indians against hostile ones. His experiences have more the character of romance than any man in the northwest.

He meets us at the wharf and says, "Come, you are my guest," and leads the way to the high, rocky bluffs overlooking the city of "The Dalles." Our entertainment was made complete through the hospitality of the lady-like, dark-eyed woman who presided at a table whereon we found an elegant supper.

We light our pipes, and stroll out to the tents of the teamsters, packers, and hands who are to accompany our expedition. An Indian boy is baking bread by a camp-fire with frying-pans. Nearby the door of the cooking-tent we see our kitchen, a chest or box,—and by its side stands a fifty-pound sack of self-rising flour, with the end open,

153

and, resting on the flour, a lump of dough.

Jimmy Kane, the Indian cook, twists off a chunk, and, by a circling motion peculiar to himself, and one would say entirely original, he soon gives it the shape of a thin, unbaked loaf. See the fellow measuring the frying-pan with his eyes, first scanning the loaf and then the pan, until, in his judgment, they will fit each other well; then, holding the limp loaf in his left hand, with the other he slips a bacon rind over the inside of the pan, to prevent the dough from sticking, and claps the latter in; and, patting it down until the surface is smooth, he pulls from his belt a sheath-knife, and makes crosses in the cake to prevent blistering. Next, the frying-pan goes over the fire a moment or two until the bottom is crusted. Meantime the cook has drawn out coals or embers, standing the pan at an angle, and propping it in position with a small stick, with one end in the ground and the other in the upper end of the pan-handle.

Meanwhile the coffee-pot is boiling, and in some other frying-pan the meats are cooking. But see that mess of dough, how it swells and puffs up, like an angry mule making ready for a bucking frolic. Jimmy takes the pan by the handle, and, with a peculiar motion, sends the now steaming loaf round and round the pan; then jerking a straw or reed from the ground, thrusts it into the heart of the loaf, and, quickly withdrawing it, examines the heated point. If no dough is there, the loaf is "done," and then Jimmy throws it on his hand, and keeps it dancing until he lands it in the bread-sack, which is stored away among bed-blankets to keep it hot; while he proceeds to put another lump of dough through the same process. Sometimes the first loaf may be stood on end before the fire while the other loaves are taking their turn in the pan.

Perhaps a dozen cakes are standing like plates in a country woman's cupboard, all on edge, while we look at the Indian cook setting the table on the ground. First spreading down a saddle-blanket, and then a table of thick sail-cloth, he draws the kitchen near, and pitches the tin plates and cups, knives, and spoons around, and, placing an old sack in the centre, sets thereon the frying-pan full of hot "fryins." But Jimmy has everything on the table, and is waiting for the boys to come.

Listen, and you will hear the tramping feet of our band of horses and mules with which we are to make our journey. They come galloping into camp, seasoning the supper with dust.

On the following morning we are on the road toward the summit of the Blue Mountain, riding over high, rolling prairies, sometimes crossing deep, dark *cañons*, and out again on the open plain. On the evening of the second day we pitched our camp in Antelope valley.

While Jimmy is preparing supper, a man approaches our camp from the open plain. He carries on his shoulders a breech-loading shot-gun, and, hanging by his side, a game-bag, through which the furry legs of Jack rabbits and the feathers of prairie chickens may be seen; and also in his left hand a string of mountain trout. The man declares himself a hunter by his spoils; but there is something else that causes us to stare at him,—the soft felt hat slouched over his face, flannel blouse, denim overalls stuffed into the top of his boots, a small pointer dog that keeps close to his heels, altogether presenting a spectacle not common in appearance.

As he comes near our camp, we recognize, in the sunburnt face and flaxen hair, a man whose heroic deeds have placed his name high on the roll of honour as a chieftain. This plain-looking, rough-clad, sunburnt hunter is George Crook, commander of the Department of the Columbia.

He is just the man that we wished to meet at this time. After a pleasant chat on every-day topics, the general threw himself down on a pile of blankets, and gave us his opinion of the Indian question, so far as concerned those we were going to meet. His experience made his views of great value, and we fully realized it within a few days.

We see, coming over the hill from Warm Springs Agency, a small cavalcade of Indians. They are to be of our party for the Snake expedition.

Foremost in the trail rode a young Indian, who had been with McKay's scouts under Gen. Crook. The general quietly extended his hand to the new-comer, in token of recognition.

This man's name was Tah-home (burnt rock). He had been successful, during the war, in capturing a little Snake Indian squaw of about twelve years of age. He had subsequently adopted her as his wife. Dr. McKay had arranged for Tah-home to bring his captive wife for the purpose of interpreter, it being presumed that she would, of course, be able to talk in her native tongue, having been only two years a captive.

It should be understood that nearly every tribe has a language distinct from its neighbours, and it was feared that some difficulty would arise in managing a council with a people who were so little known to other tribes, except by their daring acts of warfare; hence this arrangement with Tah-home and his squaw Ka-ko-na (lost child).

It required some strong promises to reassure Tah-home of the safety of this trip, in so far as it affected his property interest in the squaw; for at this time his thoughts were confined to this view of the case. When assured that, in the event the Snakes should claim his wife, and succeed in persuading her to remain with them, he should have *two horses*, he was satisfied to proceed.

One or two days after we encamped near Cañon City, and, in pity for the poorly clad squaw, we had her dressed in a full suit of new clothes. From that time henceforth Tah-home seemed to be very much attached to his wife.*"Fine feathers make fine birds"* among Indian people as elsewhere.

Pursuing our journey, we at last stand on the summit of the Blue Mountains, one hundred and eighty miles south of "The Dalles." Looking northward, spread out before us, a great high plain appears in full view, though hundreds of miles away; high mountains, looking in the distance like a wooded fringe, and their high peaks, like taller trees that had outgrown their neighbours, were clothed in snow, making a marked contrast with their shining tops. To the south an elevated plateau of open country, bleak and dreary in its aspect. A few miles on we find a boiling spring of clear water, and near it a cool one.

Passing south of the summit, about fifty miles, we reach "Camp Harney," a three-company military post established here to guard the Indians. There was a time when it was necessary. Indeed, it may be again.

CHAPTER 15

The Council With the Snake Indians—O-Che-O

On our arrival we made our camp one mile below the post, on the bank of a small stream. No Indians were visible until the day appointed for the council we had ordered. Messengers had been sent out to the several Indian camps, notifying them of our presence.

They came at the appointed time in full force, men, women, and children. The council was held near our camp, in a large army hospital tent. The Snakes were represented by their great war chiefs, We-ah-we-we, E-he-gan, and O-che-o.

Before opening council, and while arranging the preliminaries, we announced the presence of Ka-ko-na,—the captive wife of Tah-home,—and the purpose for which she had been brought along.

This announcement created great excitement among the Snake Indians. They collected around the tired little squaw, and scanned her closely, for the purpose of identification. She was frightened, and shrunk from their questions, saying to Tah-home that she was "No Snake." She had either really lost her native language, or was afraid to acknowledge that she could speak it.

Meanwhile, through the kindness of Gen. Crook, while we were encamped at Antelope valley, sending for Donald McKay, who was in government employ, we were supplied with an interpreter. Donald is not only a scout, but he is a linguist in Indian tongues,—speaking seven of them fluently,—the "Shoshone Snake," included. Ka-ko-na, satisfied that she would not be forced to go with her own people, listened to the Snake talk; suddenly, as though waking from a dream, she began talking it herself, and was soon recognized and identified as a sister of one of "O-che-o's" braves.

Her father had been killed, her mother had died, and her relatives all gone, save this one brother. Stoical as they appear to be, there is, nevertheless, deep feelings of human affection pervading the hearts of these people; especially for brother and sister, and even to cousins; but, strangely enough, they carry their ideas of practicability beyond common humanity in their treatment of mothers, by casting them off as worn-out beasts of burden when too old for labour.

This is even worse than among civilized people, who pray for the death of mothers-in-law and step-mothers.

The fathers are treated with great kindness,—at least when they are possessed of worldly goods, and even when poor they are exempt from labour,—are buried with the honours due them, and their graves held sacred as long as the graves of other fathers generally.

After the usual preliminaries of smoking the peace-pipe, both parties proffering pipes, and after drawing a puff or two, then exchanging, passing the pipes around the circle, until all had proclaimed friendly intention by smoking, Col. Otis, commander of the District of the Lakes, present, together with a number of officers from the post,—we opened the talk by saying, substantially, that we were there to represent another department of the government; that we knew all about the history of the past, and had come to offer them a home on a Reservation, and to provide for their wants; and that we were prepared to assist them in removing to the new homes at Yai-nax, on Klamath Reservation.

The chiefs were suspicious and wary, not disposed to talk, but were good listeners. After two days, passed in "making heart," they said they could not give an answer without "Old Win-ne-muc-ca," the head chief of all the Shoshones, Snakes.

The council was adjourned, and this celebrated old fraud was sent for, a distance of one hundred miles.

Meanwhile we waited for his appearance, sometimes visiting the Indian camps several miles away.

On one occasion I went on horseback and alone with We-ah-we-wa. He seemed anxious to give warning to his people of our coming, and sent runners ahead on foot for that purpose. As we rode away from our camp I had some misgivings, when I remembered that the man beside me was one of the most bloodthirsty savages that had ever led a band of braves to a banquet of blood. He it was who had directed, and assisted too, in the many scenes of robbery and murder on the Cañon City road.

He was more than an ordinary man in mental power, had in former years, while a captive, lived on Warm Springs Reservation, had learned the Chinook jargon, and could speak "Boston" sufficiently well to make himself understood.

After leaving our camp, and while *en route* to his, he told me of his capture years before; of his confinement in a guard-house, and exhibited the scars that had been made by the fetters he had worn; then of his escape and subsequent adventures, and narrow escape from recapture and death.

He did not appear to shrink from mention of his own crimes and exploits, but sought to impress me constantly that he had only acted in defence of his own rights. There was in the face of this man a cunning, treacherous look that was anything but reassuring.

On crossing a little stream fringed with willows, we came suddenly on his camp. Not a house, tent, or lodge was to be seen, but scattered around among the sage bushes were several half-circular wind-brakes, made of sage-brush and willows. The women and children ran out at our approach. The chief called them back. They came shyly, and with wondering eyes gazed on the man who had come to move them to a new home. I learned from him that *they* had never been to the post, and that few white men had ever called on him; hence the curiosity they had on being close enough to see how a white man looked. This chief was the owner of three sleek, fat, healthy-looking wives; they lived on roots, fish, and grasshoppers. The entire outfit for housekeeping was carried from one camping place to another on the backs of the squaws.

They were dressed in long loose frocks, made of deer-skins, trimmed with furs, and, woman-like, embellished with trinkets; in this instance of pieces of tin, cut by them, feathers and claws of wild animals. The sleeves were small, and in the seams a welt of dressed deer-skin, two inches deep, and cut into fringes of one-fourth inch wide. They made their toilets at the little brook beneath the willows. These people maintained all their old customs. I noticed a woman's work-basket, differing somewhat from that of those who were blessed with sewing-machines. Their needles were pointed bones, resembling an awl, and were used as such.

The threads were made of sinews of animals, cured and prepared for the purpose, very strong, but not fine enough for fancy work on silk or cambrics; and yet they make beautiful moccasins and bead-work, without other thread or needle.

The children were also clad in deer-skin clothes, as were the men; the latter being dressed with the hair and fur retained. All these people of whom I write are copper-coloured, though varying in shades about as much as white people do, some of them being much darker than others; all have black eyes, and long black hair, and smooth features, except high-cheek bones. They differ in stature; those near the sea-coast being smaller than those of the high lands; the latter averaging as large as white men. The women are much larger than white women.

Their habits are simple, and their morals beyond question, so far as the honour of their women is concerned. I learned from good authority that the Indian women who have never been contaminated by association with low white men are chaste. The law penalty of these people for violation of this virtue is death. One or two instances of the enforcement of this rigid rule have come within my own personal knowledge on reservations in Oregon.

Sixteen days after the opening of the councils, Win-ne-muc-ca arrived, and the council was again opened. The great chief spoke to his people in private, but declined to make a speech in our joint councils; the others speaking, however, for the people. O-che-o accepted our offer of a home, on the condition that we should return the captives that had been taken during the late war. This promise was made on our part. With this assurance, he and his band made ready for removal. The others did not. We used all our argumentative ability to obtain their consent, but unsuccessfully. They came to the council with war-paint on their bodies and arms concealed under deer-skin robes. Our party were armed, and all were on the keen look-out for trouble. Toward the close of the council-talks the medicine-man of the Snakes drew his knife, and, dropping his robe from his shoulders, displayed, what we well understood to be war-painting on his body and arms, and, thrusting his knife into the ground, said, "We have made up our minds to die before we will go to any place away from our country."

This action and speech brought all parties to a standing posture very quickly. The situation was a very doubtful one for a few moments. The proximity of troops prevented a fight. Had we been a few miles from assistance, I doubt not blood would have been spilled.

We-ah-we-wa himself would have consented to go to a Reservation, but the medicine-man was not willing. Their chief requested that his reasons for not complying should be made known to the "big chief" at Washington, which request was granted and complied with.

The council ended, and we made preparation to remove O-che-

160

o's band to Yai-nax, Klamath Reservation.

Before leaving camp we had demonstrated the superiority of our doctor's skill, by healing a sick Indian against the will of the Snake medicine-man.

The Snakes had demanded the return of their people who had been captured during the war. This we refused unless they would go on to the Reservation. These two circumstances had produced bad blood.

Before our departure a Snake woman, the wife of a half-breed, gave us warning that an attempt would be made to capture our party while on the way to Camp Warner. I made requisition for an escort of troops, which was honoured, and we took up the line of march. We passed safely through this wild, unsettled region, and, on arrival at Warner, O-che-o gathered his people, and, *without* escort, we continued the journey to Yai-nax.

We enjoyed the rare spectacle of seeing the medicine-man practise on a patient who was taken suddenly ill and supposed to be poisoned. The treatment was novel. He made a sage-brush fire, and waited until it had burned down to embers. Meanwhile the patient was divested of clothing. The assistants of the doctor formed in a circle around the fire, and four men were selected to manage the victim of this savage practice. The prayers, songs and dances commenced simultaneously, increasing in earnestness. The patient was lying, with his face downward, on a blanket, with a slight covering over him. The medicine-man made a sign of readiness, when the sick man was seized by the four Indians, by the hands and feet, and, amid the noise of prayers and songs and dances, he was drawn forward and backward, face down, over the hot coals, until he was burnt the length of his body, so that great blisters were raised soon after.

This man did not wince or mutter or shrink from the fearful ordeal. His faith made him whole. A day or two after he was apparently well.

Belonging to O-che-o's band was one named "Big Foot," who would, with a cane four feet long, capture sage-brush hare, incredible as it may seem, when the fleetness of these animals is considered. He would actually run on to them and knock them down with the cane.

Our route from Warner to Yai-nax led us over a high, dry country, with occasional groves of mountain mahogany, or spruce, the whole great plateau being from four to five thousand feet above the sea level. Small lakes lay basking in summer's sun or covered with winter's ice.

They are bountifully supplied with fish of the trout species.

On the day before our arrival we were met by a delegation of Klamath Indians, who came out to meet and give us welcome. It is a beautiful custom among Indians to send in runners to announce the approach of visitors, and then messengers are returned, or perhaps, as in this instance, the chief and his head men go in person to meet them.

They were impatient to "look into the eyes and see the tongue" of the new superintendent. Whether the Indians of our party had telegraphed our coming, or sent runners in advance, I do not now remember. The great Caucasian race justly honours the names of *Franklin, Morse*, and *Field*. These people of whom I write had been using fire as a medium of communication for untold generations. Spiritualism is also common among them.

We were treated with some exhibitions of this incomprehensible phenomenon while on this journey. The *séance* was not conducted with the aid of pine tables or the laying on of hands; the medium, or clairvoyant, working himself by wild motions of his arms and head into the proper condition. He announced that the Klamaths were at that minute encamped at a certain place, and designated the day on which they would meet us.

Subsequent investigation established the correctness of the prophecy. Whether the knowledge was obtained through fire-signals, or by the medium of spirit communication, this deponent sayeth not. There is a general understanding among them as to fire-signals, even when they have no knowledge of each other's language.

The meeting with the Klamaths and Snakes was one of interest to all parties, from the fact that they had been enemies, and the chiefs had not met in person since peace was restored. Living in the country intervening was a small tribe of Wal-pah-pas, who were half Snake and half Klamath. They were mediators, though sometimes fighting on alternate sides, as interest or affront gave occasion.

The Klamath chief and his people had made camp, and were awaiting our arrival. The chief first addressed me, as the high chief, stating that he had heard of me, and was anxious to "see my eyes and heart, and welcome me to Klamath." I replied by saying, "I have brought with me a man of your own colour. He comes to live on Klamath." Then, extending my hand, the chief of the Klamaths advanced and exchanged greetings with me, and also with O-che-o, chief of the Snakes. This man I consider a remarkable character. Mild-mannered, smooth-voiced, unassuming, unused to ceremonies that were not savage, he exhibited traits of character worthy of emulation by more pretentious people.

In this informal council he responded to Allen David, the Klamath chief:"I met this white man. He won my heart with strong words. I came with him. I once thought I could kill all the white men. I have lost nearly all my young men fighting. I am tired of blood. I want to die in peace. I have given my heart all away. I will not go to war. I am poor. I have few horses. I do not know how to work. I can learn. We will be friends. I will live forever, where this new chief places me. I am done."

After these greetings and the supper over, we gathered around huge fires of pine and spruce logs, and talked in a friendly manner. Singular spectacle, away out on the unsettled plains of Eastern Oregon, to see a meeting wherein were representatives of two races and seven differ ent tribes, speaking as many different languages, sitting in peace and harmony, without fear of harm, telling stories, some of which were translated into the several tongues.

To illustrate how these talks were conducted: a white man speaks in his own language, a Warm Spring Indian repeats it to his own people, who, in turn, tell it to a Klamath, he to a Modoc, and then it goes through the Wal-pah-pa's mouth to the Snake's. Often three or four sentences, of different sense, are being translated at the same time. Some wild stories are told; but oftener the white man furnishes the subject, at the solicitation of some red men asking information.

The night wears away, the fires grow dim, and, one by one, the talkers drop out of the circle, and retire to sleep unguarded. The morning sun finds the camp active, and preparation being made for moving forward. The horses and mules are driven into camp, about as motley a band as the people who were squatting around the various breakfast tables on the ground. The scenes of such a camp are enlivening indeed. Tents falling, lodges taken down, horses neighing and losing company, all bustle and confusion, while the teams are being harnessed, and the mules and Indian ponies are being saddled and packed,—the spectacle presented is an exhilarating one. But if you would enjoy the full benefit of it, take a position on the side of the camp from which we take our departure, and, while you rest your elbows on your saddled horse, take items.

See the anxiety of each to be off first, and hear the driver of the mule teams talking in an undertone until the bells on the leaders strike a note that is in tune with the road, and then each mule settles to the collar and the wheels move. Anxious squaws are jabbering to their horses, children and dogs, lazy Indian men sitting unconcerned, astride the best horses. Stand still a little longer, and see the last man run to the fire for a coal to light his pipe, and then away to overtake his company.

The camp is now deserted, the fires are burned out, and the places where tents and lodges stood look smooth, and where the weary limbs have lain the fresh broken trees tell who were there. And now our horse, with his impatient feet, bids a hasty "goodbyE" to a spot that was our home for a night; we leave it behind us to be seen no more.

Our charger, now more impatient, still hurries to join the departed throng, while we turn up our coat-collar to keep the frost from our ears. Soon we come upon the lame and lazy, and perhaps an old squaw, with her basket of household treasures that has been with her through her hard life, the basket suspended on her back by a strap around her forehead, and a stick in her hand, and her body bent forward. She plods along until the sound of approaching hoofs startle her, and instinctively she looks around and stops for us to pass. Poor, miserable old link of Darwin's mystic chain, we pity you; for you are, at least, half human, and your sons, with no filial love and no shame, are on prancing horses just ahead of you, wearing red blankets and redder paints, with feathers flying, and thoughtless of their mother; your lot is hard, but you don't know it, because in your youth you played Indian lady, while your mother wore the shoes of servitude that you are now wearing.

As we ride on, passing little squads of old people on foot, and women with baby baskets, ponies groaning under two or three great lazy boys, teams with jingling bells, we find, nearer the front of the train, the lords of this wild kind of creation, laughing and sporting as they ride, apparently unconscious of the fact that slavery and bondage have fettered old age, and compelled it to drag weary limbs over stony roads.

We arrive at Yai-nax, the future home of a war-chief, who has cost the government much of blood and treasure, though docile now. A lone hut marks the spot, near a large spring that runs off in a northerly direction to Sprague's River. A beautiful valley spreads out for miles, covered with grass and wild flax; snowy mountains lie south, west, and north, the valley ascending the mountain east so gradually that we can scarcely see where the one ends and the other begins. The cavalcade halts near the spring, and soon the throng becomes busy making preparations for the night.

The next morning's sun finds a busy camp; every able-bodied man is ordered to work; trees are falling, axes plying, and log cabins rise in rows, and the new home of the Snake Indians begins to appear to the eye a real, tangible thing.

Six days pass, and the smokes from thirteen Indian houses join in procession and move off eastward, borne by the breeze that sings and sighs, or howls in anger among the trees around Yai-nax. A council is called, and O-che-o speaks: "My heart is good. I will stay on the land you have given me. This is my home. When you come again you will find O-che-o here."

Since leaving Camp Harney nothing has been said until this evening about captives. O-che-o now raises the question again. We meet him with the assurance that all the captives that can be found shall have the privilege of returning to their people. I was not altogether prepared for the scene that was opening. O-che-o remarked, through an interpreter, that he believed me, and that he expected that I would secure the return to him of his captured son, who was somewhere in the north; but, to make his heart easy on the subject, he would try me with a case now before us; referring to Ka-ko-na.

It was a regular bombshell. We were on the eve of departure. Ka-ko-na and Tah-home had become very strongly attached to each other, and were not willing to be separated.

O-che-o had assented to the new law which I had introduced forbidding the sale of women; but he was nevertheless anxious to detain her, unless she was *paid for*. This last feature he did not avow, but I well knew the meaning of his speech. He insisted that she should be brought before the council, and in the presence of the people make her choice, to go or stay. Tah-home was almost wild with fear of losing her, and reminded me of my promise at Antelope valley. Ka-ko-na was consulted, while I was endeavouring to evade the trying scene. I was satisfied that she preferred going with Tah-home; but I well knew the mysterious power of the medicine-man, and I feared that, if she was brought into his presence, she would be so much under the power of his will, through her own superstitious faith in him, that she would not have the courage to elect to go with Tah-home.

O-che-o was informed that she preferred to go with her husband. "All right; but let her come here to say so before all the people," insisted O-che-o. I clearly saw that any further attempt at evasion would impair his confidence in my integrity.

This episode was of that kind which enlists the sympathies of all classes of men. Tah-home had won the good will of our entire party, during the trip from Antelope Valley, by his unceasing industry as a herder and camp-helper.

Ka-ko-na had also improved much in her manners, and had learned the art of laundress to some extent. No unseemly act had she committed to forfeit the respect due her as a woman; consequently now, when the two had become so thoroughly infatuated with each other that it was noticeable to even casual observers, a general feeling of pity and regret at the untoward circumstances was manifest throughout the camp.

The teamsters and other *employés* were willing to make up a purse to buy her of her people,—in fact, the project was put on foot to do so. I confess I was not insensible to the common feeling of regret, mixed with the fear for the result.

When the trying moment could no longer be delayed, Ka-ko-na and her master lover were brought into the circle. The moon was shining brightly, and, added to this, the light of the council fire made up a picture of romantic interest. Speeches were made on the occasion worthy of the subject.

An appeal was made to O-che-o's better nature, in behalf of the anxious pair. He is really a noble fellow, and, to his credit be it told, a kind-hearted man, though untrained in civil ways.

He acknowledged that it was wrong to separate those who loved each other, but said "he must look in Ka-ko-na's eyes while she made her choice." He was not willing that Tah-home should even stand beside her while the matter was under discussion.

The latter asked the privilege of speaking, which, being granted, he poured out a speech that I little thought him capable of making. It was replete with the wild poetry of love, very impassioned, and full of pathos. Finally, Ka-ko-na was ordered to make a choice,—to go with Tah-home, or stay with her people.

The Snake medicine-man took a position in front of her, and, fixing his eyes on hers, stood gazing in her face. The whole council circle was stilled. A suspense that was very intense pervaded every mind. Silence reigned; every eye was watching the movement of the woman's lips. The power of the medicine-man was more than she could stand, even when love for Tah-home was pleading.

She answered, "*I stay*," and burst into tears. Tah-home turned as white as an Indian could. The white men present felt a cold chill fall on them. Ka-ko-na and Tah-home returned to their tent, she weeping bitterly. The council was broken up, and the excited camp was again quiet, save the sobbing of the heart-broken Ka-ko-na.

An hour or two before daybreak, I was awakened by Tah-home, who, in a low whisper, made an enterprising proposition, which was no less than to elope with his wife. I dare not assent, though strongly tempted to do so. When I refused, he then wished me to prevent pursuit. This I could not do. The poor fellow returned to his tent, and the sobbing changed to paroxysms of despair.

Our next point of destination being Klamath Agency, we had despatched part of our teams the evening previous. On one of these wagons Ka-ko-na's goods had been placed by her friends, with the intention, no doubt, of making an excuse for her to follow. When the morning came for our departure, O-che-o was invited to accompany our party to the agency, and repay the visit of the Klamaths. The fact that Ka-ko-na's clothing had preceded her in wagons was urged as a reason why she should go also.

O-che-o consented. We placed the camp in charge of a trustworthy white man, and turned from this new settlement with feelings of pride, and with a prayer and hope for its success. Whether O-che-o and his people shall ever reach manhood's estate depends entirely on the policy of the government, and the men who are selected to educate them in the rudimentary principles of civilization.

Two years afterward I again visited the settlement. I found O-che-o *there*, contented. He was glad to see me, and repeated his declaration that he would "Go no more on the warpath." I found twenty-eight log houses, with chimneys, doors, and windows, occupied by the Snake Indians; also, comfortable buildings for government *employés*, and a farm of three hundred acres of land, under a substantial fence, together with corrals and barns.

This country is about forty-four hundred feet in altitude, and, consequently, the seasons are short. When not cut down by frost, wheat and barley yield abundantly, unless, indeed, another enemy should interfere,—the cricket. They are about one and one-half inches long, a bright black colour, very destructive, marching in grand armies, eating the vegetation nearly clean as they go. These crickets made their appearance in the neighbourhood of Yai-nax, and threatened destruction to the crops. The commissary in charge consulted O-che-o and Choe-tort. They ordered their people to prepare for the war on this coming army. Circular bowl-shaped basins, six feet in diameter, were made in the ground, and paved with cobble-stones; large piles of dry wood, brush and grass were collected near the pits.

All the available forces were armed with baskets, sacks, and other implements, and ordered on to the attack. The forces were put in position, and the alarm sounded, and this strange battle began. Let us stand by one of the basins, or pits, and witness the arrival of the victors, who come laden with the wounded and maimed enemies. Those in charge of the slaughter-pens, or basins, throw in wood, dry grass and sage brush, and when burnt down, the ashes are swept out with long willow brooms; then a fire is built around the upper rim of the basin, and as each captor comes with her load of thousands, they are thrown into the basin on the heated rocks. The children, especially the girls, are stationed around the circle to drive back the more enterprising crickets that succeed in hopping over, or through the fiery ring surrounding this slaughter-pen. Think, for a moment, of the helpless, writhing mass of animated nature in a hot furnace,—a great black heap of insects being stirred up with poles until they are roasted, while their inhuman torturers are apparently unconscious of the fact that these crickets are complete organisms, each with a separate existence, struggling for life.

I don't know that it was any more inhuman than a "Yankee clam-bake," where brave men and fair women murder thousands of animated bivalves without a thought of inflicting pain. The Indians had the advantage in a moral point of view, for the crickets were their enemies. When the *bake* is over they shovel them into home-made sacks, and then, sewing them up, put them to press.

An Indian cricket-press does not work by steam, with huge screws. Flat rocks are placed on the ground, and the sack full of cooked crickets is placed thereon, and then another rock is laid on the sack; finally stones, logs, and other weighty things are placed upon the pile, until the work is complete. Meanwhile, look away down the sloping plane and see the line of battle, with sprightly young squaws on the outside, deployed as skirmishers. See how they run, and laugh, and shout, until the enemy is turned, and then the victory is followed up, each anxious to secure trophies of the battle. This is one kind of war where the women wield implements of destruction quite as well as their masters.

The battle has been fought and won, and the intruders routed and driven into the rapid current of Sprague's river. The people rest from the siege contented, for the growing crop—carrots, and turnips—has been saved. This is not the only cause of gratulation, for now comes the best part of the war. The luscious cakes of roasted crickets are taken from the rude presses, and the brave warriors of this strange battle celebrate the victory with a feast of fresh crickets, and a grand dance, where sparkling eyes and nodding feathers, and jingling bells keep time to Indian drums.

Fastidious reader, have you ever been to a clam-bake, and seen the gay dancers celebrate the funeral of a few thousand sightless bivalves?—things that God had placed in hardened coffins and buried on the shore, while godlike man and woman brought them to a short-lived resurrection.

Well, then, you understand how little human sympathy goes out for helpless things, and how much of thoughtless joy is experienced in this civilized kind of feasting. The Indian has the advantage, for his roasted crickets *are sweet* and nutritious. I speak from "the card," as a Yankee would say.

O-che-o and Choc-toot are safe from want. The compressed cakes are *"cached"* away for winter use; that is to say, they are buried in a jug-shaped cellar, dug on some dry knoll, and taken out as necessity may require. The cakes when taken from the bag—as Yankee people would say, for they call everything a bag that western people call a sack—present the appearance of a caddy of foreign dates or domestic plums when dried and put in shape for merchandise.

Since my visit to Yai-nax, at the time of locating O-che-o and his people, others have been added to the station. Old Chief Schonchin, the legitimate leader of the now notorious tribe of Modocs, has taken up his residence at Yai-nax.

At the time of planting this Indian settlement, it was not known that any adverse claim could be set up to this portion of Klamath Reservation; since then, however, a military road company has laid claim to alternate sections of land, granted them by an act of the Oregon Legislature, by virtue of congressional legislation, giving lands to certain States to assist in making "internal improvements."

The government has been apprised of the state of affairs, and may take action to meet the emergency. There is, however, an embryo Indian war in this claim, unless judiciously managed.

In the treaty of 1864 this land was set apart as a home for the Klamath Indians, and such other tribes as might be, from time to time, located thereon by order of the United States. Subsequently the grant in aid of internal improvements was made. Suppose the government concedes the right to the road company to sell and dispose of these lands, to which the government has never had a title, and the purchaser takes possession; thus occupying alternate sections, of the country belonging to these Indian tribes, and giving them nothing in compensation. The result might be another cry of extermination, and another expensive spasmodic effort to annihilate a tribe who, in desperation, fight for their rights.

The land never did belong to the United States; else why treat with its owners for it? If the road company are entitled to lands for constructing a military road through this Indian Reservation, give them other lands in lieu thereof, or make the compensation to the Indians equivalent to the sacrifices they may make; otherwise more blood will be shed.

Their nationality and manhood were recognized in making the treaty by which this tract of country was reserved from sale to the United States. Let it be recognized still; treat them with justice, and war and its bloody attendants will be avoided.

CHAPTER 16

Over the Falls—First Election

Taking up our narrative, let us resume our journey to Klamath Agency, accompanied by O-che-o and a few of his head men; Tah-home and Ka-ko-na taking charge of the loose stock, and riding, for once in their lives, à la white people, side by side. This was a sad day to them; they were, human-like, more ardently in love than ever, as the hour for departure approached.

The route from Yai-nax to Klamath Agency follows down the valley of Sprague's river for twenty miles, over rich prairies skirted with timber. To the eye it is a paradise, walled in on the north and south by ranges of mountains five miles apart, traversed by a stream of clear water, and covered with bunch-grass and wild flax. It is the natural pasture land of elk, who run in bands of fifty to one hundred over its beautiful plains. Leaving the river, the road crosses a range of low hills passing down to Williamson's River,—a connecting link between the "Great Klamath Marsh" and "Big Klamath Lake." At the crossing it is one hundred yards wide; the ford being on the crown of a rocky ledge of twenty feet in width, over which the water thirty inches' depth runs very swiftly, and falls off about two feet into deeper water below.

The Indians cross on their ponies without fear; but white men with trembling limbs, with an Indian on each side. We made the trip with a silent prayer to Heaven for safety as we went through. Not so, however, with the driver of one of our six-mule teams. The wagon was partly loaded with infantry soldiers, who were returning to Fort Klamath from some duty, and had been granted the privilege of riding. The driver, when about midway, became dizzy, and for the moment panic-stricken and wild; drew the leaders' line so strongly that, mule-like, they jumped off into the boiling flood below. The soldiers leaped from the wagon before it crossed the precipice.

Soon the six mules and the driver were struggling in thirty or forty feet depth of water. The wagon rolled over and over down the water-covered, rocky slope, finally resting on the bottom. The driver and five mules were saved by the heroism of a quiet little fellow named Zip Williams. He had driven his team through, and was out of danger. Seeing the other going over the falls, he quitted his own, and throwing off his boots, drawing his knife and clasping it between his teeth, he rushed among the struggling mass of floundering mules, and succeeded in cutting the harness, thereby liberating five of the animals. The remaining one, attached to the wagon tongue, being tall, would touch the bottom with his hind feet occasionally, and, with his head and front feet out of water a portion of the time, would plead earnestly for succour; but his struggles were so furious that even the heroic Zip could not extricate him. Those present witnessed with regret this brave old mule sink beneath the flood. The wagon and part of the harness were recovered, and also the "big-wheel mule;" but the latter "was not of much account," as Zip expressed it, "except to make a big Indian feast," to which purpose he was applied.

From Williamson River our route lay through a heavy forest. The agency is situated on the east side of a small river which rises at the foot of a long ridge extending west to the Cascade Mountains. This stream runs several thousand inches of water, and would afford immense power. The buildings were made of logs, and are arranged in a row, one hundred feet apart, resembling one side of a street. The long row of twenty whitewashed houses fronting east was a welcome sight for those of our party who had for three months been almost entirely out of society, and, in fact, away from civilization.

Klamath Agency is new, it having been established in 1865; the Indians who occupy it numbering, in 1869 (the time of my first official visitation), fourteen hundred. They are "Klamaths," "Modocs," "Yahooshin," "Snakes," "Wal-pah-pas," and "Shoshone Snakes." The Klamaths number seven hundred. They were the original owners of the country; have never been engaged in wars against the white race.

They are a brave, enterprising, and ambitious people. In former times they were often in the warpath against other Indian tribes; and among their ancient enemies are those who now occupy the country in common with them.

The practice of calling the Indians together for a "big talk" on occasions of the visits of officials was also observed in this instance.

This agency has been under the management of Lindsay Applegate, of Oregon,—a man who was well qualified by nature, and a long residence on the frontier, for the office.

He had taken charge of them when they were only savages; and, during the short time he was in power, he, with the assistance of his subordinates, had advanced them greatly in civilization. Under his tuition they had abandoned the old hereditary chieftainships, and had elected new chiefs by popular vote.

They were slow to yield to the new plan; but when the election was ordered, they entered into the contest with earnestness and enthusiasm.

The manner of voting did not admit of ballot-box stuffing,—no mistake could occur,—but so natural is it to cheat and corrupt the great franchise, that even those wild Indians made clumsy imitation of white demagogues.

There were two candidates for the office of head chief,—each anxious for election, as in fact candidates always are, no matter of what race. They made promises,—the common stock in trade everywhere with people hunting office,—of favours and patronage, and even *bought votes.*

This, the first election on this Reservation, was one of great excitement. There was wire-working and intriguing to the last minute. When the respective candidates walked out and called for votes, each one's supporters forming in line headed by the candidate, the result was soon declared, and Bos-co-pa was the lucky man.

Agent Applegate named him "David Allen;" but, Indian like, they transposed the names and called him "Allen David," by which name he is known and has become, to some extent, identified with the recent Modoc war. He is a man of commanding appearance, being over six feet in height, large, well-developed head, naturally sensible, and, withal, highly gifted as an orator and diplomat.

He had met our party as we came in with O-che-o's band of "Shoshone Snakes," and, on our arrival at Yai-nax, had come on home in advance to prepare his people for the big council talk. He called them together the day after our arrival.

The weather was cold,—the ground covered with a few inches of snow. Allen David's people began to assemble. Look from the office window on the scene: here they come, of all ages less than a century; some very old ones, lashed on their horses to prevent them falling off; others who were blind, and one or two that had not enjoyed even the music of the *thunderstorm* for years; others, again, whose teeth were worn off smooth with the gums. Not one of the motley crowd was *bald*; indeed, I never saw an Indian who was. They came in little gangs and squads, or families, bringing with them camp equipages.

As each party arrived they pitched their camps. In the course of the day several hundred had come to see the "New *tyee*." Some were so impatient they did not wait to arrange camp, but hurried to pay honours to their new chief. They brought not only the old, the young, their horses and dogs, but also their troubles of all kinds,—old feuds to be raked up, quarrels to be reopened, and many questions that had arisen from time to time, and had been disposed of by the agent, whose verdict they hoped might be reversed.

The camp at nightfall suggested memories of Methodist camp meetings in the West.

Here and there were little tents or lodges, and in front of some of them, and in the centre of others, fires were built, and round them, sitting and standing, long-haired, dusky forms, and, in a few instances, the children lashed to boards or baskets.

I have selected this agency and these people to quote and write from, with the intention of mentioning, more in detail, the characteristics of the real Indian, in preference to any other in Oregon, for the reason that minutes and reports in my possession, of the councils, are more complete; also, because the people themselves present all the traits peculiar to their race. To insure the comfort of the people large pine logs were hauled up with ox-teams, with which to build fires, the main one being one hundred feet in length, and several logs high, and when ablaze, lighted up the surrounding woods, producing a grand night-scene, with the swarthy faces on each side changing at the command of the smoke and flames.

My reader may not see the picture because of my poverty of language to describe it. Suffice it to say, that these people were there to see and hear for themselves. Men, women and children came prepared to "stay and see it out," as frontier people say.

While preparations for the council were being made, a portion of the department teams, which we had used on the Snake expedition, was despatched for Warm Springs Reservation.

A high dividing ridge of the Blue Mountains separates the waters of the Klamath basin from Des Chutes and Warm Spring country.

The snows fall early on this ridge, and sometimes to great depth; hence it was necessary that the teams should leave without delay, otherwise they might get into a snow blockade, and be lost.

Tah-home was ordered to accompany the train as a guide. He remonstrated, because he had about made up his mind to remain and join O-che-o's band sooner than be separated from Ka-ko-na.

I knew if he remained it would be to his disadvantage, and probable ruin; and for that reason refused him his request, after fairly explaining the reasons therefor.

He acknowledged the validity of my arguments, and with a quick, quiet motion withdrew. I caught his eye, and read plainly what was in his mind. He had determined to take Ka-ko-na with him at every hazard.

Half suppressing my own convictions of right in the premises, I shut my eyes to what was passing; in fact, I half relented in my determination to enforce the new law in regard to buying women. I felt that the trial was a little too severe on all the Indian parties to this transaction.

The evening before the departure, in company with Capt. Knapp (the agent), I called at Tah-home's tent, and found Ka-ko-na still weeping. Tah-home was downcast and sober-faced, and renewed his petition for the privilege of remaining. I confess that was tempted to suspend the new law, but steadied myself with the belief that some way, somehow, Tah-home would succeed without my aid, and without the retraction of the law, though I could not see just how. I was "borrowing trouble," for, as I subsequently learned, the arrangement for Tah-home to get away with his wife had already been made through the intervention of a "mutual friend," and at the time I visited his camp, Tah-home and Ka-ko-na were playing a part,—throwing dust in my eyes.

This mutual friend had satisfied O-che-o by giving him one of Tah-home's horses, his rifle, and a pair of blankets, all of which had been sent off to O-che-o's camp.

The snow began falling before morning, and in the meantime Tah-home and Ka-ko-na silently left camp for Warm Springs. On the following morning, when the teams were drawn up to start, I missed Tah-home and Ka-ko-na. Of course I needed no one to tell me that at that moment they were miles away, towards the summit of the mountain.

Having, at that time, no assurance that O-che-o had been "seen," I hastened to his lodge. I found him sleeping, or pretending to sleep. On being aroused he sprang to his feet, and inquired the cause of my early visit. I think that no looker-on would have detected, in his looks or manner, anything but surprise and indignation, when the escape of

Tah-home and his wife was made known to him. Reproach was in his eyes and his actions while he dressed himself. I was alarmed lest they should be pursued.

A "*mutual friend*" is, sometimes, a handy thing in life; in this instance the "mutual," seeing that I was in the dark, and liable to make some rash promises, touched me on the arm, and called me away. I followed him, O-che-o *did not follow me*. If my memory is correct, the matter was not again referred to by either of us; but there was considerable sly laughing all over the camp, at the way in which the "*tyee*" (myself) had been outwitted by Indians.

"Such is life." We are living a lie when we seem most honest, and justify ourselves with the assurance that "of two evils choose the least," will whitewash us over to all other eyes. To the present writing, con-science has not kept my eyes open when I wished to sleep, because I shut them on Tah-home and O-che-o's trick.

The grand council was opened by Allen David, the chief, saying, "Hear me, all my people—open your ears and listen to all the words that are spoken—I have been to the head of Sprague's river, to meet the new *tyee*—I have looked into his eyes—I have seen his tongue—he talks straight. His heart is strong—he is a brave man—he will say strong words. His ears are large—he hears everything. He does not get tired. He does not come drunk with whiskey. What you have heard about him shaking hands with everyone is true. His eye is good—he does not miss anything—he saw my heart. He washed my heart with a strong law—he brought some new laws that are like a strong soap. Watch close and do not miss his words—they are strong. We will steal his heart."

The subjoined report to my superior in office was made on my return to Salem, and since it is an official communication, written years ago, it may be worthy of a place in this connection; supplement-ing which I propose to write more in detail matters concerning this visit and the series of meetings referred to. I make this statement here, because I do not wish the readers to be confused by the mixing of dates, since to finish this report in full without explanation would exclude incidents that are of interest in a book, though not justifiable in official reports.

Office Superintendent Indian Affairs,
Salem, Oregon, Jan. 20th, 1870.
Sir:—After the completion of the Snake expedition and previ-ous to starting on the Modoc trip, I held a series of meetings

and talks with the Klamaths.

I understand, and have so represented on every occasion, that President Grant meant what he said in his inaugural address: that his policy in regard to Indians would be to prepare them by civilization for citizenship. Acting from this principle, so perfectly in accordance with my own judgment, I stepped out of the track of my predecessors, and said to them that my first business is to settle the financial affairs of the agency; then, to issue such goods as I had provided; and then to deliver a message from Mr. Parker to you; that I am ready to hear any and all complaints; settle any and all difficulties; decide any and all vexed questions; to tell you about the white people's laws, customs, habits, religion, etc., etc.; in a word, I propose to remove the barrier that a condition has held between the different stations in life. Civilization may be yours—manhood—the American standard of worth. The course is clear and open to you Indian people—for the whole family of man.

I had never stood, until now, before a people just emerging from the chrysalis of savage life, struggling earnestly and manfully to leave behind them the traditions and customs of an ancestry known only to mankind by the history of bloody acts and deeds of savage heroism.

I would that I could portray these scenes: these dark-eyed men with long hair, women naturally good-looking, but so sadly debauched that virtue makes no pretensions among them; children of every *shade*,—all gathered around a huge fire of pine logs, in a forest of tall trees, in mid-winter, with the little camp fires here and there; and notwithstanding the ground was covered with snow and thermometer sometimes below zero, these people would sit, or stand, for hours, with eyes, ears, and hearts all open to hear; catching with great eagerness the story of my superior in office, to whom I made all my reports and from whom I received instructions, who, by his own energy, had elevated himself to a level with the great men of the age; and that he, Parker, was of "*their own race.*"

The Klamath chief, Allen David, arose to reply amid surroundings characteristic of Indian life,—a perfect solemn silence broken only by his voice.

I then heard the notes of natural oratory, coming in wild, but well-measured words, and recognized for the first time fully

177

that nature does sometimes produce noble men *without* the line of civilized life. I send you a verbatim report of his speech as taken by Dr. McKay; because I understand we are all trying to solve the problem of civilization for Indians. *I am not, myself, longer sceptical* on that subject; but I know that a large proportion of our public men *are*; and you would not wonder, either, could you visit some reservations and see for yourself the inside workings of moral law.

But I assert that the Indians are not to blame; let censure fall where it belongs; *viz.*, on the men who are entrusted with the care and responsibility of leading and protecting these people, yet wink at and tolerate, in subordinates, the most demoralizing habits, and may be, in some cases, participants themselves. I do not speak of this agency in particular.

Said Allen David,—"I see you. All my people see you.—I saw you at Sprague River.—I watched your mouth.—I have seen but one tongue.—I have looked into your eyes.—I have seen your heart.—You have given me another heart.—All my people will have white hearts.—When I was a little boy I lived here.—I have always lived here.—A long time ago a white man told me I could be like him. I said my skin is red, it cannot change; it must be my heart, my brain, that is to be like a white man.—You think we are low people.—Maybe we are in your eyes.—Who made us so?—We do not know much; we can learn.—Some of the officers at the fort (referring to Fort Klamath, six miles from the agency) have been good men—some of them have been bad men.—Do you think a good white man will take an Indian wife?—A white man that will take an Indian wife is worse blood than Indian.—These things make our hearts sad.—We want you to stop it.... Your ears are large.—Your heart is large.—You see us.—Do not let your heart get sick.

"Take a white man into the woods, away from a store; set him down, with nothing in his hands, in the woods, and without a store to get tools from; and what could he do?

"When you lay down before us the axes, the saws, the iron wedges and mauls you have promised us, and we do not take them up, then you can say we are '*aul-tus*'—lazy people.—You say your chief is like me—that he is an Indian—I am glad. What can I say that is worth writing down?—Mr. Parker does not know me.—When you do all Mr. Huntington promised in the treaty, 1864, we can go to work like white men.—Our hearts are tired waiting for the saw-mill.—When it is built, then we can have houses like white men.—We want the flour-mill; then we will not live on fish and roots. We will help to make the mills.—We made the fences on the big farms.—We did not get tired. . . .

"Give us strong law; we will do what your law says. We want strong law—we want to be like white men. You say that Mr. Parker does not want bad men among our people.—Is B. a good man?—he took Frank's wife—is that good? We do not want such men. Is —— a good man?—he took Celia from her husband—is that right?—Applegate gave us good laws—he is a good man.—Applegate told us not to gamble. Capt. —— won thirty-seven horses from us. He says there is no law about gambling.—Applegate said there was.—Which is right?"

Mr. Meacham said, "You need not be afraid to talk—Keep nothing back. Your people are under a cloud. I see by their eyes that their hearts are sick; they look sorrowful. Open your hearts and I will hear you; tell me all, that I may know what to do to make them glad."

Allen David said, "I will keep nothing back.—I have eyes—I can see that white men have white hands.—Some white men take our women—they have children—they are not Indian—they are not white—they are shame children. Some white men take care of their children.—It makes my heart sick.—I do not want these things.—Indian is an Indian—we do not want any more shame children. A white man that would take an Indian squaw is no better than we are.

"Our women go to the fort—they make us feel sick—they get goods—sometimes greenbacks.—We do not want them to go there—we want the store here at the agency; then our women will not go to the fort. . . . Last Sunday some soldiers went to Pompey's—they talked bad to the women.—We do not want soldiers among our women.—Can you stop this? Our women make us ashamed.—We may have done wrong—give us strong law."

Joe Hood (Indian), at a talk seven days after, said: "Meacham came here. Parker told him to come. He brought a strong law.

179

It is a 'new soap,' it washed my heart all clean but a little place about as big as my thumb-nail. Caroline's (his wife) heart may not all be white yet. If it was, my own would be white like snow. Parker's law has made us just like we were new married. I told these Indians that the law is like strong soap; it makes all clean. I do not want but one wife any more."

Allen David said: "You say we are looking into a camp-fire; that we can find moonlight. You say there is a road that goes toward sunrise. Show me that stone road. I am now on the stone road. I will follow you to the top of the mountain. You tell me come on. I can see you now. My feet are on the road. I will not leave it. I tell my people follow me, and I will stay in the stone road."

I have given you a few extracts, that you may judge from their own mouths whether they can become civilized. If Lindsay Applegate, and his sons, J. D. and Oliver, could take wild savage Indians, and, against so much opposition, in the short space of four years bring them to this state, I know they can be civilized. If good men are appointed to lead and teach them,—*not books alone*, but civilization, with all that civilization means,—men whose hearts are in the work, and who realize that, as soon as duties devolve on them, great responsibility attaches; men who have courage to *stand squarely* between these people and the villains that hang around reservations from the lowest motives imaginable; men paid fair salaries for doing duty; that will not civilize the people by "mixing blood;" married men of character who will practise what they preach, and who can live without smuggling whiskey on to the Reservation; ten years from today may find this superintendency self-supporting, and offering to the world seven thousand citizens.

I am conscious that this is strong talk, but it is surely true. I have not overdrawn this side of the case; nor will I attempt to show what *has been done*, or will be done, with superintendents, agents, and *employés* in charge placed there as a reward for political service.

The past tells the story too plainly to be misapprehended. While I am responsible for the advancement of these people, I beg to state my views and make known the result of observation and experience. As a subordinate officer of the government, I expect to have my official acts scrutinized closely. I respectfully ask that I may be furnished the funds to keep faith with a people so little understood,—people so much like children that when they are promised a saw-mill they go to work cutting logs, only to see them decayed before the mill is begun, but with logic enough to say, "When you have got us the things you promised, then you may blame us if we don't do right."

I have now no longer any doubts about President Grant's "Quaker Policy," if it is applied to Indians once subjugated. These people have mind, soul, heart, affection, passion, and impulses, and great ambition to become like white men. There are more or less men in each reservation who are already superior to many of the white men around them. At Klamath they are now working under civil law of trial by jury,—with judge, sheriff, civil marriage, divorce; in fact, are fast assuming the habiliments of citizenship.

I spent seven days, talking, and listening, and making laws, marrying and divorcing, naming babies, settling difficulties, etc., and finally started, accompanied on my journey by a large delegation of Klamaths, who insisted that I should come again and remain longer, and make *laws*, and that I would build the mills, and tell them more about our religion; all of which I promised, if possible; but realizing fully and feeling deeply how much depended on the man who is in *immediate charge* of these poor, struggling people.

I am, very respectfully,

Your obt. servt.,

A. B. Meacham,

Supt. Indian Affairs.

Hon. E. S. Parker, Commissioner,

Washington, D. C.

In Allen David's speech, he refers to the "Fort," meaning Fort Klamath, six miles distant from the agency. It was established for the protection of the settlers on the Klamath frontier. Two and sometimes three companies have been stationed at this fort for several years.

The remarks of this chief need no comment; *they tell the tale.* If confirmation was wanting of the crimes intimated in his speech, a visit to Klamath Indian Agency, and even a casual glance at the different complexions of the young and rising generation, would proclaim the correctness of Allen David's charges.

CHAPTER 17

Klamath Court—Elopement Extraordinary

The Reservation furnishes abundance of real romance, mixed with tragedy, sufficient to make up a volume. The Indians tell, and white men confirm, the story of an officer of the fort, who loved an Indian's wife, and how he sought to win her from home by presents; and, failing in this, came with armed soldiers, and, with threats of death to the husband, compelled him to give her up. This officer took this woman to the fort, dressed her in styles common among white women, and refused to return her to her husband. When the officer was "ordered away" to some other duty the squaw went home, bearing in her arms an infant not more than half Indian. Her husband refused to receive her. She was turned away from his lodge, and became a vagabond of the worst class. Fortunately for father, mother, and infant, too, the latter died a few months thereafter.

Another young officer of the United States army, who was stationed at Fort Klamath, was a party to an elopement in high life,—as all life is *high* at an altitude of forty-five hundred feet above the sea level; the other party being the wife of a handsome young Indian living on Klamath Reservation. However, they had but a few miles to travel, in order to reach a "*Chicago*" for divorces. All people without law are a law unto themselves.

The Indian husband appealed for redress, but found no one to listen to his appeals. His wife returned to him when the regiment to which the officer belonged was ordered away, bringing with her many fine clothes; her feet clad in good American gaiters, and with an armful of childhood, in which the Indian husband claimed no interest. The mother was turned away from what was once a happy home;

and today, (as at time of first publication), with her little girl, wanders from lodge to lodge, seeking shelter where she may. This woman was really good-looking, and had proved herself an apt scholar in learning the civilized arts of house-keeping and dress-making; she also learned something of our language, in which she tells the story of her own shame and the fatherhood of her child.

I am giving these statements as made to me by white men, who are responsible, and will answer, when called upon, for their authenticity. In respect to the families of these United States officers, not through fear of the men themselves, I withhold their names. In this connection I remember a conversation with a sub-chief of the Klamaths, who could speak "Boston" quite well. His name was "Blo."

He said, "Meacham, I talk to you. S'pose an Injun man, he see a white man's wife. He like her. He give presents; he win her heart; he talk to her sometime. He tell her, "Come go with me." She come. He take her away. White man come home. He no see his wife. He see him children cry. He get mad. He take a gun. He hunt 'em. He find 'em. He shoot 'em, one Injun man. What you think? You think white man law hang him?"

We were travelling horseback, and "Blo" came up close to me, leaning from his saddle, and, peering into my eyes, continued, "What you think?" I looked into his face, and read murder very plainly. Had he been a white man I might have given him a negative answer. Half savage as he was, he was seeking for encouragement to commit a bloody deed in vindication of his honour.

I replied that "the law would punish the Indians for stealing the white man's wife. But if the white man was wise he would not kill the Indian, because the laws would take hold of him." I felt that I was concealing a part of the truth, but I dared not do otherwise.

"Blo" was not so easily put off. He replied with a question that intensified my perplexity, "S'pose white man steal Injun's wife, s'pose law catch *him*?"

Harder to answer than the first one. If I said "Yes," he would have demanded that the law be enforced in his case, that had come under my own observation; and that, I knew, was impossible, with public sentiment so strongly against the Indians that white men would have laughed at the absurdity of calling one of their race to account for so trifling a thing as breaking up an Indian's family, and leaving his children worse than orphans; yet knowing full well that the whole power of the United States would have been evoked to punish an Indian for a like offence. If I said "No," I stultified myself and my government. I could only reply, "Suppose a woman run away,—let her go. Get a divorce, and then another wife."

"*Now-wit-ka, Ni-kanan-itch.*"—"Yes, I see. Law not all the time same. Made crooked. Made for white man. Aha, me see 'em now."

During the seven days' council, "Little Sallie" came into the office, and in plain "Boston" said, "I want divorce; my man, Cho-kus, he buy another woman. I no like him have two wife. I want divorce."

We had just completed the organization of a court, composed of the head chief and his eight subordinates. This was the first case on the docket, and the beginning of a new history with this people,—a new way of settling difficulties. The agent provided a book for making record of all proceedings. A sheriff was appointed from among the Indians. Each sub-chief was entitled to a constable, but, in all matters pertaining to their respective bands, as between themselves and others, neither sub-chief nor constable was permitted to take any part in the proceedings of the court.

Novel scenes indeed!—Indians holding court after the fashion of white men. The chief made a short speech on taking the middle seat on "The Bench." He removed his hat, saying "that he knew but little about the new law, but he would endeavour to make it run straight, and not run around his own people," referring to those of his band. The sub-chiefs took their places on either side, and we gave instructions to the sheriff to open court, ordering a white man to show him through, saying, "Oh-yes! Oh-yes! The Klamath Court is now open."—"*Now-witka, Now-witka, Muck-u-lux, Klamath, Mam-ook, Bos-ti-na Law, O-ko-ke, Sun,*" rang out the Indian sheriff.

"Little Sallie" was the first to appear before the bar of justice, and, without an attorney, she filed a complaint against her husband, the substance of which was to the effect, that "Cho-kus"—her master—had made arrangements to buy another wife, paying two horses; and that these horses belonged to her individually, and she was not willing to furnish horses to buy another woman, because it would leave but one horse in the family, and that Cho-kus and the new wife would claim that one, and she would be compelled to go on foot. If Cho-kus had plenty of horses she might not object; but she thought that she could dig roots, and gather "*wokus*"—wild rice—enough for the family, and Cho-kus did not need another "*nohow.*" But, if he persisted, then she wanted a Boston divorce, otherwise she did not.

Cho-kus was required to show cause why "Sallie" should not be

184

made free. He appeared in person, and expressed willingness for the separation, but asked to know who would be awarded the baby,—a little fellow twelve months old. The court decided that "Sallie" should have possession of the child. Cho-kus took it from its mother's arms, and, holding it in his own, looked very earnestly and silently into its face for a moment. His speech ran in something like the following words: "Now half this baby's heart is mine, half its heart belongs to 'Sallie.'" Then slowly drawing the little finger of one hand from its forehead down its face and body, he went on to say, "I want this child's heart, and 'Sallie' wants it; if we cut into it it will die; I can't give up my part of it."

Sallie attempted to snatch it away, saying, "I won't give up my part of the baby." This brought the husband to terms. He said he would give up taking another wife. Sallie agreed, and the court proposed that, instead of being divorced, they should be married over by "Boston law." They consented. The ceremony was deferred in order to make preparation for the approaching nuptials, under the auspices of the new law.

The white ladies of the agency, some of whom were unmarried, proposed to adorn the bride, while the *employés* furnished enough Sunday clothes to dress the husband in good style. *Employés* and Indians were notified of the important affair, and the court adjourned to the big camp-fire, in order to perform the marriage ceremony in the presence of all the people. The presiding judge *pro tem.* ordered the parties to appear.

The groom, dressed in a borrowed suit, was the first to stand up. Sallie hesitated; the husband insisted. The bride was reluctant, saying she wanted to know how long the new law would hold "Cho-kus."— "Is it a strong law? Won't he buy another wife some time?" When all the questions were answered to her satisfaction, she passed her child over to another woman, and stood beside her *lover*. Yes, her lover; for he then discovered that he really loved her, just as many a white-faced man has in similar cases, when he realized the danger of losing her.

The official reporter, on this occasion, did not furnish an account of the bride's dress, but for the satisfaction, it may be, to my young lady readers, I will say that the toilet was elaborately gotten up a-la-mode, consisting of immense tilting hoops, bright-hued goods for dress, paint in profusion on her cheeks, necklace of beads, and shells, and tresses of dark hair, "*all her own*," ornamented with cheap jewellery. This being the first marriage under the new law, the chief remarked that be wished them "tied very strong, so they could not get away from each other."

We extemporized the ceremony as follows: "Cho-kus, do you agree to live forever with Sallie, and not buy another squaw? To do the hunting and fishing, cut wood and haul it up, like white man? Never to get drunk, or talk bad to other women, and to be a good, faithful husband?" When the ceremony was interpreted, he answered, "*Now-wit-ka ni-hi;*" yes, I do.

Sallie said, "Hold on,—I want him married to me so he won't whip me anymore."

We adopted the supplement suggested, and Cho-kus again said, "*Now-wit-ka.*"

The bride said, "All right," and promised to be a good wife, to take care of the lodge and the baby, to dress the deer-skins, and dry the roots.

Cho-kus also suggested a supplement, which was, that Sallie must not "*go to the fort*" any more without *him*. She assented, with a proviso that he would not go to see "old Mose-en-kos-ket's" daughter any more.

The covenant was now completed, to the satisfaction of bride and bridegroom, and the Great Spirit was invoked to witness the pledges made; their hands were joined, and they were pronounced husband and wife. A waggish white man whispered to Allen David, the chief, that the bride must be saluted. The chief inquired whether that was the way of the new law, saying he wanted "a real Boston wedding." We said to Cho-kus, "Salute your bride." He replied he thought the ceremony was over; but, when made to understand what the salute meant, replied that it was not modest; that no Indian man ever kissed a woman in public. We urged that it was right under the new law. He remarked that somebody else must kiss her; he didn't intend to. Our waggish friend again whispered in the ear of the chief, telling him that the officiating clergyman must perform the duty to make the marriage legal. With solemn face, the chief insisted that the whole law must be met.

The parties remained standing while this controversy was going on. The bride was willing to be saluted, but the question was, *who* was to perform that part of the closing ceremony. The record don't mention the name of the individual, and it is perhaps as well. The bride, however, was saluted.

No, *I* didn't, indeed; I—don't press the question—but I di—. No, no, it was not m——, indeed it wasn't; but I won't tell anything about it. As a faithful reporter, I will only add that the happy couple received the congratulations of friends. They are still married, and Cho-kus hasn't bought another wife yet.

The next case called was a young man who had stolen the daughter of a sub-chief. He was arraigned, "plead guilty," and by the court sentenced to wear six feet of log-chain on his leg for nine months, to have his hair cut short, and to chop wood for the chiefs, who were to board and clothe him in the mean time. Care was taken to protect the convict's right, in that he should not work in bad weather or on Sundays, or more than six hours each day. He objected to having his hair cut short, but otherwise seemed indifferent to the sentence.

The chiefs were satisfied, because they saw large piles of wood in prospect. However, long before the expiration of the term of sentence they united in a petition for his pardon.

Cases of various kinds came into court and were disposed of, the chief exhibiting more judgment than is sometimes found in more pretentious courts of justice.

They were instructed, in regard to law, that it was supposed to be *common sense and equal justice, and that any law which did not recognize these principles was not a good law.*

This court is still doing business, (as at time of first publication), under the direction of a government agent. The wedding of Cho-kus and Sallie was celebrated with a grand dance. Who shall say these people do not civilize rapidly? The occasion furnished an opportunity for the Indian boys to air their paints, feathers, and fine clothes; also for Indian maidens and women to dress in holiday attire.

Chief Allen David had given orders that this "social hop," commemorating the first marriage in civil life, should be conducted in civil form. The white boys were willing to teach the red ones and their partners the steps of the new dance.

The ballroom was lighted up with great pine wood fires, whose light shone on the green leaves of the sugar pines and on the tan-coloured faces of the lookers-on. Singular spectacle!—children of a high civilization leading those of wilder life into the mazes of this giddy pastime; and they were apt scholars, especially the maidens. The music was tame; too tame for a people who are educated to a love of exciting sports.

The chiefs stood looking on, and, when occasion required, enforcing the orders of the floor-managers, who were our teamsters, turned, for the nonce, to dancing masters. I doubt if they would have been half as zealous in a Sabbath school. But since dancing is a part of American civilization, acknowledged as such by good authority, and since Indians have a natural fondness for amusements, and cannot be made to abandon such recreation, perhaps it was well that our teamster boys were qualified to teach them in this, though they were not for teaching higher lessons.

At our request we were entertained with an Indian play. No phase of civilized life exists that has not its rude counterpart in Indian life. This entertainment of which I am writing was given by *professional* players, who evinced real talent. All the people took great interest in the preparations, inasmuch as we had honoured them by making the request. The theatre was large and commodious, well lighted with huge log fires. The *foot-lights* were of pitch wood. The *boards* were sanded years before, and had been often carpeted with velvet green or snowy white. The "*Green-rooms*" were of white tent cloths, fashioned for the purpose by brown hands, and were in close proximity to the scene. The front seats were "reserved" for invited guests. The rest was "standing room." Circling round in dusky rows stood the patient throng. Nor stamps, nor whistles, nor other hideous noises gave evidence of bad-breeding or undue impatience. No police force was necessary *there* to compel the audience to respect the players or each other's rights.

As the time to begin comes round a silence pervades the assembly. No huge bill-posters, or "flyers," or other programme had given even an inkling of the play. This was as it should be everywhere, for then no promises were made to be broken, and no fault could be found, whether the play was good or bad. The knowing ones, aware, by signs we did not see, that soon the performance would commence, by motion of hand or eye would say, "Be still."

Now we hear a female voice, soft and low, singing, and coming from some unseen lodge. It grows more distinct each moment and more plaintive, and finally the singer comes into the circle with a half dance, the music of her voice broken by occasional sobs, makes the circuit of the stage, growing weary and sobbing oftener; she at last drops down in weary, careless abandonment. This maiden was attired in showy dress, of wild Indian costume, ornamented with beads and tinsel. Her cheeks and hair were painted with vermilion. The frock she wore was short, reaching only to the knee. Close-fitting garments of scarlet cloth, richly trimmed with beads, and fringe of deer-skin she wore upon her ankles, with feet encased in dainty *moccasins*.

When she sat down, the picture was that of one tasting the bitter with the sweets of life, in which joy and sorrow in alternate promptings came and went. The sobbing would cease while she gathered flowers that grew within her reach, arranging them in bunches, seemingly absorbed in other thoughts, occasionally giving vent in half-stifled, child-like sobs, or muttering in broken sentences, with parting lips, complaints against her cruel father, giving emphasis with her head to her half-uttered speech.

Following the eyes of our Indian interpreter, whose quick ear had caught the sound of coming steps, we saw a fine-looking young brave enter the ring, crouching and silent as a panther's tread, and, scanning the surroundings, he espies the maiden. We hear a sound so low that we imagine it is but the chirping of a tiny bird; but it catches the maiden's ear, who raises her head and listens, waiting for the sound, and then relapses into half-subdued silence. Meanwhile the young brave gazes, with bright eyes and parted lips, on the maiden. Again he chirps. Now she looks around and catches his eye, but does not scream, or make other noises, until, by pantomimic words, they understand they are alone.

The warrior breaks out in a wild song of love, and, keeping time with his voice, with short, soft, dancing step, he passes round the maiden, who plays *coquette*, and seems to be fully on her ground. He grows more earnest, and raises his voice, quickens his steps, and, passing close before her, offers his love, and proposes marriage, speaks her name, and, turning quickly again, passes back and forth, each time pleading his case more earnestly, until the maiden, woman-like, feigns resentment, and he, poor fellow, thinks she means what she does not, and slowly and sadly, in apparent despair, retreats to the farther side of the stage.

When he came upon the scene, clad in his dress of deer-skins, hunting-shirt and leggings, with *moccasins* trimmed with beads and scarlet cloth, his long hair ornamented with eagle feathers, and neck encircled with the claws of wild cayotes, his arms with a score of rings, his scarlet blanket girded round his waist, and reaching nearly to the ground,—swinging to his back, his quiver full of painted arrows, whose feathered ends shone above his shoulder; his left hand clasping an Indian bow, while his right held his blanket in rude drapery around him,—he was the very image of the real live young Indian brave. But now, with blanket drawn over his shoulder, covering his arms, while

189

the feathers in his hair and the arrows were held tightly to his head and neck, he seemed the neglected lover he thought himself:

Poor Ke-how-la, you do not appear to know that Ganweta is playing prude with you. Ke-how-la breaks out afresh, in song and dance, and, circling around the maiden, gives vent to his wounded pride, declares that he will wed another, and, as if to retire, he turns from her. Ganweta, as all her sex will do, discovers that she has carried the joke too far, springs up, and, throwing a bunch of flowers over his head, begins to tell, in song, that she dare not listen to his words, because her father demands a price for her that Ke-how-la cannot pay, since he is poor in horses; but that, if left to choice, she would be his wife, and gather roots, and dress deer-skins, and be his slave.

Ke-how-la listens with head half turned, and then replies that he will carry her away until her father's anger shall be passed.

Ganweta tells how brave and strong her father is, and that he intends to sell her to another.

Ke-how-la boasts of his skill in archery, and, dropping his blanket from his shoulder and stringing his bow, quickly snatches an arrow from his fawn-skin quiver, and sends it into a target centre, and then another by its side, and still another, until he makes a real bouquet of feathered arrows stand out on the target's face, in proof of his ability to defend her from her father's wrath.

Snatching his arrows, and putting them in place among their fellows, save one he holds in his hand, he motions her to come, and, bounding away like an antlered deer, he runs around the circle with Ganweta following like a frightened fawn. They pass off the scene. The braves sent by the father come on stealthily, scanning the ground to detect any sign that would be evidence that the lovers had been there. Stooping low and pointing with his finger to the tracks left, a warrior gives signal that he has found the trail, and then the party starts in quick pursuit, following round where Ke-how-la and Ganweta had passed, who, still fleeing, come in on the opposite side, and, walking slowly backward, he, stepping in her tracks, intending thus to mislead the pursuers, then, anon, throwing his arm around her, would carry her a few steps, and, dropping her on the ground, they would resume the flight.

The pursuers appear baffled; but with cunning ways they find the trail, and resume with quickened steps the chase.

Suddenly Ke-how-la stops and listens. His face declares that he has knowledge of the coming struggle,—that he must fight. Bidding

Ganweta haste away, he takes a station near a tree, and awaits the pursuers. They seem to be aware that he is there, and, drawing their bows, prepare to fight. See Ke-how-la expose his blanket, the pursuers letting two arrows fly, one of them striking it, the other the tree. A twang from Ke-how-la's bow, and a howl of pain, and a red-skinned pursuer in agony has an arrow in his heart, and then the arrows fly in quick succession, until the hero sends his antagonists to the happy hunting-ground of their fathers, and with apparent earnestness he scalps his foes.

With his trophies hanging to his belt, he calls, "*Ganweta, Kaitch Kona Ganweta!*"—Beautiful Ganweta; but he calls in vain. While Ke-how-la was fighting, a brave of another tribe carries off the shrinking maiden, and escapes to his people.

Ke-how-la takes the trail, and follows by the signs Ganweta had left on her involuntary flight, and discovers her surrounded by his enemies. He returns to his own people for assistance. He finds friends willing to follow him. Ganweta's father is reconciled with him, and gives his consent to his marriage when he shall have brought Ganweta home. A party is formed, and after the war-dance and other savage ceremonies, they go on the warpath. Then we see the warriors fight a sham battle with real war-whoops and scalping ceremonies. The arrows fly, and the wounded fall, and the victors secure the scalps and also the captive maiden, and, with wild sports, return to the lodge of Ganweta's father.

This performance lasted about three hours, and from the beginning to the end the interest increased, winding up with a scalp-dance.

I have never witnessed a play better performed, and certainly never with imitation so close to reality. It demonstrated that talent does not belong to any privileged race; that Indians are endowed with love for amusements, and that they possess ability to create and perform.

If it is urged that such plays foster savage habits among the Indians, the excuse must be that they were true to the scenes of their own lives and in conformity with the tastes of the people, as all theatricals are supposed to be.

It had one merit that many plays lack. Its actors were natural, and no unseemly struts and false steps, or rude and uncouth exhibitions of dexterity or unseemly attitudes, that make modest people hide their eyes in very shame, were indulged in by the players.

The Indians of Oregon and of the Pacific coast wear long hair; at least, until they change their mode of life, they have a great aversion to cutting it, and, in fact, it is almost the last personal habit they give up. Before leaving this agency, I proposed to give a new hat to each man who would consent to have his hair cut short. The proposition was not well received at first, because of their old-time religious faith, which in some way connected long hair with religious ceremony. It is safe to assert, that, whenever an Oregon Indian is seen without long hair, he has abandoned his savage religion. Before leaving, however, I was assured that I might send out the hat for over one hundred.

The following summer, when making an official visit, I took with me four hundred hats. When the question was brought up, and the hats were in sight, a flurry was visible among the men. The chief, Allen David, led the way, begging for a long cut. A compromise was made, and it was agreed that the hair should be cut just half-way down. With this understanding, the barber's shop was instituted, and long black hair enough to make a Boston hair merchant rich was cut off and burned up.

The metamorphosis was very noticeable. Many ludicrous scenes were presented in connection with, and grew out of, this episode. A great step forward had been made, and one, too, that will not "slip back."

When O-che-o came out of the room, after his head had been for the first time in his life under a barber's hands, he presented a comical spectacle. His children did not know him; some of his older friends did not recognize in him the chief of other days.

CHAPTER 18

Omelets and Arrows—Big Steam-Boilers

An Indian game of ball is not exactly like America's great game of base ball. It resembles, somewhat, the old game of shindy or bandy. The field is one-fourth of a mile in length, and one-eighth in width. Stakes are planted at either end, and also in the middle. The players pair off until all are chosen who desire to play. Captains are elected who command the players of each side, and take their stations at the middle stakes, arranging their men on either side, each of whom is provided with a club three feet in length, having a short crook at the lower end. The ball is fashioned out of a tough knot of wood, and is about three inches in diameter, and burnt by fire until it is charred slightly, thus making it of black colour. This game is called "*ko-ho*," and is won by the party who succeeds in knocking the ball with the club to the home base at the opposite end of the ground.

A game of "*ko-ho*" attracts much attention; old and young, deaf, dumb, and blind, all go to witness the sport; the latter, probably, to hear the boisterous shouts that attend the playing. Sometimes it is made the occasion for gambling, and then the excitement becomes intense.

Another game is played, with two pieces of wood six inches long and about one inch in diameter, securely connected by a thong of rawhide, about four inches apart; the game, as in "*ko-ho*," being to toss this plaything with straight clubs to a home base; the parties struggling as in the other game. Football is not uncommon, and great contests are had over this game also.

Civilized American gambling cards are common, and are played in games that have no existence among white people; though Indians are expert in all common games, and become, like their white brother, infatuated, and gamble with desperation. Gambling seems to be a passion among them. It is not uncommon to see the younger men of tribes that are uncivilized, seated on the ground, and, with a blanket spread over their limbs, all pointing toward a common centre, gambling with small sticks of wood, the parties alternately mixing their hands under the blanket, changing the sticks from one hand to the other while they sing a low melody; and, when withdrawing the hands, the other Indians point to the hand they suppose to be the holder of the sticks, thus indicating the one selected as the winning hand. When the bets are all made the holder opens both hands, and thus declares the result. The favourite sport of the Indians is horse-racing; but, like other people, they gamble on almost everything. Among them are natural professional gamblers. This passion is a fruitful source of poverty; and many complaints are made by young, green ones, against *red*-legged sharps.

An Indian woman filed a complaint against "Long John," an Indian gambler, charging him with having swindled her son, a boy of eighteen or twenty years of age, out of a number of horses that belonged to the family. She asserted that they were poor; that the loss was too much to bear in silence, and that, since her son was a boy, not a man, "Long John" ought to return the horses. This famous gambler was ordered to appear. The case was investigated. "Long John" pleaded guilty as charged in the indictment, but offered the old Indian law as an excuse. He finally proposed to return the horses, on condition that the boy would abandon the habit. The boy promised; the property was returned; and the old woman went away happy in the possession of her restored fortune; for it was to her what business and home are to wealthy people. Under the new law gambling is prohibited by a fine; but the Indians find ways to avoid the law, and gambling is now, and will continue to be, common among them.

These people have a beautiful country, with a cold climate, being at an altitude of four thousand feet above the sea level. Snows of two to four feet deep are not uncommon. The rivers and lakes are well supplied with fish, the mountains with game, the land with berries and wild roots.

Big Klamath marsh is situated twenty miles north of the Great Klamath Lake. It is six miles wide and twenty long, and receives its water from the south side of the Blue mountains. This marsh is covered with a growth of pond-lilies, that furnish immense supplies of *wo-cus* (seed of lily). It is a great rendezvous for several tribes who come to gather *wo-cus*. The main stem of this plant first blossoms on the top of the water, and, as the seasons advance, the flower matures and rises above the surface one or two feet, and forms a large pod, of four inches in length and three in diameter. The Indians go out among the lilies in canoes, and gather the bowls or pods while green, spread them out in the sun, and when cured they are beaten with sticks until the seeds fall out. These are put in sacks and carried home, *cached* (buried in cellars) until required for use. Then the seeds are thrown into a shallow basket, with live coals of fire, and roasted, after which it is ground by hand on flat rocks.

It is a nutritious food, and, when properly prepared, not unpalatable. The Klamaths use it in soups, and often prepare it by mixing like flour into cakes, which they bake in the ashes. This article of *wo-cus* is abundant, available, and altogether sufficient to furnish subsistence for all the Indians in Oregon. To this *wo-cus* field the natives have for generations past gone for supplies, and in the meantime to exchange slaves, gamble, and hold great councils. Many stirring scenes have been enacted at this place that would furnish foundation for romantic story or bloody tragedy.

The lakes of Klamath are great resorts for the feathery tribes, which come with the spring and sojourn through the summer. The people luxuriate on the eggs of these wild fowls. They go out into the tall *tule* (grass) in canoes, and collect them in large quantities. *"The egg season" lasts until the hatching season is over*, the Indians cooking unhatched birds, and eating them with as much avidity and as little thought of indecency as New England people cook and eat clams, oysters, or herrings.

The young fowls are captured in nets. The arrangement is quite cunning, and, although primitive in construction, evinces some inventive genius. A circular net is made three feet in diameter, and to the outer edge are attached eight or ten small rods of half-inch diameter, and about fifteen inches in length; three inches from the lower end, which is sharpened to a point, the net is attached. The upper end of the rods are bevelled on one side, and inserted into a rude socket, in the end of a shaft ten feet long.

Armed with this trap, the hunter crawls on the ground until he is within safe distance of the mother-bird and her little flock, when, suddenly springing up, the old birds, geese or ducks, as the case may be, fly away, while the little ones flee toward the water. The Indian launches the shaft with the net attached in such a way that the net spreads to its utmost size, the sharpened points of the rods pierce the ground, and, the upper end having left the socket on the shaft, stand in circular row, holding the net and contents to the ground.

The Klamath mode of taking fish is peculiar to the Indians of this lake country. A canoe-shaped basket is made, with covering of willow-work at each end, leaving a space of four feet in the middle top of the basket. This basket is carried out into the *tules* that adjoin the lakes, and sunk to the depth of two or three feet. The fishermen chew dried fish eggs and spit them in the water over the basket, until it is covered with the eggs, and then retire a short distance, waiting until the whitefish come in large numbers over the basket, when the fishermen cautiously approach the covered ends, and raise it suddenly, until the upper edge is above the water, and thus entrap hundreds of fish, that are about eight inches in length. These are transferred to the hands of the squaws, and by them are strung on ropes or sticks and placed over fires until cured, without salt, after which they are stored for winter use. This fish is very oily and nutritious, and makes a valuable food. Indeed, this country is more than ordinarily fruitful, and abounds in resources suited to Indian life.

The lakes are well supplied with various kinds of trout. They are taken in many ways; mostly, however, with hook and line. I remember, on one occasion, going to a small slough making out of the lake among the *tules*. Being prepared with American equipment of lines and flies, I was sanguine of success; but I was doomed to disappointment so far as catching trout with fly-hooks was concerned. I finally succeeded in capturing a pocketful of large black army-crickets. The first venture with this bait was rewarded by a fine trout of six pounds' weight. In one hour and a half I had twenty-four fish, whose aggregate weight was one hundred and four pounds. They were mostly golden trout, a species peculiar to Klamath Lake. They are similar to other trout, except in the rich golden colour of their bodies, and in the shape of their fins. Silver trout are sometimes caught also, they taking their name from their silver sides and the colour of their flesh. Lake trout, another species, are very dark; they are sharp biters, and very game when hooked. Salmon trout, as the name indicates, resemble salmon in every way; so much so that none but an expert could distinguish the two.

Still another kind of the trout family are also in abundance, called dog trout. They live on the younger fish of their own species; do not run in schools, but solitary and alone, devouring the small ones. I have

196

caught them with the tails of little fish sticking in their mouths. Brook trout may be found in the smaller streams; they are identical with those of New England.

The wild game consists of deer and elk, which are still abundant and furnish subsistence; and, until these people sold their birthrights and received in exchange therefore clothing and blankets,—a mere mess of pottage,—afforded material for warming their bodies. These sources of supply, together with the wild fowls, which congregate in innumerable quantities, all go to make up a country well adapted to wild Indian life, requiring but reasonable exertion to secure subsistence and clothing.

Although the country is high and cold, and the major portion covered in winter with deep snows, there are small valleys and belts of country where snow never lies on the ground for any considerable length of time, and the stock cattle and horses live through the winter without care.

When the railroad shall have been built, connecting the lake country with the outside world, it will afford large supplies of fish, game, wild fowls, eggs, feathers, ice, and lumber of the choicest kinds. Already has the keen eye of the white man discovered its many inducements and tempting offers of business.

Big Klamath Lake is twenty miles wide and forty miles long; a most beautiful sheet of water, dotted with small islands. Its average depth is, perhaps, forty feet, surrounded on two sides with heavy forests of timber; on the others, with valleys of sure and productive soil, when once science shall have taught the people how to accommodate the agriculture to the climate. This lake has a connection with those below, called Link River, a short stream of but four miles, through which vast volumes of water find outlet, over sweeping rapids, falling at the rate of one hundred feet to the mile.

The power that wastes itself in Link River would move machinery that would convert the immense forests into merchandise, and put music into a million spindles, giving employment to thousands of hands who are willing to toil for reward.

Nature has also favoured this wonderful country with steam-power beyond comparison; great furnaces underground, fed by invisible hands, send the steam through rocky fissures or escape-pipes to the surface. Near Link River, two of these escape-pipes emit the stifling steam constantly. Approaching cautiously, a sight may be had of the boiling waters beneath. Lower down the hill it arises in a stream, sufficient to run a saw-mill, coming out boiling hot, and flowing away in rippling current. Along the banks of this stream flowers bloom the year round, and vegetation is ever green for several rods from the banks. The scene from the ridge on the north that overlooks Link valley is one of rare beauty.

Standing in snow two feet deep, on a cold morning in December, 1869, my eyes first took in the landscape. Surrounded by lofty pines, and, looking southward, we caught sight of the Lost River county, the home of the Modocs, bathed in sunshine, clear, cold sunshine; the almost boundless tracts of sage-brush land, stretching away to the foot of the Cascade mountains on the right, until sage-brush plain was lost in pine-wood forest. On the left front we caught sight of Tu-le Lake, lying calmly beneath its crystal covering of glittering ice; and, still left, Lost-river mountains, and beside them the stream whose water drank up the blood of many battles in times past. Following its line toward its source, we see a mountain cleft in twain to make passage for the waters of Clear lake, after they have tunnelled Saddle mountains for ten miles, and come again to human sight.

We had been so entertained with the splendour of the winter scene, that we had overlooked its grandest feature, until our fretful horses, which had caught sight of it before we had, became restless and impatient to bathe their icy hoofs in the beautiful valley at our feet, and refused longer to wait for us to paint on our memory the panorama.

Dismounting, we, too, caught sight of one of nature's wonderful freaks. Down below us, in the immense amphitheatre, we discovered columns of steam rising from the smooth prairie hill-side, ascending in fantastic puffs, and mixing with the atmosphere; sometimes cut off, by sudden gusts of cold winds, into minute clouds, that swing out and lose themselves in strange company of fiercer breath from the mountains covered with snow and ice.

Look again to the right, and see the constant steam vapour that comes with hot breath from the boiling spring, where it runs in grandeur, and gradually warms the soil and shrubbery that surrounds its channel. Following the curve of this stream, see the clouds of steam decrease as it flows out on the plain, until, at last, its warm breath is lost to sight in the high *tule* grass of Lower Klamath Lake. Come back along the line and see the fringe of grass and flowers that exult in life, despite the winter's cold; and other of nature's children, too, are standing with feet in the soft banks, and inhaling the warm breath.

See the long line of sleek cattle and horses that have driven away the mule, deer and antlered elk, and now claim mastership of what God has done for this strange valley. Even dumb brutes enjoy this refuge from the cold storms of the plains; thus cheating old winter out of the privilege of punishing them.

Yielding to the importunity of our restless steed, we remount, and, giving rein, are carried rapidly down the mountain side, at a pace that would be dangerous on clumsy eastern ponies, until reaching the valley, and feeling the soft turf beneath us, we improve the invitation to warm our hands at this gentle outlet to one of nature's seething caldrons.

Gathering a bouquet of wild flowers from this fairy garden, surrounded by snows and ice, we resume our journey, for we are now bound for the home of Captain *Jack*.

CHAPTER 19

Modoc Blood Under a Flag of Truce

Since we are now *en route* to the Modoc country, and since they have taken a place in modern history as a warlike people, and have enrolled their names on the record of stirring events, it is well to give them something more than a passing notice.

In so doing, I shall confine my remarks to such facts as have come under my own observation, and also those that are well authenticated. In memory of the late tragedy in the "Lava Beds," in which I so nearly lost my life, I approach this subject with a full determination to present the facts connected therewith in a fair and impartial manner, without fear of criticism from the enemies of the red man, or a desire to court undue favour from his friends.

The Modocs are a branch from a once powerful tribe of the Pacific coast, and known as "La-la-cas," inhabiting the country drained by Klamath River and lakes, also including the "Lost River Basin," and extending inland from the coast proper about three hundred miles, covering the territory of what is now Siskiyou County, Cal., and parts of Jackson and Josephine counties, of Oregon. They were warlike, as most uncivilized nations are, when they become powerful. Surrounded with peoples of similar character, they were often on the "warpath."

The history of the great battles fought by the La-la-cas of olden time is a fruitful subject for Indian stories by the descendants of the Klamaths and Modocs; and from them, years ago, I learned about the rebellion so nearly cotemporaneous with the American Revolution.

That rebellion sprang from causes so nearly of the same kind as those which prompted our forefathers to take up arms against Great Britain, that the coincidence is strange indeed, though it could not have any connection with the white man's war. To those who have given the subject of Indian history a careful study, it is not new, that, while a monarch exercised arbitrary power across the Atlantic, and dictated government and law to the American colonies, many petty monarchs, also claiming the hereditary right to rule on the strength of royalty and blood, were the governing nations on the continent of America. This kind of royalty seems to have been acknowledged and disputed by turns, for many generations; and, perhaps, the La-la-cas may have passed through as many revolutions as enlightened political organizations, though no other history than tradition has made a record thereof. At all events it is part of the history of the Modocs and Klamaths, that feuds and revolutions have been of common occurrence, growing out of the desire for power. After all, human nature is pretty much the same in all conditions of society, without regard to colour or race.

The office of chief, among Indians of former times, was to the chieftain what the crown was to a king. The function of chieftain among semi-civilized Indians of today is to him what the office of President is to General Grant, or it may be likened to the position of Louis Philippe a few years ago, half attained through royal right, and half by force or consent of the governed.

This comparison is *apropos* according to the status of traditional and hereditary law.

With the La-la-cas, one hundred years ago, the prerogative of royalty, though, perhaps, acknowledged in the abstract, was often disputed in the distribution of honours.

This "bone of contention," so fruitful of blood with civilized nations, was one of the principal and moving causes of the separation of a band of La-la-cas, who are now known as Modocs, from the tribe who are now called Klamaths.

There is a curious resemblance between the political customs of savage and civilized nations. The royal house from whence came the hero of the Modoc war—Captain Jack—was not exempt from the contentions common to royal households, and it may be said, too, that while the branch to which he belonged had furnished their quota of braves for many wars, they resisted the taxes levied on them, and at last openly rebelled, and separated from their ancient tribe on account of the exactions of tyrannical chiefs.

That my readers may properly understand the subject now under consideration, it is well to state, in a general way, that Indian nations, singularly enough, follow in the footsteps of the people of Bible history. Whether they derive the custom from traditional connection or not, I leave to antiquarians to answer.

Every nation is divided into tribes, and tribes are divided into bands, and bands into smaller divisions, even down to families; each nation has, or is supposed to have, a head chief; each tribe a chief; each band a sub-chief; and so on, down, until you reach family relations.

Each tribe, band, and even family, has in times of peace an allotted home, or district of country that they call their own. They claim the privileges that it affords, and are very jealous of any infringement on their rights.

The Modocs inhabited that portion of country know, as "Lost-river Basin,"—perhaps forty miles square,—lying east of the foot of "Shasta Butte," possessing many natural resources for Indian life. It is doubtful whether any other country of like extent affords so great and so varied a supply as this district.

Lost River is a great fishing country, affording those of a kind peculiar to Tule lake and Lost River, in so great abundance as to be almost beyond belief.

But to resume the history of this band of Modocs. At or about the time indicated as cotemporaneous with "the great event" in American civilized history, the head chief of all the La-la-cas demanded of Mo-a-doc-us, the chief of the Lost River band of the La-la-cas, not only braves for the warpath, but also that supplies of fish from Lost River should be furnished.

This demand was refused. Following the refusal, war was declared; and Mo-a-doc-us issued his declaration of independence, throwing off his allegiance from and to the head chief of the La-la-cas. The war that followed was one of a character similar in some respects to the American Revolution; the one party struggling to hold power, the other fighting for freedom,—for such it was in reality.

The Modocs and Klamaths tell of many battles fought, and brave men killed; how the survivors passed their allotted time in mourning; how, at last, the La-la-cas were defeated; and though no formal acknowledgment or recognition of the independence of Mo-a-doc-us was ever bulletined to the world, yet it was, in modern political language, "an accomplished fact."

The followers of the La-la-cas have since been termed Klamaths.

Without tracing the history of the Mo-a-docs through their many wars, I pass over the intervening feuds until 1846, at which time they numbered six hundred warriors, and were subdivided into bands, governed by "Schonchin," a head chief, although his authority seems even

CAPTAIN JACK.

then to have been disputed, on the ground that he was not a legitimate descendant of the great Mo-a-doc-us, and consequently not of royal blood. He won his position as chief by his great personal bravery in battle.

The father of Captain Jack was the former chief of the Lost-river Modocs. He was killed in battle with the Warm Spring and Te-ni-no Indians, near the head-waters of the Des-chutes river, in Oregon, at which time Ki-en-te-poos (Captain Jack) was a small boy.

I have taken some pains to ascertain reliable data as to the parentage and birthplace of a man whose name has been on every tongue for the past year, and state, most positively, that Captain Jack's parents were both Modocs of royal blood, and that Captain Jack was born on Lost River, near the "Natural Bridge," and very near the ground on which was fought the first battle of the late Modoc war; and, further, that he never lived with any white man; that he never has learned to speak any other than the language of the ancient La-la-cas, or Mo-a-docs, although he may have understood many words of the English tongue.

You will have observed that the regard for royal honours was not extinct at the time of the death of Jack's father, who seems to have left in the hearts of his people the ambition to restore the ancient order of things, by re-establishing the hereditary right to the chieftainship. This sentiment, thus perpetuated, undoubtedly found a lodgement in the heart of the boy, Ki-en-te-poos.

To resume the review of the first war: As told by white men, it would appear that a wanton thirst for blood impelled the Modocs to murder defenceless emigrants. I doubt not that many innocent persons lost their lives; still, with my knowledge of Indian character, I am not ready to say that provocation was wanting. While I would be careful in making up my estimate on the validity of Indian statements, I am still willing that the Modocs' side of the causes of the first wars should be heard.

Old Chief Schonchin says that it grew out of a misunderstanding as to the identity of the *Modocs*, *Snakes*, and *Pitt-river* Indians. The emigrants had difficulties with the Snake Indians, through whose country they passed in reaching Oregon and California; and that he never knew what was the cause of the first troubles between them. The Snake Indians captured horses and mules from the emigrants, and sold them, or gambled them, to the Pitt-river Indians, who in turn transferred them, through the same process, to the Modocs; and that the animals found by emigrants in possession of the Modocs were recaptured, and hence war was at last brought about. The story seems plausible, and is certainly entitled to some respect, coming, as it does, from a man of the character of old Chief Schonchin. I know there is a disposition to discredit any statement made by an Indian, simply because he *is an Indian*, and more particularly when it comes in conflict with our prejudices to accept it as the truth. Some white men are entitled to credit; others are not. So it is with Indians, and, if it were possible, the disparity is even greater among them than among white men.

Chief Schonchin, of whom I am speaking, commands respect from those who know him best, and have known him longest. He does not deny that he was in the early wars; that he did all in his power to exterminate his enemies. In speaking of the wars with white men, he once remarked, in an evening talk around a camp-fire: "I thought, if we killed all the white men we saw, that no more would come. We killed all we could; but they came more and more, like new grass in the spring. I looked around, and saw that many of our young men were dead, and could not come back to fight. My heart was sick. My people were few. I threw down my gun. I said, I will not fight again. I made friends with the white man. I am an old man; I cannot fight now. I want to die in peace." To his credit be it said, that no act of his, since the treaty of 1864, has deserved censure. He is still in charge of the loyal Modocs, at Yai-nax station, grieving over the waywardness of his brother John and Captain Jack.

He was not in the "Ben Wright" affair, although he was near when the massacre occurred. His reason for not being present was because he mistrusted that treachery was intended on the part of Wright; and, further, that a "treaty of peace" was proposed by him, which was to be accompanied with a feast, given by the white man; but that the talk was "too good,"—"*promised too much,*"—and that, suspicious of the whole affair, he kept away; that forty-six Modocs accepted the invitation to feast with their white brethren, and that but five escaped the wholesale butchery. Of these five, the last survivor was murdered, June, 1873, during the cowardly attack on Fairchild's wagon, containing the Indian captives, near Lost River, after the surrender of Captain Jack.

Now, whether the Indian version of the Ben Wright affair is correct, or not, that forty Indians were killed while under a flag of truce in the hands of white men of the Ben Wright party, in 1852,—*there can be no doubt.* The effects of this act can be traced all the way down from that day to this, and have had much to do with making the Modocs a revengeful people.

The friends of Ben Wright deny that he committed an act of treachery; yet there are persons in California who state positively that he *purchased strychnine previous to his visit to the Modoc country, with the avowed intention of poisoning the Indians.* Others, who were with him at the time of the massacre, testify that *he made the attempt at poisoning,* and finally, abandoning it, he resorted to the "peace talk" to accomplish his purpose. The excuse for this unwarrantable act of treachery was to punish the Modocs for the murdering of emigrants at Bloody Point, a few days previous.

This unparalleled slaughter was perpetrated on the shore of Tule Lake, in September, 1852. It occurred directly opposite the "Lava Bed," at a point where the emigrant road touches the shore of the lake, after crossing a desert tract of several miles, and where the mountains forced the road to leave the high plains to effect a passage. For several hundred yards the route ran along under a stony bluff, and near the waters of the lake. The place was well-adapted for such hellish purposes.

The emigrant train consisted of sixty-five men, women, and children, and the whole line of wagons was driven down into this position before the attack was made. The Indians, secreted in the rocks at either end of the narrow passage, attacked their hapless victims both in front and rear. Hemmed in by high rocky bluffs on one side and the lake on the other, they were butchered indiscriminately. Neither age nor sex were spared, save two young girls of twelve and fourteen years of age respectively, who were taken prisoners, and one man, who escaped.

This massacre was attended with all the circumstances of savage warfare. Men were killed outright and scalped. Women were treated with indignities *that words may not reveal. Even fiendish torture was surpassed, and human language is too tame to express the horrible outrages committed on them.* Children were tortured, some of them mutilated and dismembered, while yet alive, before the eyes of their mothers. No page in all the bloody history of Indian cruelties exceeds that of the massacre of emigrants at Bloody Point, by the Modocs, in September, 1852.

The two girls who were taken prisoners were allotted to some of the brave warriors as wives. They survived for several years, and, according to Modoc stories, were reconciled to their fate, adopting the manners and customs of their captors. It is said that they taught the Modocs many things pertaining to a civilized life, and that they exercised great influence over them; that the Modoc women became jealous of their power, and put them to death.

Near the residence of Mr. Dorris, on Cottonwood Creek, is a rocky cliff overlooking the valley. It was from this cliff the unfortunate captives were thrown to the rocks below, ending their lives as victims to the jealousy of the wives and mothers of their savage captors. Evidences of this tragedy are in existence; human skulls, and, within a few years, locks of long hair, unlike that of Indians, have been found on the spot indicated as the place where these captives were destroyed.

Ben Wright was a citizen of Y-re-ka. He was esteemed as a man of good character and standing among his fellows in that early day. Born a leader, he was selected by the miners to command a company of volunteers, who were enlisted without authority of the Government of the United States, the State of California, or the County of Sys-ki-you.

This company was formed, under the common law of self-protection, in the early days of California, when Indian outrages were of common occurrence. In the absence of regular provision for protection, the miners and settlers, in a spirit of patriotism, volunteered to punish Indians as well as to guard the peace of the country. Be it remembered that the massacre at "Bloody Point" was not the only act of savage ferocity committed by the Modocs. For five years had they been murdering the worn-out emigrants who were *en route* to California and Oregon.

It was in harmony with frontier ideas of right, to punish these people for their crimes, without taking into consideration the causes that may have impelled them to bloody deeds. The victims were not responsible for the acts of their predecessors on the line of travellers. However humane and just we may feel, we cannot object to Ben Wright's motive, though all men who possess correct ideas of justice may deprecate the manner of avenging the wrongs committed. Had he slain the entire tribe in fair battle, no just condemnation could have been pronounced against him. Had he avenged their horrible crimes by ambushing them, by his skill and cunning, no man would have censured him; *but to violate a flag of truce, under pretence of peace-making, was a wrong that fair-minded men, everywhere, condemn as an outrage against humanity and civilization.*

If the Modocs had first been guilty of such acts of treachery, "extermination" would justly have been the cry. Savage warfare is unworthy of any people; but certainly it should never be surpassed by those professing Christian civilization. Even in war they should endeavour to teach the savage the higher laws that govern mankind.

Without stopping to moralize further, let us pursue the main facts, as they come following each other in succession. After the Ben Wright massacre, hostilities were continued until 1864; at which time Elisha Steel, Esq., of Y-re-ka, who was then acting superintendent for the northern district of California, made an informal treaty with the various bands of Indians, and who seems to have been more an arbitrator than a government commissioner. At all events the articles of agreement were not ratified by Congress.

This treaty did not set forth that any consideration would be paid by the government for the possession of the Modoc country. Neither did it seek to alienate the country from the Indians, but referred to the localities where certain bands of Modocs, Schas-tas, Schas-ta-scotons, and Klamaths should reside. There was also an agreement to keep peace with each other and the whites.

It was in this council that Captain Jack was first acknowledged as a chief, and then only after an election was had by the band that had repudiated Schonchin; after which Steele declared him a chief, and named him "Captain Jack," on account of his resemblance to a miner bearing that name. That the Steele treaty was somewhat indefinite and unauthorized, was given as a reason why it never was recognized by the general Government.

There may have been other and more potent reasons, however; for the Modoc country proper is about equally divided between Oregon and California, though the home of Captain Jack and Schonchin was on the Oregon side of the line. At that time the hearts of our people were much moved in behalf of the "poor Indian." Each State was anxious to furnish a home for him. Whether Steele's treaty reached Washington before or after, does not appear. The Superintendent of Oregon was instructed to "negotiate a treaty with all the Indians in the Klamath country, including the Modocs."

This council met in October, 1864. The Klamaths, and also the Modocs, were represented in the council by their chiefs; the latter by Schonchin and his brother John, who was afterwards associated with Captain Jack.

Captain Jack was recognized as a sub-chief. He participated in the council; and, when terms were agreed upon, he signed the articles of treaty in his Indian name,—Ki-en-te-poos. The idea that he was deceived in the meaning of the treaty is absurd; though it has been repeated by good men, without proper knowledge of the facts.

An unwarrantable sympathy for Captain Jack has been the result,—unless, indeed, all the Indians who were parties to the treaty are to be commiserated for having sold their birthright for an insufficient compensation. Old chief Schonchin has never claimed any other than the plain meaning of the words of the treaty; which was, substantially, that what is known as Klamath Reservation was to be the joint home of the Klamaths and Modocs. All the other country claimed by the two tribes was ceded to the United States, on condition that certain acts should be performed by the government, in a specified time. All of which has been, and is being done, to the satisfaction of the Indians who have remained on the Reservation. I assert this to be substantially correct. That they made a bargain that Captain Jack wished to repudiate is true. I do not wonder that he should do so, in view of his inherent love of royalty and his great ambition to be a chief, and the uncertainty of his tenure of office should he remain on the Reservation, the discipline of which was humiliating for one whose life had been free from restraint.

The head men of the Klamaths all agree and state positively that the treaty was fully interpreted and fairly understood by all parties, and that Captain Jack and the whole Modoc tribe shared in the issue of goods made at the council-ground by Superintendent Huntington, at the time of making the treaty. The plea that Captain Jack was deceived, as before-mentioned, is wholly unfounded. He not only understood and assented to it, but took up his abode on the Klamath Reservation, where he remained long enough to realize that Reservation life was not healthy for royalty.

Perhaps he had begun to see that he was to change his mode of life; also that Schonchin was recognized as his superior in office; and it may be that he discovered that Klamath was not as good a country for Indian life as the Lost River region. It is equally certain that he raised the standard of revolt, and finally withdrew from the Reservation, and took up his abode at his old home on Lost River; soon after which he stated to Mr. John A. Fairchilds that he had been cheated, and that "the treaty was a lie;" that he had not sold his country.

He made the same statement to Esquire Steele, of Y-re-ka, who is a man of a large and charitable heart, and who exercised great power over the Indians, and, with his former knowledge of Captain Jack, accredited his story concerning the swindle or cheat, and probably stated to Captain Jack that he would try to have the matter adjusted for him.

Steele wrote several letters to the department at Washington on this subject, and also gave letters to Jack and his people, repeating therein Jack's story about his being cheated, and commending him to the friendly consideration of white people with whom he might come in contact.

Some of these letters are still in existence. I myself have read several of them, the tenor of which was in keeping with the statement already made,—that Jack still claimed the country, and that he was a well-disposed Indian, etc.; but there was not *one line*, so far as I know, that could be construed to mean that the treaty *could or should he repudiated*.

That Steele had friendship for Jack, there can be no doubt; and that Jack recognized Steele as his friend and adviser is equally certain; and whatever influence Steele's advice may have had, it never was intended to justify Jack in removing from the Reservation to which he belonged. I have been thus particular in this matter, because Jack has used the name of Steele in a way to mislead public opinion in regard to Steele's connection with the Modoc rebellion. Jack's reason for leaving the Reservation in 1864 was, simply and substantially, that he had made a compact with which he was dissatisfied. He not only misconstrued the friendship of Steele and others, but misrepresented them in such a way as to rid himself of the responsibility as much as possible.

Following his career, we find that, in 1865, at the request of the citizens of Lost River Basin, Capt. McGreggor, commander of Fort Klamath, made an unsuccessful attempt to return Jack's band to the Reservation; and, also, that sub-agent Lindsay Applegate sought to remove him in 1866; also, that in 1867 Superintendent Huntington visited the "Modoc country," and that Capt. Jack and his warriors took a position on the opposite side of Lost River, and said to him that, if he attempted to cross over, he "would fire on him." Huntington, being unsupported, made no attempt at crossing. He reported the matter, as others had done, to the department at Washington; but no action was ordered. It will be seen that this same rebel chief had eluded and defied the authority of the government on these three successive occasions; and yet the clemency and forbearance of the government were misconstrued by him and his misinformed sympathizers.

In the latter part of 1869, while on an official visit to Klamath Agency, the Modocs first engaged my attention; and hearing then

210

the fact above referred to, as a reason why he had refused to obey the commands of the government, and believing that his return, without military force, was possible, a consultation with Agent O. C. Knapp was held. We decided to make another effort; accordingly a courier was despatched with a message that we would meet him at Link River. The reply was to the effect that if we wanted to see him we must come to his country; and, further, that he did not care to see us.

Notwithstanding this insult, we decided to visit the Modoc country in person. Believing in the power of the right to accomplish the purpose, even if force was necessary, we determined to go, "bearing the olive branch;" and, also, at the same time, recognized the necessity of being prepared for personal defence should any attack be made. A requisition was made on Capt. Goodale, commander at Fort Klamath, for a detachment of troops.

To the first request we received a doubtful answer, because "he had not the men to spare." I did not inquire of Capt. Goodale what the duties of the soldiers were; but from others I learned that they were required for "police duty," or sentry duty, which meant, probably, that one-half the soldiers were needed to guard the other half, and maybe were to wait on the officers of the fort. A few days previous, a number of enlisted men had deserted, and those sent in pursuit "had failed to put in an appearance at roll-call."

Finally, the Klamath Indians succeeded in arresting the deserters and bringing them under guard to the fort, receiving therefore a reward for so doing. This fort was built, and has been kept up at an enormous expense, to secure the peace of the country. It has been an advantage to both white men and Indians,—the one finding a market for hay and grain; the other, a market for the articles manufactured by their women,—*moccasins*, etc.; and the men an opportunity to make greenbacks by hunting and arresting deserters.

Capt. Goodale finally detailed a small squad of men, under command of a non-commissioned officer, for the purpose requested, as stated heretofore.

We left Klamath Agency on the morning of the third of December, 1869, destined for the home of the Modocs, accompanied by Agent O. C. Knapp, of Klamath, I. D. Applegate in charge of Yai-nax, and W. C. McKay, together with teamsters, guides, and interpreters; also, two Klamath Indian women. Ordering the soldiers to follow us as far as Link River, there to await further orders, we pushed on, leaving the teams with our supplies to follow into the Modoc country on the morning of the twenty-second of December, 1869.

The route from Link River is through a sage-brush plain, and following down the west bank of Lost River.

Lost River is the outlet or connecting link between Clear Lake and Tule Lake. After leaving the former, it flows underground several miles, and again coming to the surface, empties into the latter. For this reason it was named "Lost River." It is a deep, narrow stream, with but few fording-places. In March of each year it is a great fishery. None of the same species of fish are found elsewhere; it possesses the appearance of a species of white trout, excepting the head and mouth, which is after the sucker species. The flesh is rich and nutritious, and so abundant are they that they are taken with rude implements, such as sharpened sticks and pitchforks, and are even caught with the hand, when they are running over the ripples or fords.

A courier sent by the Modoc Peace Commission, with despatches to Yai-nax, having occasion to cross Lost River while en route, reported, on his return, having difficulty in crossing this stream on account of the immense numbers of fish running against the horse's legs, and frightening him. A pretty big fish story, but not incredible.

When within a few miles of the Modoc camp, we espied four Indians coming on ponies. As we approached, they, forming a line across the road, exclaimed "*Kaw-tuk!*" (Stop!) They were each armed with a rifle and revolver. Our party carried, each man, a Henry rifle and a navy six-shooter. A short parley ensued, they determining to know our business, and would allow no farther advance until their demand was recognized.

We stated, in substance, that we were anxious to see Captain Jack and his people on important business.

The Indians replied, "that they did not wish to talk with us; they had no business with us, and that we had better turn back." Three times had they defied, intimidated, or eluded officers of the government previously, and were now trying to evade a meeting by bluffing our party.

We had started to visit these people, and, in western parlance, "we were going." Pushing past the Indians, we started on a brisk gallop, they turning around and running ahead of us. After a brisk ride of four miles we came in sight of the Modoc town, situated on the western bank of the river about one mile above the "Natural Bridge," and within sight of the newly-made mounds of the State line.

The "Natural Bridge" is a ledge of rocks, twenty feet in width, spanning the river. It was used in early days of emigration, to cross the river. At the time of our visit it was two feet under water, but on either bank, approaching the bridge, were unmistakable evidences of wagon travel. On the western side the old road leads out through the sage-brush plains, and may be easily traced with the eye for several miles. This "Natural Bridge" has been gradually sinking. The early emigrants crossed over it when it was a few feet above the water; then, at a later date, the water had risen one or two feet above it; and yet neither the river nor the lake appear to be higher than they were when first vis-ited by white men.

CHAPTER 20

Blue Eyes and Black Ones, Which Win?—Tobey Riddle

The Modoc town was composed of thirteen lodges, built after the model of Klamath's Indian houses. A circular, oblong excavation, twenty or thirty feet in length and twelve wide, is first made. Then posts, two feet apart, are set in the centre and at each end. On these posts are placed timbers running lengthwise of the structure. Poles, or split logs, fifteen feet in length, are placed, with the lower end resting on the ground, while the upper end is fastened to the tops of the posts. Matting, made of "*tule* grass," is spread over the slanting timbers, and then the earth thrown out, in making the excavation, is piled upon the matting to a depth of twelve inches. No windows are made, and there is but one entrance which opens between the timbers mentioned as resting on posts at the top of the lodge. This long, narrow opening is approached from the outside by steps made in the earthen covering. From the inside hangs a ladder made of rawhide ropes. The windows, door, and chimneys are one and the same. The first glance at these houses suggests war, and a second confirms the idea that these people are always ready for an attack.

On our arrival at the town it appeared to be deserted, excepting the few Indians who returned with us. They having dismounted, one of them rushed up the rude stairway outside the largest lodge, and disappeared. This was the home of the "Chief." Our party dismounted and prepared to follow our guide. A watchman on the house-top said, "One man come! no more!" I had partly ascended the steps when the peremptory order came. It sounded ominous, and recalled "Bloody Point," and "Ben Wright." It was too late to turn back in the presence of savages.

When I reached the door, at the top of the lodge, and through the opening met the eyes of fifty painted warriors, I felt as if I was in the wrong place; but I dare not then show any signs of fear, or retrace my steps. I may not find words to express my thoughts and feelings as I descended the rawhide ladder, half expecting a shower of arrows, or bullets; half-wondering how they would feel. *I did not know then,—I have learned since.* On descending, I was met with a cold reception, that froze my blood; a feeling I cannot describe. Captain Jack looked in my face with a sullen glitter in his eye, that no white man could imitate. He refused to shake hands, to speak, or smoke, and in fact it was evident that I was not only an unwelcome visitor, but was looked upon as an enemy.

Coolly lighting my pipe, I began trying to make the best of a bad job; meanwhile enduring the stare from all eyes,—and a stare of that kind that none can understand who has never felt the same; an expression cold and scornful, but burning with hatred, was on every countenance. I have beheld but one other scene that was more indescribable, and that was the "Lava Bed" tragedy on April 11th, 1873. A terrible kind of loneliness came over me, and for a while I thought the chances *about even* whether I would get out again or not.

Finally "Scarfaced Charley" broke the stillness by asking, "What you want? What for you come? Jack he not send for you! He got no business with you! He no don't want to talk! He in his country! What for you come here? You not him *ty-ee!* He don't know you! *Hal-lu-i-me-til-li-cum,*—(you stranger)! Captain Jack want to see you, him come your home! He no want you come here! You go away! Let him 'lone! He no want talk you! You go away!"

This is substantially the first Modoc speech I ever heard. The result, however, was to break the ice, to open the way for conversation. I stated then that I was a new chief, sent by the President, to care for all the Indians, Modocs included, and that I was *their ty-ee.* I had some new things to talk about. Whether they were my friends or not, I was their friend. I had come to see my boys, and I wanted a hearing. I was not afraid to talk, not afraid to hear Captain Jack talk; I was a big chief, and did not ask my own boys when to talk. When I had ended my first speech to the Modocs, Captain Jack replied:—

"I have nothing to say that you would like to hear. All your people are *liars* and *swindlers.* I do not believe half that is told me. I am not afraid to hear you talk." I then proposed to have my friends, who were waiting outside, come in. This was agreed to, and Captain Jack

215

produced a parcel of papers, that had been given to him by various persons, including letters from "Steele," also from Esq. Potter, and John Fairchild. These were submitted to me, and treated with consideration, thereby securing a certain kind of respectful hearing, on the part of Captain Jack, to the proposition for him to provide a camp for our company.

Having thus started negotiations, Jack proffered the use of his lodge, saying that he had no muck-a-muck (meaning provision) that we could eat; that his stores afforded only roots and dried fish, that he had no flour, no coffee, no sugar, no *whiskey*, and did not think a white chief could get along without these things, etc. He, however, ordered a camp prepared for us, which was done by making small holes in the ground, two or three feet apart, with "*camas* sticks,"—a sharp-pointed instrument, of either iron, bone, or hard wood, and about three feet long, with a handle at the upper end, generally in the shape of a cross, and is used very much as a gardener does a spade, by Indian women in digging roots. Into these holes were inserted willows, eight feet in length, forming a circle twenty feet in diameter, lapping past at one point,—thus making an entrance, very much like the opening of a circus pavilion,—the whole surrounded with mattings, the upper part drawn in, thus contracting the yielding tops of the willow poles until the camp was made to resemble a huge bowl, with bottom out, in an inverted position.

This kind of work is usually done by Indian women; but, to the credit of the young men of the Modoc tribe be it said, that they, in this instance at least, assisted them, and did not allow their women to be mere help-meets, but principals in mechanical enterprises of the kind named, including also "getting wood." Sage brush is the principal fuel in this region of country; and since so much of the Great Basin lying between the Rocky mountains on the east, and Sierra Nevada, and Cascade mountains on the west, is covered with this kind of growth, and since comparatively few of my readers may have ever seen it for themselves, I may remark here, by way of explanation, that this "sage brush" is a soft, flexible shrub, the woody part being porous, and filled with a gummy substance; the bark is of a grayish colour, soft and rag-ged, and easily stripped off; the leaf is small, of such a colour, shape and taste as very much resembles the domestic plant, from which it takes its name; the body is short, crooked and forked, seldom exceeds four inches in diameter or four feet in height; burns readily, either green or dry, making a very hot fire, though of short life, yielding abundant ashes and beds of coals.

A plentiful supply of this fuel was piled up around our camp. A fresh fish was taken from the river by the Indians, which, when roasted in the sage-brush embers, made a not unpalatable meal. We spread our saddle-blankets down for bedding, placed one of the party "on guard," while the remainder slept, or went through the motion of sleeping; for we would not have cared for the Indians to know that we could not and dare not sleep. The morrow came, and the wagons having brought our supplies, we were prepared to offer a feast of coffee and sugar, hard-bread, beef, and bacon.

No Modoc would eat until our party had partaken. Some folks may think their good-breeding had taught them to defer to their superiors; but such was not the case. The reason was expressed in these few words: "Remember Ben Wright;" which was said in the Modoc language, thus explaining why they did not partake. When, however, they had witnessed that the provisions prepared for the feast were eaten by our party, they were reassured, and another point was gained.

Nothing so quickly dissolves the ice in an Indian breast as a feast. The council was opened with Frank Riddle and his Modoc woman, Tobey, as interpreter. I mention this fact, because they have become prominent characters in the history of the late Modoc war. They had been sent for by Captain Jack; in fact, he was not willing to proceed without them.

Frank Riddle is a white man, about thirty years of age, a native of Kentucky. He anticipated Greeley, going West when a very young man, and engaged in mining at Y-re-ka, Cal. Twelve years ago, on a bright morning in March, an old Indian rode up to Frank's cabin, and stopped before the door. On a small pony behind the old man sat a young Indian girl, of Modoc blood, twelve years of age.

The man was of royal lineage, being a descendant of Mo-a-doc-us, founder of the tribe, and was uncle of the now famous Captain Jack. After sitting in silence, Indian fashion, staring in the cabin door for a few minutes, he made a motion by a toss of his head, and pouted out his lips toward the young squaw behind him. This pantomime said to Frank, "Do you want to buy a squaw?"

Frank was a fine-looking, dark-eyed young fellow, and withal a clever man, of genial disposition, with native pride of ancestry, still holding to the memory of his home, and the image of a fair-haired girl who had "swung school-baskets" with him in the beach woods of Shelby County, Kentucky. He shook his head. The old man's face in-

217

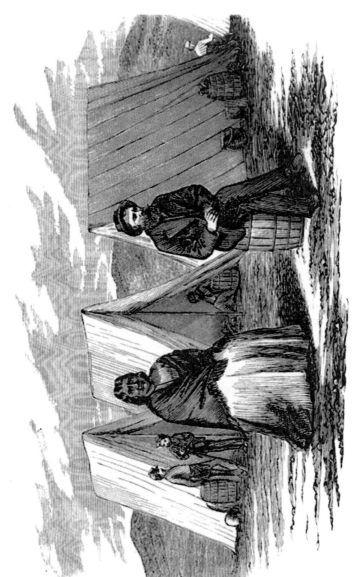

TOBEY AND RIDDLE.

dicated his disappointment. The girl on the pony slowly turned away, followed by her father.

Four days passed, and this Indian girl and her father again appeared at Frank's cabin. In sign language she made known her wish to be his slave, and that he would buy her from her father. The young Kentuckian, chivalrous as his people always are, treated her kindly; but, remembering his fair-haired girl, refused to install this Indian maiden as mistress of his home. Ten days passed; the dark-eyed girl came again, *alone*, bringing with her a wardrobe, consisting of such articles as Indian women manufacture,—sashes and baskets, shells, beads, and little trinkets.

She was attired with woman's taste, conforming to the fashions of her people. Her dark eyes, with long lashes, smooth, round, soft face, of more than usual pretensions to beauty, lithe figure, and dainty feet in moccasins, all combined to give a romantic air to the jaunty young maiden; and, when animated with the promptings of love for the young Kentuckian, made her an eloquent advocate in her own behalf. The chivalrous fellow *hesitated*. He *pitied*. He *trembled* on the brink. The dark eyes before him pleaded. The blue eyes, far away, dissolved reproachingly from view. The hopes of youth, and the air-castles that two loving hearts had built in years agone, began to vanish. They disappeared, and—and in their stead a rude cabin in romantic wilds, with a warm-hearted, loving, dusky-faced companion, became a living, actual *reality*.

The day following, the father of this Indian woman was richer by two horses. The cabin of Frank Riddle put on a brighter air. The mistress assumed charge of the camp-kettle and the frying-pan. The tin plates were cast aside, and dishes of finer mould mounted the tables at the command of a pair of brown hands.

Riddle, having broken his vows, and forsaken his boyhood idol, set to work now to make the untamed girl worthy to fill the place in his heart from which she had driven another. She was apt at learning, and soon only the semblance of a squaw remained in the dusky cheeks and brown hands. Seven years pass, and Frank Riddle and his woman Tobey appear in the Modoc council on Lost River, December, 1869.

We made the opening speech in that council, setting forth the reasons for our visit and producing the treaty of 1864. Here Captain Jack began to manifest the same kind of disposition that has been so prominent in his subsequent intercourse with government officials,—a careful, cautious kind of diplomacy, that does not come to a point, but continually seeks to shirk responsibility.

He denied that he was a party to the treaty of October, 1864, or that he signed the paper. Doctor McKay, old Chief Schonchin, and sub-Chief Blo of Klamath were brought forward, and his allegations disproved completely; we fully and clearly establishing the fact that he was present at that treaty council, and that he put his hand to the pen, when his mark was made; that he accepted and shared with the other Indians the goods issued by Superintendent Huntington in confirmation of the treaty. The amount of goods issued I cannot state; but I find that Huntington had an appropriation of $20,000, to meet the expenses of said treaty council, and, I doubt not, issued $5,000 or $10,000 worth of goods. All agree that it was a liberal supply of goods, and I believe it to be true.

Captain Jack, seeing that "he was cornered," began to quibble about what part of the Reservation he was to go on to. This was met with the proposition that he could *have any* unoccupied land. Finding his objections all fairly met, he finally said, that, if he could live near his friend, Link-river Jack, he *would go*. We began to "breathe easy," feeling that the victory was ours, when the Modoc medicine-man arose, and simply said, "*Me-ki-gam-bla-ke-tu*," (We won't go there); when, presto! from exultation every countenance was changed to an expression of anxiety, and every hand grasped a revolver.

The moment was fraught with peril. The least wavering then, on our part, would have precipitated a fight, the result of which would have been doubtful as to how many, and who, of our party would have come out alive. It is quite certain that, had a fight ensued, what has since startled our people would have been anticipated, and that the name of Captain Jack would have passed away with but little notice from among the savage heroes.

It was there I first heard those terrible words, a part of which have since become famous, uttered but a moment before the attack on the Peace Commission, on April 11, 1873—"*Ot-we-kau-tux-e*,"— meaning, in this instance, "I am done talking;" or, when used in other connections, "All ready!" or, "The time has come!" or, "Quit talking." The vocabularies of all Indian languages are very small; hence, a word depends, to a great extent, on its connection, for its meaning and power. It was just at this point that the woman, Tobey Riddle, who has since proved her sagacity and her loyalty, arose to her feet, and said in Modoc tongue to her people: "*Mo-lok-a ditch-e ham-konk lok-e sti-nas mo-na gam-bla ot-we*,"—("The white chief talks right. His heart is good or strong. Go with him now!")Frank Riddle joined the woman Tobey in exhorting the Modocs to be quiet, to be careful, using such words as tend to avert, what we all saw was liable to happen any instant, a terrible scene of blood.

Dr. McKay, whose long experience had given him much sagacity, arose quickly to his feet, saying in English, "Be on your guard! Don't let them get the drop on us." Captain Jack started to retire when I intercepted him, saying, "Don't leave me now; I am your friend, but I am not afraid of you. Be careful what you do! We mean peace, but are ready for war. We will not begin; but if you do, it shall be the end of your people. You agreed to go with us, and you shall do it. We are ready. Our wagons are here to carry your old people and children. We came for you, and we are not going back without you. You must go!"

He asked "what I would do, if he did not." I told him plainly that we would *whip him* until he was willing. He then wanted to know *where* my men were that was to whip him. I pointed to my small squad of men. I shall never forget his reply. "I would be ashamed to fight so few men with all my boys." I replied, that it was force enough to kill *some Modocs*, before we were all dead; that when we were killed more white men would come.

Not having very strong faith in his *pride* about fighting so few men, I informed him that I had soldiers coming to help us, but that we came on to try *talking first*, and then when that failed we would send for them to come; finally stating to him that he could make up his mind to *go* with us on the morrow, or *fight*, and that in the meanwhile we would be ready at any time for him to begin, if he wished to. He said then what he repeated many times to Peace Commissioners on last spring,—that "he would not fire the first shot," but if we did, "he was not afraid to die." It was finally agreed that he should have until the next morning to make answer what he would do, and that at that time he should report his conclusion.

This ended my first official council with the Modocs. Captain Jack withdrew to his lodge to have a grand "*pow-wow*," leaving our party to determine what was the next thing for us to do. We realized that we were "in great danger." No one dissented from the opinion that peril was menacing our party. Our only hope was to put on a brave front. Retreat at that hour was impossible, with even chances for escape. We despatched a messenger, under pretence of hunting our horses,—we dared not send him boldly on the mission without excuses,—with orders for our military squad at Linkville, twenty-five miles from Modoc

221

camp, to rendezvous at a point within hearing of our guns, and that, in the event of alarm, to "charge the camp," but in *no other* event to come until the next morning.

Having despatched the courier, we carefully inspected our arms, consisting of Henry rifles and navy revolvers. Captain Knapp's experience as an officer of the rebellion and McKay's longer experience as an Indian fighter, together with the frontier life of the remainder, made our little party somewhat formidable, though inadequate to what might at any moment become a fearful trial of strength.

In this connection it should be understood that at that time the Modocs were very poorly armed with old muskets, and a few rifles and old-fashioned pistols.

The Indians have great reverence and unlimited faith in their "medicine-men." This is peculiar to all Indians, but to none more so than the Modocs. While our party were invoking Almighty aid and preparing for the worst that might come, the Modoc medicine-man was invoking the spirits of departed warriors for aid. While the medicine-man was making medicine, Captain Jack was holding a council with his braves, discussing the situation, depending somewhat on the impression to be made from the medicine camp, and fully trusting therein. I have since learned that the same man, who subsequently proposed the assassination of the Peace Commission in the "Lava Bed," in 1873, made the proposition to kill our party in 1869, which, to the credit of Captain Jack, he promptly opposed at that time as he did the other.

Now, if there had been a trial of strength between the good and the bad, we should not have been worthy to represent Elijah; but the Modocs filled the position of Ahab, and they made medicine and called loudly on their gods, but failed therein, as Baal did Ahab. As men will do, our soldier squad disregarded or overlooked the instruction to await the signal to "charge camp," for the charge *was made* in a style that would have done great credit at any subsequent period in the late Modoc war. There was *spirit* at the bottom of this unexpected movement of the soldiers; not such spirits as the Modoc medicine-man invoked, but regular "forty-rod whiskey."

On leaving Link River, they had secured the "company of a bottle," and, the night being cold, they had resorted to its warming influences. The consequence was that, when they arrived at the appointed place to await orders, they forgot to stop, and came into the camp on full gallop. The horses' feet on the frozen ground, the breaking of sage brush, rattling of sabres, all combined, made a noise well calculated to produce sudden fear in the minds of all parties. Our men were all under arms and discussing the situation.

The medicine-man was going through his incantations, accompanied by the songs of the old women, whose sounds still linger on my ear, as they came to our camp, wafted by the breeze from the lake. It was past midnight, and still the great council was in session, debating the treachery proposed; it had not been voted on at that time. Subsequent reports declare that Schonchin's John had spoken in favour of the measure. Captain Jack was making a speech against it at the time the soldiers appeared.

For a few moments the scene was one of indescribable confusion; the medicine-man cut short his prayers; the war council was broken up; and Indian braves came out of the lodge without waiting for the ceremonies of even savage courtesy, but "pell-mell" they went into the sage brush, each one taking with him his arms. A guard was immediately placed, surrounding the whole camp; Capt. Knapp giving orders to allow no one to pass the picket lines.

Few eyes closed in sleep that night; daylight disclosed a complete circle of bayonets, and inside about two hundred men, women, and children; but the brave Captain Jack was not there; nor was "Schonchin's John," or "Ellen's Man," or "Curly Head Doctor;" they had retired to the "Lava Bed." We issued an order for all Indians to form in a line; they were reassured that no one should be harmed; that they should be protected, clothed, and cared for, but that all the arms must be delivered up. This request brought out professions and promises of friendship; but the order had been made and must be obeyed.

The Indians refused compliance, and a file of soldiers was ordered to seize the arms; for a few moments the excitement was intense; every man of our party stood ready for "business," while the arms of the Modocs were seized, and a guard placed over them. The aspect presented by the Modoc camp was one that will not soon be forgotten by our party; the old, the young, the middle-aged, the crippled, and ragged, nearly all making professions of loyalty, and rejoicing at the turn events had taken.

Provisions were issued for them, and order made for them to gather up the ponies and prepare for removal. This morning was the first time I heard "Queen Mary's" voice; she is a sister of Ki-en-te-poos,—Captain Jack,—and this fact gave her great power over him. She has been pronounced "Queen of the Modocs," on account of her beauty and power; she was, probably, the most sagacious individual belonging to the band. This Indian queen has had many opportunities for *improvement*, having been sold to five or six white men in the last ten years.

While she has induced so many different men to buy her of her brother, she has made each one, in turn, anxious to return her to her people; but not until she had squandered all the money she could command. It has been denied that Captain Jack was ever a party to these several matrimonial speculations; but more strongly asserted, by those who ought to know, that "Queen Mary" has been a great source of wealth to him. I am of that opinion myself, after weighing all the facts in the case.

On the morning in question Mary appeared to plead for her absent brother, that he might be forgiven, saying that he was no coward, but that he was scared; that he was not to blame for running, and that she could induce him to return. It was finally arranged that she should go to the "Lava Bed" in company with our guide, Gus Horn, and assure her brother that no harm had befallen the camp, and none would fall on them.

One day was spent in collecting the Indian ponies, taking Indian provisions from the *"caches,"* and negotiating with the runaways for their return, which was not accomplished. The following morning the camp was broken up, and all the Indians, big and little, old and young,—as we supposed at the time,—were started to the Reservation. Some were on ponies, many of them on our wagons, and perhaps a few on foot.

We reached Link River, where fires had been made, beef and flour prepared, and by nine, p.m., everybody seemed contented, except the personal friends of the runaways.

Messengers were kept on the road between our camp and the "Lava Beds" almost constantly for the three days we remained at Link river. Finally the great chief surrendered, and "came in," on assurances that "the Klamaths should not be permitted to make sport of him, and call him a coward for running from our small force." This, then, was the ultimatum, and was accepted, and, as far as possible, kept faithfully on our part.

The sight presented by Captain Jack and his men, when they arrived at Link River, if it could have been witnessed by those who have taken so great an interest in him, would have dispelled all ideas of a "Fennimore Cooper hero."

I cannot forbear mentioning an incident characteristic of the Modocs. While waiting for Jack and his remaining braves, I accidentally learned that an old woman had been left in camp on Lost River, and, asking for the reason, was told that she was too old to dig roots, or to work, and they had left her some wood and water, and a "little grub," enough for her to die easy on. A pair of new blankets, bread, sugar and meat, were prepared to send her; also a horse to ride, and volunteers asked for, to bring the old woman in. Not a volunteer came forward, save a "young buck," who was willing, *provided* he could have the blankets and pony, should he find her dead, or if she should die on the road. It needed no reflection to understand that *that* meant *murder*.

After much difficulty, the family to whom the old squaw belonged was found, and a man and woman sent after her, with the warning, that if they failed to bring her they must suffer the consequences. They insisted on being *paid* in advance for their labour. They *were not paid*, but they brought her in alive, but so weak that she had to be held on the horse, the squaw sitting behind her. It is said the Indian has no gratitude, but this old woman refuted that assertion.

On the arrival of Captain Jack's party, arrangements were made to proceed at once to Klamath Reservation. On the morning of Dec. 27th we started on our way. At the request of Captain Jack and his representative men, the squad of soldiers were sent forward to the fort; the Indians claiming that their presence made the women and children afraid; and that, having surrendered their arms, they were powerless to do harm, and had no desire to turn back. It may be thought a strange concession to make; but with their arms in our possession, we *made it*; thus proving our confidence in Indian integrity, by relieving them of the presence of the soldiers. We were safe, and had no fear of the result.

The morning was intensely cold, and the road led over a high mountain covered with snow to the depth of twenty inches. On the 28th we arrived at Modoc Point, Klamath Reservation. We were met by a large delegation of agency Indians. The meeting and peace-making of these people, who had been enemies so long, was one of peculiar interest and full of incident, worthy of being recorded. I pass over the first day, by saying that the Klamaths were much chagrined when we issued an order, at the request of Jack, against gambling.

Had we not done so, much confusion of property and domestic relation would have ensued. These people are inveterate gamblers, and in fits of madness have been known to stake their wives and daughters on the throw of a stick, sometimes a card. The second day we set apart for a meeting of reconciliation. A line was established between the Modoc and Klamath camp, and a place designated for the forthcoming meeting, at the foot of a mountain and beneath a wide-spreading pine tree.

The Klamaths formed on one side of the line, and awaited the arrival of the Modocs, who came reluctantly, apparently half afraid; Captain Jack taking a position fronting Allen David,—the Klamath chief,—and only a few feet distant. There stood these warrior chieftains, unarmed, gazing with Indian stoicism into each other's faces. No words were spoken for a few moments. The thoughts that passed through each mind may never be known, but, perhaps, were of bloody battles past, or of the possible future.

The silence was broken on our part, saying, "You meet today in peace, to bury all the bad past, to make friends. You are of the same blood, of the same heart. You are to live as neighbours. This country belongs to you, all alike. Your interests are one. You can shake hands and be friends."

A hatchet was laid in the open space, a twig of pine was handed each chieftain,—Allen David and Captain Jack,—as they advanced, each stooping and covering the axe with the pine boughs; planting their feet upon it, they looked into each other's eyes a moment, and shook hands with a long-continued grasp, but spoke no word. As each retired to his position outside of the line, the sub-chiefs and head men came forward, two at a time, and followed the example of the chieftains, until all had exchanged the pledge of friendship, and then resumed their respective places. Allen David broke the silence in a speech of great power,—and such a speech as none but an Indian orator can make. I have listened to some of the most popular speakers in America, but I do not remember ever having heard a speech more replete with meaning, or one much more logical, and certainly none exhibiting more of nature's oratory. It was not of that kind taught inside brick walls, but that which God gives to few, and gives but sparingly. I repeat it as reported by Dr. McKay.

Fixing his eye intently on Captain Jack, and raising himself to his full proportion of six feet in height, he began in measured sentences full of pathos:

I see you. I see your eyes. Your skin is red like my own. I will show you my heart. We have long been enemies. Many of our brave *muck-a-lux* (people) are dead. The ground is black with their blood. Their bones have been carried by the 'cayotes,' to the mountains, and scattered among the rocks. Our people are melting away like snow. We see the white chief is strong. The law is strong. We cannot be Indians longer. We must take the white man's law. The law our fathers had is dead. The white chief brought you here. We have made friends. We have washed each other's hands; they are not bloody now. We are friends. We have buried all the bad blood. We will not dig it up again. The white man sees us. *Soch-e-la Ty-ee.*—God is looking at our hearts. The sun is a witness between us; the mountains are looking on us. (Turning to the great tree, with a sublime gesture). This pine-tree is a witness, O my people! When you see this tree, remember it is a witness that here we made friends with the Mo-a-doc-as. Never cut down that tree. Let the arm be broke that would hurt it, let the hand die that would break a twig from it. So long as snow shall fall on Yai-nax Mountain, let it stand. Long as the waters run in the river, let it stand. Long as the white rabbit shall live in the *man-si-ne-ta* (groves), let it stand. Let our children play round it; let the young people dance under its leaves, and let the old men smoke together in its shade. Let this tree stand there forever, as a witness. I have done.

Captain Jack, on assuming an attitude peculiar to himself, with his eye fixed intently on the Klamath chief, began in a low, musical voice, half-suppressed, half hesitatingly:

The white chief brought me here. I feel ashamed of my people, because they are poor. I feel like a man in a strange country without a father. My heart was afraid. I have heard your words; they warm my heart. I am not strange now. The blood is all washed from our hands. We are enemies no longer. We have buried the past. We have forgotten that we were enemies. We will not throw away the white chief's words. We will not hide them in the grass. I have planted a strong stake in the ground. I have tied myself with a strong rope. I will not dig up the stake. I will not break the rope. My heart is the heart of my people. I am their words. I am not speaking for myself. I speak their hearts. My heart comes up to my mouth. I cannot keep it down with a sharp stick. I am done.

No doubt that, at the time of making this speech, Captain Jack really meant all he said; and if he failed to make good his promises, there were reasons that may not entitle him or his people to censure for the failure. Certainly no peace-making could have been more sincere, or promised more for the settlement of the Modoc troubles. The remainder of the day was passed in exchanging friendships (*ma-mak-sti-nas*). Preparations were completed for issuing annuity goods to the Modocs.

Other Indians had been previously served, but this was but the second time that the Modocs had ever received goods from the government, in conformity with the treaty stipulations of 1864. For five years the goods had been regularly furnished and distributed to the Klamaths and the few Modocs who remained faithful to the compact. If Captain Jack's band had not received goods, it was not the fault of the government or its agents, but because they wilfully refused to obey the orders of government officers, by remaining away from the home they had accepted.

The goods provided were of the best quality, delivered on contract, and with packages unbroken, and in presence of Capt. Goodale, U. S. Army, then in command of Fort Klamath; and they were distributed among his people. Captain Jack and his head men were seated in the midst of a semi-circle, with the other men on each side, the women in front, in half-circular rows; the children still in front of these, on either hand. When all were seated, the packages were broken, and the goods prepared for issue. Captain Jack and his sub-chiefs received two pairs of blankets each, one pair to each of his head men, and one blanket to every other man, woman, and child, except *six very small children, who were given one-half a blanket each*. They were all-wool, "eight-pound" Oregon blankets, and overweighed, by actual test, nearly one-half pound per pair.

In addition, each man received a woollen shirt and cloth for one pair of pants; each woman and child, one flannel dress pattern, with liberal supply of thread, needles, and buttons. I have been thus particular about the facts concerning this issue, because much sympathy has been manifested for the Modocs on account of the wrongs said to have been practised against them. After the distribution, the Modocs, proud of their new goods, retired to their camps, on the shores of the lake.

The "Peace Tree," under which the issue was made, was on a sloping hill-side, overlooking the valley, and commanding a view of the camp of Captain Jack. Let us see them, as they trudge homeward, with their rich prizes. They do not go like the Indians with their blankets around them, and feathers streaming in the wind. Since their retreat from the Reservation they have associated with and learned many of the manners and customs of civilized white people. Nevertheless they presented a picturesque appearance,—old and young, loaded down with goods, flour and beef, apparently happy; and I doubt not they were happy.

Their camps, scattered promiscuously along the edge of the water, were constructed of various materials. A few were ordinary tents, others made over a frame of willow poles, covered with matting, blankets, wagon sheets, and such other material as could be pressed into service. The ponies are scattered over the plain, cropping the winter grass, or tied up waiting for the owner's return.

The inside of the camps are always "cluttered,"—a Yankee word, which means in confusion and disorder. The women proceed to stow away the new dresses in baskets and sacks, or spread them for bedding; the men to smoke and wait until the feast is made ready from the supplies of flour and beef provided. They have been cheated out of what some eastern people would consider the best part of the beef,—the "head and pluck." That delectable part of the animal had been captured by the waiting Klamath squaws at the time of the slaughtering. Squaws have the smelling qualities of a war horse, "that scents the battle from afar."

At every slaughter they were sure to arrive in time to secure the aforesaid "head and pluck," which, with them, means everything except dressed meat. Even the feet are eaten. First throwing them on the fire and burning them awhile, they then cut off the scorched parts to eat. The foot is again conveyed to the fire, until fairly charred; again stripped, and so on, until but little is left, and that little does not resemble an ox's foot very much.

The head is cooked in better shape. A hole is dug in the ground, in which a fire is made, and, when burned down, the embers are removed, and the head of the old government ox is dropped in just as it left the butcher's hands. Hair, horns, and all are covered up with ashes and coals, a fire made over it and left to cook. After a few hours it is removed, and is then ready to serve up; or rather it (the head) is placed upon the ground, and the hungry Indians, each armed with a knife, surround it and proceed to carve and eat. Portions that may be too raw are then thrown on the coals and charred; even the bones are eaten. Among the old and poor people, they carefully preserve their respective ox's feet, and, when in want, throw them on the coals, and the meal is prepared in short order.

Uncivilized Indians have no regular hour for meals, but generally each one consults convenience, seldom eating together except on feast occasions. Neither have they regular hours for sleeping or rising, each member of a family or tribe consulting their own pleasure.

While we watch the novel scenes of Indians "getting wood," water, cooking, and eating, we see the enterprising young Klamaths—now released from the order forbidding their hurrying down to the Modoc camps—hasten there, some to renew old acquaintance, others to tell in soft tones to the listening ears of Modoc maidens the tale that burdened their hearts, and to negotiate for new wives; or it may be, through the mediation of a "deck" of greasy cards, to persuade the Modocs to divide goods with them.

These Klamath boys had received their new clothes a few days previous, and had soiled them enough to make them comport well with Indian toilets. While we are engaged making observations, cast the eye westward over the valley of the Klamath, and see the huge shadows approach like great moving clouds, until suddenly they start up the sloping hill-side towards us. Look closely now at the sun resting a moment on the summit of Mount McGlaughlin. See it settle slowly, as though splitting the crown of the mountain in twain, until, while you gaze, he drops quickly out of sight. Little children say he has burned a hole in the mountain, and buried himself there. But, oh, the shadows have crept over us, and we feel the chill which ensues. Look above and behind us, and see them climb the rocky crags until we are all "in the shadow."

We now see our teamster boys piling high the pitch-pine logs, and soon the crackling flames begin to paint fresh shadows round us. The dark forms of long-haired men gather in circles round the fire; for we are to have a "*cultus wa-wa*," (a big free talk). White men and Indians change their base as smoke or flame compels, and all, in half gloomy silence, wait the signal to begin. A white man speaks first of his people, their laws, religion, and habits; tells how law is made; how the white man found his religion; the history of the Bible; extols his own faith, and labours to reconcile in untutored minds the difference betwixt good and bad, right and wrong, and by simple lessons to instil the great precepts of Christianity.

The red man listens with sober face and thoughtful brow. When opportunity is made, he puts queries about many things they do not know. This is not an official council, so all feel free to speak. An old Indian, with his superstitious habits and ideas clinging to him, like a worn-out blanket in tatters, clutching the old with one hand, and with the other reaching out for the new, rises, and with great dignity tells of the religious faith of his fathers, and makes apology for their ignorance and his own, says:

I have long heard of this religion of the white man. I have heard about the 'Holy Spirit' coming to him. I wonder if it would ever come to my people. I am old, I cannot live long. Maybe it has come now. I feel like a new kind of fire was in my heart. Maybe you have brought this 'Holy Spirit.'
I think you have. When you came here first we were all in bad blood. Now I see Klamaths, Modocs, Snakes, and Ya-hoo-skins, all around me like brothers. No common man could do this. Maybe *you are a holy spirit*. When I was a young man I saw a white man on his knee telling the 'Holy Spirit' to come. Maybe the Great Spirit sent you with it.

This old man, whose name was Link River Joe, had attended a meeting held by Rev. A. F. Waller, at the Dallas Methodist Mission, twenty years before, and had still retained some of the impressions made at that time.

Old man Chi-lo-quin said he had often heard that the white man could tell when the sun would turn black a long time before it happened,—referring to the eclipse,—and inquired how the white man knew so much. This was explained until the old fellow said he thought he knew how it was; but I doubt it. Thus the last night of 1869 wore away with questions and answers. Finally we mentioned that "tomorrow will be the New Year." The question was asked, how we knew it was so. Never have I seen an audience of five or six hundred persons so eager for information. We proposed to explain, and, holding up a watch, said to them, that when all the "little sticks" on its face were in a row together, the old year would die in the west, and another would be born in the east.

The watch was passed around while the explanation was being made. Allen David requested that, since all could not see the watch, we should fire a pistol at the exact moment. After assurance that it would cause no alarm, we held the pistol upward above our heads, and announced,—"five minutes more and 1869 will be dead,—four minutes now,—now but three." The stillness was almost painful,—"Two

231

minutes more, now but one,"—and five or six hundred red men were holding breath to catch the signal,—all eyes watching the finger that was to announce, by a motion, the event; the three hands on the face of the watch were in range,—the finger crooked,—a blaze of light flashed over the dusky faces, and a report went reverberating up the rocky *cañons*, and before it died away, six hundred voices joined in an almost unearthly farewell to "1869," and, quickly facing to the east, another wild shout of welcome to "1870."

The crowd slowly dispersed, leaving one white man and an interpreter sitting by the smouldering fire, talking over the wonders of the white man's knowledge and power, accompanied by old Chief Schonchin, Captain Jack, Allen David, and O-che-o. Thus was begun the year 1870. I was surrounded then with elements of power for mischief that were only waiting for the time when accident or mismanagement would impel one of these chieftains—Captain Jack—to open a chapter with his finger dipped in the heart's blood of one of the noblest of the American army, the lamented Christian soldier, General Canby, who was then quietly enjoying a respite from the labours of the rebellion, with the honours of a well-spent life gathering in a clustering wreath around the great warrior's brow, settling down so lightly that he scarcely seemed aware that he wore a coronet made of heroic deeds and manly actions. He was looking hopefully to a future of rest in the bosom of his family, and consoling himself that life's hardest battles were over, and that when, in a good old age, the roll-call should be sounded for him, his friends would answer in salutes of honour over his grave.

While we were shedding little rays of light on the darkened minds of our hearers, a beardless Indian boy, with face almost white, was sporting with his fellows, or quietly sleeping in his father's lodge, soothed to rest by the rippling waters of Klamath Lake. This boy—Boston Charley—was to send the messenger of death through the heart of the eminent divine—Dr. Thomas. That night Dr. Thomas was with his friends, watching on bended knees before a sacred altar, waiting for the death of 1869 and the birth of a new year, little dreaming that the crimson current of his life was so soon to mingle with the blood of the other hero in recording the tragic event of the year 1873.

He, too, had fought the good fight of the cross for thirty long years, and now felt the honours of his church gathering around his gray locks, and was looking steadily forward to the hour when his Great Commander should call him to his reward; hoping quietly and peace-

232

fully to gather up his feet in God's own appointed time, and, bearing with him his sheaves, present them as his credentials to a mansion of eternal rest. While old Chief Schon-chin, with his long gray hair floating in the winds of the new-born year, was opening his heart to the influx of light, sitting quietly by the dying council fire, his brother John was brooding over his broken hopes of careless life or high ambition, sitting moody and gloomy over his own camp-fire, or dreaming of a coming hour when he might avenge the insults offered his race. It may be he was living over the scenes of his stormy life, while the hand that had that day received from my hands pledges of friendship and Government faith was in three short years to fire eleven shots at the heart that beat then in kindliest sympathy with his race.

The last hours of the dying year and the first of the new one had I given from my life for the advancement of a race, whose very helplessness enhanced the zeal with which I laboured for them. I could not draw aside the veil that hid the future, and see the gleaming eyes of Schonchin John, nor his left hand clutching a dagger while his right discharged repeated shots at my breast. I did not then see my own body prostrate and bleeding in the rocks of the Lava Bed, or my own beloved family surrounded with sympathizing friends, eagerly watching the electric sparks speaking words of hope and despair alternately; but I did see, somewhere in the future, my hand running over whited page, telling the world of the way I passed the watch-night of 1869.

CHAPTER 21

Burying The Hatchet—A Turning-Point

On the morning of January 1st, 1870, Captain Jack's band of Modoc Indians was placed in charge of Captain Knapp, under favourable circumstances. Supplies of beef and flour were secured and issued to them in sufficient quantities. Indeed, they were better fed than other Indians belonging to the agency. They had brought with them fish and roots, which, in addition to rations issued as above referred to, was altogether sufficient; and, having obtained from Agent Knapp the necessary implements, they began work in good earnest, by cutting saw logs, making rails, and hewing house logs, preparing to make a permanent settlement at Modoc Point. The arrangements had been fully explained to the Klamaths, Wal-pah-pas, Snake Indians and Modocs, at the peace-making under the great witness tree, and fully agreed to by all parties.

It was further agreed and understood, with the consent of the Link River Klamath Indians, who partially occupied the land so taken for the Modoc home, that the Modocs were to share equally with them in the use of the timber on the side of the mountains nearest to the new settlement.

The land was designated lying adjacent, and the Modocs were to select the particular tract that each might desire for a home, with the understanding that they were to be the owners thereof, and that, when allotments of land in severalty should be made, by order of the government, as stipulated in the treaty of 1864, the selection then made should be ratified and confirmed to the occupant. With this understanding, Jack and his people began improvements for a new home, and, I believe, with a full, settled determination to make it permanent.

No semi-savages ever went to work more cheerfully than did these people. Whatever may have been their faults, or what of crime attached to them since, this fact should be remembered,—that they did then acknowledge the obligations of the treaty. Mark the succession of events, and you will have some conception of the motives and reasons why the late unfortunate Peace Commissioners, with the lamented Gen. Canby, continued its labours, and protracted its efforts, to secure peace with the Modocs, even when hope seemed forlorn, and the public press were hurling denunciations against the "Peace policy," and the commissioners especially.

Gen. Canby knew all the circumstances, as did Dr. Thomas and myself, and with a firm resolve to be just, we maintained silence, recollecting a memorable saying, "Let them alone; they know not what they do."

The Modocs worked with a will, and had made several hundred rails, and hewn logs for houses, when avarice, stimulated by envy, brought about quarrels between the Link River Indians and Modocs; the former taunting the latter, calling them *hallo-e-me, tilli-cum* (strangers); claiming the timber, though admitting that they had agreed that the Modocs might cut it, nevertheless, saying, "It is our timber; you may use it, but it is ours. You make the rails, but we want some of them."

Captain Jack's people recalled the understanding on the day of peace-making. The quarrel grew warm, and Agent Knapp was appealed to, by Captain Jack, to settle the difficulties. This was one of the turning-points of a history that is reeking with blood.

Capt. Knapp was an army officer who had been assigned to duty as Indian agent. That he was a brave soldier, and had made a good record, is beyond question. In his official dealings with the Indians he was honest, I doubt not. He is the only agent that has ever had charge of Captain Jack's band since the fall of 1864.

Captain Jack and his friends have published to the world that they were starved and cheated by government agents while on Klamath Reservation in 1870.

I believe the assertion wholly unfounded. Agent Knapp came to the work having no heart in it; no knowledge of the Indian character; no faith in them or their manhood; no ambition to elevate them. It is not to be wondered at that he took but little pains with them beyond seeing that rations were issued,—which I believe was done *promptly*.

The position was unsought and undesirable, and one he wished to vacate. Had Capt. Knapp been every way qualified for this duty; had his experience given him knowledge of Indian character; had he sought the position, or been selected for it on account of his fitness for this kind of labour, and had his heart been in it; had he been fired with an ambition to do good, by elevating a poor, unfortunate race,— he would have exercised more patience when appealed to by Captain Jack in February, 1870, for redress; he would have prevented all these bloody chapters in Indian history.

Had Agent Knapp promptly interfered, tempering his action with justice, by punishing Link River Jack for annoying the Modocs, then the Modoc rebellion would have been prevented.

When Captain Jack appealed to Agent Knapp, the latter refused to admit Jack within his office, heard his complaints impatiently, and sent him away with orders to "go on with his work;" "that he would make it all right."

Jack returned to his home, and, naturally enough, the quarrel was renewed. The Link River Klamaths, having received neither reprimand nor punishment, were emboldened, and became more overbearing than before.

Captain Jack again applied for protection from further insult, and this time Agent Knapp proposed to change the location of the Modocs to a point on Williamson River, a few miles distant, and nearer the agency.

For the sake of peace, and in obedience to orders, the Modocs changed camp, and again began preparation for making homes.

This brought Klamaths and Modocs in contact, and after Jack had made a few hundred rails, and prepared a few hewn logs for houses, the Klamaths rehearsed the Link-river speeches to them,—taunting them with being poor, and claiming the country, though patronizingly saying, "You can stay here; but it is our country." "Your horses can eat the grass; but it is *our* grass." "You can catch fish; but they are *our* fish." When reminded by the Modocs of the treaty and subsequent peace-making, the Klamaths replied: "Yes, we know all that." "You can have timber, grass, and fish; but don't forget they are ours." "We will let you stay." "It is all right." Captain Jack went a *third* time to Agent Knapp, who proposed to *move them* again, remarking that "next time he would *stay moved*," he proposing to Jack to find a new location.

Jack went to search for one; but whether he could not find a location, or whether the constant annoyance on account of quarrels and removals had killed his faith both in agents and Indian friendship, makes no difference. He returned to his camp on Williamson River, called his people together, and laid the whole matter before them.

I have a report of that meeting by "Charley," a brother of Toby Riddle,—an Indian who commands the respect of all who know him personally. Although this report was made several months afterwards, I believe it to be in the main correct. The substance was, that after all were assembled, including the women and children and Link-river people, Captain Jack stated the case, mentioning the several points as already recited, and saying that he had looked at all the country, but did not find any that he liked as well as Modoc Point, and that he had made up his mind to leave the Reservation unless he could have that place for a house.

Blo, a sub-chief of the Klamaths, said, "Tell Knapp so." Jack replied that he *had talked* to Knapp already three times; and that Knapp had *no heart* for him; and that he was afraid he was a bad man; that "he would not keep the superintendent's words;" "that he intended to leave the Reservation," and asked, "Who will go with me? Who wants to stay with a man who has no heart for us?"

Then ensued a protracted discussion, Charley Riddle and Duffy insisting on remaining. The discussion was a stormy one, and continued until a late hour; but in all the speeches no charge of starving or cheating was made.

Finally the question went to a vote, and the proposition to leave was carried by a large majority. It may be here remarked that neither of the Schonchins was present, Schonchin John being at that time loyal, and opposed to the rebellion; and that is about the only thing that can be mentioned in his favour, except that he was a *poor shot*, as *I can testify*.

As soon as the vote was put and result known, active preparation was made for departure; in fact, the result had been anticipated, for the horses were all ready, the goods packed, and daylight next morning found Jack and his people retracing the road they had gone over so hopefully eleven weeks before.

I will not spend time speculating on what were the thoughts and feelings of that unfortunate band of people, while fleeing stealthily from their new homes, but will simply say, that the little cavalcade carried with them elements that have developed into hatred and revenge, which has since shocked the moral sense of mankind by bloody deeds of savage warfare that stand out on the country's history without a parallel.

Returning to the old home on Lost River, and feeling that he was not under obligations to obey law any longer, Captain Jack seems to have begun where he left off; his young men and women visiting Y-re-ka and the mining camps adjacent.

A few weeks later Jack went to Y-re-ka himself, meeting his old friends, who gave him welcome. The Modoc trade may have had something to do with the success of more than one merchant in Y-re-ka. The presence of the Modocs was hailed with pleasure, no doubt, by another class whose social status in society was little better than the Modocs themselves. To these people the Modocs told falsehoods about reservation life, and received in return sympathy for their reputed wrongs, and encouragement in repeating the falsehoods. In this way the belief that they were misused by government officials has obtained; an unjust censure has been publicly aimed against worthy men. What more natural than the fact that the dissolute portion of the Y-re-ka people should espouse the Modoc cause, and that the better part of society should form their opinions from stories circulated by friends of Modoc women?

Mankind are prone to be swayed in the direction of self-interest, and, when encouraged, any poor mortal may tell a falsehood so often that he really believes it to be true. That Jack, too, confirmed such reports is true, because in the sympathy he found were mingled words of justification. Indeed, a plain, truthful statement of the facts, as they were, was enough to insure him sympathetic advisers.

It is true, then, when Captain Jack returned to Lost River, he was strengthened and confirmed in his ideas of justification, and his determination to remain off the Reservation.

Nothing of grave import transpired until the spring of 1871, although efforts were made in the meantime by the Indian Department, and by old chief Schonchin, to induce Captain Jack to return.

A home at Yai-nax was proposed, and in order that no reasonable excuse on the part of Captain Jack could be found on account of Klamath Indians, and to remove every obstacle, the Reservation was divided into distinct agencies; the western portion being assigned to "Klamath" Indians, and the eastern portion to "Snakes," "Walpahpas," and "Modocs." A district of country was set apart exclusively for the latter. To this new home old Schonchin removed with his people; and a portion of Captain Jack's band, meanwhile, also, taking up homes. Commissary Applegate, at one time, was hopeful that the whole Modoc tribe could be induced to come to the new home at Yai-nax. Captain Jack visited it, and talked seriously of settling on this location; but while he was hesitating as to what he should do, an unfortunate tragedy was enacted, so natural to a savage state, which completely changed the current of events.

Captain Jack employed an Indian doctor to attend a sick child, and paid the fees in advance,—which, be it understood, secured from the doctor a guaranty; and in case of failure to cure, the life of the Indian doctor was in the hands of the friends of the deceased. The child died, and Captain Jack either killed the doctor, or ordered him to be killed.

Under the old Indian laws this would have been an end of the affair; but under the new order of things it was a crime. The friends of the murdered man claimed that Captain Jack should be arrested and punished under white men's laws for the offence.

An unsuccessful attempt was made to arrest him. The country was in a state of alarm; it was evident that war would be the result.

Knowing all the facts in the case, I determined to make one more effort to prevent bloodshed. Capt. Knapp had been relieved by an order of the Army Department, and I was instructed by the Indian Department to place a man in charge. Accordingly, John Meacham was sent by me to take Capt. Knapp's place. About this time I received a letter from Hon. Jesse Applegate, in regard to Modoc matters. His long experience as a frontier man gave his opinion weight. He represented the Modocs with whom he had met, as willing to meet me in council for the purpose of settling the difficulties then existing. He further suggested, that the only sure way for permanent peace was to give them a small Reservation at the mouth of Lost River,—the old home of Captain Jack. He, being a practical surveyor, furnished my office with a small map of the proposed Reservation.

Realizing how much depended then on conciliatory measures, and having confidence in Jesse Applegate's judgment, I forwarded his letter to Gen. Canby, commander of the Department of the Columbia, with a request that military action be delayed until another effort could be made to settle the difficulties then existing between Captain Jack's band of Modocs and the Reservation Indians.

Gen. Canby issued the orders desired, and the command to make the arrest was revoked.

The following letter of Instruction to Commissary Meacham will explain the situation. I associated with him on this mission, Ivan D.

Applegate, who was then in charge of Yai-nax station, Klamath Reservation. I also requested Hon. Jesse Applegate to go with them. He did not find it convenient, however, and the commissioners named proceeded under the following letter of instruction, Ivan Applegate being notified of his appointment from my office in Salem.

Office Superintendent Indian Affairs,
Salem, Oregon, August 2, 1871.
John Meacham, Commissary, Klamath Agency:—
I wish you to proceed at once to the Modoc country, and make one more effort for peace. I am induced to make this request on reading a long and intelligent letter from Hon. Jesse. Applegate, who has had a talk with Captain Jack and Black Jim.
It appears that they are anxious to see me, and that they are willing to talk this matter over, and if possible avoid bloodshed. It is impossible for me to go at present, on account of "Umatilla Council."
You can say to them that you represent *me*,—my *heart*, my *wishes*, my *words*; and that I have authorized you to talk for me.
You are familiar with all the facts in the case, and do not need especial instructions, except on one or two points: First, that I will try to get a small reserve for them in their country; but it will require some time to bring it about, and until such time I desire them to go on to any unoccupied lands on Klamath Reservation; that I will lay the whole matter before the department at Washington, and put it through, if possible; that you will protect them from insult or imposition from either Klamaths, Snakes, or whites, until such time as the authorities shall order otherwise.
I mean by this that Captain Jack and men shall be free from arrest until I am ordered to investigate the affair, and that he shall, if ever arrested, have the benefit of trial by his peers or white men, under civil law; on the condition, however, that he and his people return to Klamath, and remain there, subject to the authority of the Indian Department; that, if ordered to trial, he will surrender himself and accomplices.
You can say to him that, in the event I succeed in getting a home for them on Lost River, they will be allowed their proportion of the Klamath and Modoc treaty funds, with the privilege of the mill at Klamath Agency to make lumber, etc.; that, if I fail in

240

this, they may elect to go into the Snake country beyond Camp Warner, on the new Reservation to be laid out there this fall.

You can say further that, while I do not approve of their conduct, I am not unmindful of their bad treatment by Captain Knapp and the Klamaths, and that I do not wish to have them destroyed; but, if they refuse to accept these terms, they will be under military control and subject to military laws and commands.

You will confer with I. D. Applegate, and also with the commander at Fort Klamath. I will request General Canby to delay any order now out for the arrest of Jack until you have made this effort to prevent war.

I have requested I. D. Applegate to accompany you, and advise with you, but this you will understand,—that *you* are charged with the mission. I think going as my *brother* may give you more influence.

The Modocs can appreciate that, inasmuch as the superintendent could not come, he sent his *brother.*

I have confidence in your coolness and sense of justice, and, with I. D. Applegate as counsellor, I hope you may bring this unhappy trouble (so heavy laden with death to many persons) to a peaceful solution.

Do not take more than two or three persons with you, and, whatever the result of "the talk," you will be *faithful* and *true* to *yourself* and the *Indians.* Mr. Jesse Applegate is somewhere out in that country. He is a *safe adviser.* I have no doubt he will assist you in this hazardous undertaking. You will report the result of this visit to this office promptly.

In the event that the military commander at Fort Klamath may have already gone after Jack and opened hostilities, I do not wish you to take any desperate chances.

This matter I leave to the circumstances that may exist on receipt of this letter. I see clearly, from Jesse Applegate's letter, that hostilities are imminent, and that many good men may lose life and property unless the threatened hostilities are prevented.

I have never seen the time when we could have done otherwise than as we have; but I fully realize that we may be held responsible by the citizens of that country, who do not understand the power and duties of the Indian Department.

Go on this mission realizing that you carry in your hand the lives and happiness of many persons, and the salvation of a tribe of people who have been much wronged, and seldom, if ever, understood.

Very respectfully,

Your obedient servant,

A. B. Meacham,

Supt. Ind. Affairs.

Under the foregoing letter of instructions the commissioners appointed went into the Modoc country, having previously arranged, through Indian messengers, to meet Captain Jack and five or six of his men. No agreement was made in reference to arms, each party following the dictates of common sense,—by being ready for *peace*, but prepared for *war*. The commissioners took with them two persons, making up a party of four well-armed men. It is humane and Christian to carry always the olive-branch of peace, but it is unwise to depend on its sanctity for protection when dealing with enraged savages. Well for Commissioner Meacham and I. D. Applegate that they had forethought enough to go prepared to defend themselves; for, had they not, the list of killed in the Modoc war would have read somewhat different from its present roll of names. There is no doubt that at the time these two young men went out to meet these people, "Schonchin John," "Hooker Jim," and "Curly-haired Doctor" were in favour of assassinating them, and were only prevented by Captain Jack and Scarface Charley. The information comes through Indian lips, but I believe it to be true.

I desire the reader to note that this was the second time assassination was proposed by these people, and each time frustrated by Captain Jack; and, further, that I was subsequently informed each time of their intended acts of treachery by Tobey Riddle, through her husband.

The council was held in a wild, desolate region of country, many miles from the nearest white settlement. Captain Jack and nearly all his men were present, and *all armed*.

It should be understood that at that time, as afterward in the Lava Bed, the Modocs were suspicious of Captain Jack's firmness in carrying out the wishes of his people. This feeling was augmented by Schon-chin John, who was ambitious for the chieftainship, and constantly sought to implant distrust of Jack's fidelity in the minds of the Modocs. This accounts for more than the number agreed upon in this, and, in fact, in all subsequent meetings. Jack, nevertheless, was the acknowledged chief, but not on the old basis of theory of absolute power; he was only a representative chief. That he had not absolute control over them was owing to his own act of teaching them the republican idea of a majority ruling; or it may be that the band had demanded this concession on his part.

Nearly all of them had associated with white men, and had thereby acquired crude ideas of American political economy.

It was in this case of the Modocs a *curse*, instead of a *blessing*. Had Jack exercised the old despotic prerogative of Indian chiefs, no war would have ensued, no great acts of treachery would ever have been committed. He could and would have buried in the grave, with other wrongs, the "Ben Wright" affair; and while he would have clamoured for liberty, in its common-sense meaning, he would have held his people in check until such times as our government would have recognized his manhood and granted him the priceless boon of a citizen's privileges.

Captain Jack came into this council simply as a diplomatic representative chief, and was not at liberty to do or say more than he was authorized by the Indians in council. He set forth the grievances of his people,—which were principally against the Klamath Indians, on account of the treatment he had received while on the Reservation; and against the government, for not protecting him according to my promise made to him in December, 1869,—arguing that, since the government failed to keep its compact, he was released from his obligation to obey its laws; further, that the crime of which he was charged—killing the Indian doctor—was not a crime under the Indian laws, and that he should not be held amenable to a law that was not *his law*. He declared that he could not live in peace with the Klamaths; that his people had made up their minds to try no more, since they had made two attempts.

He said he "should not object to the white men settling in his country," and that he "would keep his people away from the settlements, and would prevent any trouble between white men and his Indians."

The commissioners again offered him a home on any part of Klamath Reservation that was unoccupied. This he positively declined. He was assured of protection, but he referred to former promises broken. A proposition was made, for him to prevent his people going into the settlement until the whole subject could be submitted to the authorities at Washington, and that a recommendation would be made to grant him a small home at the mouth of Lost River. A rude map was made, showing the proposed Reservation. With this he was satisfied, and made promises of keeping his people away until such time as an answer could be had.

The proposition was fully explained, and he was made to understand the uncertainties as to when a decision would be made in this matter; he agreeing that, if the decision was adverse to granting the new home on Lost River, his people would go on to Klamath, at Yainax.

With this agreement, well understood, the council closed, and the two commissioners reported substantially as detailed. They escaped with their lives because they were prepared to defend them.

Hostilities were averted for the time being, and would have been for all time had prudence and justice been exercised by those who held the power to do this simple act.

Ignorance of the true state of the case cannot be pleaded; the whole matter was laid by me before the authorities at Washington, and the recommendation made in conformity with the promise to the Modocs.

In my official report for 1871 (see Report Commission Indian Affairs) I used the following language:—

The Modocs belong by treaty to Klamath Agency, and have been located thereon; but, owing to the overbearing disposition of the Klamath Indians, they refuse to remain.

"Unavailing efforts have been made to induce them to return; but they persist in occupying their original homes, and, in fact, set up claim thereto. During the past summer they have been a source of annoyance and alarm to the white settlers, and at one time hostilities appeared imminent.

The military commander at Fort Klamath made an unsuccessful effort to arrest a few of the head men. Two commissioners were sent from the Indian Department, and a temporary arrangement made whereby hostilities were averted. The Modocs cannot be made to live on Klamath Reservation, on account of the ancient feuds with the Klamaths. They are willing to locate permanently on a small reservation of six miles square, lying on both sides of the Oregon and California line, near the head of the Tule lake. In equity they are entitled to a portion of the

Klamath and Modoc annuity funds, and need not necessarily be a burden to the government; but, according to the ruling of Commissioner Parker, they have forfeited these rights.

I would recommend that they be allowed a small reservation at the place indicated above, and also a *pro-rata* division of the Klamath and Modoc treaty funds for *employés* and annuities; otherwise they will doubtless be a source of constant expense to the government, and great annoyance to the white settlements near them. Though they may be somewhat responsible for not complying with the treaty, yet, to those familiar with Indian superstition, it is not strange or unreasonable that great charity should be extended to these people.

Gen. Canby was also informed in regard to the arrangement made by the commissioners; the order for their arrest was entirely withdrawn.

Thus matters were in abeyance until the spring of 1872. The Modocs, however, growing restless and impatient for a decision, began to annoy the white settlers in the Lost River country, doing various acts that were not in harmony with the compact made with the commissioners in August preceding. The white men, unwilling to endure the insolence of the Modocs, petitioned for redress. These petitions were addressed to the Indian Department, and to the Military Department, also to the civil authorities of the State of Oregon. They recited the acts of which the Modocs were accused, some of which were, "that they demanded rents for the lands occupied by white men; claiming pay for the use of the stock ranches; demanding horses and cattle; visiting the houses of settlers, and, in the absence of the husbands, ordering the wives to prepare meals for them, meanwhile throwing themselves on the beds and carpets, and refusing to pay for the meals when eaten; feeding their horses with the grain of the settlers, and, in some instances, *borrowing* horses without asking the owners."

To the credit of Captain Jack be it told that *he* was never charged with any of these outrageous acts; but he was powerless to prevent his men from annoying these people who had settled the country at the invitation of the government.

This state of affairs could lead to but *one result,*—blood. The petitions could not be disregarded. Action must be had, and that without delay. General Canby was appealed to; having rescinded the order for the arrest of Captain Jack the previous summer, he was slow to issue another looking to the same end. He believed, as I did, that any attempt to compel the Modocs to return to Klamath would endanger the peace of the country. Captain Jack had failed to keep his part of the late contract, and had thereby forfeited any claim to further clemency.

CHAPTER 22

U. S. Senators Cost Blood—Fair Fight—Open Field

While matters were thus in suspense a change was made in the office of Superintendent of Indian Affairs for Oregon, T. B. Odeneal, Esq., of Oregon, succeeding to the superintendency. He was a lawyer of ability, but had a limited knowledge of Indian character, and still less of the merits and demerits of this Modoc question.

When appealed to he laid the matter before his superior in office at Washington City, who was also a new incumbent, and had perhaps a slight knowledge of the Modoc troubles.

In a letter, dated April 11th, 1872, he instructed Superintendent Odeneal to remove the Modocs to Klamath Reservation, *or locate them on a new home*. In reply, Odeneal suggested that, since Klamath was the home set apart for them in common with other Indians, it was the proper place for them, and suggested they be removed thereto. In compliance with this recommendation, he was instructed, in a letter of September 6th, 1872, to remove the Modocs to the Klamath Reservation; *peaceably* if you can, *forcibly* if you must.

Meanwhile the Modocs were kept posted by the white men, who sympathized with them, of the proposed movements.

Captain Jack and his men sought advice of Judges Roseborough and Steele, of Y-re-ka. Both these gentlemen advised them not to resist the authority of the government, but also promised, as *attorneys*, to assist them in getting lands, provided they would dissolve tribal relations. I have sought diligently, as a commissioner, for information on this subject, and conclude that nothing further was ever promised by either Roseborough or Steele. The hope thus begotten may have caused the Modocs to treat with less respect the officers of the government, and made them more insolent toward settlers; but nothing of wilful intent can be charged to Steele or Roseborough.

It is in evidence that Superintendent Odeneal despatched messengers to the Modoc camp on Lost River, November 26th, 1872, to order Captain Jack and his people to go on to the Reservation, with instruction to the messengers that, in the event of the refusal of the Modocs to comply, to arrange for them to meet him (Odeneal) at Linkville, twenty-five miles from the Modoc camp.

They refused compliance with the order, and also refused to meet Superintendent Odeneal at Link River, saying substantially "that they did not want to see him or talk with him; that they did not want any white man to tell them what to do; that their friends and advisers were in Y-re-ka, Cal. They tell us to stay here, and we intend to do it, and will not go on the Reservation (meaning Klamath); that they were tired of talk, and were done talking."

If credit were given to these declarations, it would appear that some parties at Y-re-ka were culpable. Careful investigation discloses nothing more than already recited, so far as Roseborough and Steele were concerned, but would seem to implicate one or two other parties, both of whom are now deceased; but even then no evidence has been brought forth declaring more than sympathy for the Modocs, which might easily be accounted for on the ground of personal interest, dictating friendship toward them as the best safeguard for life and property; but nothing that could be construed as advising resistance to legal authority; and their statement in regard to advisers in Y-re-ka should not be entitled to more credit than Captain Jack's subsequent assertion that "no white man had ever advised him to stay off the Reservation." This latter declaration was made during the late trials at Klamath by the "military commission," at a time when the first proposition made to Superintendent Odeneal's messengers in regard to Y-re-ka advices would have secured the Modocs then on trial some consideration.

The only thing said or done by any parties in Y-re-ka that has come well authenticated, that could have had any influence with the Modocs in their replies to Odeneal's message, is the proposition above referred to as coming from Roseborough and Steele, to assist them as *attorneys* to secure homes *when* they should have abandoned tribal relations, paid taxes, and made application to become citizens. The high character both these gentlemen possess for loyalty to the government, and for integrity, would preclude the idea that any wrong was intended.

On receiving Captain Jack's insolent reply to his message, Superintendent Odeneal made application to the military commander at Fort Klamath for a force to "compel said Indians (Modocs) to go upon the Klamath Reservation;" reciting the following words from the honourable Commissioner of Indian Affairs: "You are hereby directed to remove the Modoc Indians to Klamath Reservation; *peaceably* if you possibly can, but *forcibly* if you must," and saying: "I transfer the whole matter to your department without assuming to dictate the course you shall pursue in executing the order aforesaid; trusting, however, that you may accomplish the object desired without the shedding of blood, if possible to avoid it."

He received the following reply:—

Headquarters, Fort Klamath, November 28th, 1872.
Sir:—In compliance with your written request of yesterday, I will state that Captain Jackson will leave this post about noon today, with about thirty men; will be at Link River tonight, and I hope before morning at Captain Jack's camp.

I am, sir, very respectfully,
Your obedient servant,
John Green,
Major First Cavalry Commanding Post.
Mr. T. B. Odeneal, Superintendent Indian Affairs.

These movements were intended to be made without the knowledge of the Modocs. Superintendent Odeneal sent messengers to warn the settlers of the proposed *forcible experiment*. Complaint has justly been made that there were several parties unwarned.

The Modocs had one especial friend in whom they relied for advice and warning. This man's name was Miller.

They called on him the day previous to Major Jackson's appearance at the Modoc camp, and he, being ignorant of the movement told them, that "no soldiers were coming." Some twelve settlers were unwarned, who lost their lives thereby.

Neglect on the part of those having the management of this matter resulted in much blood.

When Major Jackson was *en route* to the Modoc camp, some twenty-five white men from Linkville and the surrounding country assembled and proposed to accompany the expedition.

It has been said that they went for the purpose of "seeing Major Jackson and his thirty-five men get licked." At all events they were armed with Henry rifles and revolvers.

Frontier men are fond of sport, and the more it is embellished with danger the more captivating it is to *them*. I do not say this with disrespect to frontier men, but simply state a fact that is not generally understood.

While it is true that they *play* with dangerous weapons as carelessly as a city dandy does with a switch cane or ivory opera-glass, they are, nevertheless, as a class, true, honest, enterprising, great brave-hearted men, who would scorn to do a mean thing.

They have among them men who are irresponsible vagabonds, reckless fellows who are driven from the cities and towns on account of their crimes. These latter characters beget strife among the people, and when truth comes to the front and speaks out, it declares that they are the *sole* cause of any difficulty between good white men and Indians. They are the first to volunteer on occasions like this. As a class they are brave, fearless, desperate, having little regard for human life, caring not how much bad blood they evoke. But the idea that seems to prevail with eastern people, that all frontier men are rough, bad men, is outrageously false in the premises. Better men, braver men, more honourable, more enterprising men cannot be found on this continent than thousands who ride on the swelling breakers of advancing emigration. A moment's consultation with *justice* and *right* would compel the law-makers, book-writers and newspaper reporters, instead of constant, sweeping insinuations against frontier men, to say encouraging words in their behalf, and to offer them every facility to successfully plant the foundations of prosperous society on the verges of American civilization. Honour to whom honour is due.

The party of citizens who went down Lost River on the morning of the 27th of November, 1872, were, *with one or two exceptions*, good, responsible settlers. Their motives were honourable, their intentions were good; and if serious results came out of the fact of their presence it was not because they as a party were "bloodthirsty desperadoes."

They went on the opposite side of the river, and took a commanding position on a bluff overlooking the Modoc camp; which was located on the very spot where my party met Captain Jack in 1869.

The Modoc camp was divided by the river, Captain Jack, and fourteen men with their families, occupying the west bank, where the plain slopes gradually down to the water's edge; the background being covered with a growth of sage brush.

With Captain Jack was "*Schonchin John*," so named from being a younger brother of the "Old chief Schonges;" "*Scarface Charley*," so named on account of a scar on his face; "*Black Jim*," so named on account of his dark colour; "*One-eyed Mose*," so called on account of defect in one eye;"*Watchman*," who was killed in the first battle; "*Humpty Joe*," "*Big Ike*," "*Old Tails*," "*Old Tails' boy*," "*Old Long-face*," and four others.

On the east side of the river was the "*Curly-haired Doctor*," "*Boston Charley*," named on account of his light colour;"*Hooker Jim*" had lived with old man Hooker;"*Slolax*," and ten others, with their families.

Major Jackson, with his force, arrived at Jack's camp at about daybreak on the morning of the 30th November, 1872. At the same time the citizen party arrived opposite and near the camp of the Curly-haired Doctor.

The Modocs were taken by surprise,—although they had reason to expect the soldiers would come within a few days.

They have since asserted that Odeneal's messengers had agreed to come again before bringing soldiers; and, if possible, bring Supt. Odeneal with them.

It was a mistake that he did not go in person,—either with the messengers in the first instance or after their return to Linkville.

He might not have accomplished any good, but he would have prevented severe criticism, and much blame that was laid at his door; inasmuch as Jack subsequently asserted "that he would not have resisted, had Odeneal come himself to him and made everything plain." Again, they had relied on Miller for warning; hence his death.

When Maj. Jackson arrived at the camp, and while he was placing his men in position, an Indian, who was out hunting, made the discovery of Jackson's presence, and either accidentally, or purposely, discharged his gun. This called the Indians to their feet, and they instantly grasped their arms on seeing themselves so nearly surrounded by soldiers.

Maj. Jackson quietly commanded the Modocs to lay down their arms. Captain Jack complied, and told his men to obey the order of Maj. Jackson.

A parley ensued of half an hour, Captain Jack pleading for Jackson to withdraw his men, while the major was explaining his order, and assuring the Modocs that ample preparation had been made for them at Yai-nax. The whole affair seemed to be settled satisfactorily, and I. D. Applegate, who was with Maj. Jackson, went down to the banks of the river and told *One-armed Brown*, the regular messenger of the

Indian Department, who was with the citizen party on the east side, that "everything was settled."Brown mounted his horse, and started to make known the good news to Supt. Odeneal, who was awaiting the result at Linkville.

All the Modocs on the west side of the river had laid down their arms, except Scarface Charley, who was swearing and making threats. Maj. Jackson commanded him, "Put down your gun." Scarface refused; the major ordered Lieut. Boutelle to disarm him,—who, on advancing to execute the order, repeated it in emphatic words, not in harmony with savage notions of decorum and decency. "Scarface" was enraged at the vile epithets applied to him, and perhaps remembered just then that he had once seen, from a *chapparel* thicket, a sight that had haunted him from his childhood, namely, nothing less than armed white men chasing *his father* with a *lasso* and catching him. He saw them hang him without a trial, or even any proof that he was guilty of any crime. At all events, he drew his pistol, and, saying that he "would kill one white man," discharged it at the advancing officer; but so nearly simultaneous with Boutelle's pistol, that even the latter does not know who fired first. This was the opening gun of the Modoc war; the beginning of what ended on the gallows on the third of November, 1873.

Without stopping now to call up the intervening pictures, let us see how the battle went.Very soon the entire force of soldiers was firing into the Indian camps, and the fourteen Indian men were fighting back with muzzle-loading rifles.

The battle lasted three hours; the Indians, having taken cover of the sage brush, finally withdrew, carrying with them the watchman who was killed, and escaping with all their women and children.

Maj. Jackson lost ten killed and five wounded; and on the reappearance of the Indians, a few hours later, drew off his forces, leaving the Modocs in possession of the battle-field.

While all this was enacting on the west bank of Lost River, let us see how the boys who went down to "take a look" got along as spectators. Mr. Brown, hearing the report of arms, returned just in time to take an active part in a performance that was not in the programme of fun as laid out in the early morning.

The citizens and Modocs on the east side could not stand the pressure,—looking on and seeing a fair fight, within a couple of hundred yards, without taking a part. The Modocs caught up their guns and rushed down to the river, intending to reinforce Captain Jack.

252

The citizens sought to prevent them getting into their canoes; and, *somehow*, they became very much interested in matters nearer home than Maj. Jackson's fight.

Who began the battle on the east side is a question of doubt,— both parties denying it; but a lively fight was the result, and the citizens drew off, leaving *three* or *four dead friends* on the ground and—and— *one dead squaw*, with an infant corpse in her arms.

It is not in evidence who was victor, but there is the record. The major dispatched a messenger for reinforcements, who run the gauntlet of Indian bullets, and barely escaped.

From Indian lips I learn that in the first battle of which I have spoken, Captain Jack did not fire a shot himself, though he directed the fight.

On the occasion of the messenger being sent off by Maj. Jackson, Captain Jack, who was secreted in the sage brush, ran after him and fired one or two shots.

Let us look now to the Modocs with Captain Jack. They did not go on the warpath, but hastened to gather up their women and horses, and retired to the Lava Bed.

Scarface Charley remained behind, for a purpose that can scarcely be credited. Those who doubt any real genuine manhood among Indians may wonder when I declare that he remained to warn white men of the danger threatening them. In two instances he saw white men, who were his personal friends, going, as he knew, into certain death. In both instances he laid hold of the bridle-reins of the riders' horses and turned them around, and, pointing to the road whence they came, bade them "ride for life."

They lost no time in heeding the warning given, and also in notifying the settlers en route of the existence of open hostilities.

By this means John A. Fairchild was notified of the dangers that surrounded him and his family.

Mr. Fairchild's name has become intimately connected with the Modoc war; indeed, he played some of the thrilling parts of this tragic drama. He is a man of forty years of age, a native of Mississippi; went West when a boy, and engaged in mining. In the course of time he became a large stock-raiser, and went, ten years ago, with his herds of cattle and horses, into the Modoc country.

He soon learned a lesson that our government has *not*, viz., that it is cheaper to *feed* Indians than to *fight* them. Soon after his arrival he arranged a treaty with the Modocs, paying them a small compensa-

253

tion for the use of the country for stock uses. During the time, he has made the personal acquaintance of nearly every Indian of Captain Jack's band.

His home is situated on Hot Creek, near its rise at the foot of the mountains that divide the Modoc from the Shasta country.

It will be remembered that the head-quarters of the Peace Commission was at Fairchild's ranch during the first days of its organization. This was also the original home of a part of Jack's band.

At the beginning of the late Modoc war some fourteen warriors and their families were living near Mr. Fairchild's house; by his management of them they were prevented from joining Captain Jack for several days. He, together with Mr. Press Dorris, who lives near him, and is also a stock-raiser, called together these fourteen men, including "Bogus Charley" (who gets his name from his birthplace on Bogus creek), "Shacknasty Jim" (so named from his mother), "Steamboat Frank" (so called in honour of his squaw, whose name was Steamboat, because of her great size and her habit of puffing and blowing like the aforesaid vessel), Ellen's man George, and ten others,—who all distinguished themselves in the war,—and started with them and their families to Klamath Reservation. They notified Agent Dyer, of Klamath, of their coming, and requested him to meet them and take charge of the Indians.

Dyer responded, and, hastening to meet them on Klamath River, passed through Linkville *en route*. While there he heard intimations of the danger of passing through the town with the above-named Modocs.

The news of the battle had reached Linkville, and the people were aroused to madness at the sight of the mangled bodies of the soldiers and citizens that had been brought in. It is not strange that such sights should call out a demand for vengeance; that the citizens, feeling outraged, should make threats.

It is certain that a party left Linkville before Agent Dyer arrived, and went in the direction of Bob Whittle's, where Fairchild and Dorris were guarding the Hot Creek Modocs, now so anxious to reach the Reservation that they might escape any kind of entanglement with the rebels.

The party found Fairchild and Dorris fully prepared to protect those under their charge, and no attack was made, whatever may have been the first intention. On Mr. Dyer's arrival at this time, he stated his fears to Fairchild and Dorris, which the Indians overhearing, *stam-*

peded, and went directly to the Lava Beds, thus adding fourteen warriors to Captain Jack's forces. All of them were brave men, and bad men, too, as the sequel will show. The fright they had received at Bob Whittle's appears to have made them even more anxious for war than those who had been engaged in the Lost River battle, on the 30th of November, 1872.

Indian proof is abundant that Captain Jack, in anticipation of the coming of the soldiers, had advised his men to surrender rather than fight; but, even if forced to resist, in no event to attack citizens, saying, "If we must, we will fight soldiers, not white men," meaning citizens.

It is a fact that, so far as he was concerned, he sought to avoid conflict. The Curly-haired Doctor was eager for blood—or, at all events, he was rebellious, and constantly advised resistance to the authority of the Government.

His interference in the council of December, 1869, referred to in a former chapter, and his sanction to the proposition to murder our party at that time, and the subsequent proposal to assassinate the commissioners sent out in August, 1871, to arrange matters with them, all stand against him previous to the opening of the war.

But to return to the Battle of Lost River. After a sharp fight, the citizens having withdrawn to Dennis Crawley's house, the Modoc braves assembled, and, through the advice of Hooker Jim, the Curly-haired Doctor, with Steamboat Frank and three or four others, started on a mission of vengeance.

The acts of savage butchery committed by them are well known to the world,—how they went to Mr. Boddy's house with their garments covered with the life-blood of their victims, and, taunting the women, boasted of their heroism, saying, "This is Boddy's blood; but we are Modocs; we do not kill women and children. You will find Boddy in the woods. We will not hurt you."

Thus from house to house they went, after killing the husbands and fathers, until they had slaughtered thirteen persons,—Brotherton, Schiere, Miller, and others, including one small boy, who resisted them.

The reign of terror was complete. Who shall ever find words to describe the horror of the night following this treacherous butchery? The women left their homes to hunt for their murdered friends. In one instance, the presence of a team without a driver gave the awful tidings.

Leaving their dead, through the long dark night that followed, they made their way through the trackless sage-brush plains to the nearest settlement. With these people the Modocs had been on friendly terms, and had never had any misunderstandings with the Indians. On the contrary, they had shown by many acts of kindness their *good will*. They were personally acquainted with the men who composed the murderous gang. This was especially the case with Mr. Miller; he had been their steadfast friend for years, and had furnished them provisions and ammunition but a few days previously, and had further interested himself in their behalf, in conjunction with Esquire Steele of Y-re-ka, in securing to them the right to take up lands in common with other people.

The murder of Miller seems the more inhuman when it is remembered that he was killed by Hooker Jim. The latter declares that he did not know that he was shooting at Miller. Otherwise he would not have committed the treacherous deed. Miller had been on especial good terms with this *desperado*.

With my knowledge of Indian character, I am of the opinion that Hooker Jim designedly killed Mr. Miller, because he believed that the latter had purposely withheld from the Modocs the movement of Major Jackson.

Loaded with plunder, and mounted on the horses they had captured, these bloodthirsty savages made their way around the east side of Tule lake; meeting Captain Jack and his warriors in the Lava Bed. I am indebted to the Modocs themselves for many items of importance in this connection. I give them for what they are worth, with the authority announced. Some of them are doubtless correct, according to the authority quoted.

On the arrival in the Lava Bed, Captain Jack denounced the murderers for their bloody work, and particularly for the killing of Mr. Miller; he then declared that the men who committed this outrageous crime should be surrendered to the white men for trial; that a great mistake had been made; and that unless these men were given up, the whole band would be lost. The councils held were noisy and turbulent, threatening strife and bloodshed. While this matter was under discussion, the Hot-Creek Indians, who had stampeded from Whittle's Ferry, while they were *en route* to Klamath Agency, arrived in the Lava Bed, adding fourteen braves to the little band of desperadoes. The Hot-Creek Modocs, having become demoralized by the threats they had overheard made against them, and being influenced by the Curly-haired Doctor's promise of making medicine to protect them, were ready to espouse the cause of the murderers. The whole number of braves at this time was fifty-three, including the chief himself. Thus, when the discussion was ended and the question was submitted to a vote, a large majority was opposed to the surrender of the Lost River murderers.

Chapter 23

Mourning Emblems and Military Pomp

Leaving the Modocs to wrangle over their troubles, suppose we listen now to the wails of anguish and grief that burdened the air of the Lost-river country, and especially at Linkville, when the mutilated bodies of the slain citizens were brought in for interment.

When the news of the Lost River battle had spread over the sparsely-settled country, a feeling of terror pervaded the hearts of the people; but when, on the following morning, the grief-stricken, heart-broken Mrs. Boddy, Mrs. Schiere and Mrs. Brotherton, arrived at Linkville, after a long night of horrors, the excitement became intense. Armed parties, taking with them wagons, repaired to the scene of this awful tragedy.

Let those whose lives are spent where they are protected by the strong arm of law, go with me for a day, while we hunt up the victims of this wholesale murder.

Perhaps, if we are honest, and our hearts are open to conviction of truth, and we are actuated by the impulses of Christian sympathy, we may suspend our charitable emotions for the "noble red man," by the time we hear the dull thud of the clods at Linkville cemetery mingle with the sobs and shrieks of the widows and orphans.

From one who was with a party who went out on this sorrowful mission, I learned something of the scenes that met them.

On arriving at the grove of timber where Brotherton was killed, they found his body lying stark and cold, with his glassy eyes wide open. He had been pierced by four Modoc bullets. Near him was found his axe, with the handle painted with his own blood. Then another was found on a wagon, lying across the coupling poles, with his face downwards. He, too, was stripped of his clothing.

Another was found a few rods from his work, with his bowels beside him, and his heart taken from his body, and hacked to pieces. This was the work of Hooker Jim.

Thus the party went on from one to another, until thirteen bodies were found. Some of them were off from roads, where they had evidently run in their attempts to escape.

While the kind-hearted settlers were performing this sad duty, they were continually on the lookout for an attack. Let us follow this heavily-laden train of wagons, and be with them when they arrive at Linkville. Can human language depict the agony of that hour? We may tell of the outburst of grief, when the widows gather around that solemn train, preparing to unload its ghastly freight, and how, with frantic movements, they threw themselves on the remains of husband, brother and father. But we may not tell of the grief that overwhelmed their hearts in that darkest hour, when beholding loved ones mangled and mutilated by the hands that had so often received gifts from them, now so stiff and cold in death.

There are moments in life when the great fountains seem broken up as if by some terrific explosion, until even the very streams that otherwise would flow out are dried up.

Oh, how dark the world becomes to the wife and mother when the sunlights of life go out, and they stand amid the gloom, unable to recognize the hand of our heavenly Father!

Slowly and sadly the sorrowing friends start up the hill with the remains of Boddy and Schiere, while the bereaved and heart-broken widows follow the sad funeral pageant.

How can we bear to hear the cry of anguish that parts their lips when the first clod of earth falls, with sepulchral noise, on the coffin lids that cover the faces of their dead forever!

My humane, kind-hearted reader, who has a soul overflowing with kindness that goes out for "Lo! the poor Indian," look on this scene a moment, and in your mind exchange your happy home for a cabin on the frontier wilds, where you meet these Indian people, and where, from the fullness of a great heart overflowing with "good will to man," you have uttered only kind words, while you shared your homely fare with them in sympathy for their low estate. Remember how often you have almost ruined your own family that you might in part compensate them for their lost homes; how you have dropped from your hands your own duties as a wife or mother that you might teach these dark, sad-eyed savage women the little art of housewifery.

Think how many hours you have laboured teaching them the ways of civil life in dress and manners; while your memory of childhood's lessons in Christianity reconciled you to the labour and the sacrifice with this comforting assurance, "*Inasmuch as ye did it unto the least of these, ye did it also unto me.*" Remember all these, and then gaze on the dark emblems of sorrow that envelop Mrs. Boddy, Mrs. Schiere, Mrs. Brotherton, and tell me, have you still Christianity that enables you to say, "Thy will be done," nor let your lips breathe out a prayer for power to avenge your bursting heart? Will you censure now the brave and manly friends on whose arms these widows lean, while they go back to a home with the sunlight gone? If these friends, in sympathy with the bereaved, do swear to anticipate a tardy justice, do you still have hard words for the pioneers who brave danger and drink deeply from the fountain of bitter grief when in madness they cry for revenge?

It is one thing to sit through a life-time under the persuasive eloquence of ministers who have never walked side by side with such sorrow, and gradually form an ideal or real monitor in the soul, until human nature seems lost in the divine power that prepares humanity for higher life, and until we think we can at all times, when smitten on one cheek, turn the other. It is quite another thing to break old family associations, and, leaving the scenes of childhood behind you, with strong and brave hearts, open the way for emigration; plant waymarks that point to a future of prosperity; sow the seeds of civilization in unbroken wilds, fairly to represent your race before the savage, and live in the exercise of a religious faith that honest dealings and the overshadowing exercise of brotherly love will be a sure guaranty of final reward.

To go out on the bleak plains of Lost River, and by industry and economy transform the sage-brush deserts into fruitful fields, to rear the unpretentious cabins, and open your doors to the thirsty and hungry of every race and colour, and then, when you have done all this, to stand in your cabin-door and smile back at the waving fields, and listen to the lowing herds, while you rejoice in your instrumentality in making the great transformation; looking hopefully to a future, when, from neighbouring valleys, shall come up sounds of friendly recognition; longing for the hour when you may catch sight of children returning from the country school, and for the advent of the itinerant minister, who will bring with him a charter under which you may work toward a brotherhood, whose ties will bind on earth and reunite

260

in heaven,—when, suddenly, more direful than mountain torrents or heaving earthquake, comes athwart your life a scene like that enacted on Lost River, *November 30th, 1872.*

That scene, with all its horrors, has been repeated over and over again, and will continue to be until this government of ours shall come squarely up to the performance of its duty, and shall have clothed worthy men with power to do and make good its promises of fair and impartial justice to each and all those who sit down under the shadow of its flag.

Tell me truly, do you still feel scorn for the frontier people, whose lives are embellished with episodes and tragedies like these that I have here painted in plainest colours, and nothing borrowed from imagination,—no, not even using half the reality in making up the picture?

My words cannot call back the dead, or flood the rude cabins of the stricken and bereaved with sunshine and hope. No. There, on the hill, beside Linkville, the thirteen little mounds lie out in winter's storm and summer's sun; and they who prematurely sleep there will wake *no more.*

There, on the plains, stand the vacant cabins where these once lived. There, walking with the spirits of the departed by their sides, the widows go; while orphans' faces wear reproach, in saddened smiles, against a government that failed to deal justly, and who, with light and careless hand, pointed out its ministers of law without thinking once how much of human woe and misery might be avoided by a few well-studied words of command.

The dead are buried, and the notes of coming strife succeed those of bitter wailing; the winter's sun gleams from the brass mountings of officers; the zephyrs of the mountain are mingling with martial music; the great plains of sage brush are glittering with polished bayonets. The United States are at length aroused. The State of Oregon, *too*, is waxing very wroth. The doom of the Modocs is sealed; and *war! war! war!* is the word.

From the half-dozen little military posts in the Lake country is seen coming a grand army of—well—*two hundred soldiers.* "That's enough to eat up Jack's little band. Keep cool, my dear friends. Let 'em go for 'em. They need a *lickin'* bad. There won't be a grease-spot left of 'em."

(Such was the speech in a hotel not far from Linkville, Oregon.)

"Look-er here, stranger, I'll bet you a hundred head of cows, that

261

Captain Jack licks them there two hundred soldiers like h—l; so I will. I know what I'm talking about, *I do*. I tried them Modoc fellows long time ago; they won't lick worth a d—m; so *they won't*. If Frank Wheaton goes down there a puttin' on style like a big dog in 'tall rye', he'll catch h—l; *so he will*. I'm going down just to *see* the *fun*."

"You're a crazy old fool. Frank Wheaton with two hundred soldiers will wipe 'em out 'fore breakfast," suggested a listener.

"Look-er here if I'm crazy the cows aint; come come, if you think I'm crazy, come, up with the squivlents, and you can go into the stock-raisin' business cheap. *You can*.

"Major Jackson went down there tother day with forty men, and Jack hadn't but fourteen bucks with him, and he licked Jackson out of his boots in no time, and that was in open ground, and Jackson had the drap on the Ingens at that; and by thunder he got the worst lickin' a man ever got in this neck woods; *so he did*. Then another thing, Captain Jack aint on open ground now; not by a d——d sight. He is in the all-firedest place in the world. You've been to the 'Devil's garden,' at the head of Sprague river, haven't you? Well, that place aint a patchen to that ere place where the Injuns is now. I've been there, and I tell you, it's nearly litenin', all rocks and caves, and you can't lead a horse through it in a week,—and then the Injuns knows every inch of the ground, and when they get in them there caves, why it taint no use talking, I tell you, you can't kill nary an Ingen,—*you can't*. I'm a-going down just to *see* the *fun*."

The reporter who furnished me the foregoing speeches did not learn whether a bet was made, or whether any army officers overheard the talk; but the truth is, those who had this nice little breakfast job on hand were somewhat of the opinion of the fellow whose "cows were not crazy, if he was." They were willing to have *help*.

This little Modoc affair was a favourable thing for Oregon and California, in more ways than one. To the politician it was a windfall; for no matter what the cause of war may have been, it is always popular to have been in favour of the last war. It makes opportunity for brave men to win laurels and undying fame. It clothes their tongues with themes for public harangue until the last war is superseded by another. Then again it was a *heroic* thing to rush up to the recruiting office and *volunteer* to *whip the Modocs*.

It is not at all likely that the movement of armies over railroads, or toll-roads, or steamboat lines, was a desirable thing for a country where there was no money in it. Then no man was base enough to wish for war for motives so mean; neither could it be possible that any sane man, with ordinary judgment, could see any speculations or chances for greenbacks in war.

Californians did intimate that the Oregonians were a little mercenary in their anxiety for war; but with what unanimity our press repelled the mean insinuation!

Our governor very promptly sent forward two or three companies of volunteers,—California, *but one.*

Listen, ye winds, to the neighing steeds and clashing sabres, and see the uniformed officers and the brave boys, all with faces turned toward the Lava Beds, going down to vindicate the honour of the State whose soil had been *invaded* by a ruthless savage foe.

The regulars are in camp near the Modocs, waiting for the volunteers to come up. They come, with banners flying, and steeds prancing, and hearts beating triumphant at the prospect of a fight.

Some of these men were living several years ahead, when they could from "the stump" tell how they bared their bosoms to the Modoc hail; how they carried away Modoc scalps; how the ground was bathed in mingled blood of Modoc and white men.

The army now numbering four hundred, all told, of enlisted men, approaches the Lava Beds. One or two companies encamp at Fairchild's. They drill; they go through the mimic charges; they espy a few Modoc women and children encamped on the creek near Fairchild's house,—they propose to take them in. "Knits make lice,—let's take them, boys,—here goes."

A middle-sized grey-eyed man, with his whiskers dyed by twenty years' labour on "the coast," steps out and says, "No you don't, not yet. *Take me first.* No man harms defenceless women where I am, while I am standing on my perpendiculars."

"Who are you?" says one fine-looking young fellow.

"Try me, and you will find out that I am John Fairchild." These brave fellows had not lost any Indians just then, they hadn't. Bah!

"Who are your officers?" said Fairchild.

The information was furnished, and soon the grey-eyed man was reading a chapter not found in the Talmud, or the Bible either. As reported, it was *eloquent*, though not *classical.*

Preparations were being completed for a forward movement. One-half the army was to move to the attack from the south, while the other was to move down from the north. The 16th of January, 1873, the two wings were within a few miles on either side. Orders were given to be in motion before daylight the following morning. Some spicy little colloquies were had between the members of the volunteer companies; some, indeed, between officers.

One brave captain of volunteers said to another, "I have but one fear, and that is that I can't restrain my men, they are so eager to get at 'em; they will eat the Modocs up raw, if I let 'em go."

"Don't fret," said Fairchild; "you can hold them; they won't be hard to keep back when the Modocs open fire."

"I say, Jim, are you going to carry grub?"

"No. I am going to take Modoc *Sirloin* for my dinner."

"I think," said a burly-looking fellow, "that I'll take mine *rare*."

Another healthy-looking chap said he intended capturing a good-looking squaw for a—dishwasher. (Good-looking squaws wash dishes better than homely ones.)

A number of humane, chivalrous, civilizing, kind people intended to capture some little *Ingens* for servants. One fellow declared that Captain Jack's *pacing hoss* should be his.

To have heard the camp talk the night before the battle, you would have supposed that sundown, next day, would find these brave men loaded with Indian plunder and military glory, going toward home in fine style, with great speeches in rehearsal to deliver to the gaping crowds, who would hang, with breathless interest, on the words that they would deal out with becoming modesty.

That night was a long one to ambitious, noisy men; and, sad to say, a *last* one to some of the bravest of the army.

But the guard is stationed for the night, the council of officers has been held, and the moon settles slowly away; the soldiers sleep. The orders for the morrow are understood, and quiet reigns throughout the hopeful camp.

No doubt crosses the minds of the men, and, perhaps, of but few officers, so sanguine are they of success. The greatest fear expressed was, that the fight would not last long enough to give *all a fair show* to win distinction.

Rest quiet, my poor, deluded countrymen! Some of you are taking your last sleep but one,—the sleep of death.

If you had asked the opinion of Maj. Jackson and John Fairchild, or Press Dorris, they would have set your hearts at ease, about having an opportunity to fight a little on the morrow. You will have a chance to try your metal, never fear, my dear friends.

CHAPTER 24

Peace or War—One Hundred Lives Voted Away by Modoc Indians

Leaving our soldier friends to dream of glory to be won in the coming battle, let us pick our way from their camp to the headquarters of Captain Jack.

Our starting-point now is from a little grove of mountain mahogany trees on a high plateau, a few miles south of the California and Oregon boundary line, and within a short distance of the extreme southern end of lower Klamath Lake. The trees are dwarfed, stunted, and bent before the stormy winds that have swept over them so continually.

As we leave this military camp, a long, high, sharp ridge extends northward and southward, falling away at either end to hills of lesser height. Climbing to the top, and looking eastward, we see Tule Lake, named on the maps of this country Rhett Lake. It is a beautiful sheet of water, of thirty miles from north to south, and fifteen from west to east. We see also, with a field-glass, across the lake, the lone cabins where the strong hands of Boddy, Brotherton, and others have laid the foundation of future homes. They stand like spirit sentinels on the plain.

Look again at the trail leading out of the sage-brush plains; follow with your glass down to where a high stone bluff crowds against the lake, and forces the wagon trail into the edge of the water, until it disappears in the high *tule* grass.

In September, 1852, a long train of wagons, drawn by worn-out oxen, driven by hardy, venturesome pioneers, came down that trail.

They never came out again, save the two or three persons, as related in a former chapter.

265

That place is *Bloody Point.*

Turn your glass northward, and see the trail emerge from the tule grass; follow it until it turns suddenly westward and reaches the natural bridge on Lost River. Turn your glass up the river one mile, and you see the favourite home of Captain Jack, where we found him in 1869, and where Major Jackson found him on the morning of "November 30th, 1872;" and, had you been looking at that spot at 4 p.m. of the 23rd day of April, 1873, you would have descried a four-horse ambulance, with a mounted escort of six men on either side, and standing in the front end of that ambulance a woman, with a field-glass, eagerly scanning the surface of the lake. That woman shows anxiety in her blue eye and earnest face while she changes the direction of the glass, expecting each moment to catch sight of a boat crossing the lake. She is cool, calm, and self-possessed, although no other lady is nearer than twenty-four miles.

There is a reason for her presence there; and she will need all her self-command when the looked-for boat arrives. Why, that lone woman is there, on that 23rd day of April, we will tell you in good time.

Turn your glass back now to Bloody Point, and follow down the shore of the lake. Ah! there stands a white-looking object near a bluff that is black with a low growth of trees. The white object is Miller's house, just as he left it the morning before his *friend, Hooker Jim, murdered him.* The black-looking bluff near it is where *Ben Wright* met the Modocs, in a peace talk, in 1852. Swing your glass round to the right, following the shore of the lake, and, at the extreme southern end, you will see the cabins of Lou-e Land, and near them Col. Barnard's headquarters.

The white tents of the soldiers look like tiny playthings, even under a field-glass. Col. Barnard is there with one hundred "regulars," and one company of "volunteers." Look closely, and you will see that half the volunteers are red-skinned men. Their captain is a tall, fine-looking white man, who addresses them in the ancient jargon of the Klamaths,—this is Oliver Applegate.

See the Indian soldiers, with each a white badge on his head; it is not an army regulation cap, but is simply to prevent accident; that is, it is a mark to distinguish the white man's ally from his enemy.

In this camp are men about as anxious to march on the Modocs as those on the north side; some of these red soldiers are the boys who made Jack's stay on Klamath Reservation, in 1870, so uncomfortable.

266

They are *loyal*, though, to the government, and are willing to help the white men exterminate their cousins (the Modocs). Then the *pro rata* of annuity goods will be so much the larger. They don't mean any harm to the Modocs, although since 1864 they have been receiving regularly the price the government has paid for *the home of the Modocs*; except on one or two occasions, when the latter were present.

These red-skinned boys are anxious to capture the Modoc ponies; for, running with Jack's band of horses, are several that once carried these Klamath boys flying over the plains; until, in an evil moment, they were weak enough to stake them, as many a poor, weak-minded, infatuated white man has done his home, all on the hazardous chance of certain cards turning up at the right time. Well, let these fellows take rest, for they will need all their nerve before another day passes.

Move your glass round to the right, what a sight do we see! A great flat-looking valley stretches out south and west from the ragged shore line of the lake. On the further boundary see the four low buttes standing in a line; while behind Mount Shasta raises his white head, overlooking the country around on all sides for hundreds of miles.

This valley, lying so cold and cheerless, seems to have been once a part of the lake. It is devoid of timber, save one lone tree, that stands out on what appears to be a plain, of almost smooth prairie; but we forget we are one thousand feet above this valley.

Let us follow now the zigzag trail that leads to the gap just where the valley and the lake unite.

Better dismount, for wagons never have been, nor ever will go down that bluff. Horses, indeed, need a *rough-lock* to get down in safety. Oh! but this *is* steep; we are now half-way down,—let us rest, and meanwhile take your field-glass and "see what we can see." Why! it don't look as it did from the top of the bluff. Oh! I see now why you call this place the "Lava Beds." From this stand-point it presents the appearance of a broken sea, that had, when in wild commotion, suddenly frozen or crystallized; except that the surface is a grayish colour. Sage brush grows out from the crevices of the rock, and, occasionally, "bunch grass" may be seen.

Near the foot of the bluff is a small flat of a few acres that is free from rocks. A bay from the lake makes up into the rocky field; then a long point of stony land runs out into the lake.

Follow the shore-line, and another bay, or arm of the lake, runs out into the lava rocks. Look carefully, and, on the next point of lava rocks, running into the lake, you will discover a gray smoke rising. There, if you will steady your glass, you will see dark forms moving round about the fire.

They are not more than two miles from our point of observation, and this is the 16th day of June, 1873.

See that man standing above the others. He is talking. Wonder who he is, and what he is saying. Since we are talking of Indians, suppose we adopt Indian spiritualism, and in that invisible capacity we will hear and see what is going on.

We will pick our way over the dim, crooked trail, first in real person, and take items as we pass along. The trail is very dim, it is true— only seen by the rocks misplaced to make footing for the Indian ponies. Now we wind around some low stony point, and pick our way down into a rocky chasm.

Slowly rising, we climb up twenty feet of bluff, and out on a plateau. Looking carefully for the road, we follow a half-round circle of two hundred feet on the left; and, sloping from every direction, the broken lava rocks tend toward a common centre, forty feet below the level of the plateau. As we pursue our way another great basin is in sight, of similar character and proportion; and thus this plateau, that appeared almost smooth from the mountain-top, is made up of a succession of basins, all lined with broken rock, from the size of a drygoods box to that of a meeting-house.

Just ahead, we see rising above the rocky plain a craggy ledge, standing like an immense comb, the spikes of lava forming great teeth. On the right and left it looks as if the teeth-like crags are broken midway, and our trail is pointing to one of these breaks.

Before reaching it, we see on either hand where the breaks are filled with stones, piled in such a way that port-holes are left, through which the Modocs propose to fire on the advancing foes when they come to the attack.

Passing between upright spires of lava, we come out on a smooth plain of fractured stones; and, passing near the end of the second little bay, we find rough, sharp ledges rising to intercept our way.

Picking our steps, we stand on the summit of the ledge. Shut your eyes now while we pass over a chasm of thirty feet in depth, and with walls almost perpendicular. Our bridge has been made by a gorge of loose rocks that fill the chasm to its lips. Some of these have been rolled in by Indian hands, and some by old Vulcan himself, when he spilled the lava there.

Come, follow the trail,—now we stand a moment and, looking

right and left, we see great fissures and caverns that look dark and forbidding; suggesting ambush. No danger here now,—*we left the Modoc sentinel behind us*, at the huge comb-like ledge. He is not afraid of us, and all the other Modocs are in council. Climbing a cliff that overlooks a deep, wide chasm, we catch sight of the sage-brush fire, and suddenly half a hundred warriors, in half dress of "Boston," half of savage costume,—some of them are bare-armed, and have curious-looking figures on them made of paint.

This is not safe now, for sharp eyes scan the surroundings, and while this council is going on, the Modoc women are doing duty. Some of them are piling on the sage brush to keep the fire going. Others are standing, apparently pillars of stone; sphinx like, they gaze outward, for although this council is being held in a place secure from gaze of pale-faced man, the Modocs, Indian like, are ever on the alert, and do not intend to be taken by surprise. Since this is not safe for us, we had better play Indian spirit, if we would see and hear what is going on. What we lack in catching the words in the spirit correctly, we will obtain from some friendly Indian hereafter. See that fellow there; his face looks familiar; yet he is not a Modoc. Oh! yes; we recognize him now; we saw him at the peace meeting, taking the Modocs by the hand then, and afterwards taunting them with their poverty and cowardice while they were on Klamath Reservation in 1870. That fellow is *Link-river Jack*. He is a natural traitor.

He has crept cautiously into the Modoc camp to give them warning of the soldiers coming. He is the Modocs' *friend now*; he tells them that a large army is coming; that they are on the bluff almost within sight.

This was not news; for the Modocs had counted the soldiers, man by man, and knew exactly how many was in either camp. They knew, too, that half the soldiers were citizens with whom they had dealt for years. Link-river Jack tells them of the feeling outside against them; that peace may be had on the surrender of the Modocs who killed the settlers. We did not hear him tell them that if they would hold out a few days, the Klamaths and Snakes would join them; but our friendly Indian asserts that he did.

All eyes turn now to the chief, Captain Jack. He rises with stately mien and says, "We have made a mistake. We cannot stand against the white men. Suppose we kill all these soldiers; more will come, and still more, and finally all the Modocs will be killed; when we kill the soldiers others will take their places; but when a Modoc gets killed no man will come to take *his* place; we must make the best terms we can. I do not want to fight the white man. I want no war; I want peace. Some of the white men are our friends. Steele and Roseborough are our friends; they told us not to fight the white men; we want no war; soon all the young men will be killed. We do not want to fight."

Old Schonchin John arose; his face was full of war; *he* was in for a fight. He recalled the "Ben Wright" massacre; he said, "We have nothing to expect from the white men. We can die, but we will not die first. I won't give it up; I want to fight. I can't live long. I am an old man." Schonchin sat down. He had no hope for his life; his crimes were all arrayed against him, and he knew it.

Scarface Charley rose to talk. He said, "I was mad on Lost River; my blood was bad. I was insulted. I have many friends among the white men. I do not want to kill them. We cannot stand against the white men. True, I am a Modoc. What their hearts are, my heart is. May be we can stop this war. I want to live in peace."

Curly-haired Doctor, who was with the murdering gang in Lost River, arose and said, "I am a Modoc. My hands are red with white man's blood. I was mad when I saw the dead women and children on Lost River. I want war. I am not tired. The white men cannot fight; they shoot in the air. I will *make a medicine that will turn the white man's bullets away from the Modocs*. We will not give up. We can kill all that come."

The discussion is ended, and now comes the vote. They divide off,—those who were for war walked out on one side, and those who favour peace on the other. These people are democratic; *the majority rules*.

The vote is of vast importance to others than the Modocs. One hundred and fifty soldiers and many citizens are interested in that vote. Gen. Canby, Dr. Thomas, and your writer, are to be very much affected by that vote. Millions of dollars hang on the decision.

Hold your breath while each man elects for himself. The chief, Captain Jack, walks boldly out on the side of peace, but, O my God, few dare follow him. The majority vote for blood, and gather around Schonchin John, and the Curly-haired Doctor. The die is cast, war is inevitable; let us see who is with Captain Jack. There goes "Scarface Charley," "William"(the wild gal's man), "Miller's Charley," "Duffey," "Te-he Jack," "Little Poney," "Big Poney," "Duffey's Boy," "Chuckle-head," "Big Steve," "Big Dave," "Julia's man,"—fourteen men, no more.

The bloodthirsty villains who held the balance of power are, "Schonchin," "Curly-head Doctor," "Bogus Charley," "Boston Charley," "Hooker Jim," "Shacknasty Jim," "Steamboat Frank," "Rock-Dave," "Big Joe," "Curly Jack," and the remainder of the band, numbering thirty-seven, all told. There are two strange Indians there, also; they are Pitt river thieves, they do not vote. The doctor's speech has done the work. These infuriated thirty-six men believe in him, and his promise to make medicine that will turn the bullets of the white men. This has more power than the clear, logical reasoning of Captain Jack. Having turned the current of so many lives, the doctor, exulting in his success, repaired to his cave to fulfil his promise.

Suppose we follow him and see how this thing is done. He calls the singing women of the band together, and, having prepared roots and religious meats, he builds a fire, and, with a great deal of ceremony, he places the sacrifice thereon; then inhaling the smoke and odour of the burning mess, he begins his religious incantations; calling down the good spirit, calling up the bad spirit, and calling loudly for the spirits of the dead Indians to come; while the women, having pitched a tune to his words, begin to sing, and with their shoulders touching each other, they start off in a rough, hobbly kind of a dance, singing meanwhile; and a drummer, too, joins in with a hideous noise, made on a drain of peculiar shape, with but one head of dried rawhide, or untanned buckskin, drawn tightly over a rough-made hoop.

Round go the singing dancers, and louder grow the voices of the doctor and the women; both increasing in fury until exhausted nature gives proof of the presence of the various spirits.

The braves stand looking on to see what the prospects are; satisfied that the medicine is getting strong enough, they saunter back to the cave of the chief, where he sits with thoughtful brow, planning in a low voice the defence of the morrow; repeating again, "This is the last of my people; I must do what their hearts say; I am a *Modoc*, and I am not afraid to die." Then giving orders for the fight,—designating where each man should be stationed, and appointing women to carry water and ammunition to the various stations, while they fight,—he inspects the arms, and estimates how long the powder and lead will last, tells the women to mould bullets for the old-fashioned rifles; he then turns sadly away to his sister, Queen Mary, and declares that he is now going to do what he thought he never would do,—"fight the white man."

We leave the howling doctor and the sad chief and return to the soldier camp on the top of the bluff. The sentinels are walking the rounds; all is quiet, and the boys are taking their rest,—some of them their last rest save one. Ah! Jerry Crook, you jumped down from a stage-driver's box to help whip the Modocs. Your heart is beating steadily now; it will beat wildly for a few minutes tomorrow afternoon, and then its pulsations will cease forever. George Roberts, too, has left a good position to come on this mission, promising, as he fondly hopes, a dream of glory, which he will share with his comrades when hereafter he cracks his whip over the teams of the Northwest Stage Company. Enjoy it now, my dear fellow, for the vote in yonder camp has sealed your fate. Others may tell how bravely you died, but you will not live to tell of the shout of victory that the M-o-d-o-c-s will send over your dead body tomorrow night. Sleep soundly, my soldier boys; thirty of you will not answer the roll-call after the battle of the morrow.

Brave Gen. Frank Wheaton, why do you still walk back and forth, arm-in-arm with Col. John Green and Maj. Jackson? You do not feel so sanguine about tomorrow. Jackson has said something that has driven sleep from your eyes. You might find comfort in consulting Gens. Miller and Ross, and Col. Thompson, of the "Salem Press," and Capt. Kelley, of the "Jacksonville Times." They are State militia officers, it is true, but they are old Indian fighters, and can tell you how quickly you can whip Captain Jack in the morning. They are leading men, who may be *hard to restrain*, but they will take the advance. Don't say a word to Capt. John Fairchild; he knows the Modocs, as does Press Dorris. They know the Lava Beds, too; they have hunted cattle over this country, and understand the lay of it better than any white men in the camp.

They are not so *very confident.* They said, today, to some impatient boys, "Don't fret; you will get enough *to do you* before you see your mother again. The Modocs are *on it* sure!"

CHAPTER 25

Gray-Eyed Man on the Warpath

Four a.m., January 17th, 1873.—The tattoo is beaten, and the soldiers throw aside their blankets. They dress themselves; the blankets are rolled together; the men sit around, the mess-table on the ground, and partake of coffee and "hard tack." The volunteer State militia also jump out from under *their* blankets, and, making their toilets as soldiers do, prepare for *duty* and *glory*.

The weather is cold, very cold. Breakfast is over, and the order to "Fall in" sounds through the camp. The blue uniforms take places like automatons; the roll is called. "Here!" "Here!" comes out along the line. Poor fellows! somebody else must answer for some of you tomorrow; you cannot do it for yourselves.

The line of march is taken. The California volunteers, under the gray-eyed man, lead the way toward the bend of the ridge. Cautiously they approach the river. It is not daylight yet; they *must go slow.* Look over the valley below us—the day begins to dawn. Oh, yes; you are looking at the upper side of a great bank of fog. The signal that was to be given Col. Barnard "to move" cannot be made. But he will come to the attack on the south at the same time with the assault from the north.

The soldiers are unencumbered by blankets and knapsacks; they have left them with a guard at camp, *expecting* to return in a few hours. They move cautiously down the bluff into the misty scene below. The cavalry-men are dismounted, leaving their horses in camp, and answer to the call of the bugle. The two hundred men are at the foot of the bluff, at the edge of the Lava Beds.

The lines are formed; each company is assigned a position. In the dim daylight, mixed with fog, they look like ghostly mourners out on the rampart of the spirit world. Hark! "Forward—*march!*" rings out in

273

the cold morning air, and the bugle repeats "Forward—march!" The line moves, stretching out along the foot of the bluff. The regulars advance very steady, for Maj. Jackson's company that was in the Lost-river fight were in no great hurry to hear the music of battle again.

The volunteers start off rapidly, while Gen. Ross and Col. Thompson say, "Steady, boys,—steady." "Steady, my boys," repeats Capt. Kelley, of the Oregon volunteers.

"Go slow, boys, go slow. You'll raise 'em directly," says the gray-eyed man, who commands the Californians. Cautiously the line moves over the rocky plain. On, still on—no Modocs yet. On again they go through the thick fog. "Just as I expected; they've left. I knew they wouldn't stand and fight when the volunteers got after them."— "They knew we was a comin'." Such speeches were made by men who were hungry for "*Modoc sirloin.*" "Steady there; we'll raise them pretty soon," says gray eyes. "They haint run; they're *thar sure.* Go slow, boys; keep down, boys—keep down *low,* boys."

Hark! again; what is that rumble, like a train crossing a great bridge? *Bang—bang—bang—bang* comes through the fog bank. "Barnard's opened on 'em. Now we will go. Hurrah! We will take 'em in the rear. Hurrah! hurrah! hurrah for h—l," sings out a Modoc-eating fellow.

"That's right; every man hurrah for the country he's going to," comes from a quiet regular on the left.

Through the mist a gleam shoots out, and then a rattle of muskets just in front of the advancing line. Hey! what means that? Did Roberts stumble and fall? Yes, he fell, but he cannot get up again; his blood is spurting from his neck on the rocks. Look to the right. Another has fallen to rise no more.

"Fire!" says Col. Green. "Fire!" says the bugle. "Fire!" say the volunteer officers, and a blaze of light burst forth along the line. To see the flame from the guns, one would suppose they saw the enemy on some cliff above them, although the Modoc flame was on a level.

Perhaps the Modocs have changed their base. No, that cannot be, for, see! again it blazes out just in front, and, oh, see the soldiers fall.

On the right of our line, among the rocks, a level blaze follows the Modoc volley. There is somebody there who knows what he is about. "Charge!" rings out the voice of Green. "Charge!" repeats the bugle. The line moves forward at a double-quick, over the rough waves of hardened lava.

On, on, still on the shattered line moves, for several hundred yards. Still no howl of pain from Modoc lips.

MODOCS ON THE WARPATH.

"They've run," exultingly shouts a voice; but before the echo of that voice had repeated the lie, through the rocky caves another blazing line appears in front. Bang, bang, now comes from the further side; again a charge is ordered, and, climbing over chasms and caverns, the now broken line move as best they can; no groan of agony tells of Modocs with bayonets or bullets pierced. No eye has seen a redskin, but four hundred pairs of ears have heard the Modoc's war-whoop, and four hundred hearts have trembled at the sound.

The line still moves forward, firing at the rocks, and—and another brave white man falls.

The investment must be completed; junction must be made with Col. Barnard. Where are the volunteers? The gap in the line must be closed. Where is Capt. ——? The caves answered back, "Where?"

But Donald McKay, the scout, says "They are behind the ledge yonder, lying down."

"Order them up," says Gen. Frank Wheaton.

An *aide-de-camp* fails to open communication with them.

The gallant Green is trying now to close up the line. "Forward, my men," he shouts. "Mount the cliff." The foremost man falls back pierced with Modoc bullets. Green quickly leaps upon the cliff—a dozen rifles from the cave send flame and balls at him. "Come, my men. Up, up," and another man reels and falls. "Come up," again shouts the brave colonel, still standing with the bullets flying around him. Another blue blouse appears, and it, too, goes backward; thus the little mound of dead soldiers grew at the foot of the cliff, until, at last, the gray-eyed man, taking in the situation, points out to his men the Indian battery that commanded this position, and then the sharp, quick rifles, mingle smoke and bullets with the muskets and howitzers, and Green's men pass over the cliff.

The fog is lifting now, but scarce an Indian yet seen. Still the circle of bayonets contracts around the apparently ill-starred Modoc stronghold.

Take a station commanding a view of the battle. Do you hear, amid all this din of exploding gunpowder, the shrieks of mangled white men, and the exulting shouts of the Modocs? Look behind you; the sun is slowly sinking behind Mount Shasta, tired of the scene. The line is broken again, and, where a part of it had stood, see the writhing bodies in blue, half prostrate, some of them, and calling loudly for comrades to save them.

A council is called by Gen. Wheaton; the fighting goes on; the line next the lake gives back. "Draw off your men!" is the order that now echoes along the faltering lines; the bugles sound "Retreat." The men are panic-stricken. Hear the wounded, who understand the bugle-call, shouting to comrades, "Do not leave us." The volunteers halt; they return to the rescue. The Modoc fire is fearful. One of the wounded men is reached in safety, but when two of his comrades lift him up, one of them drops.

Fairchild's men now go to the rescue, crawling on their faces; they almost reach the two wounded men; one of the rescuers falls; they cannot be saved. One wounded man begs to be killed. "Don't leave me alive for the Modocs." The cry is in vain. *The army of four hundred men are on the retreat.* They fall back, followed by the shouts and bullets of the Modocs, and soon leave the voices of the wounded behind them. Is it true that our army is retreating now from fifty savages?

Is it possible that our heroes, who *were to dine on "Modoc sirloins,"* are scrambling over the rocks on empty stomachs, after a ten-hour fight? Is it true that the cries for help by wounded soldiers are heard only by the *Modocs?* Yes, my reader, it *is* true. Every effort to save them cost other lives.

Our army grope their way in darkness over the rocks they had passed so hopefully a few hours since. They climb the bluff, expecting an attack each minute; the wounded, who are brought off the field, are compelled to await surgical aid until the army can be placed in a *safe position.*

The camp on the north is reached, and, without waiting for morning, they fall back to "Bremer's" and "Fairchild's."

When the roll is called in the several companies thirty-five regulars and volunteers fail to answer. Their dead bodies lie stark and cold among the rocks. The Modoc *men* disdain to hunt up victims of the fight. The squaws are permitted to do this work. It is from Modoc authority, that they found two men alive at daylight next morning, and that they stoned them to death; finally ending this long night of horror by one of the most cruel deaths that savage ingenuity could suggest. Look now in the Modoc camp when the squaws come in, bearing the arms and clothing of the fallen United States soldiers. See them parade these before the Indian braves. See those young, ambitious fellows, with those curious-looking things. Here are "Hooker Jim," "Bogus Charley," and "Boston Charley," "Shacknasty Jim," "Steamboat Frank," and several others, holding aloft these specimens of God's handiwork and their own.

277

You ask, What are they?

Go to yesterday's line of battle, scan the rocks closely, and you will see some of them are dyed with human gore; look closely, and you will see a bare foot, may be a hand, half-covered with loose stones; examine carefully, move the rocks, and you will find a mutilated white body there, and if you will uncover the *crushed head* you will see where the articles came from that the Modoc braves are showing with so much pride.

Suppose you count the Modoc warriors now. We know they had fifty-three yesterday morning, for we have the names of all the men of the whole tribe, and we have taken pains to ascertain that every man who did not belong to Captain Jack's band was at "*Yai-nax*," under the eye of the old chief "Schonchin" and the government agent, while the battle of yesterday was going on, except three Modocs—Cum-ba-twas—and they were with Capt. Oliver Applegate's company during the fight. There is no miscount. Fairchild, Applegate, Dorris, and Frank Riddle know everyone personally. Call the roll in Jack's camp, and *every man will answer to his name,* except one man who was wounded in a skirmish on the 15th, with Col. Perry's company of regulars. This statement is correct, notwithstanding the Telegraph said the Modocs had *two hundred men in the fight.*

Listen to Curly-haired Doctor. He is saying, in his native tongue, "I promised you a medicine that would turn the white man's bullets. Where is the Modoc that has been struck with the white man's bullets? I told you 'Soch-a-la Tyee,' the Great Spirit, was on our side. Your chief's heart was weak; mine was strong. We can kill all the white men that come."

Schonchin John says: "I felt strong when I saw the fog that our medicine-man had brought over the rocks yesterday morning. I knew we could kill the soldiers. We are *Modocs.*"

The chief (Captain Jack) arose, all eyes turn toward him, and in breathless silence the council awaits his speech.

He does not appear to share in the general rejoicing. He is thoughtful, and his face wears a saddened look. He feels the force of the doctor's speech; Schonchin's also. He knows they are planning for his removal from the chieftainship.

"It is true we have killed many white men. The Modoc heart is strong; the Modoc guns were sure; the bullets went straight. *We are all here*; but hear me, O *muck-a-lux* (my people). The white men are many; they will not give up; they will come again; more will come next time.

278

No matter how many the Modocs kill, more will come each time, and we will all be killed after a while. I am your voice. My blood is *Modoc*. I will not make peace until the Modoc heart says '*peace*,' We will not go on the warpath again. Maybe the war will stop."

After the several braves have recounted the various exploits they have performed, the council adjourns.

See the squaws bringing great loads of sage brush. They are preparing for a grand scalp dance. This is to be a great demonstration. The women dress in best attire and paint their faces, while the men, now wild with triumph, prepare for the ceremonies of rejoicing.

The drum calls for the dance to commence. They form around the fire on the bare rocks, each warrior painted in *black and red*, in figures rudely made on their arms and breast, indicating the deeds they may boast of. Each bears on the ramrod of his gun the scalps *he* has *taken*. The medicine-man begins a kind of prayer or thanksgiving to the Great Spirit above, and to the bad spirit below, for the success they have won. The dances begin,—a short, upright hop, singing of the great deeds of the Modocs, the warriors meanwhile waving the ramrods with the scalps.

Round and round they move, stepping time to the rude music, until they are exhausted. The blood of the warriors is at fighting heat.

The chief takes no part. He is ill at ease; his mind is busy with great thoughts concerning the past and the future of the Modoc people.

Leaving the Modocs to exult and quarrel alternately, let us hunt up our disappointed army. A part of them have returned to Col. Barnard's camp at Lone Lands; another part, the volunteers, have collected at Fairchild's ranch. Great, unauthorized councils are being held; a hundred men give wise opinions. Gen. Frank Wheaton is declared "incompetent," and some underhand work is going on to have him relieved of his command. It will succeed, although he was brave and skilful, and did as well as any other man could have done under the circumstances.

But that is not the question now, he *must* be relieved; it is enough that he did not succeed, and it is necessary now to send a new man and let him *learn* something of the country. True, Gen. Wheaton has experience and would know how to manage better than a new man. Political power is triumphant, and this worthy man is humbled because he could not perform an *impossibility*. He had raw recruits, that were unskilled in Indian wars, and he was attacking with this force the strongest natural fortress on the continent.

Let us listen to some of the pretty speeches being made in the volunteer camp.

"I tell you aint them Modocs nearly thunder though? But the 'regulars' fired from the hip; they could not *get down* and draw a fine bead."

"It takes *Volunteers* to fight Ingens. Ruther have one hundred volunteers anytime than a regiment of 'regulars.'"

"The captain says he's going to raise a new company, picked men; and then the Modocs will get h—l. Won't they though?"

Our unpopular gray-eyed man strolled into the volunteer camp. He is a little caustic sometimes. Sauntering up to the fellow who was so brave a few days before, he said:—

"How did you like your 'Modoc sirloin,' eh? putty good, eh? didn't take it raw, did you? Where's that feller who was going to bring home a good-looking squaw for a—dishwasher? Wonder how he likes her about this time? Where's that *other* fellow who was going to ride Captain Jack's *pacing hoss*?

"Wonder if those boys who were spoiling for a fight are out of danger?

"Say, boys, there's some old squaws over there near the spring; they aint got any guns, aint no bucks there; maybe you can take *them*." Tossing his head a little to one side, a habit of his when full of sarcasm, he went on to ask the captain of a certain company, "if he found any difficulty in holding his boys back. Where was *you* during the fight, anyhow? I heard Gen. Wheaton asking for you, but nobody seemed to know where you was, 'cept Donal' McKay, and he said you was down on the point; said he saw your general there with a mighty nice breech-loading *bird gun*, and that once in a while some of you would raise your heads and look round, and then Shacknasty Jim would shoot, and you would all lie down again.

"Now, captain, let me give you a little bit of advice; it won't cost you nothing. When you raise *another* company to fight the *Modocs*, don't you take any of them fellows that you can't hold back, nor them fellows who want to eat Modoc steaks *raw*; they aint a good kind to have when you get in a tight place. Why, Shacknasty Jim could whip four of them at a time. Them kind of fellers aint worth a continental d—m for fightin' Modocs. Better leave them fellers with their mammies."

CHAPTER 26

Olive Branch and Cannon Balls— Which Will Win?

A few days after this battle Captain Jack sent a message to John Fairchild and Press Dorris, proposing a "talk," telling them that they should not be molested, and agreeing to meet them at the foot of the bluff, near the Modoc camp. Messrs. Fairchild and Dorris, accompanied by one other white man and an Indian woman (Dixie), visited the Lava Beds.

The meeting, as described by Fairchild, was one of peculiar interest. Those who *had been* friends, and *then enemies* and at war, without any formal declaration of peace, coming together in the stronghold of the victorious party, presents a phase of Western life seldom witnessed. The white men, fully armed, ride to the Indian camp with the squaw guide. The Modocs had observed them with a field-glass while they were descending the bluff, two miles away.

On their arrival, the men who had so earnestly sought each others' lives stood face to face. A painful silence followed, each party waiting for the other to speak first. The Modocs approach and offer to shake hands. "No, you don't, until we understand each other," said Fairchild; and continued, "We came here because we learned that you wanted to talk peace. We are not afraid to talk or to hear you talk. We were in the battle. We *fought you, and we will fight* again unless peace is made."

Captain Jack replied, that "the Modocs knew all about who was in the big battle, but that should not make trouble now. We are glad you come. We want you to hear our side of the story. We do not want any war. Let us go back to our homes on Lost River. We are willing to pay you for the cattle we have killed. We don't want to fight any more."

Such was the substance of Captain Jack's speech; to which Fairchild and Dorris replied, that they were not authorized to make any terms, but would do all they could to prevent further war.

These men visited the Modoc camp from humane and kindly motives; yet tongues of irresponsible parties dared to speak slanderous words against these men who ventured where their vilifiers would not have gone for any consideration. Their motives were questioned, and insinuations unworthy the men who made them, never would have been made had the characters of Fairchild and Dorris been better understood.

The results of the battle of Jan. 17th had startled the public mind, and especially the authorities at Washington City. On investigating the cause of the war, it was thought that some mistake had been made. The citizens of Oregon who were then in Washington, headed by Gen. E. L. Applegate, consulted with Attorney-General Williams on the subject of the Modoc troubles. Inasmuch as a vast amount of ink has since been wasted in expressing indignation against the Modoc Peace Commission, I herewith submit the subjoined letter from Gen. Applegate, of Oregon, to the *Oregon Bulletin*, which gives a fair, and, I believe, true statement of the circumstances attending its conception. I was not present at the conference referred to, neither was I consulted as to the propriety of the movement, either by the Honourable Secretary or the Oregon delegation. Secretary Delano is qualified to defend his own action, and I only suggest that, with the representations set forth, he acted wisely in the course he pursued.

Although I did not advise the appointment of a Peace Commission, I declare that it was right, and no blame can be justly attached to either the commission or the appointing power, if it was not a success.

The principle of adjusting difficulties by such means is in harmony with justice and right. Let those who *burned* the Honourable Secretary in effigy remember the continued stream of denunciation that was poured out against the commission by a portion of the secular press of the Pacific coast, and the reason why the peace measures failed may be better understood.

LETTER FROM WASHINGTON CITY.

How the "Peace Commission," was formed—An Account from General Applegate—His Agency in the Matter.

Washington, D. C., January 29th, 1873.

Editors Bulletin: I "arise to explain" that, since coming to this city I have been meddling somewhat with public affairs. You know the Indian question is one which I think I have a right to express an opinion upon. I ought to know something of Indians and Indian affairs; and, believing that a wrong policy in regard to the Modocs might involve the country in a tedious and expensive Indian war, without a sufficient degree of good being accomplished by it to justify the losses, delays, and expenses incurred, could not avoid undertaking such action as I believed might the most quickly hasten a settlement of the trouble.

The fame abroad of Indian wars and dangers in our State is very injurious to the cause of immigration. A great many good people are confirmed in an opinion, which has been very considerably entertained heretofore, namely, that Oregon is yet an Indian country, and that the settlements are at all times in imminent danger of the tomahawk and scalping-knife.

My policy with Indians may be denominated the *"pow-wow"* policy. A matter has not only to be thoroughly explained to an Indian, but it must be explained over and over; and the fact is, that thirty years of observation convince me that Indians can be talked into any opinion or out of it by the men in whom they have confidence, and who understand the proper style of Indian talk. Consequently, I was in favour of sending some man as a Peace Commissioner to the Modoc country to *pow-wow* with these Indians and settle the difficulty. "Jaw-bone" is cheaper than ammunition; and the fact is, that all comes round to this at last, and always has. This might just as well be done at first, it seems to me, as to go through all the ups and downs, and expense of blood and treasure and long-delayed peace, with the bad effects abroad on the State, and then come to it.

I was, therefore, in favour of sending Mr. Meacham to that country immediately as a peace officer, to turn the whole thing into a "big talk," instead of letting it go on and getting into a big war.

This policy was agreed upon by as many of the Oregonians as could be got together. Styling ourselves an "Oregon delegation," we called upon Attorney-General Williams, and submitted the matter to him. We promptly received a note from the attorney-general, stating that Secretary Delano would be glad to see us in regard to this matter, and on Saturday, the 25th, we called upon him. We found him a pleasant gentleman, with a very serious business expression about his face. He heard our statements and opinions with great patience, and requested a statement in writing of our views, for the purpose of bringing the matter before the cabinet and President. The following is the said document, which was signed by the aforesaid Oregon delegation:—

Washington, D. C., January 27th, 1873.

Hon. C. Delano, Secretary Interior:—

Dear Sir: We would most respectfully submit the following notes or memoranda, in compliance with your request, on the 25th, that we should embody in writing the views which we had just expressed on the situation of affairs in the Klamath and Modoc country, in Southern Oregon:—

The Indians and military are incompatible. They cannot peaceably dwell in contact. Soldiers should not be allowed to go on an Indian Reservation at all. An agent in charge of an Indian Reservation should have the right to determine who should be about the Reservation.

The Modocs and the Klamaths have been at war as far back as tradition knows. The Klamaths persecute the Modocs when the Modocs are on the Klamath Reservation, because this Reservation is in the country of the Klamaths. This is a most irritating cause of discontent with the Modocs. The near vicinity of the Modocs to the ancient home of their fathers adds to their discontent. Moreover, the Modocs do not understand that they have justly parted ownership with their old home. The Modocs are desperate. Their disposition now is to sell their lives as dearly as possible; not to submit to the military. Active military operations should be suspended immediately. Soldiers should remain in guard only (the regulars) of the settlements against a raid by those Indians until a peace officer reports on the situation.

Because to undertake to drive those Indians to the Reservation by force would involve a considerable loss of life and property, and great expense to the Government.

Because war and bloodshed in such close proximity to Klamath and Yai-nax would produce disaffection among all those Indians, which would continually augment the force of the insurgents, and even endanger a general uprising and breaking up of those Reservations; and discontented Indians from everywhere would seek the hostile camp, and make out of a little misunderstanding a great war.

Because to force Indians on to a Reservation by arms, and keep them there against their will, would require a standing army or a walled-up Reservation.

Because those Indians already know that the government is able to annihilate them. There is nothing, therefore, to be gained in merely making them feel its power. Their extermination would not be worth its cost. And, moreover, they look to the government to protect them against local mistake and wrong.

Because they cannot, under the present juncture of affairs, be taught by force the justice of the government; for, to them, it is an attempt by force to enforce an injustice—to force them to abandon their own home and leave it unoccupied, while they are quartered upon the Klamaths; to use the wood, water, grass, and fish of their ancient enemies, and endure the humiliation of being regarded as inferior, because dependants; and particularly so since those Indians had been quieted for some time with the assurance that their request for a little Reservation of their own would be favourably considered. They, therefore, considered the appeal to the military to be premature, as a definite answer to their petition had never been had. Different tribes of Indians can be better harmonized together where none can claim original proprietorship to the soil.

The Klamaths, Yai-nax, and Modocs all ought to be removed to the Coast Reservation, a portion of which, lying between the Siletz and Tillamook, west of the Grand Ronde, capable of sustaining a large population, remains unoccupied, abounding in fish, game, and all the products of the soil to which Indians are accustomed.

A peace commissioner should hasten to the scene of trouble as coming from the "Great Father" of all the people, both whites and Indians, with full authority to hear and adjust all the difficulties.

On account of his personal acquaintance with those Indians and their implicit confidence in him, we would respectfully suggest and recommend Hon. A. B. Meacham as a proper man to appoint as a peace commissioner for the adjustment of difficulties with those tribes and the carrying out of the policy herein indicated.—[*Signed as above stated.*]

The day following the filing of the above set of "*Becauses*" and recommendations, I received a note inviting me to the Interior Department. When notified of my appointment as Chairman of the Commission, I then expressed doubts of its success, giving, as a reason, the
intense feeling of the western people against the Modocs and any
peace measures; also as to the safety of the commission in attempting
to negotiate with a people who were desperate, and had been successful in every engagement with the government forces.

It is well known at the department in Washington that I accepted
the appointment with reluctance, and finally yielded my wishes on the
urgent solicitation of the Hon. Secretary of the Interior. The fact that I
knew the Modocs personally, and that I had been successful, while Superintendent of Indian Affairs for Oregon, in managing them peaceably in 1869, was given as one reason. Another was, the sympathy I had
for them on account of the treatment of them by the Klamaths; and
another still, humanity for the soldiers whose lives were imperilled by
the effort to make peace through blood, and charity for a poor, deluded people, whose religious infatuation and hot blood had forfeited
their right to life and liberty. My heart was in sympathy, too, with the
poor, bereaved wives and mothers, made so by Modoc treachery; but
I did not believe that doubling the number of widows and orphans
would make the griefs of the mourners less, or lighter to be borne.

The sands of the sage-brush plains had drank up the blood of a
score of manly hearts; immersing the lava rocks in blood could not
make the dead forms to rise again.

With these feelings, and fully realizing the danger attending, and
anticipating the opposition that would be raised against the commission, I left Washington on the 5th of February, 1873, with the determination to do my whole duty, despite these untoward circumstances.
The other members of the commission were Hon. Jesse Applegate, a
man of long experience on the frontier, possessed of eminent qualities for such a mission, aside from his personal knowledge of existing
hostilities, and personal acquaintance with the Modocs, and Samuel
Case, who was then acting Indian Agent at Alsea, Oregon. Mr. Case
has had long experience and success in the management of Indians;
these qualities were requisite in treating with a hostile people. *Both
these appointments were made on my own recommendation, based on a personal acquaintance with these gentlemen, believing them fitted for the difficult
task assigned the commission.*

I accepted the chairmanship more cheerfully, when informed that

Gen. Canby would act as counsellor to the commission, knowing, as I did, his great experience among Indians, and the ability and character which he would bring to bear upon the whole subject of the Modoc trouble. I knew him to be humane and wise, and I had not the slightest doubt of his integrity.

The following letter of instructions was furnished for the guidance of the commission.

With these, and the appointment of Messrs. Applegate and Case, I went to the headquarters of Gen. Canby, then at Fairchild's Ranch, twenty-five miles from the Modoc camp in the Lava Beds.

I arrived at Fairchild's Ranch on the 19th of February, where I found General Canby, Hon. Jesse Applegate, and Agent Samuel Case.

The commission was duly organized, and immediately began operations looking towards the objects sought to be accomplished.

Communication with the rebel camp had been suspended after the visit of Fairchild and Dorris. To reopen and establish it was the first work. This was not easy to do under the circumstances. There were several Modoc Indian women encamped near head-quarters; but it was necessary to have some messenger more reliable. Living but a few miles distant, was a man whose wife was a Klamath, and who was on friendly terms with the Modocs. This man, "Bob Whittle," was sent for, with a request to bring his wife with him. On his arrival, we found him to be a man of sound judgment, and his wife to be a well-appearing woman; understanding the English language tolerably well.

A consultation was had, and we decided to send this Indian woman and her husband, Bob Whittle, and "One-eyed Dixie," a Modoc woman, with a message to the Modocs in the Lava Beds. The substance of this message was, that a commission was then at Fairchild's ready to talk over matters with them. This expedition was very hazardous.

These messengers left headquarters early on the morning of the 21st of February, all of them *expressing doubt about ever returning*. Fairchild's Ranch (our head-quarters) is situated at the foot of a mountain overlooking the route to the Lava Beds, for several miles. We watched the mounted messengers until we lost sight of them in the distance, wondering whether we should ever see them again.

Talk of *heroism* being confined to race, colour, or sex! nonsense; here were two women and a man, venturing where few men would have *dared* go.

They returned late on the same day, unharmed, and reported having been in the Modoc camp; and bringing with them, in response to our message, the reply, that the Modocs were willing to meet John Fairchild and Bob Whittle, at the foot of the bluff, for the purpose of arranging for a council talk with the commission.

Messrs. Fairchild and Whittle were despatched on the following morning, accompanied by Matilda Whittle and "One-eyed Dixie." Mr. Fairchild was instructed to announce the object of the commission, and, also, who were its members, and to arrange to meet the representative men of the Modocs, on some midway ground, with such precautionary measures as he might consider necessary.

He was also instructed to explain to them the meaning of an armistice,—that *no act of war would be committed by us, or permitted by them, while negotiations for peace were going on.* The meeting with Captain Jack was had by Fairchild and party; the object stated, and the *personnel* of the commission made known. Captain Jack's reply was that he was *ready to make peace*; that he did *not wish to fight,* but he was not willing to come out of the Lava Beds to meet us. "I understand you about not fighting, or killing cattle, or stealing horses. Tell your people they need not be afraid to go over the country while we are making peace. My boys will stay in the rocks while it is being settled; *we will not fire the first shot.* You can go and hunt your cattle; no one will shoot you. We will not begin again first. I want to see Esquire Steele. I am willing to meet the commissioners at the foot of the bluff, but I don't want them to come with soldiers to make peace. The soldiers frighten my boys."

The messengers returned, accompanied by two Modoc warriors, who were to carry back our answer. These Modocs were Boston Charley and Bogus Charley. We refused to go to the foot of the bluff unless accompanied by an escort of soldiers, but proposed to meet them on open ground, "*all armed*" or "*all unarmed.*" It was agreed that Esquire Steele should be sent for. Bogus and Boston returned to the Modoc camp with the results of the interview. Steele was invited to head-quarters. Gen. Canby requested by telegraph the appointment of Judge A. M. Roseborough as a commissioner; the request was granted, and, on the morning of the 23rd, Steele and Roseborough arrived.

The commission now numbered four. The Modocs had refused to accept all propositions for a meeting that had been made them, so far. Communication was now had, almost daily, between the commissioners and Captain Jack, Frank Riddle and his wife Tobey acting as messengers and interpreters. The Modocs came to our camp in small numbers,—there they came in constant communication with "squaw men" (white men who associate with Indian women), whose sympathy was with them.

From these they learned of the almost universal thirst for vengeance,—of the indictments by the Jackson county courts against the "Lost River" murderers; the feelings of the newspaper press; the protest of the Governor of Oregon; all of which was carried into the Modoc camp by such men as Bogus and Boston Charley. I stop here to say that these two men were well fitted for the part they played in the tragic event of which I am writing. Bogus Charley was a full-blooded Modoc, whose father was lost in some Indian battle. This boy was born on a small creek, called by the miners Bogus creek; hence his name. He was not more than twenty-one years old at this time. He had lived with white men at various times,—knew something of civilized life,—was naturally shrewd and cunning; the Indians called him a "double-hearted man;" and my readers will honour them for their intelligence by the time we reach the gibbet, where Captain Jack answered for this man's crimes.

His counterpart may be found in civil life in finely dressed and smooth-talking white men,—who are the scourges of good society,— persons who are all things to all men, and true to none. Boston Charley was still younger,—not over nineteen at the time justice caught him by the neck and suspended him over a coffin at Fort Klamath, November 33d, 1873. He was so named on account of his light complexion and his cunning; and as the Indian said, "Because he had two tongues; one Indian and one white." His father, a Modoc, died a natural death. He had no personal cause for his treachery, and perhaps charity should have been extended *to him*, and his life spared, because he was "*a natural-born traitor*," according to Modoc theology, and not to blame for his acts.

However, such were the two principal messengers from the Modoc camp to ours,—plausible fellows, who could lie without the slightest scruples. They came, and were fed and clothed; they *went*, with their hearts full of falsehoods that had been told them by whiskey-drinking white villains. They, too, were plausible fellows; talked with the old-fashioned "D———n-nigger-any-how" sort of a way.

Under such circumstances it was a somewhat difficult thing to arrange a council with the Modocs on reasonable terms. True, the Modocs did say that they had been told by white men that if Gen. Canby and the commissioners ever got them in their power they would *all* be hung. But who would believe a Modoc? This was simply an excuse; and, then, no one in all that country would have done such a thing. That was a Modoc lie. Nobody but Modocs ever tell lies. On the contrary, *every white man was honest.* They all wanted *to stop the war.* Of course they did. Intimate anything else, and you would get a hundred invitations to "target practice" in twenty-four hours; or else you would *fall in a fit,* and never get up again, caused by *remorse* of conscience for injuring some unnamed individual.

On the arrival of Judge Roseborough and Esquire Steele the commission was convened; a canvass of the situation was had. The proposition was made for Mr. Steele to visit the Modoc camp. He consented to go, believing that he could accomplish the object we had in view. He was *unwisely* instructed to offer terms of peace. This should not have been done. No terms ever should have been offered through a *third party,*—Messrs. Roseborough, Case, and Applegate voting for this measure. No one questioned Mr. Steele's integrity or his sagacity, but many did question the propriety of sending propositions of peace to the Modocs through a third party. This gave them the advantage of refusal, and of the advantage of discussion in offering alternatives. Mr. Steele was authorized to say that an amnesty for all offenders would be granted on the condition of removal to a new home on some distant Reservation, to be selected by the Modocs; they, meanwhile, to be quartered on "Angel Island," in San Francisco harbour, as *prisoners* of war, and fed and clothed at government expense. Mr. Steele was accompanied on this mission by Fairchild and "Bill Dad" (correspondent of the "Sacramento Record"), and also one or two other newspaper correspondents,—Riddle and wife as interpreters.

They went prepared to remain over night, taking blankets and provisions. The Modocs received them with evident pleasure.

After the usual preliminaries were over, the peace talk began. Captain Jack made a long speech, repeating the history of the past, throwing all the responsibility on to the messengers sent by Superintendent Odeneal, denying that either he or his people had ever committed crime until attacked by the soldiers; that he was anxious for peace. Mr. Steele made the proposition to come out of the Lava Beds and go to a new home.

Steele's speech was apparently well received, and an arrangement was made whereby several Modocs were to return with him to the head-quarters of the commission. Nothing of an alarming character occurred. The party returned in the afternoon of the second day, accompanied by "Queen Mary" (sister of Captain Jack), "Bogus Charley," "Hooker Jim," "Long Jim," "Boston Charley," "Shacknasty Jim,"

"Duffy," "William," "Curly-haired Jack."

We were on the lookout, and when the now enlarged party came in sight they made an imposing appearance. Steele was in advance, and, raising his hat, saluted our ears with the thrilling words, "They accept peace." Couriers to ride to Y-re-ka were ordered, despatches prepared for the departments, and the various newspapers. A general feeling of relief was manifest everywhere around camp. We felt that a great victory over blood and carnage had been won, and that our hazardous labours were nearly over. Letters of congratulation were being prepared to send to friends, and all was happiness and joy, when our gray-eyed friend, who was with the party, put a sudden check on the exuberant feelings, by saying, "I don't think the Modocs agreed to accept the terms offered. True, they responded to Steele's speech, but *not in that way.* I tell you they do not understand that they have agreed to *surrender yet, on any terms.*"

Mr. Steele repeated his declaration, and the speeches, as reported by "Bill Dad," were read, from which it appeared they had greeted Steele's peace-talk with applause. The Modocs, who came in with Steele and his party, were called up and questioned as to the understanding. They were reticent, saying they came out to *hear* what was said, and not to *talk.*

No expression could be obtained from them. Of the success of his mission, Steele was so confident that he proposed to return the next day to Captain Jack's camp, and reassure himself and the commission. He accordingly started early the next morning, accompanied by the Modocs who came out with him, and "Bill Dad" (the scribe). Mr. Fairchild was invited, but he declined with a peculiarly slow swinging of his head from side to side, that said a great deal; especially when he shut his eyes closely, while so doing. Riddle, also, objected to going, but consented to let his wife Tobey go.

The party left behind them some minds full of anxiety, especially when reflecting on Fairchild's pantomime.

The Modocs, who were returning with Steele, reached the stronghold some time before he did. On his arrival, the greeting made his *"hair stand on end,"*—he saw fearful possibilities. It required no words to convince him that he had been *mistaken.* He realized, in a moment, the great peril of the hour. The slightest exhibition of fear on his part would have closed up his career, and the scribe's, also. Steele's long experience with the Indians had not fully qualified him to understand them in council; but it *had* taught him that *real* courage commands

291

respect even from infuriated savages.

He sought to appear indifferent to the changed manner, and extended his hand to the chief, who exchanged the greetings with great caution, though giving Steele to understand that he was still his friend.

The council was opened, the chief remarking that they had *not yet shown their hearts*; that his friend Steele had missed some of his words.

Steele replied that he was their friend, and that he would not, knowingly, misrepresent them.

Schonchin accused him of being a traitor to the Modocs, and of telling falsehoods about them; and, more by manner than by word, intimated that he was done talking peace, showing a bad heart in his action, sufficiently to enlighten Steele on the most important thing in the world to him, namely, that Schonchin did not intend to give Steele another opportunity to misrepresent the Modocs.

Steele's courage and coolness saved him. He said to Schonchin, "I do not want to talk to a man when his heart is bad. We will talk again tomorrow."

The council was dissolved, the Modocs scattering about the camp, or gathering in little squads, and talking in low tones.

The indications were, that the time for saying prayers had come, at least for Steele and Bill Dad.

Captain Jack and Scarfaced Charley demonstrated that manhood and fidelity may be found even in Indian camps. They, without saying in words that Steele and Bill Dad were in danger, told them to sleep in Jack's camp, and proceeded to prepare the night-bed. Our messengers trustingly lay down to rest, if not to sleep, while Scarfaced Charley, Jack and Queen Mary, stood guard over their friends. Several times in the night, Steele looked from under the blankets, to see each time his self-appointed guards standing sentinel in silence.

All night long they remained at their posts, and it was well for Steele and Bill Dad that they did; otherwise they would have been sent off, that very night, to the other side of the "dark river."

The morning came and the council reassembled; the signs of murder were not wanting. Angry words and dark hints told the feeling.

Steele, relying on the friendship of Captain Jack and Scarface Charley, proposed that he would return to the head-quarters of the commission, and *bring with them all the commissioners the next day*.

This strategy was successful. He was permitted to depart on his promise to lead the commission to the Modoc slaughter-pen. On his arrival at our camp he looked some older than when he left the morning previous.

He admitted that he had been mistaken, detailing, without attempt at concealment, that he had escaped only by promising that the commission should visit the Lava Beds unarmed; but with candour declared that if they went they would be murdered; that the Modocs were desperate, and were disposed to recall the Ben Wright affair, and dwell upon it in a way that indicated their thirst for revenge.

The department at Washington was informed by telegraph, and also by letter, of the progress of negotiations from time to time, and *always, without exception, by the advice and approbation of Gen. Canby.*

On Steele's return, as Chairman of the Peace Commission, I telegraphed the facts above referred to, and that it was the opinion of the commission, concurred in by Gen. Canby, that treachery was intended, and that the mission could not succeed, and that we were awaiting orders; to which we received the following reply:—

Department of the Interior, March 5, 1873.
A. B. Meacham, Fairchild's Ranch, *via* Yreka, Cal.:
I do not believe the Modocs mean treachery. The mission should not be a failure. Think I understand now their unwillingness to confide in you. Continue negotiations.
Will consult President, and have War Department confer with General Canby tomorrow.

C. Delano,
Secretary.

The camp wore a gloomy aspect. The soldiers who had been with Maj. Jackson on Lost River, and with Gen. Wheaton in the Lava Beds, were anxious for peace on any terms.

Another fight was not desirable. They were real friends to the Peace Commission. The field-glasses were often turned toward the trail leading to the Lava Beds.

Late one evening, a small squad of Modocs were seen coming. Hope began to dawn again on the camp. When they arrived, "Queen Mary," speaking for her brother, proposed, that if Gen. Canby would send wagons and teams to meet them half way, the Modocs would all come out and surrender.

The proposition was accepted, the commission decided *three to one,* to turn the whole matter over to Gen. Canby; meanwhile awaiting the confirmation of the Secretary of the Interior of the above action.

Gen. Canby, accepting the charge conferred by this unwarranted action of our board, assumed the management of affairs; and the chairman could only look on, giving opinions when requested by Gen. Canby, though confident that it was not the intention of the Department of the Interior to transfer this matter to the Department of War at that time. The telegraph station was at Y-re-ka, sixty-miles from headquarters; hence two to three days were required to receive replies to telegrams.

Gen. Canby, anxious for peace,—as, indeed, he always was, from humane motives toward his soldiers and the Indians also, because he believed in the principle,—attempted to settle the difficulties, and, knowing it to be the policy of the President, accepted the terms offered. Mary and the men who came out with her returned to the Lava Beds, with the distinct understanding that the teams would be sent *without* a squad of soldiers to a point designated, and that on the following Monday all the Modocs would be there.

When Gen. Canby assumed the control of this affair, he conducted his councils without Riddle and his wife as interpreters, although they were present, and were in government employ by the commission.

For some reason he became prejudiced against them, and did not recognize them as interpreters. This fact was observed by the Modocs, and they were anxious to know why this was so.

Before leaving, "Boston," who was with Mary, signified to Tobey (Mrs. Riddle), that she would not see him again, saying: "If you ever see me, I will pay you for the saddle I borrowed."

Tobey, feeling incensed at the treatment received, was reticent, and, Indian-like, kept quiet, saying nothing of her suspicions.

The day before the time for surrender another messenger came from the Modocs, saying that they could not get ready, that they were burning their dead, but promising that two days hence they would surely come.

Gen. Canby accepted the apology, and assured the messenger that the teams would be sent.

Meanwhile, the report went out that the war was over, much to the disquiet of those who were anxious to secure U. S. greenbacks.

The day previous to the proposed surrender, Riddle and his wife expressed to me their opinion, that if the teams were sent they would be *captured*, or that no Modocs would meet them, to surrender.

I sought an interview with Gen. Canby, giving him the opinions I had formed from Riddle's talk.

The general called Riddle and his wife to his quarters. They repeated to him what they had previously said to me. He consulted Gen. Gilliam, and concluded that Mrs. Riddle either did not know, or was working into the hands of the Modocs, or, perhaps, was influenced in some way by those who were opposed to peace.

At all events, on the morning fixed upon, the teams were sent out, under charge of Mr. Steele. Many an anxious eye followed them until they passed out of sight.

The hours dragged slowly by for their return; but so sanguine were Gen. Canby and Gen. Gilliam that tents were prepared for their accommodation, one was designated as "Captain Jack's Marquee," another "Schonchin's," and so on, through the row of white canvas tents.

Mr. Applegate was so certain that they would come that he left the head-quarters for home, and reported *en route*: "The war is over. The Modocs have surrendered."

The soldiers were ready and anxious to welcome the heroes of the Lava Beds. The sentiment was not universal that the wagons would return loaded with Indians.

Our keen-sighted, gray-eyed man shook his head. "I don't think they will come. They are not going to Angel Island, as prisoners of war, just yet."

Riddle and wife were in distress; their warning had been disregarded, their opinions dishonoured, their integrity doubted.

Every field-glass was turned on the road over which the wagons were to come. *Four o'clock p.m.*, no teams in sight. *Five,*—no Indian yet; and, finally, as the shadow of the mountain fell over the valley, the glasses discovered, first, Mr. Steele alone, and soon the empty wagons came slowly down the road.

Darkness covered the valley, and also the hearts of those who really desired peace. But a new hope was now revived in the hearts of those who, from near and afar, were clamouring for the blood of the Modocs.

Another delegation arrived from the Modoc camp, saying, "The Modocs could not agree; they wanted more time to think about it."

The truth is, that they failed to agree about capturing the teams. Jack and Scarface were opposed to it. The authorities at Washington were informed of this failure, also; and they replied to the commission, "Continue negotiations." Mr. Case resigned; Judge Roseborough returned to his duties on the bench.

Gen. Canby notified the Modocs that no more trifling would be tolerated. Recruits were coming daily,—one company, passing near the Lava Beds, *captured about thirty Modoc ponies.* Gen. Canby moved his head-quarters to Van Bremen's, a few miles nearer the Lava Beds.

I suggested to General Canby, that the capture of horses was in violation of the armistice, and that they should be returned. The general objected, saying, that they should be well cared for and turned over when peace was made.

Dr. Eleazer Thomas, of California, at the request of Senator Sargent, was added to the commission, as was, also, Mr. Dyer, agent of the Klamath Indians.

Dr. Thomas brought with him a long and successful experience as a minister of the Methodist Church. He had lived on the Pacific coast for eighteen years; but he had little experience or knowledge of Indians. Being a man of great purity of character and untiring energy, coupled with a humane heart and active hand, he threw himself into this new mission with earnestness, and was impatient to begin to do something towards the accomplishment of *peace.*

Gen. Canby was sending out exploring parties of armed mounted men occasionally,—the ostensible object of which was to obtain a better knowledge of the country around the Lava Beds, with a view to moving the army nearer the Modocs. The commission was not informed of these expeditions, or their objects, by Gen. Canby, but through other parties.

On one occasion, Dr. Thomas went out with a company, and while surveying the Lava Beds at a distance, they met several Modocs, with whom he talked, and succeeded in reopening communication.

A delegation of Indians visited the new camp at Van Bremens. Every effort made through them to secure a meeting with the Board of Commissioners and Modocs failed.

Gen. Canby notified the Modoc chief of his intention to change the position of the army, so that the communications might be more easily made; and, also, that he would not commence hostilities against them unless they provoked an attack.

Captain Jack's reply was, that he would not "fire the first shot;" but, through his messengers, he asked a return of his horses.

Indians have great love for their horses. When a small company of the Modoc women came in asking for their ponies, they were denied them, but were permitted to go under guard to the corral and see them. It was a touching scene,—those Indian women caressing their ponies. They turned sadly away, when compelled, by orders, to leave the corral.

The fact is, several of these ponies had already been appropriated for the use of *young* soldiers, at home, when the war should be over.

On the last day of March, 1873, the camp at Van Bremens was broken up, and the army was put in motion for the Lava Beds.

I was never shown any order from either department, at Washington city, that authorized this movement, though I do not doubt Gen. Canby felt justified in so doing.

The commission was notified—not consulted. We were under instructions "in no wise to interfere with the army movement, but always, as far as possible, to confer and co-operate with Gen. Canby."

Four days were occupied in moving. We arrived at the top of the bluff overlooking this now historic spot of rocks, about noon of the second day.

How little we knew then of the near future, when Gen. Canby and Dr. Thomas would be carried, in rough-made coffins, *up* the zigzag road that we went down on that day!

Our new camp was pitched near the foot of this high bluff, and immediately on the shore of the lake. From it, with a field-glass, we could see Capt. Jack's people moving around their rocky home, not more than one mile and a half, air-line, though two miles around by land.

While my memory is still green with the scenes that followed, and I have not justified and will not justify or seek to palliate the crimes of the Modocs, still I cannot forget some of the meditations of the half hour I sat with Dr. Thomas, when half-way down the bluff, up which I was not to go at all, and the doctor only as a corpse.

I have recollections yet of a part, at least, of the conversation between us. We were representing one of the most powerful governments in the world, and bearing peace and human kindness in our hearts, while passing us, as we sat, were the sinews of war,—armed soldiers by the hundred. Cannon were being dragged down the hill, tents were being erected, and all the circumstance of military power and display was at our feet or above us, hastening to compel an infuriated, misguided people to acknowledge the authority of our government.

Over yonder, within range of our glasses, were a half-hundred men, unlettered, uncivilized, and infuriated by a superstitious religious faith, that urged them to reject the "olive-branch" which we came to offer them.

We could see beyond them another army of ten times their number, camping nearer to them.

The doctor was moved by deep feeling of compassion for them, and spoke very earnestly of their helpless condition,—benighted in mind, without enough of the great principles of Christian justice and power to recognize and respect the individual rights of others. Doomed as a race, hopeless and in despair, they sat on their stony cliffs, around their caves, and counted the men, and horses, and guns, that came down the hill to *make peace* with them, turning their eyes only to see the sight repeated.

Look nearer at the boys with blue dress, as they pass us, bearing camp equipage. Many of the men are going down this hill to *stay*, unless we can make peace with the Modocs. Our hearts grow sick at the thoughts suggested by our surroundings.

Mutually pledging anew to stand together for peace as long as there was a hope, we slowly followed down to the camp.

I cannot forbear mentioning an accident of the evening.

Gen. Canby's tent was partly up when I passed near him. He said, "Well, Mr. Meacham, where is your tent?"

"It has not come," I replied.

The general ordered the men to pull up the pins and move his tent to the site we had selected for ours. It was only by the most earnest entreaty on our part that he countermanded the order, and then only on our promise to share his tent with him, if ours was not put up in time for us to occupy for the night.

On the day following our arrival a meeting was had with the Modocs. On our part, Gen. Canby, Gen. Gilliam, Dr. Thomas, Mr. Dyer and myself, Frank Riddle and Tobey as interpreters. Some of our party were armed; others were not. Riddle and his wife Tobey were suspicious of treachery, and said, as we went, "Be sure to mix up with the Modocs; don't let them get you in a bunch."

"Boston," who had come to our camp to arrange for the meeting, led the way. We saw arising, apparently out of the rocks, a smoke. When we arrived we found Captain Jack, and the principal men of his band, and about half-a-dozen women standing by a fire built in a low, rocky basin.

Dr. Thomas was the first to descend. He did not seem to observe, indeed he did not observe, that we were going entirely out of sight of the field-glasses at our camp.

The place suggested treachery, especially after Riddle's warning. I scanned the rocks around the rim of the basin, but did not see ambushed men; nevertheless, I had some misgiving; but it was too late to retreat then, and to have refused to join the council would have invited an attack. The greetings were cordial; nothing that indicated danger except the place, and the fact that there were three times as many Indians as "Boston" had said would be there. One reassuring circumstance was the presence of their women. But this may have been only a blind. After smoking the pipe of *peace* the talk opened, each one of our party making short speeches in favour of peace, and showing good intentions. The chief replied in a short preliminary talk; Schonchin also. We stated our object, and explained why the soldiers were brought so closely,—that we wanted to feel safe.

Thus passed nearly an hour, when an incident occurred that caused some of our party to change position very quietly.

Hooker Jim said to Mr. Riddle, "Stand aside,—get out of the way!" in Modoc. Some of us understood what it meant. Tobey moved close to our party and reprimanded Hooker. Captain Jack said to him, "Stop that."

This lava bed country being at an altitude of four thousand five hundred feet, and immediately under the lee of high mountains on the west, is subject to heavy storms.

While we were talking, a black cloud overspread the rocks and a rainstorm came on.

Gen. Canby remarked that "We could not talk in the rain." Captain Jack seemed to treat the remark with ridicule, though the interpreters omitted to mention the fact. He said "The rain was a small matter;" that "Gen. Canby was better clothed than he was," but "he (Jack) would not melt like snow."

Gen. Canby proposed to erect a council tent on half-way ground, where subsequent meetings could be held.

This proposition was agreed to, and just as the storm was at its height.

No agreement was made for another meeting, although it was understood that negotiations would be continued.

CHAPTER 27

Captain Jack a Diplomat—Shoot Me If You Dare

On the following day the council tent was erected in a comparatively smooth plot of land, in the Lava Beds, care being taken to select a site as far as possible from rocks that might answer for an ambuscade.

This place was less than one mile from our camp, and a little more than a mile from the Modocs. Meanwhile the signal corps had established communication between the two army camps. The signal station at our camp was half way up the bluff, and commanded a view of the council tent, and of the trail leading to it from the Modoc stronghold, as it did of the entire Lava Beds.

Col. Mason's command being on the opposite side of Captain Jack's headquarters, from our camp, the three were almost in a line. Communication was also established between the army camps, with boats going from one to the other, and, in doing so, passing in full view of the Modocs.

The Modocs were permitted to visit the head-quarters during the day, and to mix and mingle with the officers and men. The object of this liberty was to convince them of the friendly intentions of the army, and also of its power, as they everywhere saw the arms and munitions of war. They were also permitted to examine the shell mortars and the shells themselves.

On one occasion Bogus Charley and Hooker Jim observed the signal telegraph working, and inquired the meaning of it. They were told by Gen. Gilliam that he was talking to the other camp; that he knew what was going on over there; they were also informed that Col. Mason would move up nearer to their camp in a few days, and that he, Gen. Gilliam, would move his camp on to the little flat very near Captain Jack's. "But don't you shoot my men. I won't shoot your men, but I am going over there to see if everything is all right." Gen. Gilliam also informed them that, "in a few days, one hundred Warm Spring braves would be there."

These things excited the Modocs very much. Bogus Charley questioned General Gilliam, "What for you talk over my home? I no like that. What for the Warm Springs come here?" Receiving no satisfactory reply, they went to Fairchild, who was in camp, and expressed much dissatisfaction on account of the signal telegraph, and the coming of the Warm Spring Indians.

On the 5th of April Captain Jack sent Boston Charley, with a request for old man Meacham to meet him at the council tent, and to bring John Fairchild along. This message was laid before the board. It was thought, both by Gen. Canby and Dr. Thomas, to be fraught with danger. I did not, and I assumed the responsibility of going this time; inviting Mr. Fairchild, and taking Riddle and his wife as interpreters, I went.

Judge Roseborough arrived in camp, and came on after we had reached the council tent.

Captain Jack was on the ground, accompanied by his wives and seven or eight men. On this occasion he talked freely, saying, substantially, that he felt afraid of Gen. Canby, on account of his military dress; and, also, of Dr. Thomas, because he was a Sunday doctor; but "now I can talk. I am not afraid. I know you and Fairchild. I know your hearts." He reviewed the circumstances that led to the war, nearly in the order they have been referred to in this volume, and differing in no material point, except that he blamed Superintendent Odeneal for not coming in person to see him while on Lost River, saying, "that he would not have resisted him. Take away the soldier, and the war will stop. Give me a home on Lost River. I can take care of my people. I do not ask anybody to help me. We can make a living for ourselves. Let us have the same chance that other men have. We do not want to ask an agent where we can go. We are *men*; we are not women."

I replied, that, "since blood has been spilled on Lost River, you cannot live there in peace; the blood would always come up between you and the white men. The army cannot be withdrawn until all the troubles are settled."

After sitting in silence a few moments, he replied, "I hear your words. I give up my home on Lost River. Give me this lava bed for a home. I can live here; take away your soldiers, and we can settle every-

WI-NE-MAH (TOBEY)

thing. Nobody will ever want these rocks; give me a home here."

Assured that no peace could be had while he remained in the rocks, unless he gave up the men who committed the murders on Lost River for trial, he met me with real Indian logic: "Who will try them,—white men or Indians?"

"White men, of course," I replied, although I knew that this man had an inherent idea of the right of trial by a jury of his peers, and that he would come back with another question not easy to be answered by a citizen *who believed in equal justice to all men.*

"Then will you give up the men who killed the Indian women and children on Lost River, to be tried by the Modocs?"

I said, "No, because the Modoc law is dead; the white man's law rules the country now; only one law lives at a time."

He had not yet exhausted all his mental resources. Hear him say: "Will you try the men who fired on my people, on the east side of Lost River, by your own law?"

This inquiry was worthy of a direct answer, and it would seem that no honest man need hesitate to say "Yes." *I did not* say yes, because I knew that the prejudice was so strong against the Modocs that it could not be done. I could only repeat that "the white man's law rules the country,—the Indian law is dead."

"Oh, yes, I see; the white man's laws are good for the white man, but they are made so as to leave the Indian out. No, my friend, I cannot give up the young men to be hung. I know they did wrong,— their blood was bad when they saw the women and children dead. *They* did not begin; the white man began first; I know they are bad; I can't help that; I have no strong laws, and strong houses; some of your young men are bad, too; *you* have strong laws and strong houses (jails); why don't you make your men do right? No, I cannot give up my young men; take away the soldiers, and all the trouble will stop."

I repeated again: "The soldiers cannot be taken away while you stay in the Lava Beds."

Laying his hand on my arm, he said, "Tell me, my friend, what I am to do,—I do not want to fight."

I said to him, "The only way now for peace is to come out of the rocks, and we will hunt up a new home for you; then all this trouble will cease. No peace can be made while you stay in the Lava Beds; we can find you another place, and the President will give you each a home."

He replied, "I don't know any other country. God gave me this country; he put my people here first. I was born here,—my father was born here; I want to live here; I do not want to leave the ground where I was born."

On being again assured that he "must come out of the rocks and leave the country, acknowledge the authority of the government, and then we could live in peace," his reply was characteristic of the man and his race:—

"You ask me to come out, and put myself in your power. I cannot do it,—I am afraid; no, I am not afraid, but my people are. When you was at Fairchild's ranch you sent me word that no more preparation for war would be made by you, and that I must not go on preparing for war until this thing was settled. I have done nothing; I have seen your men passing through the country; I could have killed them; I did not; my men have stayed in the rocks all the time; they have not killed anybody; they have not killed any cattle. I have kept my promise,— *have you kept yours?* Your soldiers stole my horses, you did not give them up; you say 'you want peace,' why do you come with so many soldiers to make peace? I see your men coming every day with big guns; does *that* look like making peace?"

Then, rising to his feet, he pointed to the farther shore of the lake: "Do you see that dark spot there? *do you see it?* Forty-six of my people met Ben Wright there when I was a little boy. He told them he wanted to make peace. It was a rainy day; my people wore moccasins then; their feet were wet. *He smoked the pipe with them.* They believed him; they set down to dry their feet; they unstrung their bows, and laid them down by their sides; when, suddenly, Ben Wright drawing a pistol with each hand, began shooting my people. Do you know how many escaped? *Do you know?*" With his eye fixed fiercely on mine, he waited a minute, and then, raising one hand, with his fingers extended, he answered silently. Continuing, he said: "One man of the five—Te-he-Jack—is now in that camp there," pointing to the stronghold.

I pointed to "Bloody Point," and *asked him how many escaped there?* He answered: "Your people and mine were at war then; they were not making peace."

On my asserting that "Ben Wright did wrong to kill people under a flag of truce," he said: "*You* say it is wrong; but your *Government* did not say it was wrong. It made him a *tyee* chief. Big Chief made him an Indian agent."

This half-savage had truth on his side, as far as the government was concerned; as to the treachery of Ben Wright, that has been emphatically denied, and just as positively affirmed, by parties who were cognizant of the affair. It is certain that the Modocs have always claimed that he violated a flag of truce, and that they have never complained of any losses of men in any other way. I have no doubt that this massacre had been referred to often in the Modoc councils by the "Curly-haired Doctor" and his gang of cut-throats, for the purpose of preventing peace-making.

Captain Jack, rising to full stature, broke out in an impassioned speech, that I had not thought him competent to make:—

"I am but one man. I am the voice of my people. Whatever their hearts are, that I talk. I want no more war. I want to be a man. You deny me the right of a white man. My skin is red; my heart is a white man's heart; but I am a *Modoc*. I am not afraid to die. I will not fall on the rocks. When I die, my enemies will be under me. Your soldiers begun on me when I was asleep on Lost River. They drove us to these rocks, like a wounded deer. Tell your soldier *tyee* I am over there now; tell him not to hunt for me on Lost River or Shasta Butte. Tell him I *am over there*. I want him to take his soldiers away. I do not want to fight. I am a Modoc. I am not afraid to die. I can show him how a Modoc can die."

I advised him to think well; that our government was strong, and would not go back; if he would not come out of the rocks the war would go on, and all his people would be destroyed.

Before parting, I proposed for him to go to camp with me, and have dinner and another talk. He said "he was not afraid to go, but his people were afraid for him. He could not go."

This talk lasted nearly seven hours, and was the only full, free talk had with the Modocs during the existence of the Peace Commission.

I left that council having more respect for the Modoc chief than I had ever felt before. No arrangement was made for subsequent meetings, he going to his camp, to counsel with his people. We returned to ours, to report to the Board of Commissioners the talk, from the notes taken. Judge Roseborough, who had been present a portion of the time, and Mr. Fairchild, agreed with me that Captain Jack himself wanted peace, and was willing to accept the terms offered; but he, being in the hands of bad men, might not be able to bring his people out of the rocks.

Gen. Canby, Dr. Thomas, and Mr. Dyer were of the opinion that, inasmuch as Captain Jack had abandoned his claim to Lost River, which he had always insisted on previously, he might consent to a removal. We did not believe that his people would permit him to make such terms. We were all more anxious than before to save Captain Jack and those who were in favour of peace. Accordingly, it was determined to make the effort, Gen. Canby authorizing me to say, through a messenger, that, if Captain Jack and the peace party would come out, he would place the troops in position to protect him while making the attempt.

Tobey Riddle was despatched to the Modoc camp with the message, fully instructed what to say. On her arrival, Captain Jack refused a *private* conference, saying, "I want my people all to hear." The proposition was made, the vote was taken, and but eleven men voted with Jack to accept the terms, the majority giving warning that any attempt to escape would be attended with chances of death to all who dared it. Captain Jack replied to the message: "I am a *Modoc*, and I cannot, and will not, leave my people." The reason was evident—he *dared* not, knowing that his own life and that of his family would pay the penalty.

This vote in Tobey's presence gave a knowledge as to the number of peace men in the Modoc camp. On her return to our camp, one of the peace men (the wild girl's man), having secreted himself behind a rock near the trail, as she passed, said to her: "Tell old man Meacham and all the men not to come to the council tent again—they get killed." Tobey could not stop to hear more, lest she should betray her friend who was giving her the information. She arrived at the Peace Commission tent in camp in great distress; her eyes were swollen, and gave evidence of weeping. She sat on her horse in solemn, sullen silence for some minutes, refusing to speak until her husband arrived. He beckoned me to him, and, with whitened lips, told the story of the intended assassination. The board was assembled, and the warning thus given us was repeated by Riddle, also the reply of Captain Jack to our message. A discussion was had over the warning, Gen. Canby saying that they "might talk such things, but they would not attempt it." Dr. Thomas was inclined to believe that it was a sensational story, got up for effect. Mr. Dyer and myself accepted the warning, accrediting the authority.

On the day following, a delegation composed of "Bogus," "Boston," and "Shacknasty," arrived, and proposed a meeting at the council tent; saying that Captain Jack and four other Indians were there waiting for us to meet them. I was managing the talks and negotiations for

306

councils, and without evincing distrust of Boston, who was spokesman, said we were not ready to talk that day. While the parley was going on, an orderly handed Gen. Canby a despatch from the signal station, saying, "*Five Indians at the council tent, apparently unarmed, and about twenty others, with rifles, are in the rocks a few rods behind them.*" This paper was passed from one to another without comment, while the talk with Boston was being concluded. We were all convinced that treachery was intended on that day.

Before the Modocs left our camp, Dr. Thomas unwisely said to Bogus Charley, "What do you want to kill us for? We are your friends." Bogus, in a very earnest manner, said, "Who told you that?" The doctor evaded. Bogus insisted; growing warmer each time; and finally, through fear, or perhaps he was too honest to evade longer, the doctor replied, "Tobey told it." Bogus signalled to Shacknasty and Boston, and the three worthies left our camp together; Bogus, however, having questioned Tobey as to the authorship of the warning, before leaving. Riddle and his wife were much alarmed now for their own personal safety. Up to this time they had felt secure. The trio of Modocs had not been gone very long, when a messenger came demanding of Tobey to visit the Modoc camp. She was alarmed, as was Riddle. They sought advice of the commission,—they thought there was great danger. *I did not.*

A consultation was had with General Canby, who proposed to move immediately against the Modocs were Tobey assaulted. With this assurance she consented to go. In proof of my faith in her return I loaned her my overcoat, and gave her my horse to ride. She parted with her little boy (ten years old) several times before she succeeded in mounting her horse,—clasping him to her breast, she would set him down and start, and then run to him and catch him up again,— each time seeming more affected,—until at last her courage was high enough, and, saying a few words in a low voice to her husband, she rode off on this perilous expedition to meet her own people. Riddle, too, was very uneasy about her safety; with a field-glass in hand he took a station commanding a view of the trail to the Modoc camp.

This incident was one of thrilling interest. We could see that Indian woman when she arrived in the Modoc camp, and could see them gather around her. They demanded to know by what authority she had told the story about their intention to kill the commission. She denied that she had; but the denial was not received as against the statement of Bogus. She then claimed that she dreamed it; this was not

307

accepted. The next dodge was, "The spirits told me." Believers as they are in *Spiritualism*, they would not receive this statement, and began to make threats of violence; declaring that she should give the name of her informer, or suffer the consequences. Rising to a real heroism, she pointed with one hand, saying, "There are soldiers there," and with the other, "There are soldiers there; you touch me and they will fire on you, and not a Modoc will escape." Smiting her breast, she continued: "I am a Modoc woman; all my blood is Modoc; I did not dream it; the spirits did not tell me; one of your men told me. I won't tell you who it was. *Shoot me, if you dare!*"

On her return she gave an account of this intensely thrilling scene as related, and it has been subsequently confirmed by other Modocs who were present. Captain Jack and Scarface Charley interfered in her behalf, and sent an escort to see her safely to our camp. She repeated her warning against going to the peace tent.

CHAPTER 28

Who Had Been There—Who Had Not

Let us change the scene, and transfer ourselves to the marquee of Gen. Gilliam. Gen. Canby is sitting on a camp-chair, and near him Col. Barnard. On the camp-bedstead sits Gen. Gilliam, and by his side Col. Mason; the chairman of the Peace Commission on a box almost between the parties. The talk is of Modocs, peace, treachery, Ben Wright, battle of 17th January, the stronghold. Gen. Gilliam remarks, addressing Gen. Canby: "Well, general, whenever you are through trying to make peace with those fellows, I think I can take them out of their stronghold with the loss of *half-a-dozen men.*" Canby sat still, and said nothing. Gilliam continued: "Oh, we may have some casualties in wounded men, of course; but I can take them out whenever you give the order." Silence followed for a few moments.

Gen. Canby, fixing his cigar in his mouth and his eye on Col. Mason, sat looking the question he did not wish to ask in words.

Col. Mason, seeming to understand the meaning of the look, said: "With due deference to the opinion of Gen. Gilliam, I think if we take them out with the *loss of one-third of the entire command, it is doing as well as I expect.*"

The portly form of Col. Barnard moved slowly forward and back, thereby saying, "I agree with you, Col. Mason." Col. John Green came in, and, to an inquiry about how many men it would cost, he replied evasively, saying, "I don't know; only we got licked on the 17th of January like ——. Beg your pardon, general." Canby continued smoking his cigar, without fire in it. Here were four men giving opinions. One of them had fought rebels in Tennessee, and was a success there; the other three fought rebels also successfully, and Modocs in the Lava

Beds *unsuccessfully*. They knew whereof they were talking. The opinions of these men doubtless made a deep impression on the mind of the commanding general, and, knowing him as I did, I can well understand how anxious he was for peace when he had the judgment of soldiers like *Green*, Mason, and Barnard, that, if war followed, about one in three of the boys who idolized him *must die to accomplish peace through blood*.

Move over one hundred yards to another marquee; the sounds betoken a discussion there also. Young, brave, ambitious officers are denouncing the Peace Commission, complaining that the army is subjected to disgrace by being held in abeyance by it.

Their words are bitter; and they mean it, too, because fighting is their business. Col. Green, coming in, says, in angry voice, "Stop that! the Peace Commission have a right here as much as we have. They are our friends. God grant them success. I have been in *the Lava Beds once*. Don't abuse the Peace Commission, gentlemen." The fiery young officers respect the man who talks; they say no more.

Come down a little further. Oh, here is the Peace Commission tent, and around a stove sits the majestic Dr. Thomas, grave, dignified, thoughtful. Mr. Dyer is there also, quiet and meditative, with his elbows on his knees, and his face is buried in his hands; Meacham occasionally recruiting the sage-brush embers in the stove with fresh supplies of fuel. A rap on the tent-pole. "Come in," and a fine-looking, middle-aged officer enters. Once glance at his face, and we see plainly that he has come for a *growl*.

After the compliments are passed, Col. Tom Wright—for it was he—begins by saying that he wanted to growl at someone, and he had selected our camp as the place most likely to furnish him with a victim. "All right, colonel, pitch in," says Meacham.

The doctor just then remembered that he had a call to make on Gen. Canby. "Well," says the gallant colonel, "why don't you leave here, and give us a chance at those Modocs? We don't want to lie here all spring and summer, and not have a chance at them. Now you know we don't like this delay, and we can't say a word to Gen. Canby about it. I think you ought to leave, and let us clean them out."

I detailed the conversation had in Gen. Gilliam's marquee, and also expressed some doubts on the subject.

"Pshaw!" says Col. Wright. "I will bet two thousand dollars that Lieut. Eagan's company and mine can whip the Modocs in *fifteen minutes* after we get into position. Yes, I'll put the money up,—I mean it."

"Well, my dear colonel, you might just say to Gen. Canby that he can send off the other part of the army, about nine hundred men besides your company and Eagan's. As to our leaving we have a right to be here, and we are under the control of Gen. Canby; and as to moving on the enemy, Gen. Canby *is not ready until the Warm Spring Indians arrive*. I am of the opinion that no peace can be made, and that you will have an opportunity to try it on with the Modoc chief." The colonel bade me "goodnight," saying that he felt better now, since he had his growl out.

It is morning, and our soldier-cook has deserted us, and deserted the army too. It seems to be now pretty well understood that no peace can be made with the Modocs, and several of the boys have deserted. Those who have *met* the Modocs have no desire to meet them *again*. Those who have not, are demoralized by the reports that others gave; and since the common soldiers serve for pay, and have not much hope of promotion, they are not so warlike as the brave officers, who have their stars to win on the field of battle. Money won't hire a cook, hence we must cook for ourselves. Well, all right; Dyer and I have done that kind of thing before this, and we can again.

While we are preparing breakfast a couple of soldiers come about the fire. "I say, capt'n, have you give it up tryin' to make peace with them Injuns there?"

"Don't know; why?" we reply.

"Well, 'cause why them boys as has been in there says as how it's nearly litenin'; them Modocs don't give a fellow any chance; we don't want any Modoc, we don't."

"Sorry for you, boys; we are doing all we can to save you, but the pressure is too heavy; guess you'll have to go in and bring them out."

Squatting down before the fire, one of them, in a low voice, says, "Mr. Commissioner, us boys are all your fre'ns,—*we are*; wish them fellers that wants them Modocs whipped so bad would come down and do it theirselves; don't you? Have you tried everything you can to make peace?"

"Yes, my good fellow, we have exhausted every honourable means, and we cannot succeed."

"Bro. Meacham, where did you learn to make bread? Why, this is splendid. Bro. Dyer, did you make this coffee? It's delicious." So spoke our good doctor at breakfast.

"Good-morning, Mr. Meacham," said Gen. Canby, after breakfast. "Who is cooking for your mess now?"

"*Co-pi, ni-ka,*—myself."

"What does Mr. Dyer do?"

"He washes the dishes."

"Ha, ha! What does the doctor do?"

"Why, he asks the blessing."

The general laughed heartily, and as the doctor approached, said to him, "Doctor, you must not throw off on Bro. Dyer."

Explanations were made, and these venerable, dignified men enjoyed that little joke more heartily than I had ever seen either of them, on any other occasion.

CHAPTER 29

Under a Woman's Hat—The Last Appeal

The commission had on all occasions expressed willingness to meet the Modocs on fair terms, saying to them, "Bring all your men, all armed, if you wish to; station them one hundred yards from the council tent. We will place a company of equal number within one hundred yards on the other side. Then you chiefs and head men can meet our commission at the council tent and talk." To this and all other offers they objected. The commission and the general also were now convinced that no meeting could be had on fair terms. The authorities at Washington were again informed of this fact. Dr. Thomas was a man of great perseverance, and had great faith in the power of prayer. He spent hours alone in the rocks, near our camp, praying. He would often repeat: "One man with faith is stronger than an hundred with interest only."

Few men have ever lived so constantly in religious practice as did Dr. Thomas. The Modocs, having been foiled in their attempt to entrap the commission, sent for Riddle, saying they "wanted his advice." Riddle went, under instructions, and talked with them. Nothing new was elicited. Riddle again warned the commission of the danger of meeting the Modocs unless fully armed for defence. He confirmed the opinion already expressed, that *Captain Jack*, was in favour of peace; but that he was in the hands of bad men, who might compel him to do what was against his judgment. Gen. Canby, always acknowledged as having power to control the commission, nevertheless conceded to it the management of the councils. He never presided, and seldom gave an opinion, unless something was said in which he could not concur; but *no action was had*, or *message sent*, or *other business ever done*, *without his advice and approval.*

On the morning of April 10th I left headquarters, to visit Boyle's camp, at the southern end of the lake, leaving Dr. Thomas in charge of the affairs of the Peace Commission, little dreaming that action of so great importance would be had during my absence. After visiting Maj. Boyle's, I returned by Col. Mason's camp, and there learned, through the signal telegraph, that a delegation of Modocs was at the commission tent, proposing another meeting. I arrived at the headquarters late in the evening, and then learned from Dr. Thomas that an agreement had been made to meet five unarmed Indians at the council tent on the following day at noon. I demurred to the arrangement, saying, "that it was unsafe." The doctor was rejoicing that "God had done a wonderful work in the Modoc camp." The Modoc messengers, to arrange for this unfortunate council, were not insensible to the fact of the doctor's religious faith, and they represented to him that "*they had changed their hearts; that God had put a new fire in them, and they were ashamed of their bad hearts.* They now wanted to make peace. They were willing to surrender. They only wanted the commission to *prove their faith in the Modocs by coming out to meet them unarmed.*"

This hypocrisy caught the doctor. He believed them; and, after a consultation with Gen. Canby, the compact was made. The doctor was shocked at my remark, that "God has not been in the Modoc camp this winter. If we go we will not return alive." Such was my opinion, and I gave it unhesitatingly. The night, though a long one, wore away, and the morning of *Good Friday, April 11th, 1873,* found our party at an early breakfast.

While we were yet at the morning meal Boston Charley came in. As the doctor arose from his breakfast this imp of the d——, from the Modoc camp, sat down in the very seat from which the doctor had arisen, and ate his breakfast from the *same plate*, drank from the *same cup*, the doctor had used.

While Boston was eating he observed me changing boots, putting on old ones. I shall not soon forget the curious twinkle of this demon's eyes, when he said, "What for you take 'em off new boots? Why for you no wear 'em new boots?" he examined them carefully, inquired the price of them, and again said, "Meacham, why for you no wear 'em new boots?" The villain was anxious for me to wear a pair of twenty-dollar boots instead of my old worn-out ones. I understood what that fellow meant, and I did not give him an opportunity to wear my new boots.

314

From Indian testimony it is evident that in the Modoc camp an excited council had been held on the morning of the 11th. Captain Jack, Scarface Charley, and a few others had opposed the assassination, Jack declaring *that it should not be done.* Unfortunately, he was in the minority. The majority ruled, and to compel the chief to acquiesce, the murderous crew gathered around him, and, placing a woman's hat upon his head, and throwing a shawl over his shoulders, they pushed him down on the rocks, taunting him with cowardice, calling him "a woman, white-face squaw;"saying that his heart was changed; that he went back on his own words (referring to majority rule, which he had instituted); that he was no longer a Modoc, the white man had stolen his heart. Now, in view of the record this man had made as a military captain, his courage or ability can never be doubted, and yet he could not withstand this impeachment of his manhood. Dashing the hat and shawl aside, and springing to his feet, he shouted, "I am a Modoc. I am your chief. It shall be done if it costs every drop of blood in my heart. But hear me, all my people,—this day's work will cost the life of every Modoc brave; we will not live to see it ended."

When he had once assented he was bloodthirsty, and with coolness planned for the consummation of this terrible tragedy. He asserted his right to kill Gen. Canby, selecting Ellen's man as his assistant.

Contention ensued among the braves as to who should be allowed to share in this intended massacre.

Meacham was next disposed of.

Schonchin, being next in rank to Captain Jack, won the *prize*; glad he did, for he was a *poor shot* with a pistol. Hooker Jim was named as his second in this *ex parte* affair; sorry for that, for he was a marksman, and had he kept the place assigned him, someone else would have written this narrative.

Dr. Thomas, the "Sunday Doctor," was the next in order. There were several fellows ambitious for the honour, for so they esteemed it. Boston Charley and Bogus were successful. These two men had accepted from the doctor's hands, on the day preceding, each a suit of new clothes.

To Shacknasty Jim and Barncho was assigned the duty of despatching Mr. Dyer. Black Jim and Slo-lux were to assassinate Gen. Gilliam. When Riddle's name was called up, Scarface Charley, who had declared this "whole thing to be an outrage *unworthy* of the Modocs," positively refused to take any part, arose and gave notice that he would defend Riddle and his wife, and that if either were killed he would

315

avenge their death.

These *preliminaries* being arranged, Barncho and Slo-lux were sent out before daylight, with seven or eight rifles, to secrete themselves near the council tent.

The manner of the assault was discussed, and the plan of shooting from ambush was urged but abandoned, because it would have prevented those who were to conduct the pretended council, from sharing in the honours to come from that bloody scene. The details completed, Captain Jack said to his sister Mary, and to Scarface Charley, "It is all over. I feel ashamed of what I am doing. I did not think I would ever agree to do this thing."

When this tragedy was planned, another was also agreed upon. Curly-haired Doctor and Curly Jack, and a Cumbatwas, were to decoy Col. Mason *from his camp, and kill him also.*

Bogus Charley had come into our camp the evening previous, and remained until the next morning. He was there to ascertain whether any steps were taken to prevent the consummation of the hellish design. Boston's visit was for the same purpose. It is almost past belief that these two men, who had received at the hands of Gen. Canby, Gen. Gilliam, and the Peace Commission, so many presents of clothing and supplies, could have planned and executed so treacherous a deed of blood. Bogus was the especial favourite of Generals Canby and Gilliam; indeed, they recognized him as an interpreter instead of Riddle and wife. He was better treated by them than any other of the Modoc messengers. It is asserted, most positively, that *Bogus was the man who first proposed the assassination of Canby and the Peace Commissioners.*

The morning wears away and the commissioner seems loath to start out. The Modoc messengers are urgent, and point to the council tent, saying, that "Captain Jack and four men waiting now." Look at our signal station half way up the mountain side. The men with field-glasses are scanning the Lava Beds. Gen. Canby has given orders that a strict watch be kept on the council tent and the trail leading to it from the Modoc camp. The officers of the signal corps were there when the morning broke. They have been faithful to the orders to watch. The sun is mounting the sky. It is almost half way across the blue arch. Bogus and Boston are impatient; saying that "Captain Jack, him get tired waiting." Gen. Canby and Dr. Thomas have been in consultation. Riddle is uneasy and restless, and as Canby and Thomas walk slowly to Gen. Gilliam's headquarters, he says to Meacham, "Do not go. I think you will all be killed if you do."—"Then come to Gen. Gilliam's tent

316

and say so there," suggests Meacham.

The commissioners approach the tent. Gen. Canby meets Col. Green and one or two other officers, stopping at the tent door, and continued talking, while the remainder of the commissioners enter. Gen. Gilliam is reclining on his bed, he is sick this morning, *very sick*. Gen. Canby remarks from the tent door; "Go on, gentlemen, don't wait for me; I will be in presently."

Riddle again repeats the warning: "Gentlemen, I have been talking with my wife; she has never told me a lie, or deceived me, and she says if you go today you will be killed. We wash our hands of all blame. If you must go, *go well armed*! I give you my opinion, because I do not want to be blamed hereafter." Riddle retires and Gen. Canby enters. Riddle's warning is repeated to him. The general replies: "I have had a field-glass watching the trail all the morning; there are but four men at the council tent. I have given orders for the signal station to keep a strict watch, and, in the event of an attack, the army will move at once against them,"—meaning the Modocs. Dr. Thomas expressed his determination to keep the compact, saying that he is in the hands of God, and proposes to do his duty and leave the result with his Maker. He thinks Riddle and his wife are excited; that they are not reliable. "I differ from you, gentlemen; I think we ought to heed the warning. If we do go, we must go armed; otherwise we will be attacked. I am opposed to going in any other way."

Mr. Dyer says: "I agree with Mr. Meacham; we ought to go pre- pared for defence. We ought to heed the warning we have had." Gen. Canby repeats, "With the precaution we have taken there can be no danger." Dr. Thomas also saying, "The agreement is to go unarmed; we must be faithful on our part to the compact, and leave it all in the hands of God."

Previous to starting, Dr. Thomas goes to the sutler's store and pays for some goods bought for the Modocs the day previous, when this compact was made. From this act it would appear that he has doubts about the result. Indeed, to another gentleman he says that he is not *sure that he will return*; but "I will do my duty faithfully, and trust God to bring it out all right." Gen. Canby is holding council with Gen. Gil- liam and other officers. He leaves them, coming to his own marquee, says something to his faithful orderly,—Scott,—then to Monahan, his secretary, and then, in full dress he walks to the "Peace Commission tent," where he is joined by Dr. Thomas and *starts for the council tent*. Side by side they walk away.

317

The doctor is dressed in a suit of light-gray Scotch tweed. The officers and men are standing around their tents, talking of the danger ahead. They differ in opinion, and all declare their readiness to fly to the rescue in the event of treachery. Bogus is with the general and the doctor. He carries a rifle; it is his own. In that rifle is a ball that will crush through the brain of Dr. Thomas in less than two hours. Having seen them start, Bogus hastens to the council tent, scanning the route as he goes, to make sure that no soldiers are secreted among the rocks.

A few moments since, Meacham and Fairchild were in earnest conversation. Meacham says, "John, what do you think? is it safe to go?"—"Wait here a minute, and let me have another talk with Bogus; I think I can tell," says Fairchild. After a few minutes he returns, whittling a stick. Slowly shaking his head, he says, "I can't make out from Bogus what to think. I don't like the looks of things; still he talks all right; maybe it's all on the square." Meacham replies, "*I must go* if the general and the doctor do." Fairchild goes again to Bogus; but the general and doctor are starting. Bogus is impatient, and cuts short the talk. Meacham is hurrying to the tent. He seats himself on a roll of blankets, and with a pencil writes,—let us look over his shoulder and see what:

Lava Beds, April 11th, 1873.

My dear Wife:—

You may be a widow tonight; you shall not be a coward's wife. I go to save my honour. John A. Fairchild will forward my valise and valuables. The chances are all against us. I have done my best to prevent this meeting. I am in no wise to blame.

Yours to the end,

Alfred.

P. S.—I give Fairchild six hundred and fifty dollars, currency, for you.

A. B. M.

"Here, John, send these to my wife, Salem, Oregon, if I don't get back."

Mr. Dyer approaches, and says, "Mr. Fairchild, send this parcel to Mrs. Dyer."—"Mr. Dyer, why do you go, feeling as you do? I would not if I were in your place. I must go, since I am the chairman of the commission, or be disgraced." Mr. Dyer replies, "*If you go, I am going. I will not stay, if all the rest go.*"

By the tent door the Indian woman is weeping, while holding a horse by a rope. Standing beside her is a white man, and also a boy ten years old. They are talking in Modoc, and we may not know what they are saying. That little group is Frank Riddle and his wife Tobey, and their little boy Jeff. Their warning has been disregarded. They are loath to give up their efforts to save the commissioners and Canby.

"Tobey, give me my horse; we must go now."

"Meacham, you no go; you get kill. You no get your horse. The Modocs mad now; they kill all you men." She winds the rope around her waist, and throws herself upon the ground, and, in the wildest excitement, shrieks in broken sobs, "Meacham, you no go; *you no go! You get kill! you get kill!*"

Can the man resist this appeal to save his friends and himself? His lips quiver and his face is white; he is struggling with his pride. His colour changes. Thank God, he is going to make another effort to prevent the doom that threatens! He calls to Canby and Thomas. They await his approach. Laying a hand on the shoulder of each, he says, "*Gentlemen, my cool, deliberate opinion is that, if we go to the council tent today, we will be carried home tonight on the stretchers; all cut to pieces.* I tell you, I dare not ignore Tobey's warning. I believe her, and I am not willing to go."

The general answers first: "Mr. Meacham, you are unduly cautious. There are but *five* Indians at the council tent, and they dare not attack us."

"General, the Modocs *dare do anything. I know them better than you do, and I know they are desperate. Braver men and worse men never lived on this continent than we are to meet at that tent yonder.*"

The general replies, "I have left orders for a watch to be kept, and, if they attack us, the army will move at once against them. We have agreed to meet them, and we must do it."

Dr. Thomas remarks, "I have agreed to meet them, and I *never break my word. I am in the hands of God. If He requires my life, I am ready for the sacrifice.*"

Meacham is still unwilling to go, and says, "If we must go, let us be well armed."

"Brother Meacham, the agreement is to go *unarmed*, and we must do as we have agreed."

"*But the Modocs will all be doubly armed. They won't keep their part of the compact; they never have, and they won't now.* Let John Fairchild go with us, him and me with a revolver each, and I will not interpose

319

any more objections to going. Do this, and I pledge you my life that we bring our party out all right. I know Fairchild. I know he is a dead shot, and he and I can whip a dozen Indians in open ground with revolvers."

"Brother Meacham, you and Fairchild are fighting men. *We are going to make peace, not war.* Let us go as we agreed, and trust in God."

"But, doctor, *God does not drop revolvers down just when and where you need them.*"

"My dear brother, you are getting to be very irreligious. *Put your trust in God. Pray more, and don't think so much about fighting.*"

"Doctor, I am just as much of a peace man as you are, and I am as good a friend as the Indians ever had on this coast, and I know in *whom to put my trust in the hour of peril*; but I know these Modocs, and I know that they won't keep their word, and I want to be ready for trouble if it comes. I don't want to go unarmed."

"The compact is to go unarmed, and I am not willing to jeopardize our lives by breaking the compact."

"Well, since we must go, and I am to manage the talk, I will grant to them any demand they make, rather than give them an excuse; that is, if they are armed,—as I know they will be,—and more than five Indians will be there, too."

Gen. Canby replied, "Mr. Meacham, I have had more or less connection with the Indian service for thirty years, and I *have never made a promise that could not be carried out. I am not willing now to promise anything that we don't intend to perform.*"

"Nor I," breaks in the doctor. "That is why Indians have no confidence in white men. I am not willing to have you make a promise that we don't intend to keep."

"Hear me, gentlemen, I only propose doing so in the event that the Modocs have broken the compact by being armed. I don't believe in false promises any more than you do, only in such an event; and I tell you I would promise anything an Indian demanded before I would give him an excuse to take my life, or yours. I say that is not dishonest, and my conscience would never condemn me for saving my life by such strategy."

The general and the doctor both insist on making no promise that is not *bona fide.* Meacham's efforts to prevent the meeting fails. He turns slowly, and with hesitating steps goes towards the peace tent in the camp. Canby and Thomas start off side by side. Meacham turns again:—

"Once more, gentlemen, I beg you not to go. I have too much to live for now; too many are depending on me; I do not want to die. If you go, I must go to save my name from dishonour."

"That squaw has got you scared, Meacham. I don't see why you should be so careful of your scalp; it is not much better than my own."

"Yes, the squaw *has* scared Meacham; that's true. *I am afraid; I have reason to be.* But we will see before the sun sets who is the worst scared."

O my God! They refuse to turn back. Their fate is sealed. The action of these few minutes involves so much of human woe; so much blood, so many valuable lives, so much of vast importance to *two* races. Oh, how many hearts must bleed from the decision of that hour! We feel sad as they walk away. Is it true that the stately form of the gallant Christian soldier is to fall on the rocks, pierced with Modoc bullets, and that savage hands will in two short hours rudely strip from him the uniform he so proudly wears? Can it be that a Modoc bullet will go crashing through the head that has worn well-earned laurels so long? Must the noble heart that now beats with kindest throbs for even those who are to murder him so soon, beat but two hours more, and then alone on the gray rocks of this wild shore cease its throbbing forever? Can it be that the lofty form of Dr. Thomas will fall to rise no more; that the lips that have so eloquently told of a Saviour's love will turn white until the blood from his own wounds smothers the sound of his last prayer, while impious hands strip him of his suit of gray, and mock him in his dying moments?

Let us not look at that picture longer, but follow the other commissioner back to the waiting, anxious friends who gather around the door of the Peace Commission tent. He does not step with his usual quick motion; his heart is heavy, and visions of a little home, with weeping wife and children, enter his mind. Funeral pageants pass and mourning emblems hang now over his soul. But he is firm, and his closed lips declare that his mind is made up.

"Fairchild, promise me upon your sacred honour, one thing. Will you promise?"

The gray-eyed man with earnest face answered,—

"I promise you anything in my power, Meacham."

"Promise me, then, that, if my body is brought in mutilated and cut to pieces, you will bury me here, so that my family shall never be tortured by the sight. Do you promise?"

"O Meacham, you will come back all right."

"No, no; I won't. I feel now that I won't; there is no chance for that. I tell you, John, there is but one alternative,—*death* or *disgrace*. I can die; but my name never has been and never shall be dishonoured."

Fairchild draws his revolver from his side and says, "Here, Meacham, take this; you can bang brimstone out of 'em with it."

"No, no; John, I won't take it, although I would rather have it than all your cattle; but if I take that revolver, everybody will swear that I precipitated the fight by going armed in violation of the compact. No, John, I wouldn't take it if I knew I never could come back without it, and taking it would save me. I won't do it. My life would not be worth a cent if I did. I wanted you to go, but the general and the doctor objected; so there's no use in talking; I am going."

A man passes close to Meacham and drops something in a side pocket of his coat. His hand grasps it, and his face indicates hesitation. The other says, in a low tone, "It's sure fire;—it's all right." 'Tis a small Derringer pistol, and it is not thrown out of the pocket. Dyer caught sight of this little manoeuvre, and he goes into his tent and quickly slips a Derringer into his pocket.

The Indian woman is weeping still. She refuses to let go the rope of Meacham's horse, until the command is repeated, and then she grasps his coat, and pleads again: "You no go; you get kill."

"Let go, Tobey. Get on your horse. All ready? Mr. Dyer, there is no other way to do."

Riddle is pale, but cool and collected. He says, "I'm a-goin' a-foot; I don't want no horse to bother me."The Indian woman embraces her boy again and again, and mounts her horse. Meacham, Dyer, Riddle, and his wife are starting.

Fairchild says, "Meacham, you had better take my pistol. I would like to go with you, but I s'pose I can't."

"No; I won't take it. Goodbye. Keep your promise."

"Goodbye, Maj. Thomas. Cranston, goodbye. Goodbye, Col. Wright. Be ready to come for us; we'll need you."

"Don't go off feeling that way. I wouldn't go if I felt as you do," says one.

"We will have an eye out for you," says another.

They are gone, and we will follow. Canby and Thomas are just rising out of a rocky chasm near the council tent. Meacham and his party are going around by the horse trail. Words can never tell the thoughts that pass through their minds on that ride. The soldier who goes to battle takes even chances in the line of his profession; the criminal may march with steady nerve up the steps that lead him to the gallows; but who can ever tell in words the thoughts, feelings, and temptations of these men, going to meet a people under a flag of truce that had been dishonoured by their own race within sight of the spot where they are to meet these people, after the earnest warning they had received?

CHAPTER 30

Assassination—"Kau-Tux-E"

While these two parties are wending their way to the council tent, let us see what is going on around it. On the side opposite from the camp a small sage-brush fire is burning. It is not at the same spot where the fire was built when Meacham and Roseborough had the long talk with Captain Jack a few days since. Why this change? Think a moment. The council that day was in *full view of the signal station.* This fire is *behind the council tent, and cannot be seen from the station.* Around the fire loose stones are placed. This looks suspicious. But who are those fellows dressed like white men, sitting around that fire? Ah! they are Modocs waiting for the commissioners. That man with a slouched hat and well-worn gray coat,—nearest the tent, is Captain Jack. He looks sad and half melancholy, and does not seem at ease in his mind.

Near him sits old Schonchin, the image of the real savage. His hair is mixed with gray. His face indicates that he is a villain.

That fellow who appears restless, and walks back and forth, is Hooker Jim. He is not more than twenty-two; *his* face tells you, at a glance, that he is a *cut-throat.* He is tall, stout-built, very muscular, and would be an ugly customer in a fight. He is accredited with being the best "*trailer*," and the closest marksman in the Modoc tribe.

That other young fellow, with feminine face, and hair parted in the middle, is a brave and desperate man. That is Shacknasty Jim.

That dark-looking man, who reminds you, at the first view, of a snake, is Black Jim. He is of royal blood, and half-brother of Captain Jack. His hair is cut square below the ears, and, take him altogether, he is a bad-looking man.

The light-coloured, round-faced, smooth-built man, who stands behind the chief; is "Ellen's Man." He is young, and is really a fine-looking fellow. He does not *appear* to be a bad man, but he *is*; and you will think him the worst of the company before we lose sight of him.

The talk around that council fire would freeze your blood could you hear it. They are making arrangements for the carnival of death that they propose holding.

The chief is nervous, and speaks of his regret that this thing is to be. "Ellen's Man" proposes to take his place if he lacks courage. "I do not lack courage, but I do not feel right to kill those men. If it is the Modoc heart, it shall be done," replies the chief.

Walk out towards the Modoc camp forty steps, and lying behind a low ledge of rocks are two boys, Barncho and Slolux. They are very quiet, but under each one we see several rifles. They are both young, and have *volunteered* to play this part in the tragedy soon to be enacted.

Near them is another man, crouching low, and in his hand he holds a gun, with its muzzle pointing towards the tent. His face indicates a much older man than he really is. He is not there to take a part in the proceedings of the coming meeting, except in a certain contingency. There is a something about him that declares him to be a man of more than ordinary stamp. This is Scarface Charley, and if, in the slaughter that is to ensue, Riddle or his wife should fall, the rifle that that man grasps will talk in vengeful tone, with deadly effect, upon the murderer.

Look behind you at the council fire. Eight Indians are there now, and the newcomers have familiar faces. They are *Bogus* and *Boston*, just arrived from headquarters. They are telling the others who are coming, that they are all unarmed.

Boston intimates something like regret or faltering in the purpose. Bogus declares that he will "Do it alone, if all the others back out. Kill these men, and the war will stop. It will scare all the soldiers away."

Hist! here comes Gen. Canby, with the brass buttons on his coat glittering in the sunlight; and Dr. Thomas, also, who is so well worthy to walk by the side of the general. The Indians arise and greet them cordially. Gen. Canby takes from his pocket a handful of cigars, offering one to each. They accept them from his hand, while in their hearts they have determined on his death. The general and all the Indians are smoking now. The thoughts of the general will never be known; not even whether he had any suspicion of their intentions.

Meacham and his party are approaching. They ride up very near the council fire,—Meacham to the right, Dyer and Mrs. Riddle to

Gen. Canby.

the left. Riddle passes to the left of the tent, looking in as he comes to the council.

Meacham is taking off his overcoat before dismounting. Why is this? The weather is not warm. There is a reason for this strange action.

Before reaching the tent the matter had been discussed by the four persons of that party. Riddle declared that if attacked he would save himself by running, Mr. Dyer saying there was no hope of escape in any other way. Meacham considered running impracticable and hopeless, and suggested that, "if we stand together, we can, with the aid of the Derringer, get a revolver for Riddle, and then we can all be armed in quick time." Dyer and Riddle adhered to the plan of escape they had proposed, Meacham still saying that it was hopeless, and adding, "I cannot run; but I will sell my life as dearly as possible." The Derringer is in his *under coat*.

As they ride up, they see clearly that the council fire is *behind* the tent, *out of sight of the signal station*, and that the Modocs are all armed with revolvers secreted under their clothing.

The Indians welcome the party with a cordiality that is very suspicious. They are good-humoured, too; another confirmation of the worst fears. Even before the party dismount, they are saluted by the Modocs with hand-shaking and other demonstrations.

Dyer is the first to alight from his horse. He looks a little pale. Tobey quietly dismounts, securing her horse to a small sage brush near the council. Meacham still sits upon his horse, apparently listless, as if in doubt. He is fighting a battle with his pride. His family are in his thoughts, and also another family of little orphans of a much-loved brother. He glances at the face of Gen. Canby and Dr. Thomas. His mind is made up. He dismounts, dropping the halter of the horse upon the ground. He intends that "Joe Lane" (the horse) shall have a chance for escape. But "Joe Lane" is well known among the Modocs. They have seen him before, and they fix their eyes on him now, impatient to feel him flying over the plains. Perhaps they are making a calculation of his value as an offset to several of the ponies captured from them by Maj. Biddle a few days previous.

See the manoeuvring going on by both parties. The Modocs are seeking to separate themselves from the white men, while Dyer, Meacham and Riddle are seeking to prevent the formation of a tableau of white men. Canby stands erect and firm, not seeming to notice the game that is playing before his eyes. His pride will not permit him to notice or to shun what is evidently the intention of the Modocs. Dr. Thomas does not see what is going on, or, if he does, so strong is his faith in God that he does not fear. Dyer and Riddle are outside on either hand, not wishing to join the group.

Meacham, now satisfied that the party are entrapped, is walking carelessly a few steps towards the camp. Perhaps he is going to make a signal to those at the lookout. If that was his intention, he abandons it; for just beside him are a pair of small, bullet eyes that watch his every movement.

The party *feel* that not the motion of even an eye is lost by the Modocs. They see everything, and, while all are apparently on the best of terms, all are on the lookout for any sign or intimation of danger. Not a motion is made unobserved. Still, no unkindly words are spoken; indeed, all parties *appear* to be in cheerful humour.

Appearances are deceitful sometimes, and especially in this instance. One party is intending to commit an unparalleled crime; the other, suspicious of their intention, awaits the issue, not quite without hope, but almost in despair.

The white men do not seem anxious to begin the council. The Modocs are trying to appear careless.

What does that mean? Bogus is going out towards a low cliff, carrying his rifle with him. Watch him a moment. While standing on a prominent rock, he is scanning the ledge that runs towards the soldiers' camp. *Ah, yes! he is looking for sage brush with which to feed the fire.* Now he has laid down his gun and breaks off the brush and returns to the council. That, then, was the *pretended* object of his trip. Curious that in *all former councils* the Modoc women have performed this work, but that *none* of them are here *now*!

Hooker Jim is on the alert, and if you will watch his eye you will see that it glances often in the direction of the soldiers' camp. Something excites his suspicion, and the other Indians, except Captain Jack, follow his gaze; and the white men, too, discover some one's head above the rocks. All arise to their feet. Is the terrible affair to begin now? Wait a moment and keep your eyes divided, watching the *intruder* and the Modocs. The former is looking around him, as if hunting for some lost article. The latter are nervous, and a hateful fire is burning in their eyes. The moment is one of intense peril. The least motion of distrust now on the part of the white men will precipitate the bloody scene, awaiting only for a signal to begin.

Mr. Riddle recognizes the intruder as Mr. Clark, who is hunting lost horses.

"Why for he come here? We no want him," says Boston Charley.

"Mr. Dyer, will you go out to Mr. Clark and send him back?" requests Mr. Meacham.

Mr. Dyer rides out to the man, and, after explaining to him the desire of the commissioners, returns to the council fire. Oh, how near we were to witnessing a horrible murder! But it is averted for the moment, and we breathe again.

Meacham is in charge of the council talk, and finally sits down near the fire, and Captain Jack takes a seat directly opposite him, and so close that their knees almost touch. The council talk begins.

Meacham says, "We have come today to hear what you have to propose. You sent for us, and we are here to conclude the terms of peace, as your messengers of yesterday requested."

To this Captain Jack replies, "We want no more war. We are tired, and our women and children are afraid of the soldiers. We want them taken away, and *then* we can make peace."

Meacham says, "Gen. Canby is in charge of the soldiers. He is your friend. He came here, because the President sent him to look out for everybody and to see that everything goes on all right."

Captain Jack replies, "We do not want the soldiers here. They make our hearts afraid. Send them away, and we can make everything all right."

Meacham continues, "Gen. Canby has charge of the soldiers. He cannot take them away without a letter from the President. You need not be afraid. We are all your friends. We can find you a better home than this, where you can live in peace. If you will come out of the rocks and go with us, we will leave the women and children in camp over on Cottonwood or Hot Creek, and then we shall need the soldiers to make other folks stay away, while we hunt up a new home for you."

Riddle and his wife are both essential to a careful rendering of the speeches. Riddle is interpreting the Modocs' speeches into "Boston talk," and Tobey is translating the white men's speeches into the "*Mo-a-doc-us-ham-konk*"—(Modoc language). Hence they are both giving closest attention. Riddle stands now just behind the chairman of the commissioners. Tobey is sitting a little to the left. Gen. Canby seats himself upon a rock on Meacham's right, about three feet distant. Old Schonchin sits down in front of him. Dr. Thomas bends a sage bush, and, laying his overcoat upon it, also sits on the left and in the rear of

Meacham.

Hooker Jim is restless and very watchful; sometimes standing immediately behind Captain Jack, and occasionally walking off a few steps, he scans the rocks in the direction of the soldiers' camp, and saunters back again, always, however, in front of the white men. Keep an eye on him; he is making now a declaration by his acts that will stop your heart's blood.

"Joe Lane," the horse, is just behind Captain Jack, standing a mute and unsuspecting witness of the act now being played.

Watch that demon, Hooker Jim! See him stoop down, and while his eye is fixed on Meacham, he is securing "Joe Lane" to a sage bush, pushing the knot of the halter close to the ground. He slowly rises, and, while patting the horse on the neck, calling him by name, and telling him he is a "fine horse," still keeping his eye on Meacham, with his left hand he takes the overcoat from the saddle, and with a stealthy, half-hesitating motion, slowly inserts his arm in the sleeve, and then without changing his position or his eyes, quickly thrusts his right arm in the other sleeve, and with a heavy shrug jerks the coat squarely on his shoulders; and, having buttoned it up from top to bottom, smiting his breast with his hand, he says, "Me old man Meacham, now. Bogus, you think me look like old man Meacham?" My dear reader, he does not fasten that horse for Meacham. He does not put on the coat because he is cold, nor merely as a joke. No, he does not mean anything of that kind. He intends to make sure of the horse and coat, and, at the same time, provoke a quarrel, and make the way easy for the bloody attack.

Meacham fully understands the import and intention of this side-play, but, with assumed indifference, remarks, "Hooker Jim, you had better take my hat also," at the same time lifting it from his head. Watch the play on that scoundrel's face as lie replies, "*No. Sno-ker gam-bla sit-ka caitch-con-a bos-ti-na chock-i-la*"—("I will, by-and-by. Don't hurry, old man.")

This speech completes the declaration of what they intended to do. There can be no longer any doubt as to the purpose of these bloodthirsty desperadoes. O God! is there no help now? Can nothing be done to save our friends? They read their fate in Hooker's action. They realize how fearfully near the impending doom must be. Every face is blanched; but no words of fear are uttered. Dyer, with a face of marble, walks slowly to his horse, now on the right of the group, and, going to the farthest side of him, pretends to be arranging the trappings of his saddle with his face towards the council fire. Riddle, pale and aghast, makes excuse to change the fastenings of the saddle on his wife's horse, which stands behind Dr. Thomas. Tobey, who has been sitting in front of the doctor, with a half child-like yawn throws herself carelessly at full length on the ground, resting on her elbows. Every act tells, too plainly to be mistaken, how each one feels and what they are expecting.

Both Dyer and Riddle intend to be covered by their horses when they start on a run for life. Tobey evidently does not intend to be in the way of the bullets that are now lying quietly on their beds of powder in the little iron chambers of the pistols under the coats of the red devils. She sees clearly that the storm, which is evidently coming up with a great black hurrying cloud from the west, will precipitate the effusion of blood that is now leaping and halting in the veins of the doomed men who sit almost motionless, waiting, watching, listening for the signal of death to be given, wondering how it will come. Will it be from ambushed men, a volley, a sting, and a war-whoop; and then, while the soul is making its exit, will the eye, growing dim, behold the infuriated monsters, with gleaming knives uplifted, spring on the helpless body? Will the ear, as life ebbs away, be lulled by streams of blood trickling on the rocks? Are angels hovering near to convey their souls away? Is God omnipresent? Is He omniscient? Is He omnipotent? Does he hear prayer? Will not God interpose now when human aid is beyond reach?

Oh, how the mind recalls the past, outstripping the lightning flash, while it passes in review the scenes from the cradle to this hour!—all the bright and happy days; the dark clouds and direful storms that have swept over the soul, and realizing the still more awful agony of the farewell greetings of sad-faced Hope leaving the heart; for until this last act of Hooker Jim's she had lingered lovingly on the threshold undecided. Words may not tell the anguish, the gloom, the terrible loneliness without her presence. Every heart breathes a prayer for her return. "Oh, come back to us now; be with us in this expiring hour of life's last midnight!"

Thank Heaven, she comes again clad in garments, not as in days past, made up of ambitions and worldly dreams, but in shining robes of spotless purity and immortal light, and she whispers, "Be of good cheer, the journey is short, and it is but a change from one life to another;" and though the voyage be stormy and the night be dark it will end in a morning of eternal day in the beautiful sunlit summer-land where sorrows come no more.

Meacham turns towards Gen. Canby and invites him to talk. Every movement is scrutinized by the Modocs. Meacham has made an excuse to look Gen. Canby in the face. He sees plainly that the general understands the situation. Will he, oh! will he not promise to remove the soldiers on the demand that has been so often made? It would avert the tragedy. It would save the lives that are banging on his words. Will he do it? Surely, now, when convinced, as he must be, that the threat will be executed, will he not feel justified in yielding? Now that the Modocs have absolved him from all obligations to them, will he grant their request; or will the high and extraordinary sense of honour that controlled his reply to Meacham in the morning, when the latter proposed to grant "any demand made, rather than give the assassins an excuse for murder," control him now? Every eye is on him. The Modocs understand that he is chief.

He stands upright in form, and character as well. He looks the great man he is. His face alone shows the intensity of his feelings. His lip quivers slightly, as it always does under excitement. He speaks slowly:—

"Tobey, tell these people that the President of the United States sent the soldiers here to protect them as well as the white men. They are all friends of the Indians. They *cannot be taken away without the President's consent.* Tell them that when I was a young man I was sent to move a band of Indians from their old home to a new one. They did not like me at first, but when they became acquainted with me they liked me so well that they made me a chief, and gave me a name that signified 'Friend of the Indian.' I also removed another tribe to a new home; and they, too, made me a chief, and gave me a name that meant 'The tall man.' Many years afterwards I visited these people, and they came a long distance to meet me, and were very glad to see me. Tell them I have no doubt that sometime the Modocs will like me as those people did, and will recognize me as their friend."

As the general sits down, Meacham turns to Doctor Thomas, and invites him to speak. *The doctor drops forward on his knees,* and, with his right hand on Meacham's left shoulder, says, "Tobey, tell these people, for me, that I believe the *Great Spirit* put it into the heart of the President to send us here to make peace. We are all children of one Father. Our hearts are all open to him. He sees all we do. He knows all our hearts. We are all their friends. I have known Gen. Canby eight years; I have known Mr. Meacham fourteen years, and I have known Mr.

Dyer four years. I know all their hearts are good. They are good men. We do not want any more bloodshed. We want to be friends of yours. God sees all we do. He will hold us all responsible for what we do."

The doctor resumes his seat. Captain Jack is ill at ease. His men are watching him closely. They evidently distrust him.

Meacham has almost decided in his mind that when the attack is made Captain Jack will throw himself in the breach, and, if he takes part at all, it will be with the white men.

The chief is slow to give the signal to begin. He is not in position according to the programme arranged in the morning. He had hoped that the demand for the withdrawal of the troops would be complied with. He sits now with his hands on his knees, staring into Meacham's face. He meets a gaze intense as his own. What are the thoughts of his mind? He is wavering. Perhaps he may refuse to sanction the butchery. He feels that his own people are watching him. Suddenly, rising to his feet, he turns his back on the white men. He is walking away from them. See! he stops! Schonchin springs to the seat Captain Jack has left, and, with eyes gleaming with the pent-up fury of hell, begins to talk. His voice is loud, and betokens great excitement. How savage he looks now, while he says, "Give us Hot Creek for a home, and take the soldiers away."

"Maybe we cannot get Hot Creek for you," replies Mr. Meacham.

Then Schonchin says, "I have been told we could have Hot Creek."

Meacham asks, "Did Fairchild or Dorris say you could have it?"

"No," replied Schonchin; "but Nate Beswick said we could have Hot Creek."

"Hot Creek belongs to Fairchild and Dorris," says Meacham. "We can see them about it, and if we can get it you may have it."

"*Take away your soldiers and give us Hot Creek, or quit talking. I am tired of talking. I talk no more,*" shouts Schonchin in loud tones, and with eyes burning with passion.

The interpreter is rendering the speech, but, before it is finished, Captain Jack, who has returned to the group, and is standing a step behind Schonchin, gives a signal, and the Modoc war-whoop starts every one present to his feet (except Tobey, who lays close to the ground); catching the sound, and oh! the sight, too, of Barncho and Slolux coming with the rifles.

"Jack, what does that mean?" demands Meacham.

THE ASSASSINATION SCENE.

1. General Canby.
2. Colonel Meacham.
3. Doctor Thomas.
4. Tobey Riddle, reclining.
5. Frank Riddle.
6. Mr. Dyer.
7. Captain Jack.
8. Schonchin.
9. Boston Charley.
10. Shacknasty Jim.
11. Hooker Jim.
12. Ellen's Man.
13. Bogus Charley.
14. Black Jim.
15. Horse held by Riddle.
16. Horse held by Dyer.
17. Horse.

The answer came quickly. Captain Jack, thrusting his right hand under the left breast of his coat, draws a six-shooter, and shouts in a loud voice, "*Ot-we-kau-tux!*"—("All ready!")

Holding the barrel with his left hand, and cocking the pistol with his right, he points it at Gen. Canby's head, touches the trigger, and explodes the cap, but does not the powder. Quickly he revolves the cylinder, and again presents it to the petrified general, who stands unmoved. Why, oh, why does he not close on the monster, and wrench the weapon from him? Quick, general, quick! He is too late. Another instant, and a shot is passing through his head. He does not fall, but turns and flees. Jack and "Ellen's Man" pursue him until he falls on the rocks. They close on him. Captain Jack holds him by the shoulder, while the other cuts him across the neck. In the fall his chin struck on the rocks and shattered his lower jaw. The monsters strip him of every article of clothing, while he is struggling in the agonies of death. Barncho comes up now, and "Ellen's Man" snatches a rifle from his hands, and, pointing at the general, discharges it, and another ball passes entirely through his head. They turn him on his face, and leave him in the last agony of a horrible death, while, with his uniform on their arms, they go back to the council tent.

Look towards the soldiers' camp. Two men are running. The foremost one is Dyer, and following him is Hooker Jim, who fires repeatedly at Dyer, who turns, and pointing his pistol, Jim drops to avoid the shot. Dyer resumes his run for life, and the other follows until Dyer has widened the space between them so much that Hooker Jim, fleet as he is, abandons the chase, and returns to join the other murderers.

Over towards the lake two other men are running. The foremost one is Frank Riddle. The pursuer is Black Jim, who fires rapidly at Riddle; in fact, he is not trying to hit him, because he knows that Scarface Charley is watching, and if Riddle falls by a shot from Black Jim, Black Jim himself will fall by Scarface Charley's rifle.

Simultaneously with Jack's first attack on General Canby, Boston Charley's first shot struck Dr. Thomas in the left breast, above the heart. The doctor drops partly down, and catches with his right hand, and with the other uplifted towards his assassin, begs him to shoot no more, as he has already received a death-wound. Bogus joins Boston. They permit the doctor to get upon his feet, and start to run, when they trip him and he falls again. They taunt him with his religion, saying, "Why don't you turn the bullets? Your medicine is not strong." The doctor rises again and walks a few steps, when they push him down, still ridiculing him.

Again he pleads for them to spare his life. They laugh in his face and say, "Next time you believe a squaw, won't you?" Once more—and it is the last time that he will ever walk in that bruised and mangled body—the doctor rises to his feet, and, going a few steps, pleading with his inhuman tormentors for mercy, and with his Maker for mercy on them, he falls to rise no more. Slolux joins them, and Bogus, placing the muzzle of a gun towards the doctor's head, sends another bullet crashing through it. The red devils now strip him of his clothing, jesting and mocking his words of prayer, and finally turn him face downwards, while through the blood from the wounds on his lips he cries, "Come, Lord—" and the prayer is smothered forever.

When the signal for the attack was given, Schonchin was in position, and, springing to his feet, he draws a revolver from his left side, and, with his other hand, unsheathes a knife. He is so near his victim that he dare not trust to a pistol alone. He is very much excited, and is not so quick as the others in cocking his pistol.

Meacham draws his Derringer, and pushing the muzzle squarely against the heart of Schonchin, pulls the trigger, but, alas! it does not fire. Why? Oh! why? He tries again, and still the hammer does not fall. He now discovers that it is but *half-cocked*. Too late! too late! Schonchin thrusts *his* pistol forward, almost touching Meacham's face. The latter jumps back and stoops, while the ball from Schonchin's pistol tears through the collar of his coat, vest, and shirt on the left shoulder, so close that the powder burns his whiskers and the bullet bruises him. He runs backwards with the pistol now ready for use, but with Schonchin pursuing him and firing as fast as he can until his pistol is empty. Now he drops it on the ground, and, *drawing another from his right side*, he continues the attack, but dare not close on the Derringer still in the hands of Meacham.

Why does not the pursued man fire? He is a good shot. Why don't he drop the old scoundrel? He was very much frightened when the attack began, but, like a soldier in battle, he has passed that, and is terribly cool now. He dare not risk his only shot, for fear of missing Schonchin, and because of the danger of hitting Tobey, for she is now interposing for his life, and, putting her hand on Schonchin's pistol, turns it away again and again, while pleading, "Don't kill him! don't kill Meacham! He is the friend of the Indians."

Slolux joins Schonchin, and, with his gun, strikes the woman on the head, while Shacknasty, snatching it from him, says, "I'll fetch him,"

BLACK JIM

at the same time sitting down and taking deliberate aim.

Meacham, striking his breast with his left hand, shouts, "Shoot me there, you cowardly red devil!" Tobey strikes down the gun. Shacknasty threatens her, and again takes aim and fires just as Meacham leaps over a low ledge of rocks and falls.

"I hit him, high up! He is all right!" shouts Shacknasty.

Meacham now decides to fire his *only* shot, and pushing the pistol up over the rocks, carefully raises his head, with it thrown back, and just as his eye comes above the rocks, he sees Schonchin sitting with his revolver resting on his knee. Instantly a flash and a sting, and a ball strikes Meacham in the forehead, between the eyes. Strange freak of the bullet that passes under the eyebrow and out over the left eye, but does not blind the other eye. Meacham now fires at Schonchin, who leaps up and falls on the rocks, wounded. Almost at the same instant a ball passes through Meacham's right arm. The pistol drops. Another ball cuts away the upper part of his right ear, and still another strikes him on the right side of the head and glances off. He quivers, and his limbs are outstretched, denoting the death-struggle. Shacknasty is the first to reach him, and he proceeds to strip him of his clothing, first pulling his boots off, then his pantaloons, and, while taking off his coat, tears the vest down at the side and throws it away. Then he strips him of his shirt, for it is a good one, and Shacknasty saves it for his own use.

While he is unbuttoning the shirt at the neck, Slolux comes up, and, placing the muzzle of the gun close to the temple of the wounded man, sets the hammer, and as he raises it up to his face to get it in range, Shacknasty pushes it away, saying in Modoc, "You needn't shoot. He is dead. He won't get up." Hearing the voice of Captain Jack calling, they leave the scene, saying to Tobey, "There lies another of your brothers, you white-hearted squaw! Go and take care of him. You are no Modoc."

This hour seems to have inherited even the wrath of the Almighty. The blackness of unnatural night hangs over this scene of blood. Gen. Canby's limbs have straightened on yonder rocks, but a few steps to the west, and his stark body looks ghastly in the awful gloom. Twenty yards to the east the form of Dr. Thomas, his body half stripped and covered with blood, is still convulsing, while his face presses the cold rocks.

The chief calls again to the red-handed demons and bids them flee to the stronghold. They gather around him with the clothing of the slain still dripping blood upon their feet. They are exulting by wild shouts of half-satiated thirst for blood. While glancing towards the soldiers' camp they reload their arms.

"I am going to have old man Meacham's scalp to put on my shot-pouch," says Boston, passing the doctor's clothing to a companion standing near.

"*He has no scalp,*" breaks in Hooker Jim, "*or I would have it myself.*"

Boston now runs to where the bleeding man is lying, and takes from his pocket a small two-bladed, black-handled knife which had been taken from the pocket of a soldier who was killed in the January battle. The Indian woman is wiping the blood from the mutilated face, now upturned with closed eyes. Boston thrusts her aside, and with his left hand, still red with the blood of Dr. Thomas, grasps the largest locks, and makes a stroke with the knife. The woman remembers that the prostrate man over whom Boston is bending has been *her* benefactor, and that through his official action, in 1869, he compelled Frank Riddle to make her a *lawful wife,* and that, had it not been for this man, she would now, perhaps, be a *cast-off squaw.* She cannot restrain her indignation, but rushes against the red cut-throat and hurls him back on to the rocks. He rises and threatens to take her life if she again interferes, taunting her with being a "white woman." Stamping on the prostrate man's head, he places one foot on his neck, and renews his attempt to secure an *ornament for his shot-pouch,* swearing because he found no better scalp, but saying that he would take one ear with it. With his left hand resting on the head, he cuts square down to the skull a long, half-circular gash preparatory to taking off the side lock and ear, too, with his knife.

Tobey now resorts to strategy to accomplish what she cannot do otherwise. Looking towards the soldiers' camp she claps her hands and shouts, "*Bos-tee-na soldiers. Kot-pumbla!*"—("The soldiers are coming!") Boston, without waiting to ascertain the truth of the warning, starts suddenly and leaves the woman alone with the dead.

Tobey's warning to Boston has reached the ears of the band of murderers at the council fire, who, hastily putting the slightly wounded old sinner, Schonchin, on "Joe Lane," while the blood-stained uniform of Gen. Canby and the gray suit of the doctor, together with Meacham's clothes, are lashed on Dyer's horse, turn away, leaving Boston behind, who grasps the rein of Tobey's horse. She shouts to Jack, who turns and orders Boston to leave him.

Jack and his party scamper over the rocks, looking back, expecting to hear the guns of the white soldiers who are coming to the rescue.

Tobey again wipes the blood from the face of her benefactor, and, stooping down, places her hand over his heart. "It stop! It stop!" she cries. With her finger she opens his eyes. They do not see her. They are overflowing with blood from the wound in his face and on his head. Again with her dress she wipes the blood from his face. She straightens his limbs and body. Then, standing alone a moment, with three dead men in sight, she sorrowfully mounts her horse and starts for the soldiers' camp.

While this scene of terror is being enacted at the council tent, another, a little less bloody, is in progress on the opposite side of the Modoc stronghold, the plans for which have been mentioned. Curly-haired Jack (Cum-ba-twas) and Curly-haired Doctor have gone out towards Col. Mason's camp, with a flag of truce, to decoy the "Little Tyee" (Col. Mason) among the rocks. But he is an old Indian fighter, and cannot be caught by such devices.

Maj. Boyle is there, and, notwithstanding the fact that on the day before Meacham had told him of the threatened treachery, he proposes to Lieut. Sherwood to go out and meet the flag of truce. The major was Indian agent at Umatilla, and had been successful in managing peaceable Indians. He had been with Gen. Crook in Arizona, also; and, having confidence in his sagacity to manage still, he volunteered to go now.

Having obtained the consent of Col. Mason, they leave the picket-line behind them and the guard of the day on the lookout. They go cautiously, and, when within hailing distance, the Modocs, under cover of the flag of truce, ask for the "Little Tyee."

"He will not come," replies Boyle. The quick eye of the major catches sight of a musket behind the flag of truce. He turns and flees, calling on Sherwood to "Run! run for your life!"

They run. But see! Sherwood falls! A bullet from the musket of Curly-haired Jack has broken his thigh. The guard rush to the rescue. The Modocs fire a volley, and then flee to their stronghold, pursued by the guard. The signal-station at Mason's camp says, "Boyle and Sherwood attacked, under a flag of truce." Capt. Adams, of the signal corps, on the bluff above Gilliam's camp, receives and dictates it to his secretary, who, after writing, sends it to Gen. Gilliam, in the camp, one hundred yards below. The general reads the dispatch, and calls for Dr. Cabanis to come in, while he writes a message to send by the doctor, informing the commissioners of the attack on Mason's men. The general has written but a line, when Maj. Biddle, who has the other glass at the signal station, shouts, "*Firing on the commissioners!*" The officers order the men to "Fall in!" Soon the bugle repeats the assembly call. The men spring to their arms, and in a few moments the five hundred men are ready to rush to the rescue. Each company forms in line in the order in which they are encamped,—Col. Miller's company occupying the left front, Lieut. Eagan's next on the left, and Maj. Throckmorton taking his position behind Eagan's company; the cavalry companies are on the right.

Gen. Gilliam is astounded, petrified. He hesitates; he does not give the order to march; he seems bewildered. Maj. Biddle rushes down from the signal station and cries, "I saw Canby fall." The men are frantic. They do not understand the delay. The officers swear, and threaten to move *without* orders.

Gen. Gilliam now awakes from his lethargy, and gives the order, "March, and deploy from the left in skirmish line!"

"*Forward!*" shouts Col. Miller.

"Forward!" rings out along the lines, while Maj. Riddle's bugle sounds "Forward!" Maj. Thomas is ordered to remain with his battery and guard the camp.

Now that the order to march is given, the men go flying towards the scene of blood in skirmish line. Behind the army are the surgeons with the stretchers.

The newspaper reporters are there, also, and foremost among them "Bill Dad" of the "Sacramento Record." While waiting for orders Bill Dad says to a citizen, "I will give you fifty dollars to carry my message to Yreka ahead of all others. Yes, seventy-five!"

"All right," responds the man, anxious to make money out of the occasion. Other reporters engage couriers.

Col. Miller nears the council tent, urging his men on. He is behind them, pushing them forward, expecting every moment to see a Modoc blaze of fire in front. They soon after meet Dyer, who, breathless, says, "They are all killed but me." Soon after they discover Riddle, who cries, hurriedly, "They are all killed." But now they meet Tobey, who sobs, "*Canby, Thomas, Meacham, all* 'kill.'"

Thirty minutes have passed, and Meacham is struggling to get upon his feet. He hears a voice. "Up, on the left! Forward, my boys!" Faintly the sound reaches his ears. "Steady, right! Up! up on the left, you d——d scoundrels!" Distinctly and clearly he hears the words, "Steady, right! Guide, centre!" Then the sound of men's feet on the

341

rocks mingles with the words of command. The men near the centre level their guns.

"That's an Indian," says one of the men.

"Don't shoot, he's a white man!" shouts Col. Miller.

The line passes over the wounded man still in skirmish order, as they expect a Modoc volley. As they pass, Dr. Cabanis comes up and says, "Bring a stretcher here. Take Meacham. He's not dead."

"I am dead! I am dead!" murmurs the wounded man.

The soldiers lift the mutilated body on a stretcher.

"Water! water! give me water!" moans the wounded man.

The doctor puts a canteen of *brandy* to his lips. The lips refuse.

"*I can't drink brandy.* I am a temperance man," says Meacham.

"Stop your nonsense. No time for temperance talk now. Down with it! down with it!" cries the doctor.

"Am I mortally wounded, doctor?" asked Meacham. The surgeon hastily thrusts his finger into the several wounds and replies, "Not unless you are wounded internally."

"I am shot through the left shoulder," said the wounded man.

"Now, boys, for the hospital! Quick! Lose no time, and we will save him," cries the doctor.

"I hit Schonchin in the right side. He fell over just in front of me," says the man on the stretcher.

"Never mind Schonchin," says the doctor. "We'll look out for him. Here, take some more brandy. Now, boys, quick! He'll stand it until you reach the hospital."

Four pairs of strong hands grasp the handles of the stretchers, and four other pairs carry the arms, and walk beside to relieve the carriers. A soldier covers the man with his coat as they hurry along. Listen, now, to the sad wail of young Scott, Canby's orderly, who was with him through the war of the Rebellion. When he reaches the body of his beloved general, who was more than a father to him, he throws himself on the prostrate form, and, frantic with grief, raves like a madman. "Bill Dad" and a soldier lift him up and cover the body with their coats.

Men with stretchers come up, and, while they lift the general, Bill Dad cuts the side of the council tent out and covers him over. Strange that this council tent should become Gen. Canby's winding-sheet! The body of Dr. Thomas is also placed on a stretcher, and it, too, is covered with a part of the tent. It is his winding-sheet, also.

While these affairs are taking place at the scene of the terrible tragedy, the quartermaster, at the camp, is putting the hospital in order for the reception of patients, ordering cooks to prepare food for the men, packing mules with supplies, stretchers, water-casks, and such other things as are necessary for the men while fighting, never doubting but that they will be needed. The animals are ready and waiting for orders from the general commanding.

But lo! behold! The glistening bayonets above the rocks *come nearer!* The army of five hundred men are *returning to camp.* "Why is this?" ask the men. "Why did we not follow the murderers to their den?" demand the officers.

"We shall not be ready to attack them until the Warm Spring Indians come," replies the general, who a few days since thought "he could take the Modocs out with the loss of half-a-dozen men." Why did not Col. Mason follow up the Modocs who attacked Sherwood and Boyle? *Because he could not move without orders, and the orders were not given.*

Three or four horsemen are waiting while a dozen pencils are rattling over paper. The burden of each despatch is the assassination. "Modoc treachery! Gen. Canby and Dr. Thomas killed; Meacham mortally wounded; Dyer and Riddle escape." How much these hasty lines will tell, and how many hearts will feel a dark shadow fall over them when the electric tongue of fire repeats this message to the world!

"Fifty dollars extra, if you get my despatch into the telegraph office ahead of the others," says Bill Dad, as he hands the paper to his courier. Away goes the courier up the steep and rugged bluff.

"One hundred dollars if you get to the office in Y-re-ka, first," says another reporter, in a whisper, to his courier, who dashes off close behind the first.

Another rider is mounted and waiting for the word to start. Gen. Gilliam's adjutant hands this man a sealed envelope. It contains an official telegram for the authorities.

"Lose no time! Off with you!" says Adjutant Rockwell. And now three riders are urging their horses up the hill. Y-re-ka is eighty-three miles distant. A long race is before them. The evening is dark and gloomy, but the clouds pass away, and the moon shines on three men galloping together, mile after mile. Sunrise finds two of them still together. One of them, as they near a ranch, swings his hat and shouts. A man in shirt-sleeves runs to a stable and brings a fresh horse to the man who signalled him. The rider dismounts, and, while changing the saddle from his horse to the fresh one, tells the awful tidings. The other rider urges his horse on, on, for he, too, has a fresh horse but a few miles ahead. On he goes, and looking behind him sees his rival coming. He comes up and passes, saying, "Goodbye, George!"

Twenty minutes more and both are mounted on fresh horses, one leading, but now in sight of each other. One is casting an eye backwards over his shoulder; the other is pressing the sides of his horse. The gap closes up. Y-re-ka is now in sight, and they are galloping side by side. Both are sitting erect, and the music of jingling spurs is in harmony with the stride of the horses. One mile more, and somebody wins. It all depends on "bottom." The spurs cease to jingle. They are muffled in the bleeding sides of the panting horses.

What a race! One is an iron-gray, the other a Pinto horse. The rider of the gray, reaching back with his spurs, rakes his horse from the flank forward, leaving a vermilion trail where the spurs have passed. With extended head and neck, and lengthened stride, he goes ahead a few yards. With another application of spurs, the switch of the horse's tail touches his rider's back.

"Ah, ha! I've got you now!" shouts the rider of the Pinto, as he comes up like the moving of a shadow, and leaves the gray and his rider behind. One hour more, and the lightnings of the heavens are repeating the messages, and sending them over mountains and plains, to almost the farthest ends of the earth.

CHAPTER 31

Harnessed Lightning Carrying Awful Tidings

It is night, and in the solders' camp a wail of anguish is heard coming from the tent nearest Gen. Canby's late quarters. Grief weighs down the heart of Orderly Scott, who is giving vent to his anguish in stifled sobs and vows of vengeance on the perpetrators of the foul deed. He rises from his bed, and, with face half buried in his hands, looks again on the mangled form of his benefactor, and, in renewed paroxysms of grief, is borne away by his friends.

The sound of hammer and saw disturbs the midnight hour, while the carpenters are transforming the wooden gun-cases into coffins for the dead. Two are in progress, but the mechanics are economizing the rough boards, for the probabilities are that the *third* will be needed on the morrow.

The steward is holding a lamp while Drs. Semig and Cabanis are dressing the wounds of the only patient in the hospital tent. He is unconscious, while the ugly, ragged wound in his face is being carefully bound, and the long crooked cut on the left side of the head is being closed with the silver threads, and his ear is being stitched together. He flinches a little when the flexible silver probe is following the trail cut through his right arm made by the pistol ball that struck it outside of the wrist, and, passing between the bones of the fore arms, came out on the inside, midway between the hand and elbow. The left hand is laid out on a board, and the wounded man is told that "the forefinger must come off."

"Make out the line of the cut, doctor," says Meacham.

"There, about this way," the doctor replies, while with his scalpel he traces a cut nearly to the wrist.

"I can't hold still while you do that, without chloroform," says Meacham.

The doctor feels his pulse, and says, "You have lost too much blood to take chloroform."

"Then let it stay until I am stronger," rejoins Meacham.

For once doctors agree, one of them saying, "The finger would not disfigure a corpse very much."

"Please ask Gen. Gilliam to send to Linkville for my wife's brother, Capt. Ferree," comes from the bloodless lips of the wounded man.

"My dear fellow," replies the kind-hearted doctor, "the general sent a courier for him hours ago."

This thoughtful act of kindness, on the part of Gen. Gilliam, has touched the heart of the sufferer. When he awakes again Capt. Ferree was bending over him and remarking, "He will be blind if he recovers, won't he, doctor?"

"He won't be very handsome, that's a fact," says the nurse.

In the Modoc camp, when the murderous bands arrive with their scanty plunder, a general quarrel ensues, and bitter reproaches are heard against Hooker Jim for not securing Mr. Dyer, and against Curly Jack and Curly-haired Doctor, for the escape of Maj. Boyle, and on account of the clothing taken from the murdered men. Captain Jack claims the uniform of Gen. Canby. Bogus and Boston divide the clothing taken from Dr. Thomas, and Shacknasty Jim, Hooker Jim and old Schonchin are awarded the clothing and effects of Meacham.

Preparations are making for defence, as the Indians do not doubt that an attack will be made immediately. Many bitter recriminations are uttered; but it is war, war to the last man! They hush all their quarrels in the necessity for united action. They pledge themselves to fight until the *last man* is dead. The Curly-haired Doctor calls his assistants around him and begins the *Great Medicine Dance*. All night long the sound of drum and song is heard. The Modocs expect every moment to hear the signal of their sentinel on the outposts announcing the "soldiers!" No sleep comes to this camp tonight.

The morning comes, but no blue-coats are seen among the rocks. The army of one thousand men *are not ready yet*.

The Modocs exult; they are jubilant; they have *scared* the government. "*It is afraid. It will grant us, now, all we ask.*" Captain Jack and Scarface Charley do not assent to this unreasonable view of the situation.

"The soldiers will come. Our victory is not complete. We must

346

fight now until all are dead. The Modoc heart says 'We must fight!'" Captain Jack affirms.

Saturday morning, April 13th, finds the three camps side by side, and each on the lookout for an attack.

Strong hands are bearing two rough-looking boxes up the steep bluff. In the foremost one is the body of Gen. Canby; in the other, all that is mortal of Dr. Thomas. Slowly they mount the rugged hill. They reach the waiting ambulances. The bodies are each assigned an escort. Sitting beside Gen. Canby's coffin are his adjutant, Anderson, and the faithful Scott.

How changed the scene! a few hours since all were hopeful. Now, all are in despair, crushed under the affliction of the hour. While they move cautiously under escort, the terrible news is flashing along thousands of miles of telegraph lines, over mountains, under rivers and oceans. Before the sun sets the hearts of millions of people are beating in sympathy with the bereaved. Extras and bulletins are flying from a thousand presses. The newsboys of America are shouting the burden of the terrible telegram. The Indians along a thousand miles of the frontier have already learned that something of dreadful import has happened.

About the middle of the afternoon of this day a woman sitting in her room on State street, Salem, Oregon, raises her eyes, turning them towards the street. Perhaps the sound of steps on the wooden pavement attracts her attention. She sees two familiar faces turned towards her window. "Oh, see her! How pale she is!" She drops her work, and runs hastily to meet the two gentlemen.

"Is he dead? Is he dead? Tell me! Has my husband been killed by the Modocs?" the woman cries.

The gentlemen are speechless for the moment, while the lady pleads. They dare not speak the truth too plainly, now; she cannot bear it.

One of them replies, "Gen. Canby and Dr. Thomas have been killed by the Modocs, and Mr. Meacham is sli—" "mortally wounded!" shrieks the lady sinking to the floor.

Three young persons are coming home. The eldest is a young lady of eighteen. The lad that walks beside her is her brother of sixteen; and the other is an auburn-haired girl of fourteen. There is something in her appearance that connects our thoughts with the mutilated, almost bloodless man who is lying in the hospital in the Lava Beds.

They turn the corner leading out of the Plaza and in sight of

DOCTOR THOMAS

home. They see men and women hurrying across the front yard.

"Has father been killed by the Modocs?" bursts from their lips as they fly.

Dr. Hall meets them and says, "Your father is slightly wounded. He is not dead."

The three frightened children gather around the *tearless*, pale-faced mother, who says, "Don't deceive me. I am strong now. I can bear it. Tell me the worst."

The friends exchanged glances. Dr. Hall shakes his head, slightly motioning towards the elder girl, whose face is buried in the bosom of Mrs. Dr. Smith.

"George, run to the telegraph office and bring the despatch," says the mother to her son. "I must know the truth."

The boy bounds away towards the office, and is met by Prof. Powell, who says, "Come back, George. I will go home with you, and tell your mother all about it."

The two return, and the professor, with faltering voice reads the despatch: "Canby and Thomas killed. Meacham mortally wounded." The marble-faced wife arises, saying, "I am going to my husband." Her friends remonstrate with her.

"I am going to my husband. Do not hinder me," she repeats.

"My father! my father!" cries the elder daughter, as she is borne to her room.

"My father will not die. He must not die. *My father will live*," the younger daughter insists. Her brother is trying to hide his tears while he talks hopefully.

"Father is a very strong man. He may get well. I think he will," he says.

It is midnight, and sympathizing friends are in the sitting-room and parlour. The daughters and son have sobbed themselves to sleep. The mother and wife, with bloodless face, is on bended knees, and, with uplifted hands clasped, is whispering a prayer.

At this moment her brother is bending over her husband three hundred miles away, watching his breathing; while thoughts of a widowed sister and her orphan children sadden the heart of the veteran who has passed through the war of the Great Rebellion. A silent tear drops on the mangled face beneath him.

Donald McKay, "the scout," with seventy-two picked men, is dismounting at Col. Mason's camp. Leaving them, he is challenged by the picket guard and, passing in, reports himself to the officer of the day.

His men stand waiting his return. Meanwhile we will go close enough to inspect them. They are dressed in the uniform of the soldiers of the United States. Their arms are the same, and in the moonlight they appear to be "Regulars." If the wounded man in the hospital were here they would salute him with, "*Tuts-ka-low-a?*" ("How do you do, old man Meacham?") And he would reply, "*Te-me-na, Shix-te-wa-tillicums.*" ("My heart is all right.")

These boys are Warm Spring Indians, and the same men who were in the council tents in 1856, when the government swindled them and their fathers out of their homes in the beautiful "Valley of the Tygh." They were also in the revival meeting at the Warm Springs Agency in 1871, when the Superintendent of Indian Affairs, who now lies in yonder hospital, and Agent John Smith, took so many red hands in their own and recognized a brotherhood with them. They are the same men, too, who have for years past, each Sunday morning, joined their beloved agent in prayer and song. They have left behind them humble homes, in a poor country, where the government placed them, and where it still keeps them by the strong arm of the law, without consulting their wishes,—a home they cannot leave, even for a day, without a "pass."

Their manhood was acknowledged in making a treaty; but denied as soon as the compact was completed, until in 1866, when the government found it had an expensive war on hand with the Snake Indians, and then it offered these men the privilege of volunteering to whip the Snake Indians. This offer they accepted, and were rewarded for their services with a few greenbacks, worth fifty cents on a dollar, and an invitation to a new treaty council, in which they were *cheated* out of a reserved right to the fisheries on the Columbia River, near "The Dalles;" and then they were summoned back to their unsought homes, subject to the whims and caprices of government officers, who were given positions as a reward for political services. True, they agreed to the terms, and they must be made to stand by them whether their pledges were made freely and voluntarily, or under the shining bayonets of an army, and by reason of the superior diplomatic talent of the government officials who outwitted them. It makes no difference. They are Indians, and three-fourths of the people of the United States *believe* and *say* that "the best Indians are all underground."

Anxious to demonstrate their loyalty to a government that has been so good to them, and to establish their right to manhood's privileges, when an opportunity offered, they enlisted by the advice and consent of their agent, and, followed by his prayers, they are here to-night under the famous scout, Donald McKay.

He evidently is not a "Warm Spring Indian," yet they trust him, knowing, from their experience with him in the Snake campaign of 1866, that he is thoroughly reliable. Donald McKay is half brother to Dr. Wm. C. McKay. His mother was a Cayuse woman. Being a man of extraordinary endowments, which fit him for a leader, he has taken an active part in all recent Indian wars of the Northwest. His *name alone* carries a warning to refractory "red-skins."

As Donald approached his men on his return from head-quarters, several voices inquire if "old man Meacham is dead." Quietly leading their horses inside the picket line, they unpack the kitchen, mule and blanket ponies.

It is now Sunday morning, the 13th of April. The sun finds couriers on the road to Y-re-ka, bearing despatches announcing that "Meacham is sinking. The surgeons have extracted four bullets from his wounds. The Modocs cannot get away."

A sad, anxious woman is leaving the depot at Salem, Oregon, destined for the Lava Beds. At home her children are in tears, realizing how dark the clouds of sorrow may become.

The childless widow of Gen. Canby sits with *broken heart*, in her parlour in Portland, Oregon.

The family of Dr. Thomas, in Petaluma, Cal., are kneeling around the family altar, and a bereaved widow is praying for resignation to this dispensation of Providence,—is praying for strength to say *"Thy will be done on earth as it is in heaven."*

Monday morning, April 14th, opens amid the noises of camp life; the drum and bugle calls, and human voices join in songs of praise. They are strange sounds for a military camp on the eve of battle. There is an uncommon accent to them, but they sound familiar. What! The sounds come from the lips of men who were born in wild camps among the mountains of Eastern Oregon. Can it be that these red men have so far advanced in Christian civilization that they are now doing what not one of the five hundred white men have the courage to do? Yes, my reader, *it is true* that the Warm Spring Indians, who have learned from Agent John Smith these songs of praise and the honour that is due to God, are faithful to their pretensions, and *are worshipping* Him, and seeking strength to sustain them in the coming strife.

Blush, now, will you not, you who prate so loudly of the superiority of the white men! of his sense of right controlling his actions!

Here are *red men*, who are but a few years removed from savage life, *living* the "*new religion*"—Christians in real earnest, and shaming the hypocritical pretenders whose cant and whine make liberal-minded people turn away in disgust. You Christian Indian-hater, look at these red-skinned people, and learn a lesson in Christian honesty and moral courage!

The shadows of Van Bremers mountain come slowly over the Lava Beds. In the Modoc camp the "medicine-man" is conducting the war-dance and working the blood of Modoc hearts up to fighting heat. He promises his people that he will make a medicine that will turn the soldiers' bullets away. He points to the great battle of January, and its results, to inspire confidence in him. The chief is saddened, and fully realizes the situation. He is desperate, and is resolved to fight to the bitter end. He has already appointed the places for each of the war-riors. He tells his people that the hated Warm Spring Indians are now in the soldiers' camp. He reminds them that these people are their enemies; that it was the Warm Spring and Tenino Indians who killed his father. He counsels them to remember his father's death. He knows that a thousand white soldiers are there and that the "big guns" will reach his stronghold.

Some of his followers have superstitious faith enough in the med-icine-man to believe that they will outlive the war, and to believe the white men are conquered already. The chief knows better.

In the soldiers' camp preparations are making for the assault. The Coehorn shell-guns are made ready for putting on the backs of mules. Food for the soldiers has been prepared. The guard is stationed. The soldiers in either camp well understand that the morrow's sun will witness another bloody struggle. Those of them who were in former battles shrink from this one, knowing how nearly impregnable the "stronghold" will be.

"I say, old man, there is a little bit of fun going on. I wish you could be up to see it." Thus spoke Capt. Ferree to Meacham, and continued, "You know Long Jim—a Modoc prisoner—is under guard. Well, the boys are going to give him a *chance* to run for his life without the knowledge of Gen. Gilliam. They have everything all fixed, and I'll bet fifty dollars he 'makes it!' They have him in the stone corral, and the plan is to station the boys outside next to the Lava Beds and leave one or two men to guard him. They will pretend to sleep, and Jim will jump the wall, and then the boys will let him have it. Two to one he gets away! I thought I would just tell you, so you wouldn't get scared to death, thinking the Modocs were attacking the camp."

This man, Long Jim, had pretended to desert the Modoc camp during the peace negotiations. He had a bullet extracted from his back while in the commissioners' camp, several weeks before. He was afterwards caught while acting as an emissary to other Indians, and, by order of Gen. Canby, was being detained under guard as a prisoner. Hence his presence. He stoutly denied having any desire to return to Captain Jack's camp.

The officers are assembled in Col. Green's quarters. They are celebrating a half-solemn, half-sentimental ceremony that is sometimes indulged in before an engagement. To a listener who lies in a hospital it sounds somewhat as does the medicine war-dance in the middle camp. Indeed, its results are the same, although the design is different. In the Modoc camp, the dance and medicine are for the purpose of invoking spiritual aid and stimulating the nerves of the braves to heroic deeds. In the soldier camp the intention is to celebrate the stirring scenes passed, to exchange friendship, to blot out all the personal differences that exist, and pledge fidelity for the future.

They tell stories and pass jokes and witticisms until a late hour. Before adjournment they join in singing a song that is sung nowhere else and by no other voices. The wounded man in the hospital tent hears only the refrain. It sounds melancholy, and has a saddening effect.

Then stand by your glasses steady,
This world's a round of lies—
Three cheers for the dead already,
And hurrah for the next who dies—

. . . . rings out from the lips of brave men who dread not the strife of battle under ordinary circumstances; but to meet an enemy who is so thoroughly protected by chasms and caverns of rock does not promise glory that inflates men's courage previous to battle.

Col. Tom Wright and Lieut. Eagan drop into the hospital, and, sitting down beside the wounded commissioner, assure him that they will remember Canby and Thomas, and will avenge his own sufferings. They retire with expressions of hope for his recovery. They meet Maj. Thomas and Lieut. Cranston coming to pay a visit. Exchanges of sympathy and friendship follow, and they return to quarters to sleep before the battle, leaving behind them but one wounded man. He is peering into the future, wondering *who* of all the five hundred men and officers will be his *first neighbour.*

The camp is quiet. Midnight has passed. The relief guard has been stationed. In the corral Long Jim is *sleeping*. He shows no sign of any intention to escape. The guard *is discouraged*. The boys outside are impatient. What if Jim should not make the attempt? It would be a huge joke on the boys who planned this little side scene. Truth is, nearly everybody who is in the secret is cursing Jim for a fool that he don't try to escape. A consultation is held. Something must be done. "I'll fix it," says a "little corporal." Going to the corral he says, "Don't go to sleep and let the prisoner get away." Everything becomes quiet and the two guards sit down, one at each side of the corral.

"I'm so d—d sleepy I can't keep awake," says one to the other.

"Sleep, then. I won't say a word," rejoins his companion. "He can't get away from me. He's sleeping himself."

The first speaker soon hangs his head and *sleeps*. Soon the other's chin rests on his breast and he begins to *snore*. Long Jim slowly raises *his* head. All is quiet. There sit the two guards, sleeping. One is snoring. Jim listens. His love for his own people and for liberty burns in his heart. He has picked up many items that would be valuable. He knows that the attack will be made on the morrow. His friends must be notified. He listens a moment, and then, cautiously laying aside his blanket, he stands erect. One of the guards sits in the gateway of the corral. The wall around him is higher than his head. He cannot see over it. Laying his hands on the stone and summoning all his strength he *springs*. A blaze at either end of the corral, then bang! bang! go the guns outside like the firing, of a string of China crackers, only louder. Twenty shots are fired, and still Jim does not fall. He reaches the outer picket line. *Two more guns are fired off*, lighting up the track for the runaway, and still he flies. The boys reload and send a parting volley in the direction Jim went.

"*He 'made it'; and a madder set of fellows you never saw.* I knew they couldn't hit him. I've tried that thing, and it can't be done." I need not tell my readers who uttered this remark.

You may suppose that this little episode, "just before the battle," roused the camp. No such thing occurred. Gen. Gilliam, it is true, jumped to his feet, but was reassured when he was told that it was nothing—only Long Jim escaping.

Before daylight this distinguished individual was "a-tellin' the Modocs the news," as one of the sleeping guard declared. So he was, with his clothing pierced by half-a-dozen bullets, but "with nary a wound."

CHAPTER 32

Killed in Petticoats

It is four o'clock on the morning of Tuesday, the 14th of April. The men are silently falling into line. The mules are groaning under the heavy weight of "mounted pieces," or loaded with stretchers and other contrivances for carrying the dead and wounded. The soldiers do not seem to realize that some of their number will *return on these mules*, wounded and helpless, or dead. Perhaps each one thinks and hopes that it will be some one other than himself. From the immense preparations for war it would seem that Captain Jack and his followers must be taken in a few minutes. One thousand men and seventy-two Warm Spring Indians are taking position around the ill-starred chieftain's fortress. He is not ignorant of their presence. His old women and children are hidden away in the caves of the Lava Beds. The young women are detailed to attend the warriors with water and ammunition. The Modocs are better armed than during the last battle. Some of their guns were captured from fallen soldiers on the 17th of January. A large quantity of ammunition that was taken has been changed to suit the old rifles.

The men are at the stations assigned them. They are divested of all unnecessary clothing, and their limbs are bandaged by folds of rawhide. They are awaiting the attack. Each warrior holds a position made impregnable by the formation of the rocks, or the condition in which the great convulsions of nature which produced this indescribable country, left them.

The sun is driving away the darkness, and soon the battle must begin.

In the hospital a veteran of the Second Iowa Cavalry is sitting beside the wounded man, and preparing him for the shock that his nerves will feel.

"Don't get scared, old man! It will begin very soon, and you will presently have company enough," he says.

The hospital attendants are making ready to care for the wounded. Mattresses are placed in rows on either side. In a small tent, nearby, a surgeon is laying out lint and bandages.

The Iowa veteran is standing at the door, saying to Meacham, "I will tell you when it opens. I can see the fire before you will hear the sound and feel the jar. Don't get frightened, and think that the mountain is coming down on you, old man. There goes the signal rocket. Now look out!"

An instant more and the shells and howitzers join in a simultaneous demand for the Modoc chief to surrender. The earth trembles while the reports are reverberating around and through the chasms and caverns of the Lava Beds, and before they have finally died away, or the trembling has ceased, another sound comes in a continuous roar, proceeding from the left, and by the time the belt of fire has made the circuit, it repeats itself again and again. But no smoke of rifles is seen coming from the stronghold. "Charge!" rings out by human voice and bugle blast, and a returning series of bayonets converge.

On they go, nearing a common centre. No Modocs are yet in sight. The soldiers, now upright, are hurrying forward, when suddenly, from a covert chasm and cavern, a circle of smoke bursts forth. The Modocs have opened fire. The men fall on the right and left, around the circle. "Onward!" shout the officers. "Onward!" But the men are falling fast. The charge must be abandoned. The bugle sounds "Retreat!" The line widens again, the soldiers bearing back the dead and wounded. They now seek cover among the rocks. The wounded are sent to the hospital, by way of the lake, in boats or on the mule-stretchers. The battle goes on. The wounded continue to arrive. The shadows of the mountains from the west cover the Lava Beds, and still the fight goes on. A volley is heard near the hospital.

"What's that?" asked the startled patient.

"Burying the dead," quietly responds the veteran nurse.

A few minutes pass, and another volley is fired, and another soldier is being laid away to rest forever. Still another, and another yet; until five volleys announce that five of the boys who started out with United States rifles in the morning are occupying the narrow homes that must be theirs forever.

At irregular intervals during the night the fight is continued. The Modocs are constantly on duty. The soldiers relieve each other, and are in fighting condition when Tuesday morning comes. No cessation of firing through the day. No rest for the Modocs.

One of the camp sutlers, well known all over the West as a game fellow, unable to restrain his love for sport, and being Patriotic, goes to quartermaster Grier and demands a *breech-loader*, and also a *charger* to ride, saying he wanted to do something to help whip the Modocs. Mr. Grier informed *Pat* that he could *not* issue arms without an order. Pat was indignant, and made application successfully to a citizen for the necessary outfit for war. He mounted Col. Wright's mule and repaired to the scene of action.

On reaching the line of battle he looked around a few minutes, and, to a word of caution given him by an officer, replied, "Divil an Indian do I see. I came out to git a scalp, and I'm not goin' home without it."

The officer who had given him the friendly advice watched the bold sutler as he kept on his way with his "Henry," ready to pick off any Modoc who might be imprudent enough to show his head. The soldiers shout, "Come back! come back!" but on goes the fearless sutler, carefully picking his way. Look very closely, now, and we can see what appears to be a *moving sage-bush*. Slowly, almost imperceptibly, it creeps over the ledges. If Pat would only look in the right direction he could see it and have a chance at the travelling bush; and as he is a good shot, he *might* scatter the leaves, besides boring a hole through *Steamboat Frank's* head. A puff of smoke comes out of the now immovable bush, and the report mingles with the roar of battle. Pat's mule *drops* under him, and he slips off and takes cover behind a low rock. The mule recovers its feet, and, with almost human sense, makes its way back to the soldiers' line.

Pat, anxious to discover his man, raises his head above the rocks. Whiz! comes another bullet, so close that Pat drops back quietly,— indeed, so very quietly that the soldiers report him dead; and noble-hearted Pat is named among the slain. But let us see how he really is. After lying contented awhile, he again slowly lifts his head, and another shot comes so close that Pat again drops behind the rock, and a second time the soldiers shout, "They've got him this time, sure!"

Not so, however. Pat is not hurt yet. Again and again he attempts to move from behind the rock, scarcely large enough to protect him, and each time Steamboat fires. No one who knows Pat McManus ever doubted his courage, but he deserves credit, also, for remembering that "*Discretion is the better part of valour.*" He finally arranges himself for a "quiet snooze behind the rock," as he expressed it, and awaited the welcome shades of evening. He then crawls out to the soldier line. It is said that he stood the fire of the soldiers who mistook him for an Indian, until he shouted to them, "Dry up, there! It's me! Don't you know a white man on his knees from an Injun on his belly?"

Directly west of Captain Jack's stronghold is a flat an almost level plain of lava rocks of six hundred yards in width, but commanded by the stronghold, while it does not offer protection to those who attempt to hold it. To complete the investment it is necessary to take this "flat." Lieut. Eagan is ordered to the execution of this enterprise. He is a daring leader, and, calling to his men to follow, moves forward. It is known to be a hazardous undertaking, but Eagan is just the man. Away he goes, jumping from one rock to another, calling to his men: "Come, my boys! come!" he cries. But suddenly the Lava Rocks in front belch forth Modoc bullets, and the gallant lieutenant *drops*. Then a soldier, and then another. Eagan shouts, "Fall back!" Pell-mell they go, stooping, jumping and shouting, leaving the brave fellow alone, while his men take a position where they can prevent the Modocs from capturing their leader.

Dr. Cabanis,—who seems to bear a charmed life, hearing of Eagan's fall, goes to him. The Modocs open fire on him. Steadily the gallant doctor moves forward, sometimes taking cover as best he can, again moving, half bent, from rock to rock, and when he reaches the wounded man a shout goes up from the soldiers. The wound is dressed, and the doctor, unable to *carry* his patient, leaves him and returns again to the line.

While this battle is going on, two coaches of the Northwest Stage Company meet, one going north and the other south. Observing a custom common among western stage people, they halt and exchange news items. In the stage going north is the body of Gen. Canby, in charge of his adjutant, Anderson, and Orderly Scott. In the other stage is Mrs. Meacham, accompanied by a stranger. Indeed, she has found a new escort at almost every station, who would announce himself as "your husband's brother." Members of this brotherhood have been informed by telegraph all along the road that "A Brother's Wife is *en route* for the Lava Beds. Look out for her wants. See that she is escorted and send the bills to No. 50, F. A. M., Salem."

Anderson goes to the other coach. Mrs. Meacham anxiously inquires, "Did you see my husband after he was wounded?"

"I sat beside him half an hour," he replies. "He is doing well."

358

"Will he recover?" questions Mrs. Meacham. "Is he mortally wounded?"

"We hope he will get well. His wounds are not necessarily fatal," replies the adjutant. "A great deal," he continues, "depends on good treatment. *Your brother* is with him. Everything that can be done is being done."

Anderson walks sadly back to his charge of the lamented general.

The driver of the other stage dismounts and accosts Mr. Anderson as he resumes his seat.

"Is there any hope for Mr. Meacham?" he asks.

"Not the least in the world; but his wife must not know it now," replies Anderson, in a low voice; but O my God! *loud enough for the quick* ears of Mrs. Meacham to catch the words.

The drivers take up the lines. The stages pass. In one Gen. Canby's body is being borne to his heart-broken wife. In the other a heart-broken wife is going to her husband, with the thought that she would be northward borne in a few days, with her husband confined in a dark coffin. The southern-bound stage reaches Jacksonville. The strange gentleman assists Mrs. Meacham to alight, and attends to her baggage while the change of coaches is being made. He then introduces another stranger to Mrs. Meacham as "your husband's brother, who will go to Y-re-ka with you."

It is Wednesday evening when the stage is slowly climbing Siskiyou mountain. The occupants are but two, one a lady. She does not speak. *She has no hope now.* The gentleman is silent. He, too, has lost hope in the recovery of the lady's husband.

Lieut. Eagan is being carried to his tent. The hospital is full of patients groaning with pain. Near the door lies a Warm Springs Indian scout. The surgeons are probing his wound, while he laughs and talks to the attendants, making sarcastic remarks about "the Modocs using powder that couldn't shoot through his leg."

The Iowa veteran announces to his brother-in-law that his wife will be in Y-re-ka that night.

The Modocs are out of water. The ice they had stored in the caves is exhausted. They determine to cut their way to the lake, but a few hundred yards distant. They concentrate their forces, and, enveloped in sage brush, they crawl up near the line of soldiers and open fire in terrible earnest. Soldiers fall on right and left. The Modocs yell and push their line. The white soldiers are massing to resist. The fire is awful. Peal after peal, volley after volley, and still the Modocs hold

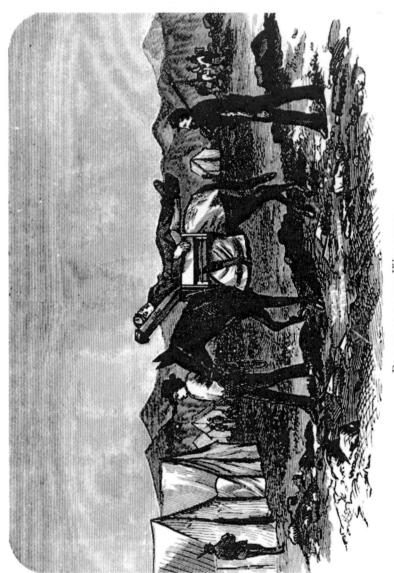

Bringing in the Wounded

their ground. All night long the Modoc yell mingles with the rattle of musketry, and the shouts of defiance from the soldiers. One party is fighting in desperation; the other from duty.

While this battle is raging, the stage-coach from the North arrives at Y-re-ka, and stops at the hotel. A gentleman says a few words to the driver. The street-lamp before Judge Roseborough's door throws its light on the faces of several ladies and gentlemen who stand waiting to receive the lady passenger. She is met with warm-hearted kindness, although every face is new. Supper is waiting. Every effort is made for the lady's comfort. She weeps now, although this great sorrow of her life had seemed to dry up the fountain of tears until the warm hearts and kind words of strange voices had touched, with melting power, her inner soul. A short sleep, and she arises, to find a four-horse carriage awaiting to bear her to the Lava Beds. A new escort takes his place beside her.

Just after daylight, and while leaving the Shasta valley, a few miles out of Y-re-ka, the driver announces a courier coming from the Lava Beds. As he approaches, he draws from his "*cantena*"—a leather pocket carried on the saddle-front—a paper, and, waving it while he checks his panting horse, says, "For Mrs. Meacham." Oh, the power of a few words! How they can change darkness into light! The letter read as follows:—

Lava Beds, Tuesday Eve., April 15.
Dear Sister: Your husband will recover. His wounds are doing well, but he will never be very handsome any more.
Your brother,
D. J. Ferree.

This inveterate joker cannot resist the temptation to mix the colours of the rainbow in all he does. But we forgive him.

This morning, as the sun dispels the darkness, the Modocs abandon the attempt to reach the lake. For two days and nights they have fought without sleep. They are suffering from thirst and long-continued fighting; but *no signs of surrender are anywhere visible*. The chief has called a council. It is decided to evacuate on the approach of night, and the braves are ordered to hold their fire unless to resist a charge.

A few of the Modocs have passed outside the lines by way of the "open flat," and are crawling towards the soldiers' camp at the foot of the bluff. Gen. Gilliam, Dr. McEldry and others have passed over the route unharmed. The horse-stretchers have passed and repassed with their mangled freight. The pack-ponies are all busily engaged, and the team horses, that were ordered by the quartermaster into service, are employed in carrying the dead. The pack-trains and teams belong to private citizens, and have been employed by the government in carrying and hauling supplies. It was not expected, however, that they would be required to carry bleeding and mangled human freight.

"*Necessity knows no law.*" In the beginning of the battle, the citizen teamsters were ordered to this place for duty. Among them was a fair-haired boy of nineteen years of age, who had trained his team horses, on the first and second days of the battle, to walk between the poles that made the mule-stretchers. The poles were about twenty feet long, and at either end a stout strap was attached to each. These straps were thrown across the saddles on the horses, one being immediately in front of the other, and between them canvas was secured to the poles, thus constituting a "horse-stretcher." This boy had proved himself very efficient, and had won the commendation of the officers, and the gratitude of the wounded men. Dr. McEldry had requested the quartermaster to continue young Hovey in the service, because in managing the stretchers he was careful and trustworthy.

A presentiment had this morning filled the mind of this noble young fellow with dread. He made application to Quartermaster Grier to be excused from further duty with the stretchers, stating his reasons. Mr. Grier expressed his sympathy with him and endeavoured to allay his fears, remarking that Dr. McEldry had paid him a high compliment for his efficiency and requested him—Mr. Grier—to send him out again this morning.

The boy—*too brave to refuse,* although no law could have compelled him to go, though his horses might have been pressed into service—assented, remarking that, notwithstanding he had made *several trips safely,* he should *not get back from this one.*

After preparing his horses for this unpleasant labour he goes to a citizen friend, and gives him his watch and other valuables, saying that he *did not expect to return,* as he had had a presentiment that he would not; and he gave to this friend a message to his father, another for his mother, and mentioning the names of his *brothers and sisters,* left a *few words of love for each.* The grandeur of character and heroism exhibited by this boy stand out among the few instances that are given to mankind in proof of the divinity that controls human action. Nothing but godlike attributes could have sustained young Hovey when calmly performing those manly actions which entitle his name to be enrolled among the heroes of the age. So let it be recorded, and let it stand with the nineteen summers he had lived, *accusing* and *condemning* those who so *wildly howled* for blood when the Peace Commissioners were labouring to prevent what might have been only a terrible phantasmagoria, but which has become an awful reality.

Young Hovey, accompanied by one assistant only, started on his way to the battle-field with four horses and two stretchers. No guard was deemed necessary, because it was understood that the Modocs were surrounded and "could not escape," and it was so reported, by the general commanding, to his superiors. Hovey and his companion had passed by the scene of the tragedy of the Peace Commissioners but a few rods, and but a few hundred yards behind Gen. Gilliam, when, from the cover of the rocks, a Modoc bullet, shot by Hooker Jim, went with a death-dealing power through his head. The monsters, not content with his death and the capture of his horses, rush upon him, and while he is yet alive, scalp him, strip him of his clothing, and then, with inhuman ferocity, the red fiends crush his head to a shapeless mass with huge stones. His companion escapes unhurt.

This outrage was committed almost within sight of the army, which was investing the stronghold, and the camp at the bluff.

Having despatched young Hovey, the Modocs then turned towards the latter camp. Lieut. Grier, who was in command, immediately telegraphed to Col. Greene, in command at the Lava Beds, that "The Modocs were out of the stronghold and had attacked the camp." He, also, called together the citizens and his own forces, as Assistant Acting Quartermaster, and, arming them, prepared to resist. But a few shots were fired by the Indians; however, one or two balls landed among the tents near the hospital. The Modocs presently withdrew.

The day is passing away with the almost useless expenditure of powder and shells. However, there was a shell sent in yesterday that did not explode when delivered, and the Modocs are anxious to see what is inside of it. How to do so is a question in the Modoc mind. Several plans are tried unsuccessfully, until an old Cum-ba-twas, with jaws like a cougar, taking it in his hands and clinching the plug with his teeth, produces a combustion that *he does not anticipate. That shell does execution. In fact, it is worth about five hundred thousand dollars to the government*, rating its services pro rata with the total cost of killing Modoc Indians. When the plug starts, the head of the old fellow who is holding it goes off his body in a damaged condition. Another younger man, who stands by waiting the result of the experiment, is blown all to pieces, cutting his scalp into convenient sizes for the soldiers to divide to advantage.

Two or three old Indian women pass through the lines to the water. A young brave dons woman's clothes and comes to the line. After slaking his thirst he starts to return. Something in his walk creates a suspicion.

"That's a man," says a soldier.

The Indian runs. *A dozen rifles command, "Halt!" The Indian halts.* The soldiers *take five or six scalps off that fellow's head*, and would have taken more, had the first ones been less avaricious. However, soldiers are kind-hearted and unselfish fellows, and the scalps are *again divided*, so that, at last, ten or twelve are happy in the possession of a scalp.

It is now five p.m. Let us see how the several parties are situated at this time. Couriers are *en route* to Y-re-ka with despatches, telling the world about the terrible slaughter, and, *by the authority* of the general in command, assuring the powers that be, in Washington, "The Modocs cannot escape. They are in our power. It is only a question of time. We have them 'corralled.'"

In Portland, Oregon, an immense concourse of citizens are awaiting the arrival of the train bearing the remains of Gen. Canby. The streets are hushed. The doors of business houses are closed. A general feeling of sorrow is everywhere manifest. Officers of the army and a delegation from a Great Brotherhood are there. On every hand flags are at half mast. Emblems of sorrow meet the eye. The grief-stricken widow sits in her room, cold, comfortless, inconsolable.

The Fraternal and Church Brotherhoods and thousands of mourning friends crowd the wharf in San Francisco, eagerly watching the coming of a steamer from Vallejo with flags at half mast. This boat is bringing home for interment the body of another great man, whose spirit went to its Maker in company with the Christian general, for whom the city of Portland, Oregon, mourns. Nearest to the dark tabernacle two young men are standing. They are the sons of Dr. Thomas.

While the two cities of the western coast are exchanging telegraphic words of sympathy, kind-hearted friends are filling a parlour where three sorrowing children are weeping without the presence of parents. The friends are repeating the hopeful telegrams of the Iowa veteran, and assuring them that their mother is with their father by that time as she left Y-re-ka the previous morning.

At this hour a young physician is hurrying to the bedside of an aged man, who has passed threescore years and ten, near Solon, Iowa. A glance at his face and we are reminded of the wounded Peace Commissioner in the Lava Beds, three thousand miles away. Five days ago he had read the telegram that said, "Meacham mortally wounded." He threw himself on his bed then, saying, "If my son dies I never can rise again,—my first-born soil who went with me through all my dark hours on the frontier, twenty-five years ago. Must he die? Can I bear it? *Thy will be done, O Lord!*"

For five days has he laid hanging between life and death. His physician has watched the telegraph, and now, with the words of the Iowa veteran, he is hurrying to the bedside of his patient.

"Your son will recover!" the doctor exclaims before reaching him.

The white-haired man rises on his elbow, saying, "Do I dream? Is it true, doctor? Will my son live?"

About this hour, away up on Wild Horse Creek, Umatilla County, Oregon, a young man is writing a letter that seems to come from an overcharged heart submerged in grief. The letter runs as follows:—

> Meacham Ranch, Wild Horse Creek, April 17th, 1873.
> My dear Nephew:—I have just heard of the death of your father. . . . Eleven months since we kneeled with him beside your Uncle Harvey's coffin and pledged our lives to care for his widow and orphan children. . . . You and I, George, are all that are left to care for two widows and two families of orphans. . . . The stroke is heavy to be borne. . . . I will try to be a father to them. We must be men.
> Your uncle,
> John Meacham.

Again we stand on the bluff, at this hour, overlooking the Lava Beds. In a little tent among the hundred others the Iowa veteran is telling his brother-in-law that his wife will be in camp by seven. A courier arrives saying that the Modocs are hanging about the trail leading down the mountain. The officers are aware of the near approach of Mrs. Meacham. They decide that she cannot come to the camp with safety. A detachment is ordered to escort Commissioner Dyer up the mountain to meet her and take her to Linkville.

While he is working his way under escort, the Modocs are seen creeping towards the road. At the top of the mountains Dyer meets the ambulance. He assures the woman that she cannot reach the camp; that her husband is well cared for, and that she must go back to a place of safety.

She remonstrates, saying, "I must—I *will* go to my husband." She alights from the ambulance and starts on foot, but is intercepted and forced to go again to the ambulance, with the assurance that "*her husband will be sent out to her within a day or two*".

No language can portray the feelings and emotions of this woman when, after travelling three hundred miles on stages and in ambulances over the Cascade mountains, through a hostile country, she is compelled to turn back when within three miles of her wounded husband, with those ominous words saying, like a funeral dirge, "*Your husband will be sent out to you in a few days*".

While she is yet pleading for the privilege of seeing him the mountain's sides reverberate with the sounds of rifle shots coming up from a point half way to the camp, volley answering volley. While she is in a half-unconscious condition, the team drawing the ambulance is turned about, and the guard take their places on either side, and the team moves away towards the frontier.

When the woman returns to consciousness, she exclaims, "Take me to my husband! I must see him before he dies."

The kind heart of Mr. Dyer is moved. He pleads with her to abandon the attempt, consoling her with Christian assurances that "God does all things well." With the guard in skirmishing order the party hurries away.

The mutilated body of young Hovey is lying stark and cold, beside the road where he fell.

Sundown is announced by the repeated volleys of musketry at the cemetery, as the bodies of the soldiers are laid away in their last sleep.

The friends of the young lad obtain permission, and the necessary facilities, from the quartermaster, to bring in his body. A coffin is prepared, and in it is placed what was, a few hours since, a noble-hearted youth full of life.

A part of the army is resting, and a part is bombarding the Modocs. Captain Jack has kept the "flat" cleared, and now, while the shot and shell are being tumbled in around his camp, he draws his people out under cover of darkness, and leaves the soldiers to fire away at his empty caves until morning, when another order to charge is made, and the lines close slowly up with great care, like fishermen who feel sure they have a big haul, until they land the seine, and discover that a great rent has let the prize escape. See the soldiers' line! How carefully it contracts to the centre, the soldiers expecting each moment that the Modocs will make a break, until, at last, the lines come together like a great draw-string, only to reveal the fact that *no Indians are there*, except one old man, whom all declare to be Schonchin, who was wounded by Meacham's Derringer last Friday. *He shall not escape*, and a dozen bullets pass through him. He falls over, and the men gather around and scalp the old fellow.

"Meacham shall have a lock of his hair," says one; and he cuts it from *one of the scalps*.

Then the old Indian's head is severed from his body, and kicked around the camp like a football, until a surgeon interferes, and saves it from further indignities by sending it to the camp, where the face was carefully skinned off, and "put to pickle" in alcohol. The men shout and hurrah while exploring the caves, expecting to find Captain Jack, like a wolf at bay, somewhere, determined to *"die in the last ditch."* Instead of Modocs, they find the remains of soldiers who have been killed, ammunition that had been captured, and dried beef that had not been required; but no evidence of any *"Modoc bodies having been burned."*

While they were rejoicing in the capture of this great natural fortress of the Modoc chief, *he* was in a new position with his people, resting and recruiting from the three days' battle, and so near his old "stronghold" that he could hear the reports of the soldiers' muskets when they finished up the supposed Schonchin.

CHAPTER 33

Fighting the Devil With Fire a Failure

The expectant man has waited, watched, listened for the sound of a voice that would bring joy to him. His attendant carefully breaks the disappointment, fearing the consequences.

Friday morning, and a Warm Springs soldier is sitting beside the commissioner. A look at his face, and we recognize him as the man who stood out so long in the meeting at Warm Springs Agency, in 1871.

Pia-noose had come in to vent his feelings and to express his friendship. After the usual ceremony of salutation on his part, he remarked that the white men did not know how to fight Modocs. "*Too much music.* Suppose you take away all the music, all the big guns, all the soldiers, and tell the Warm Springs, 'Whip the Modocs,' *all right.* Some days we get two men, some days we get more, and by and by we get all the Modocs. Warm Springs don't like so much music,"— referring to the bugle.

This morning Gen. Canby's remains are lying in state in Portland, and a whole city weeps with the widow who does not—cannot look on the beloved face.

In San Francisco bells are tolling, and a vast concourse of sad-hearted citizens are following the dark-plumed hearse that conveys the Rev. Dr. Thomas to his last resting-place in Lone Mountain Cemetery.

Mrs. Meacham is sitting in a small parlour at Linkville, and expecting each moment the arrival of a courier that will confirm her worst fears. Mrs. Boddy—whose husband was murdered last November by the Modocs—is with her. The two mingle their tears. They are kindred, now that sorrow has united them.

Gen. Gilliam has called a council of war, and plans for future operations are being discussed. The hospital gives out a sad murmur of mingled moans, curses, and groans. Two soldiers are going toward the burying-ground; one carries a *spade*, the other a small, plain, straight box, in which is the leg of a soldier going to a waiting-place for him. Riddle and his wife, Tobey, are cooking and washing for the wounded. Riddle often calls on Meacham, bringing refreshments prepared by his wife. Col. Tom Wright calls on Meacham this morning. A spicy colloquy ensues. He remarks that the Modocs are nearly "h—l."

Meacham says, "Where is your two thousand dollars now? Suppose you and Eagan took them in fifteen minutes, didn't you?"

Col. Wright: "Took 'em, *not much*,—we got the prettiest licken ever an army got in the world."

Meacham: "What kind of a place did you find, anyhow, colonel?"

Col. Wright: "It's no use talking; the match to the Modoc stronghold has not been built and never will be. Give me *one hundred picked men*, and let me station them, and I will *hold* that place against *five thousand men,—yes, ten thousand*, as long as ammunition and subsistence last. That's about as near as I can describe it. Oh, I tell you it is the most impregnable fortress in the world! Sumter was nowhere when compared with it."

Meacham: "What kind of a fighter is Captain Jack, colonel?"

Col. Wright: "Fighter; why, he's the biggest Ingen on this continent. See what he's done; licked a thousand men, killed forty or fifty, and has not lost more than *three* or *four* himself. We *starved* him out, we *didn't whip* him. He'll turn up in a day or two, ready for another fight. I tell you, Jack's a big Ingen."

Let us see where this distinguished individual and this gallant band of heroic desperadoes are at this time. From the signal-station on the mountain side, above Gilliam's camp, we can look over the spot, but they are so closely hidden that we cannot locate them; not even a curl of smoke is seen. Follow the foot of the bluff around three miles, and then strike off south, or left, two miles more, and amid an immense jumble of lava rocks we find them. Go carefully; Indian women are on the picket-station, while the warriors sleep. Since sundown last evening they passed *between* the soldier camp and the council tent and brought water to the famishing. A man sits upon a jaded horse, at the gate of a farm-house, near Y-re-ka. Children are playing in the front yard. A watch-dog springs to his feet and gives warning by loud bark-

369

ing. A stout-built man looks out from a barn to ascertain the meaning, while a middle-aged woman comes to the kitchen door. The whole, together, is the picture of a western farmer's home,—happiness and contentment. The horseman takes in the scene, and while he views the photograph he recognises in it the home of young Hovey. A painful duty is his. He hesitates. He knows that his words will send a dark shadow over this household. The farmer comes towards him. The dog is hushed; the children cease their sports; the mother stands waiting, waiting, listening, and the throbbing of her own heart prepares her for the awful tidings.

"Is this Mr. Hovey?" the horseman says, while from his inside coat pocket he withdraws a letter.

"That is my name," the farmer replies.

"I have a letter for you, Mr. Hovey?"

The children gather around the father, looking attentively at him and the horseman, while the latter, with trembling hand, passes the envelope that is so heavy ladened with sorrow. "Where's the letter from?" asks the anxious mother, while the father tears it open.

"The Lava Beds," replies the horseman, turning away his face.

The paper shakes in the hands of the farmer, while his face changes to ashy paleness. "What is it, father? Oh, what does the letter say?" cries the mother, as she comes to his side and glances over his arm. Let us not intrude on this scene of sorrow.

Hanging to *Hooker Jim's* belt is a fair-haired scalp, still fresh; the blood of young Hovey still undried upon Hooker's clothing, giving him no more concern than if it had come from the veins of a deer or an antelope. The lock of hair had once been blessed by the hands of a tender mother, who for nineteen years had watched over her first-born son. Now it is dishonoured, used only as a record by which a savage makes proof of excellence in performing feats of fiendish heroism.

The "Iowa Veteran," with an eye always out for sport, remarks, "Old man, there's going to be some lively fun in a few minutes; wish you could see it. There's fourteen Indians going for water, and a company has started out to capture them. Two to one the Modocs lick 'em." Taking a station at the tent door, he continued: "I'll keep you posted, old man; keep cool. The Modocs are taking position. They aint more than *eight hundred* yards from here. Now look out,—the fun will begin pretty soon." *Bang, bang*, and there is a rattling of rifles mixed with the Modoc war-whoop. "Here they come back, *carrying* three men; but the Modocs are following up. Don't that beat the devil and the Dutch?" remarks the irate veteran;"you've seen a big dog chase a cayote until the cayote would turn on him, and then the big dog would turn tail and run for home with the cayote after him, haven't you? Well, that's exactly what's going on out here now. This whacks anything I ever witnessed, by Jupiter! *Two* to one, the Modocs take the camp. By gorry, old man, don't know what we are to do with you. You can't run; you can't fight; you are too big for me to carry; *wish I had a spade, I'd bury you now until the fun* is all over; but it's too late. Can't help it, old man, you needn't dodge; it won't do any good; just lay still, and if they come, *play dead on 'em again. You can do that to perfection,* and there aint a darn bit of danger of their trying to get another scalp off of you. Too big a prairie above the timber line for that. 'Boston' was a darn fool to try it before."

While this speech is being made, the Modocs are coming towards the soldier camp, firing occasional shots in among the tents. "By Goshens, we'll have fun now. They're a-going; shell 'em; ha! ha! ha! Shell a dozen Modocs! *Ha! ha! ha! don't* that beat *sulphur king* out of his boots? Ha! ha! ha! Steady, old man, steady now. Keep cool. They're ready to fire. The Indians are in plain sight! Yip-se-lanta; there it goes, screeching, screaming, right in among the rocks where the Modocs are, and explodes." The smoke clears up. The Indians come out from behind the rocks, and, turning sideways to the soldier camp, pat their shot-pouches at the Boston soldiers. Shell after shell is fired and each time the Modocs take cover until they explode, and then, with provoking insolence, they pat their shot-pouches at an army of five hundred men,—that is, what is left of that army.

"Cease firing!" commands Gen. Gilliam, from the signal-station. The shell guns are covered with the nice canvas housing. The Modocs now organize an artillery battery, and, taking position, elevating their rifles to an angle mocking the shell guns, Scarfaced Charley stands behind and gives the order, "Fire!" and the Modoc battery is now playing on a camp where there are no rocks for cover. Several shots spit down among the Boston soldiers.

"I went with Grierson through Alabama, with Sherman through Georgia, but that whacks anything ever I saw. *Two* to one they attack the camp, by thunder! and if they do they'll take it sure. B'gins to look pretty squally, old man. If they come, your only show is to play dead. You can do it. I don't like to leave you, but I'll have to do it, no other chance. We'll come back and bury what they don't burn up."

The gray-eyed man, Fairchild, comes to the tent-door and engages the veteran in a talk. "I say, captain, don't you wish we had Capt. Kelly's volunteers here now? Wouldn't they have a chance for Modoc steaks, eh? They're the fellows that could take the Modocs. I've been out home and just come in. Where are the Warm Springs' scouts all this time?"

The veteran—Capt. Ferree—replies: "Oh, they are out on the other side of the Lava Beds *surrounding* the Modocs; to keep them from getting away."

Fairchild: "They aint going to leave here, no fear of that. But did you ever see anything like this morning's performances?—fourteen Indians come out, kill three men, insult the whole camp, mock the shell guns, threaten the camp, scare everybody most to death, and then retire to their own camp. That caps the climax. Say, old man Meacham, how you making it, anyhow? Going to come out, aint you? You wasn't born to be killed by the Modocs, that's certain. That old bald head of yours is what saved you, old man, no mistake."

Veteran: "I've just been telling him that I'll have a spade on hand next time the Modocs come, so I can *bury* him until the fun's over."

Fairchild: "Bully! that'll do; just the thing. I think you had better *have* the hole *ready*. No telling what *might happen*. Them Modocs mighty devilish fellers; just like 'em to attack the camp; and if they do they'll take it, sure; wish we had the Oregon volunteers here now to protect us."

Four p.m.—and a long line of carriages are returning from Lone Mountain, leaving Dr. Thomas with the dead.

Another long line of mourners are following a hearse down Front street, Portland, to the steamer *Oriflamme*, which has been detailed by Ben Holliday to bear the remains of Gen. Canby to San Francisco. The widow is supported by the arms of officers. Anderson and Scott walk beside the hearse. A city is weeping, while they pay respect to the memory of the noble-hearted Christian General, who hears not the signal gun of departure. Couriers are bearing despatches to Y-re-ka.

"The Modocs cannot escape; we have them surrounded. The Warm Springs scouts are out on the outpost. The Modocs cannot escape. Lieut. Sherwood died last night. Lieut. Eagan, improving. Meacham may recover, though badly mutilated and blind."

The salute of honour over the grave of young Hovey announces his burial by the kindly band of army officers.

"Extermination to the Modocs!" says Gen. Sherman.

"Extermination," repeat the newspapers.

"Extermination," says an echo over the Pacific coast. Extermination is the watchword everywhere. "It does look like extermination, that's a fact, with half a hundred upheaving graves filled with soldiers near the camp; a hospital overflowing with wounded; an army demoralized, and lying passive seven days after the assassination of Gen. Canby and Dr. Thomas; while every day the Modocs waylay and kill unguarded men almost in sight of camp, strip and scalp them, and then heap rocks on their bodies. This looks like extermination, but not of the *Modocs*. Perhaps it suits those who were so free with denunciation of the Peace Commission. But whether it does, or not, this condition of the plan of *extermination* is to some extent attributable to the infuriated, senseless, cowardly, and unmanly opposition that was made against Canby and the Peace Commissioners, who *saw* and *felt how costly in human life a peace made through the death-dealing bullets must be.*

Saturday morning, and Modoc emissaries are crawling into the camps of the *Klamaths*, *Snakes*, and *Wall-pa-pahs*, endeavouring to induce these people to join the Modocs in the war. They paint in glowing colours the great success they have had, and declare that the time has come when red men should unite against a common enemy. It cannot be denied that in every Indian camp along the frontier line *there were sympathizers with the Modocs*; but nowhere were they in sufficient force to precipitate a general war, although the new religion proclaimed by "*Smoheller*" had found followers everywhere, and was gaining strength by every victory won by Captain Jack. How nearly the frontier came to witnessing a great Indian war is not understood by the people of the Pacific coast.

A Warm Springs Indian, who does not belong to the scouts, is going carefully along the northern shore of the lake. His destination is Linkville. His mission is to bear a letter to Mrs. Meacham. The letter contains a message that will cause her almost to leap for joy:—

Lava Beds, Saturday, April 19, 1873.
. . . Hire an escort and meet us at the mouth of Lost River tomorrow at noon, and we will deliver your *handsome husband* over to you in pretty good shape . . . We will cross the lake in a boat. Be on time. . . .

D. J. Ferree.

Saturday passes away without an episode that is worthy of record. Not a Modoc has been seen. The scouting parties have brought no

373

tidings of them. The sentinels walk the rounds. The surgeons are visiting the wounded. The hospital gives out moans, and furnishes another victim for the graveyard, and a volley of muskets says, "Farewell, comrade!" Meacham is counting the hours as they pass. He is impatient. The long night wears away, and morning breaks at last. Another messenger is stealing away along the lake shore. An ambulance, with a mounted escort of citizens, is drawing toward the mouth of Lost River.

"Are you ready to take me to meet my wife?" says a voice in a small tent.

"No; the surgeon says *the air is raw, and the lake is too rough.* We have sent a message to your wife that we can't go," replies Capt. Ferree.

After a few minutes' silence the disappointed man replies, "*That is not the reason. The wind does not blow.*" Very serious thoughts are passing through the minds of both the hearer and the speakers. "I want to know why I am not going."

"The doctor says you could not stand it to go; the lake is too rough."

"You and the doctor are cowardly. You think I am going to die."

"If you force me to be candid, I must tell you the truth. The doctor says you have not more than *twenty chances in a hundred to recover.*"

Another silence of a few minutes, and the invalid replies, "*I'll take the twenty chances.* I must live; I have so many depending on me."

"If you pass midnight, the doctor says you *may live.*"

The ambulance, with the mounted escort, is standing on the battle-ground of November 30th, 1872. A woman is in the front end, with a field-glass, scanning the lake. No boat is in sight. Her hopes and fears alternate, when she suddenly catches sight of the messenger on the lake shore. The glass drops from her hands, and she sinks down on the seat and waits the coming of the messenger. He holds out the letter. The woman grasps it, and as she reads, her lips quiver. "Why, oh why is this? *The air is not chilly. The lake is not rough.*" Words are too poor to express the torturing suspense that follows while the ambulance carries her back to Linkville. Hope sets alternately with despair in the heart. For ten days has this woman felt the presence of each as circumstances bade them come and go. Two more days is she yet to walk beneath a sky that is half hidden by dark clouds. 'Tis midnight, Sunday. The surgeon, De Witt, and Capt. Ferree are sitting beside the woman's husband.

"I can tell you in another hour. If he comes out of this well, he is all right." Dr. De Witt, with his finger on the patient's pulse, nods to Ferree, "He is all right."

The patient awakes, and finds the doctor there. "How am I, doctor, shall I live?"

"I think you will, my dear fellow. *You have passed the crisis.*"

"Thank God!" comes from every lip.

"Keep quiet; don't get excited. We can save you now, but you had a very close call. *If you had been a drinking man all the surgeons in Christendom could not have saved you.* Rest quiet until morning, and I will come in again." Oh, what a change a few hours have wrought! Yesterday the sun went behind a dark cloud, and the invalid withstood the shock of "*Twenty out of a hundred*" for life. Now the sun of life comes again, and makes the vision clear of a loving family, home and friends. The transitions from despair to hope have been so frequent with this man that he can scarcely realize that he is again led by the angel of hope.

It is morning. Dr. De Witt and Capt. Ferree are in council. "I think he is on the safe side if he is careful," remarks the doctor. Another messenger is despatched to Linkville, with a letter making another appointment at the mouth of Lost River for the next day.

Donald McKay is in camp to receive orders. He reports that his scouts have circled the Lava Beds. "The Modocs have not escaped; they must be in there somewhere." Couriers arrive bringing newspapers, containing obituary notices of Gen. Canby, Dr. Thomas, and *A. B. Meacham.* Fairchild, Riddle, and Ferree were in Meacham's tent, reading.

Ferree remarks, "See here, old man, they have had you dead. You can know what the world will say about you when you *do* die. Some of them say very nice things. Here's one fellow that knows you pretty well. . . . 'Meacham *was* a man of strong will and positive character, who made warm friends and bitter enemies.'"

"There, that will do; when I die I want those words put on my tombstone," replies Meacham.

"Here, how do you like this? . . . '*Served him right.* He knew the Modocs better than any other man; why did he lead Canby and Thomas to their death? On his skirts the blood must be,' . . . Here is another that's pretty good. This fellow has found out you aint dead, and he is mad about it. It's a Republican organ, too, at that. . . . 'If Meacham could be made to change places with Canby or Thomas few tears would be shed. He is responsible for all this blood. *He knew* the Modocs. *They* did not. We are not disappointed. We expected that this

375

fanatical enthusiast would do some foolhardy thing, and we can only regret that he did not suffer instead of innocent men.' . . . There, how do you like that, old man? That's what you get for not being a general or a preacher. They pay you a high compliment,—sending Canby and Thomas to their death. Big thing, old man! You are somebody. Now, I'll tell you if you don't get through to straighten this thing out I'll do it, if it costs my life."

"Call on me, captain, I know that Meacham did all in his power to prevent the meeting," says Riddle.

Fairchild remarks, "If they had listened to Meacham, they would have been alive now. I know what I am saying, I know all about the whole thing, and I know that Meacham did his best to keep them from going. I can tell those newspaper men some things they would not like to hear. They abused Meacham all the way through, while Canby escaped their slander, when he was in truth as much a peace man as Meacham, and more too. I have been with the commission. All I have to say is that it was a d——d cowardly contemptible thing from the beginning to the end the way the Oregon papers '*went for*' the peace policy. I guess they are satisfied now. They wanted war, and they've got it. The *Modoc-eating* Oregon papers and volunteers haven't lost any Modoc themselves. Better send some more volunteers down here to eat up the Modocs, like Capt. ——'s company did the day that Shacknasty Jim held a whole company for seven hours in check, d——n 'em."

Capt. Ferree replies, "Fairchild, you had better go slow. Almost every editor in Oregon is a *fighting man*. Two or three of them were down here once, and they may come again for more Modoc news, and if they run across you you're gone up." Fairchild: "Yes, they're '*on it*,' seen 'em try it. Shacknasty tried 'em. One of them came down here looking for Squire Steele, of Y-re-ka, and when a man pointed out Steele to him, this fighting editor rode out of his way to keep from meeting him. It's a fact! Another one was going to scalp old Press Dorris. He didn't fail for the same reason that Boston Charley did on the old man there,—cause he hadn't any hair;—no, that wasn't the reason. He rode *too good a horse himself*; that's why. Press was around all the time. He didn't keep out of the way; fact is, Press was anxious for the scalping to begin. If any of those fighting editors come down here, well, set Shacknasty after them, and then you'll see them *git*. Bet a hundred dollars he can drive any two of them before him.

"Look here, here's something rich," says Ferree, turning the paper:

. . . "'Gov. Grover will call out volunteers to assist the regulars. They will make short work of it. The regulars are eastern men, and cannot fight Indians successfully.'"

Fairchild says, "*That's rich. One thousand soldiers here now*, and more Oregon volunteers coming, to *whip fifty Modocs*. All right; the more comes the *more scalps* the Modocs will take; that's about what it'll amount to."

Monday passes slowly away to join the unnumbered days of the past. No sound of war is heard. Quiet reigns until the sunset volley announces that the decomposed lava is covering up another one of the fruits of the demand for blood, and the cry for vengeance went up so loudly that even the Modocs in the Lava Beds heard it.

Tuesday morning. The ambulance is leaving Linkville, escorted by a mounted guard of citizens, destined to the Lost River battle-ground. Hope is leading the woman who is making this second journey to this historic place. The miles are long to her who has been so many days alternating between joy and sadness. Surely, she will not be disappointed this time.

"Old man," Dr. DeWitt says, "*you cannot go this morning.* I think it is unsafe, and it may cost your life."

"*I'm going; I'll take the risk. I cannot bear to disappoint my wife again.*"

A stretcher is brought to the side of the mattress whereon the speaker lay. Strong arms lift the mattress and man upon it. When he was carried on the stretcher, a few days since, he weighed one hundred and ninety-six pounds, less the blood he left on the rocks. Now he weighs one hundred and fifty pounds. "Lieut. Eagan's compliments, with a request for Mr. Meacham to *call on him before leaving.*"

The stretcher is carried into Lieut. Eagan's tent, and set beside the wounded officer's cot. The salutations commonly given are omitted, or half performed. Eagan lays his hand on Meacham's arm and says, "How do you make it, old man?"

"First-rate, I guess. I am going home. Are you recovering from your wound?"

"Very fast. Be about in a few days. Want to help finish up this job before I go home.

"Goodbye, Eagan."

"Goodbye, Meacham."

These men were old-time friends, and this parting was suggestive of sad thoughts. Both wounded. Will they ever meet again?

As the latter is being borne to the shore of the lake, a half cry is heard from Tobey. "I see him, Meacham, one time more. May be him die. I no see him 'nother time." A small white hull boat is waiting in the little bay. Lieut. M. C. Grier, A. A. Q. M., is managing the preparations for the departure. With thoughtful care every possible arrangement is made. Mattresses, awnings, oarsmen, buckets for bailing, and arms for defence are provided; and while many officers of the army gather around the boat, the wounded man is carried on the stretcher and carefully laid on a mattress. "Old Fields" is placed in command. Dr. Cabanis sits in the stern; the veteran beside the wounded. The departure is made with "God bless you!" from the officers. A small squad of armed men are starting up the lake shore to prevent the possibility of the Modocs capturing the party in the boat.

Steadily the soldier oarsmen pull along near the land, while the inveterate jokers, Dr. Cabanis and Capt. Ferree, beguile the time in story-telling and witticisms; some of them at the expense of the man on the mattress. "Say, Meacham, what will you give me not to tell *how much brandy* you drank the other day while you was on the stretcher at the council tent? It's all right for you to humbug the Good Templars by saying that you never drink; but you can't pull the wool over my eyes. No man ever drank a *canteen full* the *first drink*, as you did that day; it won't do, Meacham."

Suddenly a dark cloud moves up, and a strong wind comes off the shore. Landing is out of the question; to put to sea in a whitehall boat with eight men in it, and nearly to the edge, is hazardous. But there is no alternative. The prow cuts across the waves, the water leaps over the bow. Fields, Ferree, and two of the oarsmen, bail for life, now, while Cabanis holds her head to the sea.

"Steady, boys, or we'll swamp her," says Fields.—"Old man, *playing dead* won't save you this time; if we swamp her you had better *pray like old Joe Meek did*. Promise the Lord to be a good man if he will save us this one time more."—"Save the brandy, doctor, we may need it if we get out into the water," says Fields, and continues, "Steady, boys, steady! I'll be —— if she don't swamp. Look out, boys, what you're doin'."

The waiting woman in the ambulance catches sight of the boat as it rises on the crest of a wave and sinks again into the trough of the sea. Language is not competent to describe her emotions as she holds the glass on the threatening scene before her. One moment, hope,—another, *despair*, there, again, as the boat comes in sight, she thanks God; a moment more, and prayer moves her lips. "Can it be that he could live through all he has suffered only to be drowned?"

"Fear not, brave woman, the Hand that was let down out of the dark cloud that passed over the bloody scene when your husband was in a storm of bullets, will calm these waters. Your husband's work is not yet finished!"

"That was a close call, boys. *I tell you it was*; but we are all right now," says old Fields.

"They are there waiting for us," remarks Ferree. "Is Mrs. Meacham there? Can you see her?"

"Yes, yes, old man; she is there, standing in the wagon, looking at us with a glass. Lay still, old man, she is there. You'll be with her pretty soon."

"Thank God!" goes up from the mattress. "How far off are we now, Fields?"

"'Bout a mile. Be patient. Yes, old man, there's your wife, sure. She is standing on the ground now, looking through a glass. Be patient, old man; I'll introduce you to her. She wouldn't know who it was,—if I didn't tell her."

The "old man" was wondering if it is possible; shall I see her again? Am I dreaming? Is this a reality? Won't I wake and find it all a delusion? Oh, how slow this boat! "How far now?"

"Only a little piece; keep cool, you'll be there in a few minutes," quietly remarks Fields. Ferree, putting his finger on his lips, nods and smiles at his sister.

That smile has lifted despair once more from this woman's heart. But a moment since she had caught sight of the whitened face of her husband, so motionless and pale. She felt a pain in her heart, for she thought him dead. Now, her brother's smile has reassured her; but "Why does my husband lie so still?" The keel of the boat grinds on the gravelled margin of the river. Fields jumps ashore, with rope in hand. The woman stands beside the ambulance; she does not come to meet the party. Her joy is too great; she must not, dare not, now express her feeling.

"Well, Orpha, here's the old man; he is not very pretty, but he's worth a dozen dead Modocs yet." The "old man" is carried to the ambulance, and placed on a mattress, and his wife sits beside him, reunited after a separation of five months, during which time one of them had passed so close to the portals that death had left the marks of his icy fingers upon him; and the other through a terrible storm of grief and suspense. The driver mounts his box; the veteran beside

379

him. The escort mount their horses and range themselves on either side. The Modocs have not been heard of for several days and may be looking around their old home to waylay travellers. "Old Dad Fields" calls his crew; Dr. Cabanis cautions the driver about fast-driving, and also "the old man" about humbugging temperance people. The boat leaves the shore, the oars dip the waters. The driver cracks his whip, and one party is returning to the soldiers' camp; the other is crowding forward to Linkville, half expecting to see a blaze of rifles from the sage bush. Twenty-five miles yet tonight. Over all the smooth road they go at a gallop.

At midnight a light glimmers in the distance. It is Linkville. The moon is up, and shines now on *thirteen little mounds* by the roadside, beneath which sleep thirteen men who were killed by the Modocs last November. Uncle George's nurse is waiting at the hotel door to receive the old man Meacham once more. Thank God for big, noble-hearted men like Uncle George and his partner, Alex. Miller! "The old man" is sleeping, but wakes up with a start as he has done every hour since the eleventh of April. The glaring eyes of old Schonchin, the horrid yells, the whizzing bullets, all come fresh to the brain when left without direction of his will. He wakes with a sudden start to find himself in a comfortable room, a soft hand on his brow; a familiar voice of affection reaches his ear, and he falls away to sleep again, soothed by the low murmur of a woman's prayer.

CHAPTER 34

Betrayed

Ten o'clock, Wednesday morning, April 22nd, Meacham is being transported to Ferree's ranch at the south end of the Klamath Lake twelve miles from Linkville. We have been here before. It was on the 27th of December, 1869, when conducting Captain Jack's band on to Klamath Reservation. *Then* Captain Jack acknowledged the authority of the government and was endeavouring to be a man. *Now he is an outlaw.* After a stormy passage across Tule lake last night, Fields and Dr. Cabanis landed at Gilliam's camp. The surgeons are visiting the hospitals. Some of the patients are improving, but on one poor fellow we see the signet of the grim monster. The sunset gun tonight will not disturb him.

Lieut. Eagan is still improving. Fairchild is in camp, and assuring Gen. Gilliam that as "soon as the Oregon volunteers arrive, the Modocs will throw down their guns and come right out and surrender;" Riddle and wife in camp also, and assisting to care for the sick. "Muybridge," the celebrated landscape artist, of San Francisco, is here with his instruments, photographing the "Lava Beds," the council tent, and the scene of the assassination. "Bunker," of the *San Francisco Bulletin*, is on the ground reporting for his paper. "Bill Dad," with his long hair floating in the wind and a pipe in his mouth, slipshod and sloven, still hovers around to keep the readers of the *Record* posted.

Gen. Gilliam is consulting with his officers; they are indignant at the inaction manifested. Donald McKay and his Warm Springs Indians are scouting under the direction of army officers. Both Donald and his men are disgusted with the *red-tape way of fighting* Modocs.

Captain Jack and his people are quiet this morning. They are so closely hidden that even the sharp eyes of Donald McKay cannot discern their whereabouts. Captain Jack's men are anxious to be on the warpath; but the chief restrains them. They, in turn, reproach him with want of courage. He insists that they must act on the defensive. Bogus, Boston, Shacknasty Jim and Hooker Jim are rebellious and threaten to desert. Couriers are bearing despatches to Y-re-ka announcing that *"the Modocs cannot escape."*

A gun from the deck of the *Oriflamme* tells the people of San Francisco of her arrival with the remains of Gen. Canby. An immense concourse of citizens escort the hearse to the headquarters of the army.

The widow sits in a carriage, with unmoistened eyes, while the populace pay homage to the great character of her husband. The body of Dr. Thomas is quietly resting with the dead, while he in spirit is enjoying the glories of eternal life; his last sermon preached, his trials over.

The three children of Meacham are drying their tears, and thanking God that they are not fatherless, and for the love of a brotherhood that brings to their home sunshine in the faces and words of Secretary Chadwick and Col. T. H. Cann, who have called this morning.

Away up in Umatilla, a young man, who has been bowed down with grief over a second great bereavement, this morning reads to the little orphans that climb on his knees, and their widowed mother, the telegram signed by Capt. Ferree, announcing the recovery of his brother. His joy is unbounded. A great load has been lifted from his shoulders and his heart.

Midway between the oceans and near Solon, Iowa, in the sitting-room of an old homestead, a group is kneeling around a family altar. The bent form of a silver-haired man is surrounded by his aged second wife, his two living daughters; and perhaps, too, the invisible presence of *two* daughters and two sons that have gone before, and *their own* mother, are also there. His voice is tremulous while he leads in prayer and recounts that half of his family has gone and half remains; blesses God that the dark sorrow that threatened them has passed away, and invokes Heaven's blessings on the living loved ones.

Thursday morning, and we are in a cabin at Ferree's ranch. The proprietor enters, holding a letter in his hand. "See here, old man, I don't know but what you have jumped out of the frying-pan into the fire. How does this suit you?"

Klamath Agency, Thursday morning, April 23.
Friend Ferree:—Be on your guard. The Klamath Indians were in war council last night. . . . We have sent our women and chil-

dren to Fort Klamath for safety. . .

L. S. Dyer,
Agent Klamath.

"That don't look wholesome for us, old man; but you are all right, you can *play dead* on 'em again, and they *can't scalp you nohow*. We are pretty well stockaded and well armed. We can play them a merry string, if they do come. If we have to fight, why, you can't do much, that's so, except as old man Jones did at the camp-meeting last year. He said he couldn't *preach*, he couldn't pray *much*, but he could say *Amen* as well as anybody; and all through the meeting old Father Jones was shouting 'Amen!' '*A-men!*' until they stopped the old fellow. Didn't I never tell you about that? Well, brother Congar was preaching brimstone pretty lively, and Father Jones was shouting Amen occasionally. Brother Congar was saying to the congregation, 'If you don't repent and be baptized, you'll all go to hell, shure as you're born,'—'Amen! Thank God!—Amen!' shouts Father Jones.

"Brother Congar stops. 'Father Jones, you didn't understand what I was a-sayin,'—'Yes, I guess I did, Brother Congar, you told me if we come over here that, whenever you said anything powerful smart, I was to say 'Amen!' You said you couldn't preach *worth a cent* unless I did, and I've done it, so I have. If it aint satisfactory, I quit and go back home,'—'Amen!' shouted brother Congar, and went on with the preaching. Now all we will ask of you, 'old man,' is to say 'Amen,' but don't act the fool about it like Father Jones did, that's all. We'll tend to administering sulphur in broken doses, if they try to take us in. Don't think there's any danger though. Dyer isn't over the scare he got in the race with *Hooker Jim* yet."

Friday morning, April 24th.—The army at the Lava Beds is performing some masterly feats of inactivity that would have been a credit to Gen. McClellan on the peninsula. The wild fowls that fly over the Lava Beds look down on the army of a thousand recuperating after the big battle of last week. Col. Miller is in charge of Captain Jack's stronghold. The Warm Springs are divided up, and assigned to duty with the different squadrons of cavalry. Quartermaster Grier is having a coffin made and a grave prepared for a soldier that is dear to somebody somewhere, who is in blissful ignorance of his fate.

Ferree's Ranch, Sunday morning, April 25, '72.—A horseman arrives, and, taking Ferree aside, he informs him that a reliable friendly Indian had come in to Linkville and reported that it was understood that Meacham had killed Schonchin, and that some of Schonchin's friends had been to Yai-nax—an Indian station on Klamath Reservation—and learned that Meacham was at Ferree's. Further, that it was thought advisable that he be immediately removed to Linkville, lest the Modocs should make an attack on the ranch, seeking revenge for the death of Schonchin. The ambulance is ordered out, and the convalescent Peace Commissioner was again on wheels. Here we take leave of our inveterate joker—the Iowa veteran—Capt. Ferree leaving him to administer "*saltpetre* and *blue-pills*" to the red skins in the event of an attack.

Lava Beds, Gilliam's Camp, Sunday morning, April 26th.—Something is to be done today. The location of the Modocs has been ascertained through the efforts of the Warm Springs Indian scouts. A reconnoissance of the new stronghold is ordered. The detachment designated for this purpose consisted of sixty-six white men and fourteen Warm Springs Indians under McKay; the whole under command of Capt. E. Thomas of 4th Artillery. First Lieut. Thomas Wright—spoken of in this volume as Col. Wright of Twelfth Infantry, a son of the gallant old General Wright—is of the party, and in immediate command of his own and Lieut. Eagan's companies.

Lieut. Arthur Cranston and Lieut. Albion Howe of Fourth Artillery, Lieut. Harris also of the Fourth, Assistant Surgeon B. Semig, H. C. Tichnor as guide, Louis Webber, chief packer, and two assistants; the whole, exclusive of Warm Springs scouts, seventy-six. I may be pardoned for making more than mere mention of this expedition and the manner of its organization, because of its results; to understand it fairly, it should be stated that the parties named, except the Warm Springs scouts, were all of the army camp at the foot of the bluff, the head-quarters of Gen. Gilliam, commander of the army in the Modoc campaign.

The Warm Springs scouts were encamped near the old Modoc stronghold, and had been ordered to join the command of Capt. Thomas, while *en route*, or at the point of destination, which was a low butte or mound-like hill, on the further side of the Lava Beds, from the several camps. The outfit of this reconnoitring party, aside from the men and arms, consisted of a small train of pack mules. This train of packs was suggestive. Tacked on to the *apparahos*—pack-saddles—were subsistence and medical stores for the party, and also several *stretchers*. The object of the reconnoissance was to ascertain whether the field-pieces could be planted so as to command the new position of the *Modoc General, Jack Kientpoos*. Shells had done *wonderful execution* in the three days' battle, and, of course, were *the thing to fight* Modocs with; provided, however, that the fools of the Modoc camp were not all dead; for it is an undoubted fact that out of only two or three hundred tossed into the Modoc stronghold, *one of them had done more execution* than *all the bullets fired by the soldiers* in the three days.

Capt. Thomas was instructed, in "no event, to bring on an engagement." The point of destination was in full view of the signal station at Gilliam's camp, and not more than three miles distant. The command proceeded with skirmishes thrown out, and proper caution, until their arrival at the foot of the butte. The Warm Springs scouts had not joined the command. Capt. Thomas remarked that, since no Indians were to be seen, the command would take lunch. Lieut. Wright replied, that "*when you don't see Indians is just the time to be on the lookout for them*." The skirmish guards were called in, and the whole command, except Lieut. Cranston and twelve men, sat down to bivouac for an hour; Cranston, in the meantime, remarking that he "was going to raise some Indians," proceeded to explore the surroundings. In so doing he passed entirely out of sight of the main party. The foot of the butte is similar to other portions of the Lava Beds, thrown into irregular ledges, or cut into chasms and crevices.

Now Cranston has passed over a ledge, when suddenly from the rocks, that had been so quiet, a volley of rifles opens on both parties. It is not known whether Cranston and his men all fell on the first fire; it is, however, probable that *he* did not, as his remains were afterwards found several rods from where he was last seen by the survivors. Capt. Thomas's party were thrown into confusion. He ordered Lieut. Harris to take a position on the hill-side, and when the point was reached, Harris found that the enemy was *still above* him and commanding his new position. His men were falling around him, and he was compelled to fall back, leaving two dead and wounded.

In making the retreat, Lieut. Harris was mortally wounded. The scene that followed is without a precedent in Indian warfare. Every commissioned officer was killed, except Surgeon Semig, who was wounded; and of the sixty-six enlisted men but *twenty-three* reached headquarters.

Donald McKay and his scouts hurried to the scene, and arrived in time to prevent the annihilation of the entire party. That the soldiers were demoralized at the suddenness of the attack, there is no doubt. It

WARM-SPRING INDIAN PICKETS.

seems to have had an unusual combination of circumstances attending the carnage. That Capt. Thomas should have permitted himself to be surprised by an enemy, for whose destruction he was at that time seeking a location for the batteries, is strange, especially after the warning suggestions of Lieut. Wright, whose long experience on the frontier—of almost a life-time—should have given weight to his views. Strange, too, that *every officer* should have fallen so early in the attack, and that Donald McKay, with his Warm Springs, should have been thirty minutes behind time, and then, when coming to the rescue, should have been held off by the fire of the soldiers, who mistook him and his men for Modocs, and compelled them to remain out of range so long that the soldiers were nearly all killed or wounded before Donald was recognized.

Singular that this butchery should have continued three hours in sight of the signal station before reinforcements were ordered to the rescue. Indeed, it is stated on good authority, that soldiers who escaped made their way into camp one or two hours before Col. Green was ordered to go to the scene with his command. Singular, indeed, that fifty-three men were killed or wounded by twenty-four Modocs, on ground where the chances were even for once, and *not one of the twenty-four Modocs was wounded.*

What is still more unaccountable is, that the Modocs should have become *surfeited* with the butchery, and desisted from satiety, calling out in plain Boston English,—"*All you fellows that aint dead had better go home. We don't want to kill you all in one day.*"

This speech was heard by soldiers who still live, and for the truth of which abundant evidence can be had. We have it on Modoc authority that Scarface Charley made this speech, and repeated it several times, and that he insisted that the Modocs should desist, because his "heart was sick seeing so much blood, and so many men lying dead."

Follow the advancing wave of civilization from ocean to ocean, and no parallel can be found living, on printed page, or tradition's tongue. *Seventy-six well-armed men*, with equal chances for cover, shot down by a mere handful of red men, until in charity they *permitted twenty-three* to return to camp!

Can we understand how this was done? It seems incredible, and yet it is true. While we shudder, and in our rage vow vengeance on the perpetrators, we are compelled to admit that there was behind every Modoc gun *a man* who was far above his white brother in fighting qualities. Much as we are inclined to underrate the red man, we are forced to admit that *twenty-four men* leaving a stronghold, and going out among rocks that gave even chances against them, was an act of heroism that if performed by white men would have immortalized every name, and inscribed them among the bravest and most successful warriors that this country has produced. Performed by a band of red-handed Indians, it is scarcely worthy of mention. While we do most *emphatically* condemn all acts of treachery, no matter by whom committed, we are not insensible to emotions of admiration for acts of bravery, no matter by whom performed.

In speaking of this battle Gen. Jeff. C. Davis says:

> It proved to be one of the most disastrous affairs our army has had to record. Its effects were very visible upon the morale of the command, so much so that I deemed it imprudent to order the aggressive movements it was my desire and intention to make at once upon my arrival, in order to watch the movements of the Indians.

What, is it so, that with all the slaughter reported from time to time, Captain Jack still has men enough left to cause an army of *one thousand* to wait for recuperation and reinforcements before again attacking him?

This battle was fought on the 26th of April, ten days after the three days' battle. Curious that "the press," or that portion of it that was so loud in denunciation of the Peace Commissioners, did not find fault, and enter *"protest"* against the delay. The commission has been *"out of the way"* since the 11th inst., and three days' battle has been fought, and one day's slaughter withstood, and it has not cost much over half a hundred lives, that were required to satisfy the clamour for vengeance, and now why not raise your trumpet notes again, brave editors, and a proportionate howl for vengeance? You are safely seated behind your thrones, where no shot could reach you.

Why don't you howl with rage because a few *"cut-throats"* have murdered ten *per cent.* of an army of a thousand, *"who were hired to fight and die if need be"? You did not want peace except "through war."* You have done your part to secure the shedding of blood. Are you satisfied now when, through the failure of the Peace Commission, so many men have yielded up their lives? This short apostrophe is intended for those who *appropriate* it; not for the really brave editors who were fearless enough to defend "The humane policy of the President and Secretary Delano," in the face of a clamour that filled the country from the 1st of February to the 11th of April 1873.

BATTLE OF DRY LAKE.

Morning of the 10th, of May, 1873.—Fourteen days have passed, and Gen. Canby has been placed in his tomb, Indianapolis, Indiana. The widow, grief-stricken and heart-broken, is with her friends. Orderly Scott has been ordered to report at Louisville, Kentucky; Adjutant Anderson, to head-quarters, Department Columbia. The emblems of mourning are everywhere visible around the home of Dr. Thomas. Meacham is at his home in Salem, Oregon, recovering rapidly, and with a heart full of gratitude and kindly feelings to Dr. Calvin De-Witt, U. S. A., who brought him safely through the hospital at the Lava Beds.

The mother of Lieut. Harris is sitting beside her wounded son, in the hospital at Gillam's Camp. Gen. Jeff. C. Davis has assumed command of the expedition against the Modocs. Captain Jack and his people have left the Lava Beds. Dissensions are of every-day occurrence among them. Bogus and Hooker Jim, Shacknasty, and "Ellen's man" are contentious and quarrelsome.

Read the telegram of Jeff. C. Davis to Gen. Schofield, and we may know something of what has occurred:—

Headquarters in the Field, Tule Lake, Cal., May 8, 1873. I sent two friendly squaws into the Lava Beds day before yesterday; they returned yesterday, having found the bodies of Lieutenant Cranston and party, but no Indians. Last night I sent the Warm Springs Indians out. They find that the Modocs have gone in a southeasterly direction. This is also confirmed by the attack and capture of a train of four wagons and fifteen animals yesterday P.M. near Supply Camp, on east side of Tule lake. The Modocs in this party reported fifteen or twenty in number; escort to train about the same; escort whipped, with three wounded. No Indians known to have been killed. I will put the troops in search of the Indians with five days' rations.

Jeff. C. Davis,
Col. Twenty-Third Infantry, Com. Dept.

In his final report, Nov. 1st, 1853, he says:—

Hasbrouck's and Jackson's companies, with the Warm Springs Indians, all under command of the former, were immediately sent out in pursuit, and signs of Indians were found near Sorass

Lake, where the troops camped for the night. On the morning of the 10th the Indians attacked the troops at daylight; they were not fully prepared for it, but at once sprang to their arms, and returned the fire in gallant style. The Indians soon broke and retreated in the direction of the Lava Beds. They contested the ground with the troops hotly for some three miles.

The object of this hasty movement of the troops was to overhaul the Indians, if out of the Lava Beds, as reported, and prevent them from murdering settlers in their probable retreat to another locality. This object was obtained, and more. The troops have had, all things considered, a very square fight, and whipped the Modocs for the first time. But the whole band was again in the rocky stronghold. . . .

Gen. Davis does not state all the facts in the case. While it is generally admitted that Captain Jack *was whipped* this *time*, it is also true that Donald McKay and his Warm Springs Indian boys turn up *at the right time again* and assist in driving the Modocs three miles, recapturing the horses that were taken from the escort a few days since. Two Warm Springs scouts were killed in this fight, but their *names have never been reported*.

Captain Jack appears in this fight in Gen. Canby's uniform. One Modoc was certainly killed this morning, because *his body was captured*. There can be no mistake; several persons saw it with their naked eyes,—so they did, oh! This Modoc, whose name was George, "Ellen's man," was Captain Jack's assistant in the murder of Gen. Canby. His death was the signal for new quarrels among the Modocs, which ultimated in the division of the band, and made it possible for the *thousand* men to *whip* the *remainder*. The seceding Modocs, who are double-dyed traitors, were *Bogus Charley, Hooker Jim, Shacknasty Jim, Steamboat Frank*, and ten others, mostly Hot Creek Indians, and the same, except Hooker Jim, who were driven back to the Lava Beds after they had started under escort of Fairchild and Dorris to the Klamath Reservation, last December, ten days after the Lost River Battle, by the howl for blood that came up from every quarter.

At that time they had committed no crimes; had not been in battle or butchery. After joining Captain Jack they had espoused the cause of the murderers who killed the Lost River settlers. They were not indicted, and had less excuse than any other Modocs. Their home in "Hot Creek" was several miles from any scene of slaughter on either side. They had steadily opposed every peace measure offered, while Bogus had played his part so well that he was the favourite of the army officers, and had friends among the white citizens; he had instigated the assassination of the Peace Commissioners, laid the plans, and even slept in the camp of Gen. Canby, and ate his breakfast off the general's table, and to his friend Fairchild declared, even after Canby and Thomas had started for the Lava Beds, that there was no intention of killing the Peace Commissioners.

The cause of the quarrel between these men and Captain Jack was the fact that the few deaths that had occurred among the Modocs had been of those who did not belong to Jack's immediate family or band. They accused him of placing the outside Indians—Hot Creek and Cum-ba-twas warriors—in the front of the battles.

He replied that they had voted every time for war and against peace proposals. The quarrel increased, and after the defeat at Dry Lake, Captain Jack rebuked them for forcing the band into that fight against their will. The death of "Ellen's man" brought the crisis. We see the band who started into the war with fifty-three braves, after having accomplished more than any band of an equal or proportionate number of men, of any race or colour, in any age or country, quarrelling among themselves, now divided into two parties; one of whom, with *fourteen* men, *every one of whom had* voted for war, turning traitor to his chief, and offering themselves as scouts against him *without promise of amnesty* or other reward. Such perfidy stands unparalleled, and *alone*, as an act that has no precedent to compare it with. The succeeding events are clearly told in Gen. Davis' report.

"The chief could no longer keep his warriors up to the work required of them, lying on their arms night and day, and watching for an attack. These exactions were so great, and the conduct of the leader so tyrannical, that insubordination sprang up, which led to dissensions, and the final separation of the band into two parties; they left the Lava Beds bitter enemies. The troops soon discovered their departure, and were sent in pursuit. Their trails were found leading in a westerly direction. Hasbrouck's command of cavalry, after a hard march of some fifty miles, came upon the Cottonwood band, and had a sharp running fight of seven or eight miles. The Indians scattered, in order to avoid death or capture. The cavalry horses were completely exhausted in the chase, and night coming on he withdrew his troops a few miles' distance to Fairchild's ranch for food and forage.

391

Indians captured in this engagement expressed the belief that this band would like to give themselves up if opportunity were offered. When given this, through the medium of friendly Indians, they made an effort to obtain terms, but I at once refused to entertain anything of the kind; they could only be allowed safe-conduct through the camp to my headquarters when they arrived at the picket-line. They came in on the 22nd of May, and laid down their arms, accompanied by their old women and children, about seventy-five.

To learn the exact whereabouts of the Indians was now very important, and I determined to accept of the offered services of a Modoc captive; one who, up to the time of their separation, was known to be in the confidence of his chief, and could lead us to the hiding-place of the band. He was an unmitigated cut-throat, and for this reason I was loath to make any use of him that would compromise his well-earned claims to the halter. He desired eight others to accompany and support him, under the belief his chief would kill him on sight; but three others only were accepted, and these of the least guilty ones. They were promised no rewards for this service whatever. Believing the end justified the means, I sent them out, thoroughly armed for the service.

After nearly three days' hunting they came upon Jack's camp on Willow Creek, east of Wright Lake, fifteen miles from Applegate's ranch, to which I had gone, after separation from them at Tule lake, to await their return and the arrival of the cavalry.

The scouts reported a stormy interview with their angry chief. He denounced them in severe terms for leaving him; he intended to die with his gun in his hand; they were squaws, not men. He intended to jump Applegate's ranch that night (the 28th), etc.

On the return of these scouts, I immediately sent Capt. E. V. Sumner, *aide-de-camp*, back to the rendezvous, at Tule lake, with orders to push forward Capts. H. C. Hasbrouck's and James Jackson's commands to Applegate's ranch, with rations for three days in haversacks, and pack-mules with ten days' supply. All arrived and reported by nine o'clock a.m., the 29th, under command of Maj. John Green, their veteran cavalry leader since the commencement of the Modoc war, in excellent spirits. The impenetrable rocky region was behind them; the desperado and his band were ahead of them, in comparatively an open country.

After allowing the animals an hour's rest the pursuit was renewed, and about one o'clock p.m. Jack and band were "jumped" on Willow

Creek near its crossing with the old emigrant road. This stream forms the headwaters of Lost River. It was a complete surprise. The Indians fled in the direction of Langell valley. The pursuit from this time on, until the final captures, June 3rd, partook more of a chase after wild beasts than war; each detachment vying with each other as to which should be first in at the finish.

Lieut. Col. Frank Wheaton, Twenty-first Infantry, reported to me, in compliance with his orders, from Camp Warner, on the 22nd, at Fairchild's ranch. He was placed in command of the District of the Lakes, and the troops composing the Modoc expedition.

After making necessary disposition of the foot troops and captives at Fairchild's ranch, he came forward to Clear lake, and joined me at Applegate's with Perry's detachment of cavalry; these troops were at once sent to join the hunt. Most of the band had by this time been run down and captured; but the chief and a few of his most noted warriors were still running in every direction.

It fell to the lot of these troopers to catch Jack. When surrounded and captured he said his "legs had given out." Two or three other warriors gave themselves up with him.

Though called for, no reports have been received of these operations from the different detachment commanders; hence details cannot be given.

As soon as the captives were brought in, directions were given to concentrate the troops, and all captives, etc., at Boyle's camp on Tule Lake. There the Oregon volunteers, who had been called into the field by the governor, turned over a few captives they had taken over on their side of the line. It is proper to mention, in this connection, that these volunteers were not under my command. They confined their operations to protecting the citizens of their own State. Yet on several occasions they offered their services informally to report to me for duty in case I needed them. No emergency arose requiring me to call upon them.

By the 5th of June the whole band, with a few unimportant exceptions, had been captured, and was assembled in our camp on Tule Lake, when I received orders from the general of the army to hold them under guard until further instructions as to what disposition would be made of them. It was my intention to execute some eight or ten of the ringleaders of the band on the spot; these orders, however, relieved me of this stern duty,—a duty imposed upon me, as I believed, by the spirit of the orders issued for the guidance of the commander of the Modoc expedition, immediately after the murder of the Peace Commissioners; as well as by the requirements of the case, judging from my stand-point of view, a commander in the field. I was glad to be relieved from this grave responsibility. I only regretted not being better informed of the intentions of the authorities at Washington, in regard to these prisoners after capture. In accordance with instructions, as soon as the attorney-general's decision was received, I ordered a military commission for their trial, and with that view moved them to Fort Klamath, as a more suitable place to guard and try them. Six were tried and convicted of murder; four have been executed; two have had their sentences commuted to imprisonment for life by the President.

A few days after these executions took place at Fort Klamath, on the 3rd *ultimo*, the remainder of the band was started to their new homes in Wyoming territory; they are probably there by this time.

The number of officers killed in this expedition is eight; wounded, three; total, eleven. Enlisted men killed, thirty-nine; wounded, sixty-one; total, one hundred. Citizens killed, sixteen; wounded, one; total, seventeen. Warm Springs Indian scouts killed, two; wounded, two; total, four. Grand total, killed and wounded, one hundred and thirty-two. A large number of the killed were murdered after being wounded and falling into the hands of the Indians.

During the Modoc excitement many of the Indian tribes of Oregon, Idaho, and Washington territory showed a very discontented feeling, and strong sympathies with the hostile tribe. The settlers seemed much alarmed in some localities. To meet this state of affairs I thought it best to organize as large a force as practicable, and make a tour through the country *en route* to the proper stations of the troops. The march was made through Eastern Oregon and Washington territory; it was about six hundred miles. The cavalry was commanded by Maj. John Green, the foot-troops by Maj. E. C. Mason. The march was well conducted by these commanders, and well performed by the troops. I was gratified to see that with the capture of the Modoc band the excitement ceased. All the tribes throughout the department are now perfectly quiet"

CHAPTER 35

Modoc Butchers Outdone

For an account of the immediate circumstances attending the final surrender of the Modoc chieftain, I subjoin the following from the pen of Samuel A. Clarke, of Salem, Oregon, who was on the ground, and had abundant opportunity to learn the facts and incidents connected therewith. He was correspondent for the *New York Times*, from which paper of June 17, 1873, this graphic account of one of the most important events of 1873 is taken:—

> Boyle's Camp, Tule Lake, Modoc Country,
> Tuesday, June 3, 1873.
> The Modoc campaign is considered at an end. The eight or ten of the lately hostile band who have not been captured dare not commit any depredations, and efforts are being made to secure them without further contest. It remains to sum up the last few days, and present the facts of the capture of Captain Jack and his band, and I am now prepared to give a full and complete statement of the closing movements of the campaign.
> The beginning of the end was when Bogus Charley and his band of Cottonwoods and Hot Springs Indians, which means those who were brought up in the vicinity of Dorris' and Fairchild's ranches, which are on the creeks so called, came in and surrendered, about two weeks ago. The attempt made to surprise the train and camp at Sorass Lake, over three weeks ago, was a failure, and though the Indians inflicted some damage, they still suffered defeat, being driven off with the loss of most of their own horses and their loads. This discouraged them, and disaffection took place. The troops followed them up persistently; many who had supported the war with reluctance com-

plained of their fate; bickerings led to separation, and Captain Jack was left with scarce more than half his force to carry on the desperate struggle as he could.

I have described the manner of the campaign in former letters, and told how three squadrons of cavalry and artillery mounted, accompanied by detachments of Warm Springs Indians, have been put in the field. Then came the startling proposition from Bogus Charley, Steamboat Frank, Hooker Jim, and Shacknasty Jim, that they would join the troops and act as guides, and lead them to Captain Jack. They gave it as their opinion that Jack and his men would be either at Willow Creek, in the *cañon* east of Clear lake, or at Cayote Springs, south-east of there, or at a place ten miles from Boiling Springs, on Pitt River, hard to find and easily defended; or, fourth, at a *cañon* near Goose Lake, much further off, on the very verge of Modoc territory. They inclined to the opinion that he was at Willow Creek, because it is a strong natural position, and in a good neighbourhood for a supply of roots, herbs, game, and fish; and the result proved that their first surmise was correct.

General Davis and a squad of cavalry left with them eight days ago, and proceeded to Boyle's camp, east and south of the Lava Beds, whence the four renegades proceeded on their way Tuesday, a week ago, to hunt for the Modoc trail. They were entirely successful, and returned the next day with an interesting account of their expedition. Striking out south of Tule and Clear Lakes, they found and followed the trail to Willow Creek *cañon*, fifteen miles east of Applegate's ranch on Clear lake. As they approached they found Modoc pickets out four miles in advance; the pickets went with them to within about a quarter of a mile of the Modoc camp, and the Modoc warriors, twenty-four in all, came out and formed a line.

Jack ordered the spies to give up their guns; but they refused to do so, and retained their guns in their hands during all the talk that followed. The Modocs wanted to know what they came for, and who sent them; they recognized that they rode Fairchild's horses, and wanted to know how that came. The four Peace Commissioners gave for answer the precise facts that had occurred; stated the fact of the surrender of Fairchild's place, of all the Cottonwoods, and the way they had been treated, and advised them all to give up the war and do the same.

At that point Bogus Charley and his comrades wanted to have a free talk with their old friends, but Captain Jack forbade it. He said he would never surrender; he didn't want to be hung like a woman, without resistance, but was determined to die fighting with his gun in his hand, as a warrior should. He told them not to talk any more about surrender, to go back to the whites and stay with them if they wanted to, but never to come back to him again, for if they did he would certainly kill them. He wanted to receive no more messages and hear no more talk.

But Jack's power was evidently on the wane; he was no longer a dictator, with unlimited confidence and authority. Scarfaced Charley and some of the rest very deliberately declared they would talk; they told Bogus they were tired of fighting, and didn't want to be driven around all the time, afraid of their lives, and obliged to live like dogs. They complained bitterly of their hardships and poverty, and that they could not see their friends as of old time. Bogus told them that the soldiers and Warm Springs Indians were coming right after them; that Gen. Davis had ordered them to hunt the Modocs down, and they would do so. Then they wanted to know when the soldiers would come; the answer was, at any place and at any moment. Some of them bitterly asked if they four were intending to bring the soldiers there; but Bogus evaded that by saying the soldiers would come anyhow.

Despite Jack's command, and his refusal to talk, the four spies had a long, free conversation with their old associates, and the result was to greatly increase the demoralization existing in their ranks. The talk ended without any promise being made, and the four spies returned the next afternoon, and were intercepted at Applegate's ranch, on Clear Lake, Gen. Davis having in the mean time removed to that place. The spies were detained there, and word was sent to have the troops immediately move, and the next morning (Thursday), at daybreak, they were in motion, bound for the last Modoc stronghold.

The Modoc spies seem to have acted in the most perfect good faith. They, with Fairchild in company, went with the troops, which were under command of Col. Green, and led them directly to the place, warning them as they drew near that they might be ambushed, and advising every necessary precaution. The troops, in three squadrons, each with a detachment of Warm

Springs Indians, moved to within three miles of the Modoc camp about eleven o'clock Thursday morning, and were then divided. Hasbrouck and his command, guided by Hooker Jim, taking the north side of the *cañon*; Col. Green and the remaining force, with Steamboat Frank as their guide, going on the south side; Fairchild and the other two spies being in company. The Modocs seem not to have dreamed that the troops could reach them so soon, and had no strict watch out.

No one was seen until within less than a mile of Jack's centre, when the troops ran on four Modoc sentinels. Frank gave advice to surround the camp by sending men around and over a little mountain, and, this being done, a march was ordered and the Warm Springs got within three hundred yards of three Modocs, who hallooed not to shoot, and wanted to know what they were bringing so many men there for; they wanted to talk. Fairchild and the Modoc guides were sent for, and a talk had. Boston Charley came over to see Fairchild, and laid his gun down; the Warm Springs Indians all laid their guns down, and came over and shook hands with him in the most amicable manner. Movements were stopped to give opportunity for the surrender of the band, and a talk was progressing, when an unfortunate accident made the Modocs scatter in apprehension. Modoc Frank, one of the guides, happened to have his gun accidentally discharged by the hammer catching as he turned his horse.

The Modocs evidently supposed that Boston Charley, who had been sent to talk, had been shot, and that caused a stampede, and prevented the surrender that evening. Boston said they all wanted to quit the fight, and he was told to go back and tell them all to come in and lay down their arms. While he was attempting to do this, Hasbrouck's men closed up on the other side and made him prisoner, not knowing the errand he was engaged on. Donald McKay sent word over to let him go free, as the Indians wanted to come in; but Boston had been delayed an hour and a half, and he came back at dark with word that the Indians had all run away, except seven squaws, including Captain Jack's sister and some children, who were captured.

At early day, on Friday, the troops moved up each side of the *cañon*, skirmishing for three miles, when scouts came in and reported that the trail led off north, toward Gainox, and laid on high ground, where it was difficult to track. The troops followed it until noon, when they struck Langell's valley in twelve miles. The Modocs were in scattered bands. About one o'clock Fairchild, the Modoc guide, and some Warm Springs Indians struck a plain trail, and followed it for about six miles northeast, and discovered three bucks ahead, who called back and then ran away. They were headed off, and ran down into a *cañon* and hid. During the day thirteen bucks and a number of women got into the same *cañon*, and were discovered by the Warm Springs Indians.

A few shots were fired by Captain Jack himself, but it was thought that he didn't try to hit anybody, and only fired to keep them off. They called to each other, and Scarfaced Charley came down off the bluffs and talked with Dr. Cabanis. Scarface said Captain Jack was there, and they all wanted to give up. Dr. Cabanis went up and talked with Jack, who wanted to know what they would do with him. He said he would surrender the next morning; it was late then, and their women were tired. He said they were out of food and clothes; that their feet were sore, and that all hands would come in in the morning and give up their guns.

That happened on Friday evening, the 30th of May. The troops then went down to Lost River, five miles, and camped. Dr. Cabanis and Modoc Mose, one of the captured Indians, afterwards went back to the Modoc camp, and carried them a supply of bread, and stayed all night. They returned the next morning with the word that Jack had gone before their return, and left behind some pretext that he went to find a better camp on the bluff. But that morning Scarfaced Charley came in and laid his gun down, and did it with an exceeding sorrowfulness, as if he felt and understood all that he surrendered in doing so. Scarface is more respected than any other Indian, and there is much sympathy felt for him among the whites, as he went to war unwillingly, and has done his work in open warfare, and not been engaged in any savage and merely murderous work. He is considered the best and bravest of the entire Modoc band of braves.

Next came Sconchin John, the old villain, who drove the tribe to war more than almost any other man, and who is considered responsible for many of the inhuman acts committed. He laid down his repeating rifle, with a look of the most profound and savage mistrust and gloomy sorrow. His manner was untranslatable, for he had much to dread, and all his fears and half his hate of white men were visible in his sullen manner. The lesser lights then came up in turn, and went through the form of surrender. There were twelve or thirteen in all who gave up their guns, and all of them gave evidence of gloomy terror. They were shown a place to camp on Lost River, in Langell's valley, and the next morning were sent with Fairchild, Lieut. Taylor, of the artillery, and sixteen mounted light-battery men, to Gen. Davis' quarters, at Jesse Applegate's, on Clear Lake.

In the meantime Gen. Davis had sent Maj. Trimble, with his squadron, including some Warm Springs scouts, with young Applegate and Jesse Applegate's nephew, Charley Putnam, as guides, to intercept Captain Jack, in an easterly direction. They struck the trail ten miles north-east, and followed it five miles south, back to the Willow Creek *cañon*, below the first Modoc place of retreat or stronghold. Then part of the force crossed to the south side and skirmished up the *cañon*. The scouts soon discovered a Modoc man, named Humpy Joe, a hunchback, who is half-brother to Captain Jack. He asked for Fairchild, and Charley Putnam told him he was on the other side of the creek, and asked where Captain Jack was. Humpy said he was down the creek, hid in the rocks, and would surrender tomorrow. Charley said they had him surrounded, and he must surrender now. He and Maj. Trimble went with Humpy Joe, who called for Captain Jack to come forth, and the famous chief stepped boldly out on a shelf of rock, with his gun in his hand. He showed no timid fear or trepidation, and his conduct commanded the admiration of those who were his captors, for a certain sort of native dignity was apparent, and even in defeat, and at the moment of his surrender, the great Modoc chief was self-possessed, and acted a manly part. Major Trimble went up to him and demanded his gun. He also asked if Fairchild was there, and, learning that he was near, gave up his trusty Springfield rifle, a remodelled breech-loader.

Thus ended the Modoc war, for its soul and leading spirit of evil stood there a captive, with his arms given up, and powerless for future evil. There were two others with him, and four squaws and their children made up the list of prisoners taken at that time. Captain Jack had two wives, and one of them had a bright little girl of six years old.

Captain Jack then walked coolly up to where the Warm Springs Indians were, and they, with a commendable spirit of forbearance, and no doubt with an appreciation of the heroism that had so long and successfully resisted them, laid down their guns, and all around shook hands with the Modoc chief. They talked some with him; but he is not much of a talker either in English or Chinook, and his half brother, Humpy Joe, did most of the talking. Captain Jack then called up the squaws and children, and they were all mounted behind the Warm Springs Indians, and started for Gen. Davis' camp, ten miles distant. It would seem as if the Modoc chief must have felt crestfallen, and have been humiliated to find himself mounted in the same manner; but those who saw it say that, mounted behind a Warm Springs Indian, he still bore himself with dignity, and sat there like a Roman hero, as my informant graphically expressed it. He never moved a muscle or bore evidence in his look that he felt humiliated at his defeat. He bowed to Fairchild as he passed him, but made no other sign.

Captain Jack was looking rather shabby when discovered, and was allowed to don his better suit before being taken to headquarters; for it is not too much to say that the chieftain was in a very dirty guise; his favourite wife, too, was looking rather untidy; the wife improved her attire by the very simple process of donning a new delaine dress, not exactly made in the latest style, but she put it on over the plainer calico, which was too much soiled to be presentable. I do not learn that any portion of Gen. Canby's dress was found when he was taken.

He was taken, under guard, to the Modoc camp on Clear Lake, where the rest of the prisoners were placed. This happened Sunday afternoon, June 1. The Warm Springs Indians were jubilant over the fact that they had finally run the fox to earth. Captain Jack's stoical fortitude must have been sorely tried as he rode, a captive, behind one of them; for, as the procession moved, it assumed the appearance of a triumph, and he formed a part of and listened to the triumphal chant, the song of victory, that swelled along the line of his captors as they bore him away to await his fate. But they who saw it say he gave no token, by look, or word, or act, that would have shown that he was in-

SCHONCHIN AND JACK IN CHAINS

terested, or that he resented the rejoicing over his defeat. Again the song of triumph rose and swelled as they approached the camp on Clear Lake, and rode into the presence of Gen. Davis and Gen. Wheaton.

The commander-in-chief can certainly congratulate himself that his well-directed efforts have been successfully rewarded, and that the efficiency of the army has been maintained under extraordinary circumstances. The Warm Springs band came up to headquarters, ranged in a long line, with their strange, wild chant ringing on the air, and delivered their prisoners, who were ordered under guard with the rest.

A greater humiliation still awaited the discomfited Modoc chief. Gen. Davis ordered leg-shackles to be made for Captain Jack and Schonchin, and toward evening they were led out to be ironed. Great excitement pervaded the Modoc camp as these leaders were taken from it, and led away, they knew not where. They were taken to the blacksmith under a guard of six men, and for the first time Jack showed apprehension. As his guards passed where Fairchild stood, he stopped and asked his old friend where they were taking him. I allude to Fairchild here as his friend, because, while he has never excused their war conduct, he has been always, for many years, well acquainted with them, and has possessed great influence over them. They have learned to place great confidence in him, and have never found it misplaced.

So in all their movements of surrender they have wanted to have him present, and have done it at his advice when otherwise no one could have induced it. He gave Captain Jack no answer but to tell him kindly to go on with the men, and he went on unhesitatingly. He may have thought he was going to execution, but he went on nevertheless. At Fairchild's suggestion, Scarface Charley was sent for to act as interpreter. Scarface speaks good English, and he explained to Jack and Schonchin that they were to be shackled to prevent any attempt at escape. They made the most earnest protestations that they had surrendered in good faith; that they had no desire to get away, and under no circumstances should make such an attempt.

It was really an affecting scene to witness the grief with which they submitted to have the shackles placed on them; but when they saw that their fate was inexorable, they made no complaint or resistance, though they keenly felt the indignity, but stood silently to let the rivets tighten to bind them in chains they will never cease to wear, for it is probable they will be tried by a military tribunal, and that they will suffer the penalty of their crimes as soon as the form of a trial and securing of evidence to convict them can be gone through with.

The short and decisive campaign that has resulted in practically ending the Modoc war has been a rough one. The troops were fully equipped, and the horses all shod and in good order; but the ten days' scouting through a terribly rough country has left men and horses considerably worse for wear. It is now ordered that the troops under Col. Mason shall move to this place from Fairchild's ranch. This place will be headquarters until the whole matter is wound up. There are still eight or ten Modoc warriors out; but they will not undertake to make a fight, and only time and good management are required to lead them also in and bring the end.

Captain Jack maintains a gloomy reserve, and will not converse with his captors on any subject. It is safe to say that he will make no explanation or revelations, but die and make no sign. Bogus Charley says all the men expect to die, and await their fate without fear. Captain Jack himself has no fears of what the result may be, and waits it with stoical fortitude. He will die heroically, I have no doubt, for he has evidently less regard for life than the rest of the Modoc warriors.

This was substantially the end of the great Modoc War. The closing scenes were very exciting. Some of them are worthy of mention as having an immediate bearing on the question of Peace and War as between the *superior race* and the original *inheritors* of the soil.

Time, June 8th, 1873. Location of the scene, Rocky Point, near the mouth of Lost River.—Characters in this tragedy: first, *Civilized Christianized white men*; second, Helpless Modoc captives.

James Fairchild—a brother to John A., the "gray-eyed man"—left Fairchild's ranch on the morning of the 8th, with a four-mule team, and a wagon filled with Modoc *men, women*, and *children*, who had surrendered and were entirely unarmed.

Very little things sometimes turn the current of great events. When leaving Fairchild's ranch on the morning in question, the entire party consisted of seventeen Modoc captives and the brothers Fairchild.

Among the captives were Bogus Charley and Shacknasty Jim. Before arriving at Lost River the party divided, James Fairchild driving the team and going by a longer route, on account of crossing Lost River at a wagon ford; John A. Fairchild, together with Shacknasty Jim and Bogus on horseback, going by a shorter route. The latter party, not mistrusting danger, continued on their way, not waiting for the team to come up to the junction of the roads.

While James was crossing the river he encountered a body of Oregon volunteers, under command of Capt. Hizer. The soldiers gather around the wagon and question Fairchild. He explains to them that the Indians under his care are Modoc captives, all of them Hot Creeks; that he is taking them to the headquarters of General Davis on "the peninsula," to deliver them up; that none of them have been accused of being parties to any murder or assassination. This seems to satisfy the soldiers, and they retire to their camp. Fairchild passes on towards his point of destination. After proceeding a few miles he sees two men going towards the road, with the evident intention of intercepting him.

The Indians in the wagon also make the discovery, and beg Fairchild to turn back, to save them. He feels that trouble is brewing. He looks in vain for his brother John and the Indians that are with him. The two men have halted by the roadside. Fairchild comes up to them. They order him to halt, and accompany the order with a heavy *"persuader"* in close proximity to his head. The music made by *"spring steel"* under the manipulation of a man's hand has but two notes,—a short tick and a long click; and then the *"persuader"* is ready for business. Fairchild, hearing this kind of music, *halts*, and to the "Get down, you old white headed ——," etc., demands, "By whose authority?"

"By mine. I am going to kill them Ingens, and you too, —— you!"

One of the civilized white men cuts the mules clear of the wagon. Fairchild leaps to the ground, still clinging to the lines. The unarmed captive women beg for mercy. They plead with Fairchild to save them. They raise imploring hands and cry, "Don't kill! don't kill!"

The four Indian warriors are mute; they know resistance is in vain. Fairchild entreats the white men to desist. The muzzle of a needle-gun is within six inches of his ear. A shot, and *"Little John's"* brains are scattered over the women and children. Another, and *"Te-hee Jack"* is floundering among them. Another, and *"Poney's"* blood is spurting over his wife and children. Still another shot, and *"Mooch"* falls among

405

shrieking squaws. One more, and *"Little John's" wife* is shot through the shoulder. The five are writhing in the death agony together, and the blood of the victims is streaming through the floor of the wagon and dropping in puddles on the ground beneath. A dust is seen rising from the road. The civilized white murderers decamp in haste, leaving Fairchild holding to his mules, while the uninjured Modoc women are extricating themselves from the dead bodies which had fallen on them. The blood of this civilized butchery still drops from the wagon.

Sergeant Murphy and ten men, Battery A, of the Fourth Artillery, came upon the scene. The civilized *butchers* are fleeing. *No effort* is made to arrest them. Sergeant Murphy had not been ordered to arrest them, and, of course, he had no right to arrest *white men without an order.* Capt. Hizer's company of Oregon volunteers is within a few miles also. The country is open; the murderers have but a few miles the start. But Capt. Hizer has *no orders* to arrest white men either. He is not there for that purpose; and no one can censure him because he did not catch the civilized *white murderers.* Those men were seen by Fairchild before and behind the wagon. They were on the watch for *John Fairchild.* Had he and his party been with the team when the attack was made, the census return of that county would not have been quite so large as it is, especially on the Anglo-Saxon civilized list. *Pity he was not there,* for *he* is "a dead shot." The commiseration is due, however, to the community that furnished homes for the fellows who covered themselves with glory by performing this heroic feat. True, they dare not boast of it *now,* but they will by and by. The grand jury of Jackson County *did not* find bills of indictment against them. No effort has ever been made to discover the names of the perpetrators of this deed.

True, there were those that claimed to know who the persons were, but they never tell; neither would they tell, if placed on the witness stand. I would not have my reader suppose that the *people* of Oregon approved of the crime—very far from it. They condemned it in unstinted terms, and with one voice shouted, "Shame! Shame!" So they would have done if the tables had been turned. No State in the Union has a more orderly, law-abiding, peace-loving people than Oregon; none that venerates justice more highly. True, they have sometimes been lenient to the white men of bad character. But no more so than other States where votes are necessary to elevate men to power. Like all other peoples they are tender-hearted towards *all* men who control votes.

As a people they are brave, without a doubt; but among them occasionally may be found specimens of *cut-throats*, who kill unarmed people; and once in a great while, just as in the States of Massachusetts or New York, an editor who does the same kind of work with his pen, when he thinks he can do it with impunity. But the respectable editors, there as elsewhere, have learned sense enough to let a man alone when he is down, until they are sure he can't get up before they kick him. With great unanimity those of Oregon and the whole Pacific coast denounce the killing of helpless, unarmed Indians, as they did the killing of settlers after the Battle of Lost River, Nov., 1873,—only not quite strong enough to *justify* the authorities in making *any* efforts to bring the offenders to *justice*.

The scene changes to a military camp on the "peninsula," at the south end of Tule Lake. A hundred white tents declare this to be the headquarters of the army that whipped the Modocs,—that is to say, the army to whom the Modoc traitors turned over their chief. One hundred and twenty poor, miserable specimens of humanity are under guard. There is great rejoicing over the victory. The Modoc women and, children are contented, in one sense at least,—they are well fed, and have rest. The government teams have just arrived from the mountains with timber. The quartermaster's forces are engaged in rough carpenter work. Curious-looking building they are erecting,— looks something like a country butcher's windlass; but it is not that, for there is more of it. The Modoc captains wonder what it is for. They are unsophisticated in civilized modes of appeasing outraged justice.

Scarface Charley asks a soldier, "What for that thing they make?"

"To hang Modocs," laconically replies Mr. Soldier.

A wail of savage woe breaks the air. The medicine-man says he "can beat that thing."

"May be so, Curly-haired Doctor; but unless some other medicine interferes you can have a chance to try it, and, in the meantime, to reflect on the inhuman manner in which you and Hooker Jim killed Brotherton, Boddy, and others."

Not far from the gallows we see an artist with his camera, and going toward it two men under guard. One of them shouted "*Kautux-ie*" at the council tent the 11th of April. The other one was his right-hand man then. They are inseparable now, as they have been for years past; but this time a few links of log chain, as well as bloody crimes, unite them. They cast anxious eyes towards the gibbet. They meet John Fairchild, and ask him where they are going. "Go on; it's all right," he replies. They take places before the camera. The artist lifts his velvet cloth, and Captain Jack looks squarely at what appears to him to be "a big gun." To his surprise the big gun is again covered up, and he is then assured that it will not shoot. It was under such circumstances that the likeness of Captain Jack, which accompanies this book, was taken. Old Schonchin is next made a target. They smile when led away, for they had *expected to die*.

Some satisfaction to know that the old fellow endured suspense, even if it was temporary. They are taken back to the guard-house, and, as they march under escort, they see Hooker Jim, Bogus Charley, Shacknasty Jim, and Steamboat Frank, walking around unfettered, unguarded, well clothed, well fed, and well armed. The chief restrains himself until he arrives at the tent used for guard-house, then he gives way to a tempest of passion, and, in true Indian style, declaims against the injustice of what he sees and feels. True, Captain Jack, you are wearing chains that *properly belong to those villains*. True, you pleaded with all your eloquence for peace, and against the assassination of the commissioners. True, they voted against you. True, that Bogus first proposed to kill Gen. Canby, and that he was also first to betray you to your enemies. It is also true, that for this double treachery he is now being rewarded with liberty. True enough, that that cut-throat, Hooker Jim, is the very man that put the woman's hat on your head, and taunted you to madness, until at last you yielded against your judgment, and consented to commit the first great crime of your life. True, that he was the man who followed your trail, day and night, like a hound, until he pointed the steps of the soldier to your last hiding-place.

It is for this *damnable act of treachery to you that he is now being rewarded*. True, also, that Steamboat Frank and Shacknasty Jim fired as many shots at the commissioners as you did; and that they, too, voted against you while you were trying to make peace, and that they boast yet of the number of soldiers they have scalped. They joined Bogus and Hooker Jim in hunting you, carrying each a breech-loading rifle, and wearing the uniform of the United States soldiers, and were with your captors when your star fell. It is for these last-named heroic acts that they are now enjoying the boon for which you have pleaded all your life, from the same government that pets them, and almost fawns upon them as heroes. Certainly your cup is full of grief, while theirs runs over with joy. If you were a *white man* we would commiserate you, and half the people of America would join in an effort to save

408

you; but you are an Indian.

No Indian can be an "honourable man;" the idea is an insult to every *Irishman*, and *German*, and the whole Caucasian race besides. You are simply unfortunate in being born in the land of the free, and the home of the brave, with a *red skin*. Better you had been born across the sea, and with any brogue in the world on your tongue. If you had only been blessed with a *white skin*, and had that kind of manhood that would have permitted you to wear some rich man's collar, fawn upon and toady to the whims and caprices of your masters, at the sacrifice of your own self-respect, and that of the rest of mankind, then your crimes might have been condoned. But you are *now* a *citizen*, and you may enjoy a citizen's privilege of being punished for other men's crimes as well as your own.

Gen. Davis has invited the settlers of the Lost River country, to "come in and identify the murderers, and stolen property captured from the Modocs." Among others who availed themselves of the opportunity are two women. We have seen them before,—the first time on the afternoon of November 29th, 1872, when the red-handed villain who walks around camp, the *lion* of the day,—Hooker Jim,—came to them with his hands red with the heart's blood of their husbands; and again, when a funeral procession was slowly wending its way to the Linkville cemetery. We recognize them as Mrs. Boddy and her widowed daughter, Mrs. Schiere. Gen. Davis, with the heart of a true man and soldier, receives them kindly, and assigns them to a tent; patiently listens to the sad story of their great bereavement.

He calls on them again, taking with him Hooker Jim and Steamboat Frank. Mrs. Boddy identifies Hooker as one of the Indians concerned in the massacre. When questioned as to the robbery of Mrs. Boddy's house, Hooker Jim replies, "I took the short purse, and *Long Jim* took the other purse."

The women are much excited and are crying. They lose self-control. Mrs. Boddy, drawing from her pocket a knife, dashes at Hooker Jim's breast. Mrs. Schiere, with a pistol, attempts to shoot Steamboat Frank. The man who would not brook insult from Gen. Nelson could not see these women commit a crime; with almost superhuman strength and agility he disarms both women before they have sipped from the cup of revenge, accidentally receiving a slight wound in one hand from the knife held by Mrs. Boddy. The savages stand unmoved and make no effort to escape. Let the reader be charitable in judgment on the actions of these widows. They were alone in the world. Their protectors had fallen by the hands that have since been washed by a *just government*, when in its dire necessity it accepted their services as traitors.

Ah! double traitors to a reluctant, but brave leader. If the men who killed the unarmed captives in Fairchild's wagon yesterday can go unpunished after killing Indians that had not harmed them, let charity extend to these broken-hearted women, nor censure them for a thirst for vengeance, especially when they realized that justice has hid her face to these inhuman monsters who are reeking with blood, and guilty of the most damnable treachery. True, these are women; but the accident of sex does not change nature, and never should be urged against those whose wrongs drive them to desperation.

The quartermaster's carpenters are putting on the finishing strokes to the extempore instrument of a *partial* justice to be administered without even the farce of an *ex-parte* trial. The *trap* is being arranged. Eight or ten ropes are hanging from the beam. Gen. Davis is preparing a statement of the crimes committed by the captives, and, also, his verdict, which he proposes to read to these unfortunate subjugated warriors before he tests the strength of the dangling ropes with live-weight. A courier arrives from Y-re-ka. A message is received by Gen. Davis, ordering him to hold the prisoners subject to further instructions from Washington.

The work on the hanging-machine is suspended. The Modoc medicine-man assures his friends that he has won another victory. Gen. Davis is thoroughly chagrined. *The disappointment is great.* Modocs enjoy it; white man does not. The brittle thread of life has been strengthened for the temporary benefit of a few vagabonds whose existence is no blessing to mankind outside of the Modoc blood; whose death would cause a shout of joy over the civilized world. Not because it would bring back the dead, and cause them to stand in the flesh again, but because justice has been done to a man with a red skin who dared claim the privileges of manhood; and, being denied, had resisted a good government in which he had no part.

The scaffold stands untried. Nobody knows whether it is a good hanging-machine or not. The camp is broken up; the war is over, and the Modocs are *now* where they can be *controlled*. They are *en route* to Fort Klamath, under guard.

The chieftain who, a few weeks since, was over-matching the best military talent of the army, holding in abeyance twenty times the number of his own forces, and defying a great, strong government, is now a captive and in chains, compelled to travel under an *escort* over the route he had passed so often in the freedom of days gone by. Familiar objects greet his eyes as he raises them from the last look he will ever take of the scene of his glory as a chief, and his shame as an outlaw.

The first place of historical interest on this last ride of the Modoc chief, as he leaves "the peninsula," is where Ben Wright killed nearly as many warriors as Captain Jack has had in his command. If the angel of justice accompanies this conquering army with its dejected captives, she will cover her face while it passes the spot where Modoc blood watered the ground *under* a *flag* of *truce*, when she remembers that the perpetrators of that deed were *honoured* for the act. A few miles only, and the vacant cabin of Miller stands, accusing Hooker Jim, the murderer of its builder and owner, for *his* treachery, and upbraiding a government that excuses *his* crimes, because he can be made useful in hunting to the death the chief who led where such a villain forced him to go.

Justice uncovers her face when this army reaches Bloody Point, for now she remembers that it was here that a train of emigrants were waylaid and cruelly butchered, and she shows no favours to the descendants of those who committed the crime. Again the eye of the conquered chief glances over the scene of his childhood, and, too, over the field where he fought his first battle. Since it would be pronounced sickly "sentimentalism" to ponder over the scenes of such a man's boyhood, and lest we should offend some *white man's* fine sense of pride that he is a white-skinned man, though he may have little else of which to boast, we pass along up Lost River, with simply recalling the fact, that this man's—Captain Jack's—early home abounds with *traditional literature* connecting his name with the savage scenes of the past, and linking it with the tragic events of 1872-3.

The conquering army marches over the spot where the white murderers "wiped out" some of the wrongs committed against *our race*. The tramping of soldiers' feet and the iron-shod hoofs of mule teams erases the dark spots in the road, where the tokens of requited vengeance were painted by the dropping blood from Fairchild's wagon on the eighth of June.

This blood does not cry out loud enough to catch the ear of the sober, honest-faced angel who has been perching on the victorious emblem of the free white American! No danger that those dark spots will ever trouble that great angel. The blood that made them was drawn from the wrong kind of veins for that.

While the army marches over the trail, effacing footprints of the fleeing avenger, a shot is heard. Quick almost as lightning flash every soldier's hand grasps his arms. The thought that the Modocs are attempting escape passes through every mind. "Halt!"—rings out the cavalry bugle. Above one of the government wagons a small puff of smoke is rising in the clear morning air, while behind and beneath it the spattered drops of blood announce that another tragedy is now being enacted. The wagon halts, and now through the floor the current runs in streams, while its splashing on the ground makes melody for ears of white men and soothes the dying senses of *Curly-haired Jack*.

A few words of explanation, and the fact is established that *treason* is still among the Modocs, treason to the Government of the United States, committed *by Curly-haired Jack*, in blowing out his own brains, thus cheating the aforesaid government out of the great privilege of hanging him for the murder of Lieut. Sherwood, under a flag of truce, on the eleventh of April, 1873.

Poor, conscience-stricken self-murderer! his body is mixed up again with his native land, and his friends are denied the privilege of mourning for him.

The army, with its costly coterie of famous guests, encamps at Modoc camp on Klamath Reservation. This is the spot where Captain Jack and his people settled in the beginning of 1870. How changed the fortunes of this man! *Then* his limbs were free, though his manhood was half disputed; *now* every motion of his limbs rings clanking music in his ear, constantly reminding him that his manhood has obtained recognition at the cost of life and liberty. *Then* he was restless under the restraints of civilization, because it denied to him a clear pathway to its privileges and blessings; *now* he is passive under the persuasive influence of a power that compels his crushed spirit to submission. *Then* he was the hero chief of Hooker Jim and Bogus Charley, and the daring band that surrounded him; *now* he is the humbled, crestfallen victim of *their treachery*.

He sits behind a guard whose glittering bayonets warn him of the folly of resistance. *His betrayers*, unfettered, ramble over the ground where the Modocs had begun their new home in 1870.

He steals glances at the great witness tree where Modocs and Klamaths buried the hatchet. *They* dance with joy over the results of its resurrection.

The army moves out of camp. The captive chief catches sight of four rough-hewn timbers on the left of the road. These were once designed for use in making that chief a house, wherein he was to have passed through probation, looking toward his ultimate attainment of citizenship under the "Humane Policy of the Government."

The Klamaths, who badgered him into the abandonment of his new home in 1870, have not disturbed the house-logs referred to. They never will; and the probabilities are that these logs will remain as monuments, marking the sepulchre of broken hopes.

A few miles before reaching Fort Klamath the cavalcade passes through *Council Grove*,—the place where Klamaths and Modocs made the treaty of 1864 with the United States.

At last the shattered companies of soldiers reach the fort, having left behind them many of their comrades; but having in charge a distinguished prisoner and his companions. When they pass inside the irregular circle of forest trees that shut Fort Klamath up into a grand amphitheatre, the outside is shut out from four, at least, of the prisoners forever.

CHAPTER 36

Weakness Under Chains

A portion of Fort Klamath, mentioned in the last chapter, is used as a court-room. A long, narrow table stands near the middle of the hall. At the farther end of the table sits Lieut.-Col. Elliott, First Cavalry, to his right Capt. Hasbrouck of Fourth Artillery, and Capt. Robert Pollock, Twenty-first Infantry. On the left, Capt. John Mendenhall, Fourth Artillery, and Second Lieut. George Kingsbury, Twelfth Infantry. These officers are all in new uniform, and make a fine impression of power. At the other end of the table sits Maj. H. P. Curtis, Judge Advocate; also in uniform near him, Dr. E. S. Belden, short-hand reporter. To the right of Col. Elliott, sitting on a bench, four men,—*red men,*—Captain Jack, Schonchin, Black Jim, Boston Charley. All these men were at the council tent the 11th of April last, and participated in the murder of Gen. Canby and Dr. Thomas. Lying on the floor are two others. They are the men who jumped from the ambush with the rifles, and uttered the yell that sent terror to the hearts of the Peace Commissioners,—Barncho and Slolux. Behind Maj. Curtis two other familiar faces,—Frank Riddle and his wife Tobey.

At a side table reporters are sitting. At either end of the room a file of soldiers stand with muskets ornamented with polished bayonets. These are necessary, for the prisoners might kill somebody if the bayonets were not there! Hooker Jim, Bogus, Shacknasty and Steamboat are standing near the door, unfettered and unguarded. *They* don't need guarding, for they are soldiers now themselves, and have done more to close up the Modoc war than the "Army of a Thousand."

They are real live heroes, and they feel it too. If anything is yet wanting to make this scene complete, it is fully made up by the soldiers, who now enjoy a safe look into the eyes of the Modoc chief.

Fort Klamath, July 5, 1873.

The commission met at 10 a.m., pursuant to adjournment.
Present, all of the members of the commission, the judge-advocate, and prisoners.

The proceedings of the last meeting were read and approved.
The judge-advocate then read before the commission the order convening the commission, which is interpreted to the prisoners.

The commission then proceeded to the trial of the prisoners: Captain Jack, Schonchin, Black Jim, Boston Charley, Barncho (alias One-Eyed Jim), and Slolux, Modoc Indian captives, who being called before the commission, and having heard the order convening it read, it being interpreted to them, were severally asked if they had any objection to any member present named in the order, to which they severally replied in the negative.

The members of the commission were then duly sworn by the judge-advocate; and the judge-advocate was then duly sworn by the president of the commission; all of which oaths were administered and interpreted in the presence of the prisoners.

The judge-advocate asked the authority of the commission to employ T. F. Riddle and wife as interpreters, at $10 a day, which authority was given by the commission.

T. F. Riddle and wife (Tobey) were then duly sworn to the faithful performance of their duty in the interpretation of the evidence and proceedings as required, in the presence of the prisoners, which oath was interpreted to the prisoners.

The judge-advocate then presented to the commission E. S. Belden, the official short-hand reporter, who was then duly sworn to the faithful performance of his duty; which oath was duly interpreted to the prisoners.

The prisoners were then severally asked by the judge-advocate if they desired to introduce counsel; to which they severally replied in the negative; and that they had been unable to procure any.

The prisoners were then severally duly arraigned on the following charges and specifications:—

Charges and specifications preferred against certain Modoc Indians commonly known and called as Captain Jack, Schonchin, Boston Charley,

Black Jim, Barncho, alias One-Eyed Jim, and Slolux, alias Cok.

Charge First.—"Murder in violation of the laws of war." The specification in substance was the murder of Gen. E. R. S. Canby and Dr. Eleazer Thomas.

Charge Second.—"Assault with intent to kill in violation of the laws of war." Specification second. "Assault on the Commissioners. Attempt to kill A. B. Meacham and L. S. Dyer."

"All this at or near the Lava Beds, so-called, situated near Tule Lake, in the State of California, on or about the 11th day of April, 1873."

To which the prisoners severally pleaded as follows:—

To first specification, first charge, "Not guilty."
To second specification, first charge, "Not guilty."
To first charge, "Not guilty."
To first specification, second charge, "Not guilty."
To second specification, second charge, "Not guilty."
To second charge, "Not guilty."

T. F. Riddle, a citizen and witness for the prosecution, being duly sworn by the judge-advocate, testified as follows:—

Question by judge-advocate. Were you present at the meeting of the commissioners and General Canby, referred to in the charges and specifications just read? *Answer.* Yes, sir.
Q. On what day was it?
A. On the 11th of April, I believe, as near as I can recollect.
Q. Were the prisoners at the bar present on that occasion?
A. Yes, sir.
Q. You identify them all?
A. Yes, sir; I identify all but Barncho and Slolux. I saw them, but I didn't know them. They were some seventy-five yards behind me; they came up behind.
Q. Is Captain Jack the principal man in this Modoc band?
A. Yes, sir.
Q. What is he? Describe him.
A. He is a chief amongst them. He has been a chief since 1861, I believe.
Q. What position did Schonchin hold among the Modocs?
A. I never knew him to be anything more than just a common man amongst them until, within the last year, he has been

classed as Captain Jack's sub-chief, I believe; they call it a "Sergeant."

Q. Black Jim?

A. He has been classed as one of his watch-men, they call them.

Q. Boston Charley?

A. He is nothing more than a high private.

Q. Barncho?

A. He is not anything.

Q. Slolux?

A. He is not anything.

Q. Are they all Modocs?

A. Yes, sir; they are classed as Modocs; one of them is a Rock Indian, or a "Cumbatwas."

Q. Were they all present at this meeting of the 11th of April?

A. Yes, sir. Barncho and Slolux was not in the council. They came up after the firing commenced.

Q. What connection did you have with the peace commissioners from the beginning?

A. I was employed by General Gilliam to interpret, and then from that I was turned over to the peace commissioners; but I acted as interpreter all of the time—all through their councils.

Q. Did you ever receive any information which led you to suppose it was a dangerous matter for the commissioners to interview these men?

A. Yes, sir; the first that I learned was when I stopped at Fairchild's. They agreed to meet the wagons out between Little Klamath and the Lava Beds, and all of them come in, women and children. They said Captain Jack sent word that if General Canby would send his wagons out there, they would send his women and children in.

Q. Where you present at the killing of General Canby and Mr. Meacham?

A. Yes, sir.

Q. Had you received any information which led you to think that it was dangerous?

A. Yes, sir, I had; my woman, some week or ten days before that, went to carry a message into Jack's cave, where he was living, and there was an Indian called William—he followed her after she started for home back to camp, he followed her out.

Q. How do you know this?

A. My woman told me.

Q. In consequence of some information which you received, what did you then do? Did you speak to the commissioners about it?

A. Yes, sir; I told them I received information, and then I went to the peace commissioners and told them it was dangerous to go out there anymore to meet them, and I advised them not to go. While I was at Fairchild's, this Hooker Jim, he came there and took me out one side and told me, "If you ever come with them peace commissioners to meet us anymore, and I come to you and push you to one side, you stand back one side and we won't hurt you, but will murder them."

Q. Do I understand you to say you then cautioned the commissioners?

A. Yes; I told them of it.

Q. What did you say?

A. I told them what Hooker Jim told me; and I said I didn't think it was of any use to try to make peace with those Indians without going to the Lava Beds, right where they were. I said, "I think the best way, if you want to make peace with them, is to give them a good licking, and then make peace."

Q. Did you tell them what Hooker Jim said?

A. Yes, sir; and at another time, I believe it was the very next time after we were out in the Lava Beds—after General Gillam had moved over to the Lava Beds—we met, and Hooker Jim came to me after we got to the ground where we were to hold our council, and he took hold of me and said, "You come out here and sit down;" and he pushed me as he said he would. I said "No."

Q. When was this?

A. I don't remember the date; it was sometime in April.

Q. The first or second meeting?

A. The first meeting after Hooker Jim had told me this at Fairchild's.

Q. Where they the same, or other commissioners?

A. It was General Canby, Dr. Thomas, and Mr. Dyer, and Judge Roseborough, I believe, was along, if I am not mistaken; I won't be positive. Hooker Jim came to me and caught hold of me, and pushed me one side, and said, "You stand out here." I told him "No;" that I had to go and talk and interpret for them; and my woman here spoke up to him to behave himself, and not go doing anything while he was there; and he then said, "Well, go and sit down."

Q. Did you visit the Lava Beds before the massacre; and, if so, did you go alone, or with some ne else?

A. The first time I went in there was with Squire Steele. Fairchild—

Q. (Interrupting.) Very shortly before the massacre, did you?

A. Well, I was in there.

Q. State why you went in there.

A. I was in there on the 10th of April. My woman and me went in there, and took a written message in there from the peace commissioners. I read and interpreted it to Captain Jack, and I told him then, after I interpreted it to him, that I gave him a notice; and I told him to bring it the next day when he met the commissioners, to bring it with him. He threw it on the ground, and he said he was no white man; he could not read, and had no use for it. He would meet the commissioners close to his camp—about a mile beyond what they called the peace tent. He said he would meet them there and nowhere else.

Q. A mile nearer the Lava Beds than the peace tent?

A. Yes; he said that was all he had to say then. I could hear them talking around, and sort of making light of the peace commissioners—as much as to say they didn't care for them.

Q. What was the tenor of this message you say you read?

A. It was a statement that they wished to hold a council with them at the peace tent next day, to have a permanent settlement of the difficulties between the whites and the Indians; they wanted to make peace, and move them off to some warm climate, where they could live like white people.

Q. Where is that note you carried?

A. It is lost.

Q. Did Captain Jack say anything about arms in reference to the meeting?

A. Yes, sir; he said he would meet them five men without arms, and he would do the same—he would not take any arms with him.

Q. That he would meet them at the place he fixed—one mile nearer the Lava Beds?

A. Yes, sir; one mile nearer the Lava Beds.

Q. Five men, without arms, and he would also go without arms?

A. Yes, sir.

The Court. Five, including himself?

A. Yes, sir.

The Judge-Advocate. What did he say about the proposition to move him from the Lava Beds?

A. He said he knew no other country only this, and he did not want to leave it.

Q. Did he say anything about a desire for peace?

A. Yes; he said if they would move the soldiers all away he would make peace then, and live right there were he was, and would not pester anybody else; he would live peaceably there.

Q. Was Captain Jack alone in this interview when you talked with him?

A. No, sir; these other men were around with him, sitting down.

Q. These prisoners here now?

A. Some of them.

Q. Did he do all or only a part of the talking?

A. That evening he done all of the talking—that is, he was the only one that had anything to say to me in regard to this affair.

Q. Did you see anything there which led you to suppose that they intended hostilities?

A. Yes, sir; I did; I saw that they had forted up all around the cave.

Q. Did they seem to be well provisioned?

A. They had just been killing several beeves there that day.

Q. Which of these men were there at the time?

A. Boston was there—most all of these that are here.

Q. Can't you name them?

A. There was Boston, Black Jim was there, and Barncho; I don't remember whether Schonchin was there or not at the time the conversation was going on.

Q. Did you go back to the commissioners then?

A. Yes, sir.

Q. State the facts about it. State what followed after your return to the commissioners.

A. I went back and went to the peace commissioners' tent with

Jack's message that he would meet them five unarmed, and he would do the same; he would have five men with himself, and go without arms; and I told him they were forted all around there, and they had been killing beef; and I thought it was useless to try to make peace any longer; and if Captain Jack would not agree to meet at the tent, and if I were in their places I would not meet them anymore.

Q. What did the commissioners then reply or decide upon? What decision did they come to?

A. They held a council between themselves. I was not at their council.

Q. Was your visit the day before the assassination?

A. Yes, sir; I seen General Canby that evening,; and I told him I had a proposition to make to him. He was out, and I met him, and he wanted to know what it was; I told him that if I was in his place, if I calculated on meeting them Indians, I would send twenty-five or thirty men near the place where I expected to hold the council, to secrete themselves in the rocks there; that they would stand a good show to catch them, if they undertook to do anything that was wrong. General Canby said that that would be too much of an insult to Captain Jack; that if they knew of that, they might do an injury then; he would not do that.

Q. Did you hear him say that?

A. Yes.

Q. Did they determine to meet him, or not?

A. they sent to me the next morning, then, to come down to the peace commissioners' tent.

Q. Was Captain Jack informed that they would not go to that place one mile nearer?

A. Yes, sir; Bogus Charley went in that evening before the murder, right ahead of me, into General Gilliam's camp and stayed all night. He staid at my camp, and the next morning the peace commissioners decided that they would not meet Captain Jack in this place where he wanted to meet them, and sent a message out by Bogus and Boston for them to meet him at the peace commissioners' tent, the peace tent, and they were gone about an hour; and they came back again and said that Captain Jack was there with five men.

Q. (Interrupting). You heard it?

A. Yes.

Q. Jack was to meet them where; he was where?

A. He was at the peace tent.

Q. Captain Jack sent back a message then by Bogus and Boston that he would meet them at the peace tent with five men?

A. Yes, sir; but they were not armed, and he wanted the peace commissioners to go without arms.

Q. He sent that message, and you heard it?

A. Yes, sir.

Q. What advice, if any, did you then give the commissioners?

A. My woman and me went down to the peace commissioners' tent and she went to Mr. Meacham; I saw her myself at the first, though I told him not to meet them.

Q. Were you at the peace commissioners' tent when you gave them this advice?

A. The peace commissioners' tent in General Gillam's camp.

Q. Not the large peace tent?

A. No; the peace commissioners' tent. He wanted to know why, and I told him they intended to murder them, and that they might do it that day if everything was not right; and my woman went and took hold of Mr. Meacham and told him not to go; and held on to him and cried. She said, "Meacham, don't you go!"—I heard her say so myself—"for they might kill you today; they may kill all of you today;" and Dr. Thomas, he came up and told me that I ought to put my trust in God; that God Almighty would not let any such body of men be hurt that was on as good a mission as that. I told him at the time that he might trust in God, but that I didn't trust any in them Indians.

Q. Did any of the other commissioners make any reply?

A. Mr. Meacham said that he knew there was danger, and he believed me, every word I said, and he believed the woman, and so did Mr. Dyer. He said he believed it; and he said that he felt like he was going to his grave. I went then to General Canby and asked him if General Gillam was going out. He said "No." I said, I want your commissioners then to go to General Gillam's tent with me.

Q. Did they go?

A. Yes, sir.

Q. Was Tobey with you?

A. No, sir; she was not with me then; she was standing holding her horse.

Q. State what occurred at General Gillam's tent.

A. We went down with Mr. Meacham, General Canby, Dyer, and Dr. Thomas; and General Canby walked down with us. General Canby did not go into the tent, but the other three went in; that is, Mr. Dyer, Meacham, and Dr. Thomas, and I went in to General Gillam and said, "General Gillam, these men are going out to hold council with them Indians today, and I don't believe it is safe. If there is anything happens to them, I don't want no blame laid on me hereafter, because I don't think it is safe for them to go, and after it is over I don't want nothing laid on me;" said I, "I am not much afraid of the Indians; but I will go before I will be called a coward."

Q. State what followed then.

A. Well, before we got through the conversation there, General Gillam—that is, there was not anything more—and then General Gillam gave a big laugh, and said if the Indians done anything, that he would take care of them, and we started out, and General Canby and Dr. Thomas started on ahead; Mr. Meacham went to Tobey (my wife), and asked her if she thought the Indians would kill him; and she said, "I have told you all I can tell you;" she said, "they may kill you today, and they may not."

Q. You heard this?

A. Yes. "But," says she, "don't go." By that time General Canby and Dr. Thomas had got some one hundred yards ahead of us. Bogus Charley walked out; General Canby and Dr. Thomas walked; Mr. Dyer, Meacham, and Tobey rode horseback.

The Court. Did Bogus Charley walk out with you?

A. Yes; him and me were behind.

The Judge-Advocate. Where was Boston Charley at this time?

A. If I am not mistaken he was with General Canby and Dr. Thomas.

Q. Did you finally arrive at the peace tent?

A. Yes, sir.

Q. And whom did you find there?

A. I found Captain Jack, Schonchin, and Black Jim (Ellen's man), who is dead, they say, Shacknasty Jim, and Hooker Jim.

Q. Were there any others?

A. There were no others; well, Boston, he went out with us, and

Bogus Charley; there were eight of them there.

Q. Eight were there in the party?

A. In the council; yes, sir.

Q. What took place after you met these Modocs whom you have named—between the commissioners and they?

A. Well, we all sat down around a little fire we had there, built, I suppose, some twenty or thirty feet from the peace tent. There was some sage brush thrown on, and we were all sitting around the little fire, and General Canby gave them all a cigar apiece, and they all sat around there and smoked a few minutes, and then they went to talking; General Canby, I think, though I won't be certain, made the first speech, and told them that he had been dealing with the Indians for some thirty years, and he had come there to make peace with them and to talk good; and that whatever he promised to give them that he would see that they got; and if they would come and go out with him, that he would take them to a good country, and fix them up so that they could live like white people.

Q. Did you interpret all of this to the Indians?

A. Yes, sir.

Q. So that they understood it?

A. Yes, my wife and me did together.

Q. Was that the summary of General Canby's speech?

A. That was about the substance of his speech, with the exception that he told them that he had a couple of Indian names; that he had taken Indians on to a reservation once before, and that they all liked him, and had given him a name.

Q. General Canby said that?

A. Yes. They sat and laughed about it. I disremember the name now.

Q. Do you know who spoke next?

A. Mr. Meacham spoke next, and he told them he had come there to make peace with them; that their Great Father from Washington had sent him there to make peace, and wipe out all of the blood that had been shed, and to take them to some country where they could have good homes, and be provided with blankets, food, and the like.

Q. That was Mr. Meacham's speech?

A. Yes, sir. Dr. Thomas, he said a few words. He said the Great Father had sent him there to make peace with them, and to wipe out all the blood that had been shed, and not to have any more trouble, to move them out of this country here,—that is, the place where they were stopping.

Q. Mr. Riddle, do you know whether the Lava Beds are in the State of California?

A. Yes, sir; they are. I could not be certain what the extent of them is; it may be possible a small portion of them is in Oregon.

Q. How near the Lava Beds was General Gillam's camp?

A. It was about two miles and a half from Jack's stronghold.

Q. How near to the Lava Beds was the peace tent?

A. It was right on the edge of it.

Q. What distance from General Gillam's quarters or camp?

A. I think about three-quarters of a mile.

Q. Did any Modocs reply to those speeches?

A. Captain Jack spoke.

Q. What did he say; can you remember?

A. Yes, I can recollect some of what he said. He said that he didn't want to leave this country here; that he knew no other country than this; that he didn't want to leave here; and that he had given up Lost River; and he asked for Cottonwood and Willow Creek; that is over near Fairchild's.

Q. Is Cottonwood Creek the same as Hot Creek?

A. They are two different creeks.

Q. What did he mean by giving up Lost River?

A. He said there was where the fight had taken place; and that he didn't want to have anything more to do there. He said he thought that was what the fight took place about,—that country there; he said the whites wanted it.

Q. What fight do you refer to?

A. The first fight, where Major Jackson went down to bring them down on the Reservation; that was in November, 1872.

Q. Did Captain Jack demand Willow Creek and Cottonwood Creek?

A. Yes, sir.

Q. That is, the land around this place?

A. Yes.

Q. To live on?

A. Yes, sir; he wanted a reservation there.

Q. Then what was said, or what occurred?

425

A. Mr. Meacham, then he made another speech, and he told Captain Jack: "Jack, let us talk like men, and not like children," and he sort of hit him on the knee or shoulder,—probably hit him on the shoulder once or twice, or tapped him,—he said, "Let us talk like men, and not talk like children." He said, "You are a man that has common sense; isn't there any other place that will do you except Willow Creek and Cottonwood?" And Mr. Meacham was speaking rather loud, and Schonchin told him to hush,—told him in Indian to hush; that he could talk a straight talk; to let him talk. Just as Schonchin said that, Captain Jack rose up and stepped back, sort of in behind Dyer's horse. I was interpreting for Schonchin, and I was not noticing Jack. He stepped a few steps out to one side, and I seen him put his hand in his bosom like—

Q. (Interrupting). Did you perceive, as soon as you got there, that these men were armed?

A. Yes, sir; I did; I could see some of them were.

Q. In what way did you observe that?

A. I saw these sticking out of their clothes.

Q. You saw what?

A. They were revolvers.

Q. Did Captain Jack at this interview represent this band?

A. Yes, sir.

Q. And these other men listened and appeared to concur?

A. Yes, sir.

Q. Were they there as representatives of the band?

A. Yes, sir; I suppose they were.

Q. You say Captain Jack got up and went to the rear, and you saw him put his hand to his breast?

A. Yes, sir.

Q. What then occurred?

A. Well, he stepped back and came right up in front of General Canby, and said, in Indian, "All ready, boys,"—and the cap bursted, and before you could crack your finger he fired.

Q. You say this?

A. Yes, sir; and after the cap bursted, before you could crack your finger, he fired and struck General Canby under the eye, and the ball came out here (showing). I jumped and ran then, and never stopped to look back any more. I saw General Canby fall over, and I expected he was killed, and I jumped and ran

426

with all my might. I never looked back but once, and when I looked back Mr. Meacham was down, and my woman was down, and there was an Indian standing over Mr. Meacham and another Indian standing over her, and some two or three coming up to Mr. Meacham. Mr. Meacham was sort of lying down this way (showing), and had one of his hands sticking out.

Q. You saw General Canby fall, you say?

A. Yes, sir.

Q. Did he continue to lie where he fell?

A. He was not when they found him; he was about thirty or forty yards from there. I did not see him get up.

Q. As soon as Captain Jack fired, what then occurred?

A. They commenced firing all around. I could not tell who was firing except Schonchin here; I see him firing at Mr. Meacham, but the others were kind of up in behind me, and they were firing, and I did not turn around to look to see who it was. I thought it was warm times there.

Q. Did any other Indians come up?

A. Just as the fire commenced I see two Indians coming up packing their guns.

Q. What do you mean by "packing their guns"?

A. They were carrying them along in their arms.

Q. How many had each man?

A. I could not tell; it looked like they had some two or three apiece.

Q. Can you identify those men?

A. No, sir, I cannot. I did not stop to look to see who they were. I saw they were Indians.

★★★★★★

Tobey, Riddle's wife, an Indian, called for the prosecution, being duly sworn, testified as follows:—

Question by the judge-advocate. What is your name; is your name Tobey?

Answer. Yes.

Q. Did you think they were going to kill the commissioners that day?

A. Yes.

Q. What made you think so?

A. There was one of the other Indians told me so.

Q. Who told you?

A. William; Whim they call him.

Q. How long before the meeting did Whim tell you this?

A. It was about eight or ten days.

Q. What did Whim say to you?

A. He said not to come back any more; to tell the peace commissioners not to meet the Indians any more in council; that they were going to kill them.

Q. Did you tell General Canby not to go?

A. I did not tell General Canby; I told Meacham and Thomas.

Q. Did Mr. Meacham believe you?

A. Yes, sir.

Q. Did he say he believed you?

A. Yes.

Q. What was done with the bodies of Dr. Thomas and General Canby?

A. They stripped their clothes off of them.

Q. Did you see them do that?

A. I seen them strip Dr. Thomas. I saw Steamboat Frank taking Dr. Thomas's coat. Steamboat Frank was one of the three that came up.

★★★★★★

The above questions and answers were duly interpreted to the prisoners by the sworn interpreter, Riddle.

The judge-advocate then asked the prisoners severally if they desired to cross-examine the witness, to which they replied in the negative.

The commission had no question to put to the witness.

L. S. Dyer, a citizen, called for the prosecution, being duly sworn, testified as follows:—

Question by the judge-advocate. State your name.

Answer. L. S. Dyer.

Q. What is your business?

A. I am a United States Indian agent.

Q. Of the Klamath agency?

A. Yes, sir.

Q. Does that include the Modocs?

A. Yes, sir.

Q. Do you recognize the prisoners at the bar?

A. I do.

Q. Do you recognize them all?
A. No, sir.
Q. Who is that one with a handkerchief on his head?
A. Captain Jack.
Q. Who is the next one this way?
A. John Schonchin.
Q. And this one?
A. Boston,—sometimes called Boston Charley.

★★★★★★

Question by commission. I understood you to say that Superintendent Meacham got these Modocs back into the Reservation once or twice before.
Answer. Once before.
Question by commission. With or without the assistance of the military?
Answer. He had a few soldiers. I only know this from the records and reports in the office.

★★★★★★

The foregoing questions and answers were all duly interpreted to the prisoners.
The commission thereupon adjourned to meet on Monday next, the 7th instant, at 10 a.m.

H. P. Curtis,
Judge-Advocate of Commission.

THIRD DAY

Fort Klamath, Oregon, July 7, 1873.
The commission met pursuant to adjournment.
Present, all the members named in the order, the judge-advocate, and the prisoners.
The proceedings of the previous session were read and approved.
Shacknasty Jim, a Modoc Indian, a witness for the prosecution, having been first cautioned by the judge-advocate of the punishment of false swearing, was then duly sworn.

Question by judge-advocate. What is your name?
Answer. Shacknasty Jim.
Q. Do you remember when General Canby was killed?
A. Yes; I know.
Q. Were you present.

429

A. Yes.

Q. Did you know that he and the commissioners were to be killed.

A. Yes.

Q. How did you know it?

A. They had a talk at night.

Q. When was this talk? How long before?

A. The evening before.

Q. Who talked?

A. Most of the Indians; the two chiefs were talking.

Q. What two chiefs?

A. Captain Jack and Schonchin.

Q. Did you hear them state they meant to kill them?

A. I didn't hear them say they were going to kill them.

Q. What did you hear them say?

A. I heard them talking about killing the commissioners: that is all I heard them say. I didn't hear them say who was going to do it.

Q. How long before the meeting of the peace commissioners when General Canby was killed was this talk?

A. I almost forget. I don't want to lie. I have forgotten how many days it was.

Q. What Indians were at that meeting of April 11, when General Canby was shot?

A. Schonchin, Captain Jack, Ellen's man (dead). I was there, and Black Jim, Boston, Bogus Charley, and Hooker Jim; there were eight.

★★★★★★

Steamboat Frank, a Modoc witness for the prosecution, duly sworn, being duly warned against the consequences of perjury.

Question by judge-advocate. What is your name?

Answer. I am called Steamboat Frank.

Q. Were you present at the death of General Canby?

A. Yes.

Q. How did you get there?

A. I was about as far as from here to the end of the stables (about four hundred yards) when the firing commenced.

Q. Whom, if any one, were you with there?

A. With Scarfaced Charley.

430

★★★★★★

The judge-advocate now called Bogus Charley as witness for the prosecution, who, being first cautioned of the consequence of perjury, was duly sworn, and testified as follows:—

Question by judge-advocate. What is your name as commonly called?
Answer. Bogus Charley.
Q. Were you present at the death of General Canby?
A. Yes.

★★★★★★

Hooker Jim, a Modoc, a witness for the prosecution, being first cautioned of the consequence and punishment for perjury, was duly sworn.

Question. What is your English name?
Answer. Hooker Jim.
Q. Were you present when General Canby was killed?
A. I was.
Q. Did you know he and the commissioners were to be killed?
A. I did.
Q. Are you now a friend to Captain Jack?
A. I have been a friend of Captain Jack, but I don't know what he got mad at me for.
Q. Have you ever had a quarrel or fight with him?
A. I had a quarrel and a little fight with him over to Dry lake, beyond the Lava Beds.
Q. How did you know the commissioners were going to be killed?
A. Captain Jack and Schonchin—I heard them talking about it.
Q. Where were they when you heard them?
A. At Captain Jack's house.
Question by commission. What part were you detailed to take in it, if any, in murdering the commissioners?
Answer. I ran Dyer and shot at him.
Question by commission. Had you agreed to kill one of the parties before the attack?
Answer. I said I would kill one if I could.
Question by judge-advocate. Do you like Captain Jack now, or

431

dislike him?

Answer. I don't like him very well now.

★★★★★★

The judge-advocate then asked each one of the prisoners, successively, if they desired to cross-examine this witness, to which they replied in the negative.

★★★★★★

William (Whim), Modoc, called for the prosecution, and warned against the penalties of perjury, was then duly sworn.

Question by judge-advocate. What is your name?
Answer. Whim, or William.
Q. Were you with the Modoc Indians in the Lava Beds?
A. Yes.
Q. Do you remember when General Canby was killed?
A. Yes, I know that they went to kill him.
Q. Did you know that he was going to be killed?
A. Yes, I knew they were going to kill him.
Q. Did you know they were going to kill the peace commissioners?
A. Yes.
Q. Were you at the killing?
A. No, I didn't go.
Q. How did you know they were going to kill them?
A. I heard Jack and Schonchin talking about it.
Q. Anyone else?
A. That is all that I heard say anything about it.
Q. How long was this before the killing?
A. I don't know exactly, but it was eight or ten days.
Q. Did you speak to anybody about it?
A. Yes, I told about it.
Q. Whom?
A. I told this woman here (Tobey, Riddle's wife).
Q. What did you tell her?
A. I told her to tell the peace commissioners not to come; that I did not want to see them killed.

★★★★★★

The judge-advocate then asked each prisoner, successively, if he desired to cross-examine this witness; each answered in the negative. The commission desired to put no questions.

★★★★★★

While this man is under examination as a witness, A. B. Meacham enters the court-room. The prisoners fix their eyes on him steadfastly. Until now, they had doubted his recovery from his wounds.

★★★★★★

A. B. Meacham, citizen, called for the prosecution, duly sworn, testified as follows:—

Question by judge-advocate. What is your name?
Answer. Alfred B. Meacham.
Q. Are you a citizen of the United States?
A. I am.
Q. What position did you hold in connection with the late war with the Modocs?
A. I was appointed by Secretary Delano as chairman of the peace commissioners, as special commissioner.

★★★★★★

Q. Now state what occurred next.
A. During the day the propositions that were made by Boston, that is, on Thursday, were accepted by Dr. Thomas, and an agreement made to meet Captain Jack and five men, unarmed, at eleven o'clock; all parties unarmed at the council tent on Friday. I knew this agreement to have been made by Dr. Thomas on the evening of the 10th, on my return from Boyle's camp that night.
Q. Did he give it to you officially?
A. Yes, sir. When I started on the visit to Boyle's camp, I said to Dr. Thomas, if occasion requires my presence in any business, you will act in my capacity as chairman of the commission; and as acting chairman of the commission he made this arrangement, and so notified me.
Q. After that what followed?
A. I protested against the meeting, but subsequently yielded to the opinions of Gen. Canby and Dr. Thomas,—Mr. Dyer and I dissenting.
Question by judge-advocate. Had General Canby a weapon on his person?
A. Not that I am aware of.
Q. Had Dr. Thomas?
A. I know he had not.

433

★★★★★★

All the foregoing testimony was faithfully interpreted to the prisoners.

The commission thereupon adjourned to meet at 9:30 a.m. tomorrow morning.

The prisoners are remanded to the guard-house. They hesitate, and cast anxious glances at Meacham, who is exchanging salutations with members of the court.

Meacham. "Have the prisoners no counsel?"

Col. Elliott. "They have been unable to obtain counsel. The usual question was asked them."

Meacham. "It seems to me that, for the honour and credit of the government, and in order to have all the facts drawn out and placed on record, counsel should have been appointed."

Col. Elliott. "We are perfectly willing, and would much prefer it; but there is no lawyer here, and we must go on without."

Meacham. "I have no disposition to shield the prisoners from justice, but I do feel that to close up all gaps, and make the record complete, all the circumstances should be drawn out. Not because anything could be shown that would justify their crimes, but because it is in harmony with right and justice. Sooner than have it said that this was an ex-parte trial, I will appear myself as their counsel,—by your consent."

Col. Elliott. "Certainly, we are willing, and if you say you will appear as their counsel, we will have your name entered on the record. Certainly, Mr. Meacham, we are more than willing. It would be an act of magnanimity on your part that is without a precedent. You know all the facts in the case and could, perhaps, bring them out better than any other man."

Meacham. "I know that my motives would be misconstrued, and I would have another storm of indignation hurled upon me by the press. But that does not intimidate me; I only fear my strength is not sufficient. It is only sixty days since the assassination, and I have been twice across the continent, and am still feeble. However, I will report to you tomorrow morning my conclusion."

Judge-Advocate Curtis remarks: "Mr. Meacham, I wish you would take hold of this matter; there is no one else that can; and, if you will, every courtesy shall be extended to you. The witnesses can be recalled for cross-examination. I should be better satisfied to have counsel for the prisoners."

Meacham. "I will take the matter under consideration, and in the mean time I desire an interview with the prisoners."

Col. Elliott. "Most certainly, you can apply to the 'officer of the day,' and he will make the necessary order."

In the guard house, Captain Jack and Schonchin are brought out of the cell chained together. There is music in the clanking chain that sounds harsh, severe, and causes a shudder, which soon gives way before the logic of justice. These chieftains come with slow steps and eyes fixed intently on Meacham. They extend their hands in token of friendly greeting. Meacham refuses. "No, Captain Jack, your hands are red with Canby's blood; I cannot, now."

Schonchin still holds out the same hand that fired repeated shots at Meacham.

"No, Schonchin, *your* hands are red with my own blood; I cannot, I will not now."

Schonchin places his hand on Meacham's arm. He presses it slightly. An Indian grunt signals his satisfaction with his experiment. He *now realises that Meacham is not dead. Up to this time he had been doubtful.* He looks with intense interest at the wounds he had made in his effort to kill this man on the 11th April.

Captain Jack is anxious to talk about the trial. Meacham inquires, "Why did you not have a lawyer to talk for you?"

Captain Jack. "I don't know any lawyer that understands this affair. They could not do me any good. Everybody is against me; even the Modocs are turned against me. I have but few friends. I am alone."

Meacham. "You can talk yourself. The newspapers say, '*Captain Jack has spoken for his race*; now let extermination be the cry.'"

Captain Jack. "I know that the white man has many voices: they tell one side, they do not tell the other."

Meacham. "Tell the other yourself. You can talk: Now speak for your race. Tell the other side. The world will read it."

Fixing his eye on Meacham very intently Captain Jack says, "Meacham, you talk for me."

Meacham. "No, Captain Jack, I cannot talk for you. I saw you kill Gen. Canby. I cannot talk for you. If you had shot me as Schonchin did, I would talk for you. As it is, I cannot. I will not talk for Schonchin; he was all the time in favour of blood."

Schonchin breaks in, saying, "I did not kill you; you did not die. I am an old man. I was excited; I did not shoot good. The others all laughed at me; I quit. You shoot me. You don't want me to die. You did not die."

Captain Jack. "I cannot talk with the chains on my legs. My heart is not strong, when the chain is on my leg. You can talk strong. You talk for me."

An hour later, Meacham is in consultation with his friends, including the army surgeon. There is but one opinion in regard to Meacham offering himself as counsel for the Modocs, aside from the newspaper comments,—that it will cost him his life. He is not sufficiently recovered from the shots of the Lava Bed tragedy of April 11th.

JULY EIGHTH. FOURTH DAY.

Military commission assembled. Meacham has decided that he *cannot* appear as *counsel* for the prisoners.

They are brought into court; proceedings of previous meeting read and approved; H. R. Anderson, lieutenant of Fourth Artillery, duly sworn. His evidence was chiefly in regard to Gen. Canby's relation to the government, the army, and the Peace Commission.

Q. What command did he hold, if any, at the time of his death?

A. Department of the Columbia, and adviser to the peace commission under telegraphic instructions from Washington.

Q. Was he in receipt of instructions from any source as to the course he was to pursue; was he receiving instructions from time to time?

A. Yes, sir, from time to time; from commanding General of the Army.

Q. What kind of instructions were they? Did you see them yourself?

A. Yes, sir; generally telegraphic instructions.

Q. What was their nature? What did they instruct him to do?

A. Instructed him to use his utmost endeavours to bring about a peaceable termination of the trouble.

Q. What relation did he hold with the peace commissioners?

A. He was ordered down there to consult and advise with them.

Q. Do you remember General Canby's initials?

A. E. R. S.; his full name was Edward Richard Sprigg Canby.

★★★★★★

Henry C. Mceldery, assistant surgeon U. S. A., called for prosecution, sworn, testified as follows:—

Question by judge-advocate. Did you see the body of General Canby after his decease?

A. I did, sir; I saw it on the field on the evening of April 11.

Q. Was the general dead?

A. Yes, sir; he was quite dead when I saw him.

Q. Please describe his condition.

A. He had been entirely stripped of every article of clothing. He had three wounds on his body, and several abrasions of the face. One of the wounds, apparently made by a ball, was about at the inner *canthus* of the left eye. The edges of that wound were depressed, as if the ball had entered there. . .

Q. Did you see Dr. Thomas's body?

A. I saw him. There were several gunshot wounds in his body, but I don't recollect sufficient to swear to the exact locality of each one.

Q. What was your opinion as to the cause of his death?

A. I think the gunshot wound over his heart was the cause of his death.

Q. Did he die of wounds received on that day?

A. I think the wounds that I saw were sufficient to cause his death; yes, sir.

TESTIMONY FOR DEFENCE.

Scarface Charley is sworn, and testifies at length; the main feature of which is that they have been encouraged by the Klamath Indians to resist the government.

Dave—a Modoc—is next called. His testimony is of similar character, endeavouring to involve other Indians with the Modocs....

One-eyed Mose is sworn for defence; nothing new is elicited from this witness. Captain Jack states that he had no further testimony to offer. He is informed by the court that he is at liberty to make a statement. He rises with some hesitation; first casting his eyes at his chains, he mutters in his native tongue, that he "cannot talk very well with the irons on his legs;" he proceeds to scan the court and spectators deliberately. The sight of uniforms and bayonets does not inspire the chieftain. It is evident that he feels the hopelessness of his cause; that he is no longer the brave, strong man that he was when free and untrammelled. There were elements in this man's character, before his subjugation, that qualified him to make a strong effort. He is now

437

SCARFACE CHARLEY

unmanned, and the chief who has made so great a name as a warrior is now a mere pettifogger. Few passages in his speech are worthy of a place in history.

The whole burden of it is to shift the responsibility from his own shoulders. He does not refer to his troubles on Klamath Reservation; censures his own people; censures Major Jackson for the manner of the first attack, exonerates Roseborough and Steele of ever giving him bad advice; asserts positively that he was always in favour of peace; that the Hot Creek squaws reported that the Peace Commissioners intended burning him and his men; that he had reason to believe that they intended to kill him. Hooker Jim was the leader of the war-party; asserts that he was constantly ridiculed by Hooker and others; called a "squaw" and a coward; that the scouts, Hooker, Bogus, Steamboat Frank and Shacknasty, were all in favour of killing the commissioners; Hooker especially "wanted to kill Meacham;" finally, that the majority of the tribe have overruled him and driven him against his judgment into crime. Take his speech all in all, it was not up to the record he made as a fighting man. He concludes by saying he did not know how to talk in such a place with irons on his feet.

Schonchin makes a short speech, blaming others for his misfortunes, especially the Klamath Indians. Major Curtis reviews only so much of the testimony and speeches as refer to Maj. Jackson, clearing his name from unfair imputation.

The court again adjourns, a few minutes after which Col. Lewis, a lawyer of Colusi, Cal., arrives, and is much chagrined to find "the trial over," as he intended to offer his services as counsel for the prisoners. Too late. The trial is closed. It would not have changed the result, although it might have changed the record of testimony. So ends the trial of the murderers of Canby and Thomas. The findings of the court cannot be doubted, although they are not made known. This trial has been conducted with fairness on the part of the government; but it was, after all, a one-sided tribunal, from the fact that the prisoners had no counsel. Those who constituted the court were all men of character; exhibited no partiality or injustice toward the unfortunate red men, whose lives were in their hands.

While no censure rests on the court, it is, nevertheless, a cause of complaint that Hooker Jim, Bogus Charley, Steamboat Frank, and Shacknasty Jim, who were the worst men of the Modoc tribe, should be allowed to go free from arrest and trial. Gen. Davis had made no promises. He expected they would be tried and convicted, and sentenced to imprisonment for life. The argument that was used by Judge Advocate Curtis, that they had been of invaluable service as scouts, and had done so much to bring the Modoc war to an end, is not based on sound principles of right; but for these very men Canby and Thomas would not have died; peace would have been made, and more than one hundred lives would have been saved. That it was policy to pardon these men as an encouragement to other Indians to betray their people is not good logic, when it is understood that they were the real instigators of the treacherous deeds of the Modocs.

If the Modocs were a nation at war with the government, all were alike entitled to be treated as prisoners of war. If they were simply part and parcel of the people of the United States, then they were not enemies, and no action of a military judge-advocate could absolve them from the crime of murder, committed on the citizens of Oregon in Nov., 1872.

As the matter was settled, no one had a voice in regard to putting them on trial except the judge-advocate, and he exercised only a presumptive prerogative.

The finding of the court has been approved. Captain Jack, Schonchin, Black Jim, Boston Charley, Barncho and Slolux, are sentenced to death. The third of October has been designated as the day for the execution.

Gov. Grover, of Oregon, has demanded the attention of the government to the subject of the indictments. If any action has ever been taken it has not been made public.

CHAPTER 37

The Execution

The Modocs, men, women, and children, who were not placed on trial, were confined in a stockade near the fort, except the traitor scouts, who enjoyed the liberty of the camp, and were the heroes of the day.

At various times between the trial and the execution, the prisoners were permitted to visit the stockade. Their families were also allowed to visit them occasionally in the "guard-house."

On leaving Fort Klamath, after the trial and before the execution, I visited the prisoners, and shook hands with them, in token of forgiveness as far as I was concerned.

I was satisfied that justice would be meted out to those who had been placed on trial. Captain Jack seemed to correctly anticipate the result, and questioned me as to his fate, expressing a great dread of being hanged.

He said that but one side of the story had been told; that he had no friends to talk for him. I assured him that he had been fairly dealt with; that the officers who had tried him were all good men and had not done and would not do him injustice, and that I would write out a fair statement of all the facts for everybody to read.

He clung to my hand to the last moment. I left him with feelings of commiseration for him, and with a firm resolution to keep my promise, to tell his story for him.

It is now October 2nd, 1873. A long scaffold is erected; a more finished machine than the one on the peninsula. Ghastly and gloomy, it stands out on the open plat of meadow, with six ropes hanging from the beams.

The traitor scouts seem to take great interest in this instrument of death, which they have unjustly escaped.

Whether conscience troubles these worthies is a matter of some doubt; but that they were exempt from execution was a very satisfactory arrangement to them,—though to no one else, except their own families.

On the day before the execution, Gen. Wheaton, accompanied by a Catholic priest (Father Huegemborg), Post Chaplain, with Oliver Applegate and Dave Hill, a Klamath Indian, as interpreter, visited the prison for the purpose of informing the doomed men of the sentence.

The venerable father opened the painful interview by shaking hands with the convicts. He told them that Christ died for all men; that if they accepted him they would be saved. The prisoners listened attentively to every word. This was especially the case with Captain Jack, and Schonchin.

Gen. Wheaton then requested the chaplain to inform them of the decision of the President. He did so in a few feeling words. While it was being interpreted to them not a muscle moved; no sound was heard save the voice of the speakers.

The scene was a very impressive one. After a few moments of awful silence, the lips of the fallen chief began to move. His voice was soft, low, and scarcely audible:—

I have heard the sentence, and I know what it means. When I look in my heart I see no crime. I was in favour of peace: the young men were not ready for peace,—they carried me with them. I feel that while these four men—Bogus, Shacknasty, Hooker, and Steamboat—are free, they have triumphed over me and over the government. When I surrendered I expected to be pardoned, and to live with my people on Klamath land.

When asked by Gen. Wheaton, which member of the tribe he wished to take charge of the people, he evinced some emotion. After a short pause, he replied, "I can think of no one; I cannot trust even Scarfaced Charley." He asked if there was no hope of pardon. When assured that the sentence would be executed, he again asked if both sides of the case had been laid before the President.

On being told that the President had been informed of all that had been done, and that he need not entertain any hope of life, but to pay attention to what the chaplain said, he replied, "I know that what he says is good, and I shall follow his advice. I should like to live until I die a natural death."

Slolux, one of the young Modocs who carried the rifles to the council tent on the morning of the assassination, was next to speak. He denied any part in the terrible crime, as did Barncho.

Black Jim, half-brother to Captain Jack, spoke next. He was anxious to live that he might take care of the tribe; saying, "I don't know what Captain Jack and Schonchin think of it." Jack shook his head. Jim continued, "If the white chief's law says I am guilty of crime, let me die. I am not afraid to die. I am afraid of nothing. I should like to hear the spirit man's talk."

Captain Jack again asked that the execution be delayed until his speech could be laid before the President, as perhaps he did not know who it was that instigated the murder of Canby and Thomas. This request also was denied. Boston Charley was the speaker; he created a sensation:—

A Guilty Indian

You all know me; during the war it seemed to me that I had two hearts—one Indian and the other white. I am only a boy, and yet you all know what I have done. Although a boy I feel like a man, and when I look on each side of me I think of these other men as women. I do not fear death. I think I am the only man in the room. I fought in the front rank with Shacknasty, Steamboat, Bogus and Hooker. I am altogether a man, and not half a woman. I *killed* Dr. Thomas, assisted by Steamboat and Bogus. Bogus said to me, "Do you believe that these commissioners mean to try to make a peace?"
I said, "I believe so."
He said, "I don't; they want to lead us into some trap."
I said, "All right—I go with you." I would like to see all my people and bid them goodbye today. I would like to go to the stockade to see them. I see that if I were to criminate others it would not amount to anything. I see it is too late. I know that other chief men were not at the bottom of that affair, and they did not take so prominent a part in the massacre as the younger men. I know but little, but when I see anything with my eyes, I know it.

Boston's Reasons for the Massacre

Boston was then asked why they killed Canby. He said that all the presents they had received had no influence on them, and they suspected Canby and the commissioners of treachery,

Boston Charley

and their hearts were wild. After the young men had decided to kill the commissioners, he told Bogus he was afraid. Bogus said, "Don't be afraid; I can kill him." After that Captain Jack said he would go and prevent it. The object of Bogus going in that night to camp was to remove any suspicion from General Canby's mind. The young warriors thought that Canby, Thomas, Meacham, and Gillam were powerful men, and that the death of these *tyees* would end all further trouble. When they saw Dyer coming in place of Gillam, they decided to kill them all. When Bogus came into the soldiers' camp he told Riddle's squaw that he was going to kill Canby and the commissioners. She said, "All right; go and kill them." I am telling what I know to be the truth—nothing more.

Boston's reference to the part taken by the chief caused Captain Jack to speak once more, and it was his last that has found record. He seemed anxious to have Hooker and Bogus put on trial,—finally concluded, "If I am to die I am ready to go to see my great Father in the spirit world."

Schonchin was the last to speak:—

The Great Spirit, who looks from above, will see Schonchin in chains, but He knows that this heart is good, and says, "You die; you become one of my people."

I will now try to believe that the President is doing according to the will of the Great Spirit in condemning me to die. You may all look at me and see that I am firm and resolute. I am trying to think that it is just that I should die, and that the Great Spirit approves of it and says it is law. I am to die. I leave my son. I hope he will be allowed to remain in this country. I hope he will grow up like a good man. I want to turn him over to the old chief Schonchin at Yainax, who will make a good man of him. I have always looked on the younger men of our tribe as my especial charge, and have reasoned with them, and now I am to die as the result of their bad conduct. I leave four children, and I wish them turned over to my brother at Yainax. It is doing a great wrong to take my life. I was an old man, and took no active part. I would like to see those executed for whom I am wearing chains.

In the boys who murdered the commissioners I have an interest as though they were my own children. If the law does not kill them, they may grow and become good men.

I look back to the history of the Modoc war, and I can see Odeneal at the bottom of all the trouble. He came down to Linkville with Ivan Applegate; sent Ivan to see and talk with Captain Jack. If Odeneal came by himself, all the Modocs would go to Yainax. I think that Odeneal is responsible for the murder of Canby, for the blood in the Lava Beds, and the chains on my feet. I have heard of reports that were sent to Y-re-ka, Ashland, and Jacksonville, that the Modocs were on the warpath, and such bad talk brought Major Jackson and the soldiers down.

I do not want to say my sentence is not right; but after our retreat from Lost River I thought I would come in, surrender, and be secure. I felt that these murders had been committed by the boys, and that I had been carried along with the current. If I had blood on my hands like Boston Charley, I could say, like him, "I killed General Canby"—"I killed Thomas." But I have nothing to say about the decision, and I would never ask it to be crossed. You are the law-giving parties. You say I must die. I am satisfied, if the law is correct.

I have made a straight speech. I would like to see the Big Chief face to face and talk with him; but he is a long distance off,—like at the top of a high hill, with me at the bottom, and I cannot go to him; but he has made his decision,—made his law, and I say, let me die. I do not talk to cross the decision. My heart tells me I should not die,—that you do me a great wrong in taking my life. War is a terrible thing. All must suffer,—the best horses, the best cattle and the best men. I can now only say, *let Schonchin, die*!

This was the last speech made by the Modoc convicts.

The chaplain came forward and offered a most eloquent prayer, full of pathos and kindly feeling for the condemned.

Let us look on this scene a moment; it may humanize our feelings. The prison is but a common wooden building, 30 by 40 feet, and known as the "guard-house." It is on the extreme left of and facing the open "*plaza*" or "parade-ground," in the centre of which stands a flag-pole, from whose top floats the stars and stripes. A veranda covers the doorway, before which are pacing back and forth the sentries.

Before entering cast your eye to the right, about one hundred yards, and a square-looking corral arrests your attention. This is the stockade. It is constructed of round pine poles, twenty feet long, standing upright, with the lower ends planted in the ground. Through the openings we see human beings peeping out, who appear like wild animals in a cage. A partition divides this corral. In the further end Captain Jack's family and a few others are encaged; in the nearer one the Curly-haired Doctor's people. In front walk the sentinels. Outside, at the end of the stockade, nearest the guard-house, there are four army tents; in these four tents are the families of Hooker Jim, Bogus Charley, Steamboat Frank, and Shacknasty Jim, and these Modoc lions are with them, probably engaged in a game of cards. Scarfaced Charley also enjoys the privilege of being outside; but he does not engage in sports, or idle talk, oftenest sitting alone in gloomy silence.

Passing the guards as we enter the room, a board partition stands at our right, cutting off one-third of the guard-house into cells; the first cell has been the home of Boston, Slolux and Barncho, since their arrival at the fort. The next is where Captain Jack and Schonchin have passed the long, painful hours of confinement, meditating on the changes of fortune that have come to them.

In front, and running alongside the opposite walls, are low bunks raised twenty inches from the floor. Sitting around on these bunks are the thirteen Modoc Indians,—prisoners,—six of whom have just learned from official authority their doom.

Gen. Wheaton is in full uniform. The white-haired chaplain is near the centre of this curious-looking group. Oliver Applegate and Dave Hill are with him. Officers and armed soldiers fill up the remaining space. Outside the building are soldiers, citizens, and Klamath Indians, crowding every window.

The tremulous voice of the kind-hearted chaplain breaks the solemn stillness with a short sentence of prayer. Applegate translates the words into Chinook to Dave Hill, who repeats them in the Modoc tongue. Sentence after sentence of this prayer is thus repeated until its close.

The good old man who has performed this holy ministry bursts into tears, and bows his head upon his hands. In this moment every heart feels moved by the eloquence of the prayer, and a common emotion of sympathy for those whose lives were closing up so rapidly.

Gen. Wheaton terminates this painful interview by assuring the convicts that, as far as possible, their wishes should be respected.

In the name of humanity, do we thank God for noble-hearted men like Gen. Wheaton, who rise superior to prejudice, and dare to extend to people of low degree the courtesies that all mankind owe the humblest of our race, when, in life's extremities, the heart is dying within the body. The women and children are coming to take a last farewell of their husbands and fathers. Who that is human could look on this grief-stricken group, while listening to the notes of agony making a disconsolate march for their weary feet on this painful pilgrimage, and not bury all feelings of exultation and thirst for revenge toward this remnant of a once proud, but now humbled race; notwithstanding to the ear come despairing sobs of woe from the lips of Mrs. Boddy, Mrs. Brotherton, Mrs. Canby and Mrs. Thomas, on whom the great calamity of their lives burst like a thunder-bolt from a clear sky, shattering their hearts, and leaving them sepulchres of human happiness, illuminated only by the rainbow of Christian faith and hope, spanning the space from marble tomb to pearly gate?

These semi-savage Modoc women, with crude and jumbled ideas, made up of half-heathen, half-Christian theology, had not the clear, well-defined hopes of immortality that alone bear up the soul in life's darkest hours.

True, they had been cradled through life in storm and convulsions. For eleven months they have heard the almost continuous howl of a terrible tempest surging and whirling around and above them. They have listened to rattling musketry, roaring cannon, and bursting shells. They have seen the lightnings of war, flashing far back into their beleaguered homes in the rocky caverns of the "Lava Beds;" but with all these terrible lessons, they were not prepared to calmly meet this awful hour.

Human nature, unsupported by a living, tangible faith, sunk under the overshadowing grief, and struggled for extenuation through the effluence of agony in wild paroxysms of despair.

We might abate our sympathy for them in the reflection that they are lowly, degraded beings, incapable of realizing the full force of such scenes; but it would be an illusion, unworthy of a highly cultivated heart.

God made them too, with all the emotions and passions incident to mortality. Circumstances of birth forbade them the wonderful transmutation that we claim to enjoy. When we pass under the clouds of sorrow, the angel Pity walks beside us, arm in arm with sweet-faced Hope, whose finger points to brighter realms; with *them*, Pity, alone.

The sun is setting behind the mountains; the grief-stricken group are returning to the stockade, leaving behind them the condemned victims of treachery.

Their betrayers—Hooker, Bogus, Shacknasty and Steamboat—are invited by the officers to an interview with their victims; all decline, save Shacknasty Jim. This interview roused the nearly dead lion into life again; the meeting was characterized by bitter criminations. The other heartless villains, after declining the interview, requested Gen. Wheaton to give them a position where they could witness the execution on the morrow.

Let us drop the curtain over this sad picture, and turn our attention to the quartermaster and his men, who are just in front of the guardhouse. He has a tape line in his hand, and, with the assistance of one of his men, is measuring off small lots, squaring them with the *plaza*; see him mark the spot, while a soldier drives down a peg; and then another, about seven feet from it. He continues this labour until *six* little pegs are standing in a row, opposite another row of like number.

Hooker, Steamboat, and Bogus Charley are leaning on the fence, looking at the men who are now with spades butting the soil in lines, conforming to the pegs.

Bogus asks, "What for you do that?"

"Making a new house for Jack," answers a grave-digger, lifting a sod on his spade.

This is a little more than Bogus could stand unmoved. He turns away, and, meeting the eyes of Boston, who looks out between the iron bars of his cell, Bogus mutters, in the Modoc tongue, a few words that bring Barncho and Slolux to the window.

The three worthies look out now upon a scene that very few, if any three men in the world ever did—that of the digging of their own graves. It is but a thin partition that separates these convicts from their chiefs, Captain Jack and Schonchin, who are aroused from the condition into which the parting scene had left them, by a tapping on the wall. If the last trial was crushing on them, what must have been the force of Boston's speech, through that wall, telling them that the earth was already opening to receive their bodies.

The sheriff of Jackson County, Oregon, is on hand, and he has a business air about him too.

Justice sent him on this mission, after the red demons, who want a front seat at the show tomorrow. Will justice or power triumph? We shall see, when he presents his credentials to Gen. Wheaton, whether a State has any rights that the *United States* is bound to respect.

An offer of *ten thousand* dollars is made to Gen. Wheaton for the body of Captain Jack. He indignantly spurns it. This accounts for the future home of the Modoc chief being located under the eyes of Uncle Sam's officers. It is now nearly ready for occupation; the mechanics are putting on the finishing touches to his narrow bed; he is not quite ready yet to take possession; he is waiting for Uncle Sam to arrange his *neck-tie*, and read to him his title-deed.

Boston looks out through the iron bars, and sees the sods upthrown, that are to fall on his lifeless heart tomorrow.

What a contemplation for a sentient being; watching the grave digger hollowing out his own charnel-house!

Barncho and Slolux also share in this unusual privilege. How the thud of the pick, with which the earth was loosed, must have driven back to the remotest corner of each heart the quickened blood!

The retreat sounds out far and wide over the camp and fortress, and sweeps its music through the cracks of the stockade and prison cells, mingling with the weird, wild shrieks of the despairing Modoc women and children.

Midnight comes, and still the prayers are offered up, and incantations are going on; sleep does not come to weary limbs.

The morning breaks. Fortress and camps, stockade and prison cells, are giving signs of life.

The sun is climbing over the pine-tree tops, and sending rays on the just and the unjust, the guilty and the innocent.

The roads leading to the fort are lined with the curious, of all colours, on wheels and horse. At 9.30 a.m., the soldiers form in line, in front of the guard-house.

Col. Hoge, officer of the day, enters and unlocks the doors of the cells, and bids the victims come forth. Every day, from the 20th of February to the 11th of April, had this command, and even invitation, been extended to them. *Then* it was to come forth to *live* free men; *now* it is to come forth to die as felons. To the former they turned a deaf ear, and answered back with insult, strange as it may appear. To the latter they arose with chains rattling on their limbs, and, with steady nerve, turned their backs on their living tombs, to catch a sight of their new-made graves yawning to receive them.

Then they were surrounded with daring desperadoes, whose crimes bade them resist. Now, by no less brave men, whose polished arms compel submission. Then the chief was pleading for his people, surrounded, overruled by traitorous villains. Now, he is surrounded by men who will soon take his life, and let the villains live to chide justice

450

by their blood-covered garments and double-dyed treason.

A four-horse team stands in front of the guard-house, in which are four coffins; the six prisoners mount the wagon. The chief sits down on one of these boxes, Schonchin on another, Black Jim on the third, and Boston Charley on the fourth, Barncho and Slolux beside him. A glance over the heads of the guards shows six open graves; there are but four coffins in the wagon. What means this difference? But few of all the vast assembly can tell. The chief's thoughts are busy now trying to solve the problem. Perhaps he is not to die; an uncertain glimmering of hope lights up his heart. The cavalcade moves out in line passing near the stockade. The prisoners catch sight of their loved ones; they hear the cries of heart-broken anguish.

Gen. Wheaton refrains from the use of the Dead March. The column goes steadily on, marching for one hundred yards, then turns to the right, and the scaffold comes in view; it marches square to the front, then turning to the left, directly towards it, and when within a few yards, the column opens right and left, while the team with the victims of crime drives to the foot of the steps that lead to the ropes dangling in the air above. It stops. Again the stern, manly voice of Gen. Wheaton commands. The first time the Modocs heard that voice was on the 17th of June, 1873, when supported by loud-talking guns. Then they answered back defiance from the caverns of the stronghold. All day long he coaxed them then with powder and shell; now he speaks with the silent power of a hundred glittering sabres backing his words, and the Modocs answer with the clashing chains on their legs. "The first shall be last, and the last shall be first."

This royal-blooded chief was the *last* to enter the vortex of crime; he is the *first* to rise on the ladder of justice.

The chains are now cut from his limbs. He stood unmoved when they were riveted there; he is equally firm now.

Again the problem of the four coffins and six graves engages his mind, while the chisel parts the rivets. Schonchin is next to stand up while his fetters are broken. Then Boston, next Black Jim; and the good blacksmith wipes the perspiration from his brow with his leathern apron, straightens himself ready for this kindly work to Barncho and Slolux.

Behind are *six* graves,—above are *six* ropes,—in the wagon are *four* unchained men and *four* empty coffins. The suspense is ended by a word from General Wheaton to the blacksmith, and a motion with his sword towards the ladder, while his eyes meet first the chief, then

Schonchin, next Black Jim, and rest a moment on Boston Charley. Steadily the four men march up the seven steps that lead to the *six* dangling ropes. Barncho, with Slo-lux, still sits in the wagon below.

The mourning Modoc captives in the stockade have an unobstructed view of the scene, three hundred yards away; they count *four* men going up the ladder,—they see *six* ropes hanging from the beam above them.

"*Four loyal Modoc lions, who did so much to bring the war to a close,*" are standing with folded arms within the hollow square near the scaffold. Scarfaced Charley is sitting on a bench on the opposite side of the stockade, with his face buried in his hands. He will not witness the death-struggles of his dying chieftain.

It is now 10 a.m., October 3rd, 1873. The four men are led on to the drop; their arms and legs are pinioned. Captain Jack is placed on the right; next to him, Schonchin, then Black Jim, and then Boston Charley. Four hempen cords hang beside them,—*two* swing clear to the left; the *two* villains who broke the long armistice on the eleventh of April with a war-whoop are resting on other men's coffins in the wagon below.

The four men are standing on a single strand that holds the drop. One stroke of an axe would end this terrible drama, now. The polished blade is waiting for the dreadful work. Justice perches with folded wings on the beam above. Her face is blanched. She says, "My demands would be satisfied with imprisonment for life for these helpless, blood-stained men,—'twould be more in harmony with my Father's wishes; but those whom he has sent me to serve, clamour for blood, for life. If this must be, why the two men in the wagon below? Why the four unfettered villains yonder? I cannot understand by what authority I am compelled by my masters to witness this partiality. *Here, over these betrayed victims do I enter my solemn protest.* I see before me another power that evokes my presence, the State of Oregon, represented by Sheriff McKenzie, in whose hands I see a paper signed by Gov. Grover, and bearing my own countersign." With faith in the power of the general government, she folds her wings and sits calmly watching Corporal Ross of Co. G, twelfth Infantry, adjust the instrument of death to Captain Jack's neck. It differs from the one used by this chief on Gen. Canby, but is equally sure; and the chief's nerves are even steadier now than they were when he shouted, "*Kau-tux-a.*"

Corporal Killien measures the diameter of Schonchin's neck with the end of another rope. The old chief's eyes do not glare now as they did when he drew from his side a knife with one hand, and a pistol with the other, and shouting, "Blood for blood!"—*chock-e la et chock-e la,*—fired eleven shots at the chairman of the "Peace Commission." He was excited then; *he is cool now.*

Private Robert Wilton is putting a halter on Black Jim's neck, while Private Anderson is fixing a "neck-tie" that will stop the voice that taunted Dr. Thomas, in his dying moments, with the failure of his God to save him.

Justice smiles on Anderson's hand while he performs this worthy act in vindication of her honour.

The ropes are all adjusted; the soldiers who have performed this last personal act walk down the steps.

Forty millions of people, through a representative, read a long list of "wherefores" and "becauses," including the finding and sentence of the courts, to the patient men standing on the drop, thousands of eyes watching every movement.

At last the adjutant reads the following short paper from the *forty million,* to the *four* men on the scaffold; the *two* men in the wagon.

Executive Office, August 22, 1873.
The foregoing sentences, in the cases of Captain Jack, Schonchin, Black Jim, Boston Charley, Barncho, alias One-eyed Jim, and Slolux, alias Cok, Modoc Indian prisoners, are hereby approved; and it is ordered that the sentences in the said cases be carried into execution by the proper military authority, under the orders of the Secretary of War, on the third day of October, eighteen hundred and seventy-three.

U. S. Grant,
President.

While the words are being interpreted the adjutant draws another paper from a side pocket in his coat. In a clear voice he reads sentence by sentence, while the majestic form of Oliver Applegate repeats, and Dave Hill interprets into the Modoc tongue:—

(GENERAL COURT MARTIAL ORDERS, NO. 84.)
War Department, Adjutant-General's Office,
Washington, September 12, 1873.
The following orders of the President will be carried into effect under the direction of the major-general commanding the Division of the Pacific:—

453

Executive Office, September 10, 1873. The executive order dated Aug. 22, 1873, approving the sentence of death of certain Modoc Indian prisoners, is hereby modified in the cases of Barncho, alias One-eyed Jim, and of Slolux, alias Cok; and the sentence in the said cases is commuted to imprisonment for life. Alcatraz Island, harbour of San Francisco, California, is designated as the place of confinement.

U. S. Grant,
President.

By order of the Secretary of War.

E. D. Townsend,
Adjutant-General.

Justice whispers, "What does that mean?" Those two men voted for the assassination on the morning of the 11th of April, and volunteered to bear the guns to the scene of slaughter.

The chaplain offers a prayer, the last notes of Dave Hill are dying on the air as he finishes the words in the Modoc tongue.

A flash of polished steel in the sunlight and the axe has severed the rope that held the trap, and the thread of *four* stormy lives at the same instant, and *four* bodies are writhing in mid-air. An unearthly scream of anguish rises from the stockade, much louder, though no more heart-rending, than escaped the lips of Jerry Crook and George Roberts on the 17th of Jan., or from young Hovey on the 18th of April, while Hooker Jim and Bogus Charley were scalping him and crushing his head with stones.

The four bodies are placed in the four coffins, and Barncho and Slo-lux ride back to the guard-house beside them.

The sheriff of Jackson County presents to the commanding officer the requisition of the governor of Oregon for Hooker Jim, Curly-haired Doctor, Steamboat Frank, and other Modocs. The following telegrams explain the result:—

Jacksonville, Oregon, October 4, 1872.
To Jeff. C. Davis, U. S. A., Commanding Department of Columbia,
Portland, Oregon:—
At the hour of the execution of Captain Jack and his co-murderers at Fort Klamath, on yesterday, the sheriff of Jackson County was present with bench-warrants and certified copies of the indictments of the Lost River murderers, and demanded

their surrender to the civil authorities of this State for trial and punishment. A writ of *habeas corpus* has also been issued by Justice Prime, of the circuit court of Jackson County, commanding that the indicted murderers be brought before him, and cause be shown why they are withheld from trial. I respectfully ask that you communicate the proceedings to Washington, and that final action in the premises be taken by order from there.

L. F. Grover, Governor, Oregon.

To which was received in reply:—

Shown by the secretary to the President in Cabinet today. It is understood, the orders to send all the Modocs to Fort E. A. Russell, as prisoners of war, given the 13th September, 1873, will be executed by Gen. Schofield, and no further instructions are necessary.

Signed, E. D. Townsend,
Adjutant-General.

Thus was the matter disposed of, no further action being taken in regard to this question.

Gov. Grover expressed what he believed to be the wishes of the people of the Pacific coast, when he demanded the surrender of the Indians who had been indicted by the local authorities. The President and cabinet were actuated, doubtless, by humane and charitable motives in thus disposing of a serious question.

Knowing all the facts in the case, I do not believe it was just, or wise, to cover the worst men of the Modoc tribe with the mantle of charity, for turning traitors to their own race, and at the same time to sanction the sentence of death on the victims of their treachery.

The terrible tragedy is closed,—it only remains to dispose of the survivors, after having placed the four dead bodies in the ground, and filling up the two empty graves, sending the intended occupants to San Francisco Bay. The living are ordered to the Quaw-Paw Agency, Indian Territory. Here is the official statement:—

Fort McPherson, Neb., November 1, 1873.
Edward P. Smith, Indian Commissioner, Washington, D. C.:—
Modocs consist of thirty-nine men, fifty-four women, sixty children. Detailed report by families forwarded to department headquarters October 30.

J. J. Reynolds, Colonel Third Cavalry.

Thirty-nine men! Why, Captain Jack had *never* more than fifty-three men with him, all told. Call the roll, let us see where they are now:—

1. *Captain Jack.* A voice from—well, it's uncertain where,—a slanderous rumour says, from a medical museum, Washington city,—answers, "*Here.*"

2. *Schonchin.* "*Here,*" comes up from one of the graves in the parade-ground, Fort Klamath.

3. *Boston Charley.* "*Here,*" whispers a spirit, hanging over one of the graves in the same cemetery.

4. *Black Jim.* "*Here,*" comes up through the thick sod beside "Boston."

5. *Ellen's Man.* "*Here,*" answer scattered bones that were drawn off the Dry-lake battle-ground, by a Warm Springs scout, with a reatta, and now bleaching in among the rocks of the Lava Beds.

6. Shacknasty Jake, from a skull which furnished several scalps during the three days' battle, when its owner was killed in petticoat, comes in hollow voice, "*Here.*"

7. Shacknasty Frank; the ashes of a warrior who was wounded in a skirmish on the fifteenth of January, and died in the Lava Beds, answers, "*Here.*"

8. *Curly-haired Jack.* The answer comes from the bones of a suicide, muttered up through the blood of Sherwood, "*Here.*"

9. *Big Ike.* The remnants of a brave who stood too near the valuable shell, on the third day of the big battle, answers in broken accents, "*H-e-r-e.*"

10. *Greasy Boots.* "*Here,*" is answered by the ghost of the brave killed the day before the battle of January 17th.

11. *Old Chuckle Head.* On a shelf, in a certain doctor's private medical museum, a skeleton head rattles a moment, and then answers, "*Here.*"

12. *One-eyed Riley.* The bones of the only brave who fell in Lost-river battle answer, "*Here.* I fell in fair battle; I don't complain."

13. *Old Tales.* The ghost of Old Tales answers, that he was killed by a shell, and murmurs, "*Here.*"

14. *Te-he Jack*—

15. *Mooch*—

16. *Little John*—

17. *Poney*—

A dark spot in the road between Fairchild's ranch and Gen. Davis

456

camp shakes, upheaves, and with thunderous voice proclaims in the ears of a Christian nation, "*Here* we fell at the hands of your sons after we had surrendered. 'Vengeance!'"

Fifty thousand hearts, in red-skinned tabernacles on the Pacific coast, respond, "Wait."

Seventeen voiceless spirits have answered the roll-call who were sent off to the future hunting-ground by United States *sulphur, saltpetre and strong cords.*

Seventeen from *fifty-three,* leaving *thirty-six,*—the returns say, *thirty-nine.*

How is this? Look the matter up, and we shall find that "*Old Sheepy*" and his son Tom Sheepy, who never fired a shot during the war,—in fact, was never in the Lava Beds,—are compelled to leave their home with Press Dorris and go with the party to Quaw-Paw.

Another,—a son of Old Duffey,—who remained at Yai-nax during the war, sooner than be separated from his friends, joins the exiles on their march. Now all are accounted for, and the record here made is correct.

The other side we have told from time to time in the progress of this narrative. The cost of this war has not yet been footed up.

CHAPTER 38

The Two Gibbets

A gloomy picture fills the eye from the height of the bluff whence we took our first view of the Lava Beds, Jan. 16th, 1873. The whited tents are there no more. The little mounds at the foot rest heavy on the breasts of the fallen. No curling smoke rises from savage altar, or soldier camp. The howl of cayote and cougar succeed the silver bugle, calling to the banquet of blood. Wild birds, instead of ascending ghosts, fill the air above, and their screams follow the weird wild songs of the medicine-men. The caverns answer back to bird and beast—no more to savage war-whoop, or bursting shell. The cannon are cooled by a winter's frost, while a winter's storms have given one coating to the scars left on the lava rocks by the iron hail. The dark spots, painted by mad hands, dipped in the blood of heroes, grow dim. A rude, unfinished gibbet stands out on the deserted promontory of the peninsula, a reproachful proof of a soldier's unwarranted haste, a token of a nation's prudence; while another rude scaffold, which justice left half-satisfied, also remains at Fort Klamath, defiant and threatening, and upbraiding her ministers for unfair dispensation in sparing the more guilty, while writing her protest on the blood-stained hands of the felons who provoked her wrath, as she follows them to the land of banishment.

The lone cabins, made desolate by the casualties of war, are again inviting the weary traveller to rest. The ranchmen of the Modoc country follow the cattle trails without fear. The surviving wounded are trying to forget their scars, or hobbling on crutch or cork. Tall grasses meet, fern and flowers bloom over the graves of loved ones, bedewed with the tears of the widows and orphans of a nation's mistake in refusing to recognize a savage's power for revenge, until recorded by scars on the maimed hands and mutilated face of his biographer, and proclaimed by the marble shaft whose shadows fall over the breast of the lamented Canby, near *Indiana's* capital, and by the tomb of the no less lamented Dr. Thomas, which keeps silent vigils with those of Baker and Broderick, on the hallowed heights of Lone mountain, San Francisco.

The broken chains of the royal chief hang noiseless on the walls of his prison cell. His bones, despised, dishonoured, burnished, sepulchred in the crystal catacomb of a medical museum, represent his ruined race in the capital of a conquering nation; and the survivors of his bloodstained band, broken-hearted, mourn his ignominious death, shouting their anguish to listless winds in a land of exile. He lives in memory as the recognized leader in the most diabolical butchery that darkened the pages of the world's history for the year eighteen hundred and seventy-three.

The Congress of the United States devotes itself to the payment of the cost of the war; while the results stand out ghastly monuments, calling in thunder-tones on a triumphant nation to stop, in its mad career; *to think*; upbraiding it for the inhuman clamour of power for the blood of heroic weakness, until it thwarted President Grant's policy of doing right, *because it was right*; at the same time applauding him for his courage in proposing, and his success in consummating, a settlement on peaceful terms with a powerful civilized nation, with whom we had cause of estrangement.

If it was bravery that courted the accusation of cowardice, while it grandly defied impeachment by proposing to settle a financial difference, involving questions of national honour, in the case with England, on amicable terms; it was infinitely more patriotic, more humane, more just, and more godlike, boldly to declare that a weak and helpless people should be treated as men,—should be tendered the olive-branch, while the cannon were resting from their first repulse.

The civilized world joins in honouring him in the former case; cowardly America burns in effigy his Minister of the Interior for failure in the latter; while on neither magistrate nor minister should fall the blame. On whom, then, should it fall? Where it belongs,—on the American people as a nation. If you doubt it, read the history written by our own race, and you will blush to find from Cape Cod bay to the mouth of the Oregon, the record of battle-grounds where the red man has resisted the encroachments of a civilization that refused him recognition on equal terms before the law. You will find that these battle-grounds have been linked together by trails of blood, marked out by the graves of innocent victims of both races, who have fallen in vindication of rights that have been by both denied, or have been slain in revenge by each. You will find scarce ten miles square that does not offer testimony to the fact that it has been one continuous war of races, until the aborigines have been exterminated at the sacrifice of an equal number of the aggressive race.

You will find that in almost every instance where the white man and the Indian have met in conference, the latter has been over-matched with diplomatic schemes, plausible and captivating on the surface, while behind and beneath has always lurked a hidden power, that he dared not resist in open council.

You will find that notwithstanding the Indian has made compacts under such circumstances as have alienated his home and the graves of his fathers, he has been almost always true and faithful to his agree-ments, until justified by *his* ethics, in abandoning them on account of the *breach* by the *other party* to the compact.

You will find that a few bad white men, who have always swung out in the van of advancing immigration, and have without commis-sion or authority represented the white race socially, have offered the Indian the vices, and not the virtues, of Christian civilization; and when the facts are known, you will find that these few bad white men have been the real instruments of blood and treachery, nearly always escaping unpunished, while the brave and enterprising frontiersman has unjustly borne the stigma and censure of mankind; if, surviving the tomahawk and scalping-knife, he has stood up in defence of a home, to which his government invited him.

As I proposed in the outset to *confine* myself to facts of personal knowledge, or those well authenticated from other sources, and to write of the Indians of the North-west, and of Oregon especially, I leave it to others to review the history of other portions of the coun-try, and, in pursuance of my own plan, I beg to introduce a witness to sustain the assertion, that civilization has refused the Indian admis-sion on equal terms with other races,—a witness who was born and raised on the frontier line; whose whole life has been spent in Oregon; one whose statement will not be questioned where he is known,— Captain Oliver C. Applegate, who has given me, on paper, a few of the many incidents coming under his own personal observation, which he has in times past related to me around camp-fires in the wild region of the lake country of Oregon.

Hon. A. B. Meacham:—

Dear Friend,...A Klik-a-tat Indian, named Dick Johnson, came to my father's house in the Willamette valley, and worked for him on his farm, prior to the year 1850. In that year my father removed to the Umpqua valley, and soon after Dick Johnson, with his wife (an Umpqua), and mother and step-father, called the "Old Mummy," followed up and asked permission to cultivate a small portion of my father's farm. This they were allowed to do. They cultivated these few acres in good style, and found time to labour for father and other farmers, for which they received good remuneration.

In 1852, Dick Johnson, under the encouragement of my father, Uncle Jesse, and other friends, took up a claim in a beautiful little valley about ten miles from Yoncalla, where my people resided. This place was so environed by hills that it was thought the whites would not molest Dick there. Aided by the old man and his brother-in-law, Klik-a-tat Jim, who came from the upper country to join him, Dick improved his farm in good style, built good houses and out-buildings, and fenced hundreds of acres. He was frugal, enterprising and industrious, and emulated the better white people in every way possible, and was so successful in his farming enterprises that he outstripped many of his white neighbours. His character was above reproach, and, beside sending his little brother to school, he was always seen with his family at church on the Sabbath day.

Unfortunately, there were greedy, avaricious white men living in the vicinity of Dick Johnson, who coveted his well-improved little farm. Eight of them—disguised—went to his place late one afternoon, and found Dick chopping wood in the front yard. They shot him in cold blood, and, as his lifeless body fell across the log on which he was chopping, his step-father ran from the house unarmed, and was shot also. The women, after being beat over the heads with guns and revolvers, finally made their escape to the woods, and took refuge under the roof of a friendly neighbour.

Klik-a-tat Jim—who came from mill about the time the old man was shot—was fired on several times, some bullets cutting his clothing, but, jumping into his house at a window, he got his gun, and the cowardly assassins fled. Although there was im-

461

mense excitement throughout the country when this outrage was committed, and a hundred men assembled to bury Dick Johnson and the old man like white men, as they deserved, an ineffectual attempt was made to bring the offenders to justice, and *they actually lived for years upon the farm, enjoying the benefits of poor Dick Johnson's labour.*

Our laws then scarcely recognized the fact that the Indian had any rights that were worthy of respect, and this most atrocious crime had to go unpunished, thus encouraging the Columbia Indians to greater desperation under Old Kam-i-a-kin, in the war of 1866–1867. Well it would be, for the good name of the American people, if we could point to but one isolated case of this kind; but truth and candour compel us to admit, that too many Indian wars have been occasioned by the greed and ruffianism of our own race.

★★★★★★

Many years ago, during the first Modoc War, the Klamaths say that a band of Modocs was pursued by troops from the Modoc country, out by Yainax, and to the vicinity of Silver lake, where the Modocs managed to elude their pursuers. The troops (probably a detachment of Gen. Crosby's California Volunteers), not liking to be foiled in their efforts to take a few scalps, returned by Klamath Marsh, Williamson River, and Big Klamath Lake, butchering in cold blood several unresisting Klamaths. Even this did not occasion trouble with the Klamaths, many of whom tried to incite the nation to a war of revenge. . . .

Ever truly yours,

(Signed)   O. C. Applegate.

To sustain the declaration that the Indian has been overmatched and outwitted in treaty council, I propose to introduce a witness whose long life on the frontier qualifies him to speak; whose great talents, and intimate acquaintance with the politics and wants of the North-west, secured him a seat for six years in the Senate of the United States, and who is now (1874) a member of Congress; one who was also a Superintendent of Indian Affairs in Oregon, and knows whereof he speaks. I refer to Hon. James W. Nesmith. In his official report for the year 1857, page 321 Commissioners' Report, he says:—

My own observation in relation to the treaties which have been made in Oregon leads me to the conclusion that in most instances the Indians have not received a fair compensation for the rights which they have relinquished to the government.

It is too often the case in such negotiations that the agents of the government are over-anxious to drive a close bargain; and when an aggregate amount is mentioned, it appears large, without taking into consideration that the Indians, in the sale and surrender of their country, are surrendering all their means of obtaining a living; and when the small annuities come to be divided throughout the tribe, it exhibits but a pitiful and meagre sum for the supply of their individual wants.

The Indians, receiving so little for the great surrender which they have made, begin to conclude that they have been defrauded; they become dissatisfied, and finally resort to arms, in the vain hope of regaining their lost rights, and the government expends millions in the prosecution of a war which might have been entirely avoided by a little more liberality in their dealings with a people who have no very correct notions of the value of money or property. A notable instance of this kind is exhibited in the treaty of September 10, 1853, with the Rogue River Indians. That tribe has diminished more than one-half in numbers since the execution of the treaty referred to. They, however, number at present nine hundred and nine souls.

The country which they ceded embraces nearly the whole of the valuable portion of the Rogue River valley, embracing a country unsurpassed in the fertility of its soil and value of its gold mines; and the compensation which those nine hundred and nine people now living receive for this valuable cession is forty thousand dollars, in sixteen equal annual instalments of two thousand five hundred dollars each, a fraction over two dollars and fifty cents *per annum* to a person, which is the entire means provided for their clothing and sustenance.

When those Indians look back to the valuable country which they have sold, abounding, as it does, with fish and game and rich gold fields, it is but natural that they should conclude that the $2.50 *per annum* was a poor compensation for the rights they relinquished. It is true that the government can congratulate itself upon the excellence of its bargains, while the millions of dollars subsequently spent in subduing those people have failed to convince them that they have been fairly dealt with.

Even the treaties which have been made remain, with but few

exceptions, unratified, and of the few that have been ratified but few have been fulfilled.

Those delays and disappointments, together with the unfulfilled promises which have been made to them, have had the effect to destroy their confidence in the veracity of the government agents; and now, when new promises are made to them for the purpose of conciliating their friendship, they only regard them as an extension of a very long catalogue of falsehood already existing. . . .

That the Indian has been overcome by power may be established by the fact, that in the treaty council of 1855, whereby "*The Confederate Bands of Middle Oregon*" were compelled to accept Warm Springs Reservation as a home, by the threats and presence of an armed force of the government. This I state on the authority of Dr. Wm. C. McKay, who was secretary for the council.

That the Indian has been faithful to his compacts, I submit the testimony of a veteran, who has fought them forty years,—General Harney.

HUMANE TREATMENT OF THE INDIANS.

General Harney, before the House Committee on Military Affairs, today, gave his opinion that if the Indians were treated fairly there would never be any difficulties with them. He had known but two instances in which they ever violated the treaty stipulations, and in these the Indians were to be excused, for the treaties had grown old before they were sought to be enforced, and the chiefs and head men who made them were all dead. The troubles with the Indians were principally caused by fraudulent agents and by whiskey dealers.

That the Indian has not been the aggressor in the wars of Oregon, I refer to one of the bloodiest that has ever cursed this young State, in proof.

From Hon. George E. Cole, now Postmaster, Portland, Oregon, I learned some of the facts in this case. No man stands fairer than Mr. Cole as a man of integrity and honour. In proof of this assertion his present position, in one of the most respectable federal offices in the State, is cited.

In the fall of 1851, a party of miners, returning from a successful gold-hunting expedition to California, encamped on an island in Rogue River. All was peace and quiet. *No war, no blood, no treachery.* The Indians were in joint occupation of the beautiful valley of Rogue River with the white men, whose cabins and farms dotted the more beautiful portions of the country.

After the miners have made camp two Indians visit them,—a common thing for Indians to do. They are invited to partake of the supper,—an act of courtesy never omitted in wild life,—and they accept. The day passes into night. The Indians prepare to return to their own camps. The miners object, and, *through fear that they* might be surprised in the night, demand that the Indians remain. The Indians remonstrate. The miners are more solicitous for them to stay, their anxiety to leave being *construed* as ominous of intended treachery. The Indians, also, suspecting the same thing on the part of the miners, *break to run,* and both of them are shot down and scalped.

The miners resume their journey. The friends of the Indians miss them. Their scalpless bodies are found on a timber drift in the river below. The Rogue River war, with all its horrors, was the result.

That it was the most terrible that has ever devastated Oregon, let us call to the stand another unimpeachable witness,—Gen. Joel Palmer,—and we shall learn something of the reasons why it was so. Gen. Palmer, in his annual official report as Superintendent of Indian Affairs for the year 1856, page 200, says in speaking of this Rogue River war:—

In every instance where a conflict has ensued between volunteers and hostile Indians in southern Oregon, the latter have gained what they regard a victory. It is true that a number of Indian camps have been attacked by armed parties, and mostly put to death or flight; but in such cases it has been those unprepared to make resistance, and not expecting such attack. This, though lessening the *number* of the Indians in the country, has tended greatly to exasperate and drive into a hostile attitude many that would otherwise have abstained from the commission of acts of violence against the whites.

The avowed determination of the people to exterminate the Indian race, regardless as to whether they were innocent or guilty, and the general disregard for the rights of those acting as friends and aiding in the subjugation of our real and avowed

465

enemies, have had a powerful influence in inducing these tribes to join the warlike bands.

It is astonishing to know the rapidity with which intelligence is carried from one extreme of the country to another, and the commission of outrages (of which there have been many) by our people against an Indian is heralded forth by the hostile parties, augmented, and used as evidence of the necessity for all to unite in war against us.

These coast bands, it is believed, might have been kept out of the war, if a removal could have been effected during the winter; but the numerous obstacles indicated in my former letters, with the absence of authority and means in my hands, rendered it impracticable to effect it.

★★★★★★

A considerable number of the Lower Coquille bands had been once induced to come in, but by the meddlesome interference of a few *squaw men* and reckless disturbers of the peace, they were frightened, and fled the encampment. A party of miners and others, who had collected at Port Orford, volunteered, pursued, and attacked those Indians near the mouth of Coquille, killing fourteen men and one woman, and taking a few prisoners. This was claimed by them as a *battle*, notwithstanding no resistance was made by the Indians.

This witness clearly establishes the fact, that unarmed and unresisting Indians were attacked and shot down like wild beasts, and that "extermination" was the war cry of the white men. He confirms, too, the statement in regard to the rapidity with which intelligence is transmitted from one tribe to another, and its effect.

Do you wonder at the Modocs refusing to surrender, with so much to remind them of the white man's bloodthirsty deeds? See the last quotation from Gen. Palmer, and remember that these fourteen men and one woman were killed *after* the surrender, and in the attempt to escape.

White men were accustomed to regard the Indian as the synonym for treachery and savage brutality. Let us see how this matter stands in the light of what has been already written, after adding one or two other instances from the many that crowd thickly forward for a place on the witness-stand.

Judge E. Steele, a lawyer of high character, a resident of Y-re-ka,

Cal., since 1851, and also an ex-superintendent of Indian Affairs, in reporting an Indian difficulty in 1851, relates:—

That while hunting for two Indians who had committed some offence, we fell in with Ben Wright, who, learning from a squaw with whom he was living that the Indians had taken that course, he, with a band of Shastas, had started in pursuit and intercepted and captured them. We came in together, and took the Indians to Scott valley, and there gave them a fair trial, proving their identity by both white men and Indians, and the Indian testimony and their own story, all of which was received in evidence. One was found guilty, and the other acquitted and set at liberty. Our present superintendent of public instruction, Professor G. K. Godfrey, was one of the jury.

During our absence the people remained under great excitement, as all kind of rumours were afloat; and our company was so small, and I had started into a country inhabited by hordes of wild Indians, and those of Siskiyou mountain and Rogue River valley notoriously hostile and warlike. Old Scarface, learning of the difficulty at Rogue river, contrary to advice given him when we left, had come out from the *cañon*, appeared on the mountain lying east of Y-re-ka, as the Indians afterward told me, for the purpose of letting the whites know the trouble, as the roads were guarded by the Indians on the mountains, so that travellers could not pass. As soon as he was seen, a wild excitement ensued, and a company started in pursuit. Scarface, seeing the danger, fled up the Shasta valley, on foot, his pursuers after him, well mounted. After a race along the hills and through the valleys for about eighteen miles, he was finally captured and hung upon a tree, at what is now called Scarface Gulch."

In speaking of a trip to Rogue River valley he says:—

We had got out of provisions, and when, at the mouth of Salmon river, we made known our destination to the chief, Euphippa, he took his spear and caught us some fish, but would take no pay.

In 1854 or 1855 there was one more excitement in Scott's valley by the whites fearing an attack from the Indians, from the fact that they had held a dance and gone back into the hills. Here it may be well to state a custom among all those upper country Indians, which, not being generally understood by our people, has led to much difficulty. It is, at the commencement of the fishing season, and at its close, they hold what is called a fish-dance, in which they paint and go through all the performances of their dances at the opening and closing of war. They also hold a harvest dance, when the fruits and nuts get ripe, but this is of a more quiet character, more resembling their sick dance, when they try to cure their sick by the influence of the combined mesmerism of a circle of Indians, in which they are in many instances very successful.

But to return to my subject. Hearing of the gathering of the whites, and knowing the danger to our people and property if a war was then inaugurated, I got on my horse and rode to the place of rendezvous. After consulting, it was determined to fall upon the Indian camp at about daylight next morning, as it was thought that at that hour they could be mostly killed and easily conquered. I returned to my house, took my young Indian, Tom, and started, by a circuitous trail in the mountains, for the Indian camp, and before morning had them all removed to a safe place. In a few days all fears were quieted and harmony restored without the loss of any lives or destruction of property.

About this time a young Indian from Humbug creek, visiting the Scott-valley Indians, had stopped at an emigrant camp and stolen two guns. Word was brought to me. I sent for Chief John, and required him to bring the guns and Indian, which he did. I tied and whipped the Indian, and then let him go. Late in the fall, afterwards, I was sitting near the top of the mountain back of my house, witnessing a deer drive by the Scott-valley Indians on the surrounding hills, when I heard a cap crack behind me in a clump of small trees. Getting up and immediately running into the thicket, I discovered an Indian running down the opposite slope of the mountain. I returned to my house, and sent Tom after Chief John, and from him learned that when he left, this Humbug Indian was there. I directed him to bring him to my house, which he did next morning.

The Humbug Indian told me it was not the first time he had tried to kill me, but that his gun had failed him, and now that he and all the Indians thought that I had a charmed life. I gave him a good talk, which impressed him much, and then unbound him, and told him to go and do well thereafter. He was never known to do a bad act afterward, but was finally killed by the Klamath-lake Indians, about a year afterwards.

Of another affair, occurring in 1855, he says:—

Learning of the difficulty, and judging the Indians were not wholly to blame, I proposed to Lieutenant Bonicastle, then stationed at Fort Jones, and Judge Roseborough to accompany me, and with Tolo, another Indian, to visit their company, and arrange terms of peace. We went and spent two days with them before arriving at a solution of the difficulty. During this time they several times pointed their guns at us with a determination to shoot, but as often were talked into a better turn of mind, and finally agreed to go and live at Fort Jones, and remain in peace with the whites. The third day thereafter was settled upon for their removal, when Bonicastle was to send a company of soldiers to escort and protect them.

In the next day a white man, who had a squaw at the cave, went out, unknown to us, and told the Indians he was sent for them, and thereupon they packed up and started for Fort Jones with him, one day ahead of time agreed upon. On their way in at Klamath River, about twenty miles from Yreka, they were waylaid, and their chief, Bill, shot from behind the brush and killed. They kept their faith, nevertheless, and came in, when I explained it, so they were satisfied. This was *known to the Modocs, and they talked of it on our last visit to the cave.* Occasionally thereafter I was applied to only on matters of trifling moment and easily arranged, until my appointment to the Indian superintendency, in the summer of 1863, for the northern district of California.

In this narration I have passed over several Rogue River wars without notice, as I had nothing to do with them; also the Modoc war of 1852, which took place whilst I was away at Crescent City; therefore all I know of that was hearsay; but I know it was generally known that Ben Wright had concocted the plan of poisoning those Indians at a feast, and that his interpreter Indian, Livile, had exposed to the Indians, so that but few ate of the meat, and that Wright and his company then fell upon the Indians, and killed forty out of forty-seven and one other died of the poison afterward. There is one of the company now in the county who gives this version, and I heard Wright swearing about Dr. Ferrber, our then druggist (now of Vallejo), selling him an adulterated article of strychnine, which he said the doctor wanted to kill the cayotes.

That the plan was concocted before they left Yreka defeats the claim now made for them, that they only anticipated the treachery of the Indians. Schonchin was one of the Indians that escaped, and in late interview then he made this as an excuse for not coming out to meet the commissioners. The story of the Indian corresponds so well with that I have frequently heard from our own people, before it became so much of a disgrace by the reaction, that I have no doubt of the correction in its general details. At the time others, as well as myself, told Wright that the transaction would at some time react fearfully upon some innocent ones of our people; but so long a time had elapsed that I had concluded that matter was nearly forgotten by all, and nothing would come of it, until the night of my second visit in the cave, when Schonchin would get very excited talking of it as an excuse for not going out.

The history of that night you have probably seen as it was given by an article in the *Sacramento Record* and *San Francisco Chronicle*, for which paper he was corresponding; he was made wild; he was with me the whole time after.[1] A final peace was made with the Modocs, but the year is now out of my mind; but about 1857 or 1858 they came to Yreka with horses, money, and furs to trade and get provisions and blankets. On their way out they were waylaid at Shasta River, as was claimed by Shasta Indians, and seven killed, robbed and thrown into the river. Many of our citizens thought white men were connected with this murder, and it is probably so. The Shasta Indians retreated; they claim that but few of their people were engaged in the massacre, but it was mostly done by the white people, in their negotiations for peace in the spring of 1864, mentioned hereafter.

Col. B. C. Whiting, another ex-superintendent of Indian Affairs, says:

In 1858 a party of white men went to an island in Humboldt bay, California, and murdered, in cold blood, one hundred and forty-nine men, women, and children, who were *suspected* of being connected with other Indians who were at war with white men; . . . . . no effort was ever made to bring the murderers to justice.

---

1. Refers to the Ben Wright massacre.

One more witness,—one whose statement was made with chains on his limbs, and while he was on trial for his life at Fort Klamath, July, 1873. Captain Jack says:—

> I wanted to quit fighting. My people were all afraid to leave the cave. They had been told that they were going to be killed, and they were afraid to leave there; and my women were afraid to leave there. While the peace talk was going on there was a squaw came from Fairchild's and Dorris's, and told us that the peace commissioners were going to murder us; that they were trying to get us out to murder us. A man by the name of Nate Beswick told us so. There was an old Indian man came in the night and told us again.

> *The Interpreter.* That is one of those murdered in the wagon while prisoners by the settlers.

> *Captain Jack* (continuing). This old Indian man told me that Nate Beswick told him that that day Meacham, General Canby, Dr. Thomas, and Dyer were going to murder us if we came to the council. All of my people heard this old man tell us so. And then there was another squaw came from Fairchild's, and told me that Meacham and the peace commissioners had a pile of wood ready built up, and were going to burn me on this pile of wood; that when they brought us into Dorris's they were going to burn me there. All of the squaws about Fairchild's and Dorris's told me the same thing. After hearing all this news I was afraid to go, and that is the reason I did come in to make peace.

Add to all this the fact, that the popular cry was war, of which the Modocs were aware, as they were of all the incidents referred to in this chapter; and the further discouraging knowledge that no efforts had ever been made to punish offenders for crimes committed on their race; and a candid mind may be enlightened as to the cause of the failure of the Peace Commission sent out by President Grant in 1873.

The seed was sown while he was carrying on business at Galena, or fighting rebels around Vicksburg. The harvest came while he was in power. It was rich in valuable lives. It was costly in treasure.

It was a natural yield. It came true to the planting. The seed was sown broadcast, and harrowed deep into human hearts by the constant repetition of insult and wrong, irrigated often by the blood of the Indian race. It slumbered long (sometimes apparently dead, save here

471

and there an outcropping giving signs of life), so long, indeed, that Judge Steele thought "the matter was nearly forgotten by all," until Schonchin called it up during one of Steele's visits to the Lava Beds in 1873.

If the harvest *was* delayed in part, it was none the less prolific when it came. The *reapers* were few, but their *sheaves* were many, and bound together with the lives of the humble, the great, the noble, the good.

Does my reader yet understand why the policy, under which we settled a great matter of difference with a great nation, was not successful in settling a small matter with a small nation? Does he see, now, on whom the blame rests?

I hear someone answer:—

"On the frontier men, of course."

Not too fast, my friend. While it is true that each succeeding wave of immigration to the border line has borne on its crest a few bad men mixed with the good, it is also true that the great majority of the frontier men were of the latter class,—brave, fearless pioneers as God has ever created for noble work; rough, unpolished men and women, with great hearts that opened ever to their kind. I assert here, in re-iteration, that nowhere in all this broad land can be found men and women of larger hearts and nobler aims than frontier people. As far as their treatment of the Indian tribes is concerned, I assert, fearless of contradiction, that three-fourths of them are the Indians' best friends; and that, if dissensions arise, they are caused by bad white men, who mix and mingle with the Indians, and, by their wilful acts of dissipation, provoke quarrel and bloodshed, thereby involving good citizens. When once blood is spilled, the Indian too often feels justified, by his religion, in wreaking vengeance on the innocent. They retaliate; and hence border warfare reigns, and the bloody chapter is repeated over and over again, until "Extermination" rings along the frontier-line, and both races take up the cry.

The question has been asked twice ten thousand times, What is the remedy? For two hundred years, political economists, statesmen and philosophers have been proposing, experimenting, and failing in schemes and plans for the Indian. Never yet have they come squarely up to duty as American citizens and Christian patriots should, and recognized the manhood of the Indian, treating him *as a man*, dealing justly and fairly with him, redressing his wrongs, while punishing him for his crimes.

In plain words, we have never, as a nation, experimented in our management of the Indian race of America, with a few plain laws that were first written on the marble tablets of Sinai, and sent along down succeeding ages, between the 12th and 19th verses of the 20th chapter of Exodus. Nor have we always remembered the 31st verse of the sixth chapter of St. Luke:—

"And as ye would that men should do to you, do ye also to them likewise."

If, as we proudly assert, we, as a nation, are the rich inheritors of the priceless boon of liberty, then let us be the champions of human rights.

If we are the friends of the weak and oppressed, let us protect those whose claim upon us is based upon a prior inheritance, and whose weakness has been our strength.

If we would welcome the exiled patriot from other lands, let us give the hand of fellowship to those whose birthright to this land cannot be disputed.

If our civilization is the most exalted on the face of the earth, then let us be the most magnanimous in our treatment of the remnants of a people who gave our fathers the welcome hand.

If we would be just, then let us remember that our civilization has refused them, and *them alone*, its benefit.

If we honour bravery, let us remember that they have resisted *only when oppressed*.

If we reverence the high and noble principles of fidelity in a people, let us not forget that, of all the nations of the earth, the Indian is the most faithful to his compact.

Let us as a nation, reading our destiny in the coming future by the light of the hundred stars upon our flag, be true to God, true to ourselves, and true to the high trust we hold.

While we shake hands with the Briton and our brothers of the South, over the battle-fields of the past, let us not withhold from these people our friendship.

While we forget the crimes of others, let us bury in one common grave all hatred of race, all thirst for revenge.

While we are strong enough and brave enough to defy the taunts of the civilized world for proclaiming the advent of the hour when the song of the shepherds on the plains of Bethlehem shall become the motto of a Christian nation,—"Peace and good will to men,"—let us not live a lie, and prove our cowardice by shouting "EXTERMINATION" against a race fast fading away.

Let us not fall from our high estate by debasing a grand national power in a triumph over a civilization inferior to our own.

Let us gather up and care for these people, redeem the covenant of our fathers, fulfilling our high mission.

Let us uphold the hands of our rulers who declare a more humane policy, and let it be the crowning glory of the American statesman to proclaim to the world that the glad time so long foretold has come, when "The wolf, also, shall dwell with the lamb, and the leopard shall lie down with the kid; and the calf and the young lion and the fatling together; and a little child shall lead them."

Appendix to Chapter Six

Oneatta, Yaquina Bay Agency, October 1, 1871.
Sir:—I have the honour of submitting this my eighth and last annual report of the affairs of Siletz agency.

I closed my term of service as agent on the 1st day of May, 1871, at which time, as you are already aware, I turned over the agency to my successor, Hon. Joel Palmer. Since then I have been busily engaged in making up my final papers. This task, I regret to say, is not yet entirely finished. The delay has been owing to some irregularities, occasioned by a change of *employés*, and to other causes over which I have had no control. I shall now, however, push the work forward with all possible dispatch, and shall soon have my papers fully completed. I ask, for that purpose, your indulgence, and that of the department, for a short time.

I presume it will hardly be expected that I should at this time enter into the usual details concerning the affairs of the agency. All the important facts which have not been communicated to the department by myself heretofore will, undoubtedly, be embodied in the first annual report of my successor. He will find it convenient, if not necessary, in introducing himself officially to the department, to give some sort of a summary of the condition of the affairs of the agency at the time he took charge. I feel, therefore, that it would be altogether a work of supererogation for me to go over that ground in detail.

As this is my last report, after a somewhat protracted term of service in charge of Siletz agency, I think it not inappropriate that I should present here a few statements of facts in the history of the dealings of the government with these Indians, in order to show some of the difficulties with which I have had to struggle. I shall also presume somewhat upon your indulgence by offering some suggestions, prompted by my own experience, concerning the future management of the Indians over whom I have so long had control.

I have had charge of Siletz agency for eight years, and in that time have had to encounter many stubborn obstacles to the successful management of its concerns. I think, too, that I may say, without vanity, that I have *overcome* many such obstacles. It is not an easy matter, even under the most favourable circumstances and with all possible helps, to conduct successfully the affairs of an Indian agency. To a race accustomed, as the Indians have been, to the licentious freedom of the savage state, the restraints and dull routine of a reservation are almost intolerably irksome. It is not wonderful, therefore, that they should be often fractious and impatient of control, or that, even when reduced to complete submission to the regulations imposed upon them, they should, in many instances, become sullen and unteachable. To manage such a people in such a condition with any degree of success requires unceasing, anxious labour.

Yet this is the duty imposed upon almost every Indian agent in the United States. But in addition to these difficulties, which are incident to Indian management everywhere, there are some which are peculiar to Siletz agency. There are at this agency some fourteen tribes and parts of tribes of Indians, numbering, in the aggregate, at the time I took charge, about 2,000. Separate treaties were made with all of these different tribes in 1855, at the conclusion of what is known as the "Rogue River War," in Southern Oregon. Some of these treaties have been, in part, confirmed and complied with by the United States Government, but most of them have been entirely and persistently disregarded.

In expectation, however, of the immediate ratification of all the stipulations entered into, the Indians were all removed from their lands in the Rogue River country to Siletz reservation at the close of the war above referred to. Here they have been kept ever since as prisoners of war, supported by a removal and subsistence fund, appropriations for which, varying from $10,000 to $30,000, have been annually made by Congress. For sixteen years this scant, irregular, and uncertain charity, doled out to them from time to time, has been the only evidence

476

they have received that they were not utterly forgotten by the government.

For sixteen years they have been fed upon promises that were made only to be broken, and their hearts have sickened with *"hope deferred."* For sixteen years they have seen the white man gathering in annually his golden harvests from the lands which they surrendered; and for all those sixteen long, weary years they have waited, and waited in vain, for the fulfilment of the solemn pledges with which the white man bought those lands. What wonder is it that, suspicious and distrustful as they are by nature, they should, under such tuition, cease to have any faith in the white man's word, or to heed his solemn preachments about education and civilization? Who can blame them if, after such an experience, they come to regard the whole white race, from the Great Father down, as a race of liars and cheats, using their superior knowledge to defraud the poor Indian? And is it amazing that, with such an eminent example before them, they should grow treacherous and deceitful as they grow in knowledge; or that they should use every possible exertion to escape from the restraints which, as they believe, the white man has imposed upon them only for the purpose of defrauding them? In my judgment it is safe to assert that by far the greater part of their restiveness and indocility is justly attributable to this cause. I am fully satisfied that it has more than doubled the difficulty of controlling and managing them for the past eight years. So thoroughly have I appreciated this fact, that I have again and again urged, in my annual reports, the necessity of entering into treaties with the Indians at this agency who are not now parties to any stipulations. Feeling as I do that the neglect with which these Indians have been treated in this particular has been most unwise as well as grossly unjust, I cannot permit this last opportunity of expressing myself officially on the subject to pass without again earnestly urging a speedy correction of this grievous error and wrong.

Notwithstanding the many embarrassments with which I have had to contend in the management of the affairs of this agency, I am fully satisfied that no Indians on this coast have made any more rapid advancement than those under my charge, in industry and civilization. When I entered upon the discharge of my duties as agent, eight years ago, I found the Indians in almost a wild state, kept together and controlled by military force. This condition of things rapidly disappeared; and for the past four or five years I have succeeded in keeping the Indians generally upon the eservation, and in controlling them without any other aid than a very small corps of *employés*. And when I turned over the agency to my successor the state of discipline was far better than it was at any time when the agent had the assistance of a detachment of soldiers to enforce his orders. Besides, the Indians have, many of them, attained a comparatively high degree of proficiency in the useful arts.

About all the mechanical work needed on the reservation can now be done by them. Indeed, so great has been the improvement among them in every respect that, in my judgment, many of them are today capable of becoming citizens of the United States, and should be admitted to citizenship as soon as circumstances will permit. Knowing as I do the liberality of your views on the subject of the equality of men, I feel confident that you will spare no effort in your power to bring about this state of things at as early a day as possible.

Before closing this report permit me to make one suggestion as to the management of the Indian agencies under the system lately adopted by the government. I am satisfied that, under this system, it would be a matter of economy, as well as a benefit to the Indians, to place the whole subject under the immediate control of the superintendent, doing away with agents entirely. Each reservation could be managed by a sub-agent appointed by the superintendent, and subject to his supervision and control. The superintendent should then be held strictly responsible for the management of the reservations or agencies within his jurisdiction, and the various sub-agents and *employés* should be made accountable to him alone. The disbursements could be made by the superintendent, and the accounts for the whole superintendency could be kept in his office.

The advantages of this system would, undoubtedly, be great. It would reduce considerably the machinery of the Indian Department, and would simplify all its processes. Besides, it would render those who had the management of the different reservations amenable for their conduct not to a distant authority, but to one at home. Their acts would thus be judged, and condemned or approved, as the case might require, in every instance by one who would have, to a great extent, a personal acquaintance with all the circumstances. Under the present arrangement the Indian Department is little better than a gigantic circumlocution office, in which everything is done by indirect and circuitous methods.

Every agent renders his account, and is responsible (nominally) to the central office at Washington, and not to his immediate superior. In this labyrinth of routine and red-tape official incompetency and dishonesty may often hide securely. On the other hand, wise management and worth frequently escape notice altogether, or receive censure instead of commendation. In fact, there are in each superintendency so many different centres of power and influence, each of which must be watched from the head of the department, that the view is distracted and bewildered, and official accountability degenerates into a mere farce.

The superintendent, though he has a sort of supervision of the different agencies, is yet really powerless to correct abuses which may come to his notice. His subordinates are not responsible to him, and he can do no more than report their incompetence or misconduct to the common superior of all, and then await the tedious processes of circumlocution. His jurisdiction is, in fact, merely formal, rather than actual, and he is not responsible for the conduct of his subordinates; there is but little motive for him to exercise even the slight power which he has. The only remedy is to give him full authority over all the agents and sub-agents, and to make him personally accountable for their official acts.

I think that the necessity for this change is now more urgent than ever before. As a religious element has been infused into the management of Indian affairs, and as agents are appointed upon the recommendations of the different churches, there is danger that, in the search for piety in those who aspire to office, certain other very respectable and necessary qualities may be lost sight of. It is quite as needful that appointees should have some talent for affairs as that they should have the spirit and form of godliness; yet the former does not always accompany the latter. Many very good and pious men are but children in the business of the world.

It is also a fact of common experience that if religious bodies are left to select men for responsible positions of any sort, they are apt to choose them more on account of their zeal in the service of God or of some gift of exhortation or prayer, than on account of capability for business. I know that thus far the President has been very fortunate in his selections of men to carry out his new "Indian policy;" but depending, as he must, upon the recommendation of church organizations in these matters, he is liable hereafter to make the mistake I have mentioned, and appoint men to office whose piety constitutes their only fitness for the positions they are called upon to all. It is in view of this danger that I particularly recommend the propriety of making the change suggested above.

With many thanks for the distinguished consideration which I have received at your hands in my official dealings with you, I have the honour to be, your most obedient servant,

Ben. Simpson,
Late United States Indian Agent.

Hon. A. B. Meacham,
    Superintendent Indian Affairs in Oregon.

Appendix to Chapter Eight

Office Supt. Indian Affairs, Salem, Oregon, May 23, 1870. Sir:—Having just returned from an official visit to Grand Ronde Reservation, I desire to call attention to a few items that are of importance:—

First. The Indians have an unusual crop in prospect.

Second. They fully realize the advantages to result from having lands allotted in severalty, and therefrom arise questions which I propose to submit. (See paper marked "A.")

Third. The mills built fifteen years since are totally unfit for service, for the reason that they were not located with good judgment, in this that they were built on a low, flat, muddy piece of river bottom, composed of alluvial deposit that washes away almost like sand or snow, having neither "bed rock nor hard pan" for foundation, constantly settling out of shape and damaging machinery, besides being threatened with destruction at every overflow.

The lower frames of both mills, but more especially that of the saw-mill, are so rotten that they would not stand alone if the props and refuse slates from the saw were removed.

The flour mill is a huge, unfinished structure, supported on wooden blocks or stilts, and double the proper dimension, with an old patched-up wooden water-wheel that has been a constant bill of expense for ten years; machinery all worn out, even the bolting apparatus rat-eaten and worthless, but with one 42-inch French Burr, that, together with mandril, are as good as new.

The saw-mill is the old-fashioned "Single Sash" with flutter wheel, only capable, when in best repair, of making 600 to 1,000 feet of lumber per day; but utterly worthless at present for several reasons, the chief of which is want of *water*. The "dam" was originally built about one-quarter of a mile above the mills, at an enormous expense to government, across a stream (that is four times as large as need be for such mill purposes), with soft, flat alluvial porous banks and mud bottom.

The history of said dam is, that it has broken *twenty times* in fourteen years, each time carrying away *mud* enough at the ends of the dam to make room for each successive freshet.

I *believe that history*, since inspecting the "works," as evidence is in sight to show where thousands of days' work have been done, and many greenbacks "sunk."

I called to my assistance Agent Lafollette and George Tillottson, of Dallas, Polk County, a man acknowledged to be the most successful and practical mill-builder in our State, who stands unimpeached as a gentleman of honesty and candour. The result of the conference was, that it would require $5,000 to build a dam that would be permanent; that all the lower frame-work of both mills would require rebuilding at a cost of $2,000, and that at least $1,000 would be required to put machinery in good working condition; and, when all was done, these people would have only tolerable good old mills, patched up at a cost of $8,000.

But mills are indispensable civilizers, and *must* be built. I am determined to start these Indians off on the new track in good shape.

There are three several branches coming in above the old mills, any one of which has abundant motive power. On one of these creeks a fall of thirty feet can be obtained by cutting a race at the bend of a rocky cascade, taking the water away from the danger of freshets, and building the mills on good, solid foundations, convenient of access by farmers and to unlimited forests of timber.

Mr. Tillottson estimates the total cost of removing the old mills and such parts as are useful, and rebuilding on the new site a first-rate No. 1 double circular saw-mill, with Laffelle turbine water-wheel, all the modern improvements attached; same kind of water-wheel for flour-mill, with new bolting apparatus, etc., at about $4,000, exclusive of Indian labour.

I submitted, in full council, to the agent and Indians, the proposition to apply funds already appropriated for the repair of agency buildings, a portion of the Umpqua and Calapooia School Fund, that has accumulated to upwards of $5,000, and so much of Annuity Fund as may be necessary to this enterprise, on the condition that the Indians were to do all but the "mechanical work."

The matter was fully explained, and, without a dissenting voice, they voted to have the mills, if furnished tools, beef and flour.

The agent has now on hand a considerable amount of flour. For beef, I propose to use a number of the old, worn-out oxen, as they are now fifteen or twenty years old, worthless for work and dying off with old age.

To sum up, I have put this enterprise in motion, and propose to have the new saw-mill making lumber in sixty days, and the flour-mill grinding in ninety days.

I now ask permission to apply the funds I have named to this object, fully satisfied in my own mind that it is for the benefit of these people. If it cannot be granted, then I will insist on funds, that may be so applied, being furnished from the general funds of the department. These Indians *must* have a mill; besides, it would reflect on the present administration of Indian affairs, to turn them over to the world without that indispensable appurtenance of civilization.

Klamath Mill is a monument of pride, and has done much to redeem the reputation of our department; and I propose, when I retire, to leave every reservation supplied with substantial improvements of like character. Klamath flour-mill is now under way, and will grind the growing crops.

Going out of the ordinary groove, and wishing you to be fully posted about such transactions, is my apology for inflicting this long communication.

Very respectfully,

Your obedient servant,

A. B. Meacham,

Supt. Indian Affairs in Oregon.

Hon. E. D. Parker,

    Commissioner, etc., Washington, D. C.

★★★★★★

"A."

I respectfully ask for instruction in regard to Indian lands; and as the time for allotment is near at hand, it is necessary that some points be settled, for instance:—

First. Where there is more land suitable for settlement on a reservation than is required to fulfil treaty stipulations, shall more than the said stipulated number of acres be set apart to the individual Indian?

Some of the reservations will have an excess, and others will fall short of the amount required to comply with treaty stipulations. In some instances, where the excess is small, it would seem proper to divide *pro rata*. It does not appear that any of these tribes are on the *increase*; hence no necessity exists for lands to be held in reserve to any considerable amount for future allotment. When possible, I would favour giving them more than the treaty calls for.

Second. When less land than is necessary to comply with treaty is found, must the number of acres be cut down so that a proportionate allotment can be made? Or may unoccupied government lands outside be allotted to Indians belonging to the reservation?

Instances will occur of this kind, as at Warm Springs, where insufficient lands can be found, and a few families who are well advanced and capable of taking care of themselves could be located outside. I am in favour of that plan, and suggest, if approved, some instructions be given the land officers, so that said location can be legally made.

Third. May Indians not on reservation be allotted lands on reservation, and may they be allotted government lands not on reservation?

There are Indians in this State, that have never yet been brought in, that can be induced to locate under the system of allotment. And when all parties consent, they should be allowed to do so. Again, some of these people have advanced sufficiently, by being among white persons, to locate and appreciate a home. And there are a few instances where the whites would not object to their being located among them.

They *must have homes* allotted them somewhere, and the sooner it is done the better for the Indians.

Fourth. Are not Indians who have never been on reservation, citizens, under late amendments to the constitution; and have they not the right, without further legislation, to locate lands, and do all other acts that other citizens may rightfully do?

I am fully aware of the political magnitude of this question; but while I am "superintendent" for the Indians in Oregon, they shall have all their rights if in my power to secure them, whether on or off reservations.

Fifth. Are white men or half-breeds, who are husbands of Indian women, who do now belong, or have belonged, to any reservation, considered as Indians, by virtue of their marriage to said Indian women in making the allotment of lands?

I understand that all half-breed men living with Indians on reservations are considered Indians (but always allowed, nevertheless, to vote at all *white men's elections*). But there are several Indian women, in various parts of the country, who are married to white and half-breed men, and the question is asked, whether they are not entitled to land.

Again, there are Indian women living with white men, but not married, who have children that should have some provision made for them.

Sixth. May the allotment be made immediately on completion of survey, without waiting for survey to be approved?

For many reasons it is desirable that the allotment be made as early as possible, so that the people may prepare for winter. They are very impatient, and I hope no unnecessary delay will be made.

Seventh. Is a record to be made by and in local land office of surveys and several allotments? Is record of allotment to be made in county records, and if so, how is the expense to be met?

These people are soon to be as other citizens, and stand on equal footing. I have no doubt about the propriety and necessity for making these records, but so as to close up all the gaps, I want to be instructed to have it done.

A. B. Meacham,
Superintendent Indian Affairs in Oregon.

Department of the Interior, Office of Indian Affairs,
Washington, D. C., June 28, 1871.

Sir:—I have received your communication of the 23rd *ultimo*, asking, among other things, instructions concerning certain questions which present themselves for settlement in the allotment of lands in severalty to Indians upon reservations in the

State of Oregon.

In reply to the first inquiry therein propounded, you are informed that, where there is more land suitable for settlement on a reservation than is required to fulfil treaty stipulations, more than the number of acres named in said treaty cannot be set apart to each individual Indian, but the excess must be held in common for the benefit of the whole tribe or band occupying the reservation.

Secondly. Where less land is found upon a reservation than is necessary to give to each individual or family the full quantity specified in the treaty, the number of acres so allotted may be reduced so as to give each person or family a proportionate share of the entire quantity available for purposes of allotment; but unoccupied government lands lying outside of the boundaries of the reservation cannot be used to complete the quantity required to fulfil the treaty stipulation.

Thirdly. Indians not residing on a reservation cannot receive allotments of lands thereon, neither will unoccupied public lands be allotted to them.

Fourthly. Indians residing on a reservation, and living in a tribal capacity, do not become citizens of the United States by virtue of any of the recent amendments to the constitution of the United States. Their political status is in no wise affected by such amendments.

Fifthly. In case where white men or half-breeds have married Indian women, and said white men or half-breeds have been adopted into and are considered members of the tribe, and are living with their families on the tribal reservation, allotments may be made to them in the same manner as if they were native Indians.

In cases where Indian women are married to white or other men, and do not now live on or remove to a tribal reservation previous to the time of making the allotments, they will not be entitled to receive land in severalty.

The children of Indian women living with but not married to white men will not be allowed selections of land unless they shall take up their residence with the tribe upon the reservation.

Sixthly. The allotments must not be made until subdivisional surveys are completed and approved by the proper authority.

Seventhly. No record is necessary to be made in the local land office, or the county records of the county or counties wherein the several reservations are situated of the survey or allotment thereof.

Your suggestions regarding the erection and repair of mills and mill-dams, etc., and the application of funds therefore, will be made the subject of a future communication.

Very respectfully,

Your obedient servant,

E. S. Parker,
Commissioner.

A. B. Meacham, Esq.,

    Supt. Indian Affairs, Salem, Oregon.

Office Supt. Indian Affairs, Salem, Oregon, May 30, 1870. Chas. Lafollette, *Agent Grand Ronde:*—

Sir,—Mr. Tillottson reported to this office on yesterday. We have decided to proceed with the saw-mill as soon as you can have Indian labourers to assist. It is desirable that we push this enterprise, and, in order to do so, it would seem necessary for you to "*call in*" enough to make a gang of say twenty workingmen; and as soon as this is done notify Mr. Tillottson at Dallas. I have ordered all the tools required to be forwarded to you at Dayton; and have no doubt they will be awaiting your orders. I think you can send immediately without fear of disappointment. In the mean time you will arrange *subsistence* for the Indian with my parties. It would be well also to assist Mr. Tillottson about a boarding-place.

My arrangement is, that "the mechanics are to board themselves" with him; he to have the entire control of the works, we to furnish the labourers. When he is dissatisfied with the services, to certify to the time through your office, and forward to me for payment. I think it best not to transfer funds until an answer is obtained from the commissioner in regard to diverting the funds.

We cannot expend or anticipate a fund not yet remitted, as I find a rule laid down to that effect. If we meet with a favourable reply we will then proceed with the flouring-mill. You may find employment, while waiting for tools for Mr. Reinhart, at such wages as you may agree upon. Hoping you will give this enterprise sufficient attention to secure success, etc.,

I am respectfully,

Your obedient servant,

A. B. Meacham,
Supt. Indian Affairs, Oregon.

Office Supt. Indian Affairs, Salem, Oregon, Dec. 19, 1874.
L. S. Dyer, Esq., Commissary in charge Grand Ronde:—
Sir,—Col. Thompson, surveyor, has been employed by me to assist you in making the allotment of lands on Grand Ronde.
Herewith find the only instructions furnished this office, which, together with the copies of treaties in your office, it is hoped may be sufficient guide in making the allotment.

As arranged during my late visit, all matters of dispute about priority of rights, etc., must be settled by a Board, consisting of Commissary L. S. Dyer, Col. D. P. Thompson and W. P. Eaton, or any other you may designate; if Mr. Eaton is unable to act; and, on request of the Indians, you will add to said Board three Indians, who are not *interested* parties in any matter under consideration by your Board.

Great patience may be required in settling the differences that will arise, and I trust that you will, at all times, bear in mind that you are labouring for a race who are docile and reasonable when they are made fully to understand the wherefore, etc., of any proposition.

I regret that the Commissioner of Indian Affairs has not furnished this office with more specific instructions in the premises.

This order to make allotment is in anticipation of orders from the commissioner, which, I have no doubt, will be forwarded at an early day. At all events, the necessity of immediate action is obvious.

July 20th, Wm. R. Dunbar was instructed to enrol all the Indians of Grand Ronde Agency, including those of Nestucker and Tillamook. Mr. Dunbar reported the enrolment complete, a copy of which you will find in your office.

It is possible that some changes have occurred in the arrangement of families, of which you will take note, and correct the same in making statement of allotment.

You will also be particular to see that the original and present name and tribe, together with sex, estimated age, and relationship to families with whom they are residing at the time of allotment, be identified with the number of the particular tract allotted to such person or family.

In this connection it is necessary, in cases of plurality of wives, that each man shall designate one woman to be his legal wife, and all others to be members of his family, with the privilege of forming other marriage relations, taking with them the lands allotted in their respective names.

Orphan children, who are *attached* to families, must have the same rights.

It would seem proper that, so far as possible, these people should be allowed to retain their present homes, and to adjust their respective rights among themselves; but it will be necessary, in some cases, to assume control and adjudicate differences.

Inasmuch as there are several treaties in force with the Grand Ronde Indians, in the complications arising therefrom I would advise that the treaty with Willamette Valley Indians be adopted as the guide, without regard to the other treaties.

Let the allotment be uniform to all persons entitled to lands, as per instructions of commissioner in reply to queries, and above referred to.

Should any number of your people elect to remove to Nestucker, and there take lands in severalty, it would seem right, perhaps, to do so. Land will be ordered, surveyed at the places above referred to, and possibly also at Salmon River.

I do not know of any other instructions or laws to guide you, except this: In absence of law, do justice fairly and impartially. Law is supposed to be in harmony with justice and common sense; and, if it is not, it is *not good law*.

Fully realizing the difficulties in your way in fulfilling this order, and having confidence in your integrity and ability, I can only say, in conclusion, push this matter through, and furnish this office, at an early day, full report of your doings, together with statistical table of allotments made under the rules and instructions furnished you.

It may be observed, by reading the several treaties, that the amount of land stipulated to be allotted differs somewhat in the amounts specified.

From surveyors' reports, it appears that there is some deficiency of lands suitable for Indian settlement, and since the several tribes are mixed up, and to avoid confusion, I have indicated the treaty with the Indians of the Willamette Valley as the proper one to govern your action.

Now, if the question should be raised by the Umpquas, and they refuse to accept the amount named in the treaty referred to (Willamette Valley), you will propose to the Umpquas to have the excess claimed by them set off to them of timber lots; or otherwise let the whole matter stand for further instructions. Should the question come up at an early day please notify me, and, if possible, I will in person adjust the matter.

I think, however, that if you make the proposition to the Indians to settle it *before* allotment, they will agree to the Willamette treaty, and I will arrange for the acknowledgment, on their part, of the fulfilment of treaty on the part of the government hereafter.

> Very respectfully,
> Your obedient servant,
>
> A. B. Meacham,
> Superintendent Indian Affairs in Oregon.

CPSIA information can be obtained at www.ICGtesting.com
Printed in the USA
LVOW08s0100281114

415967LV00001B/55/P